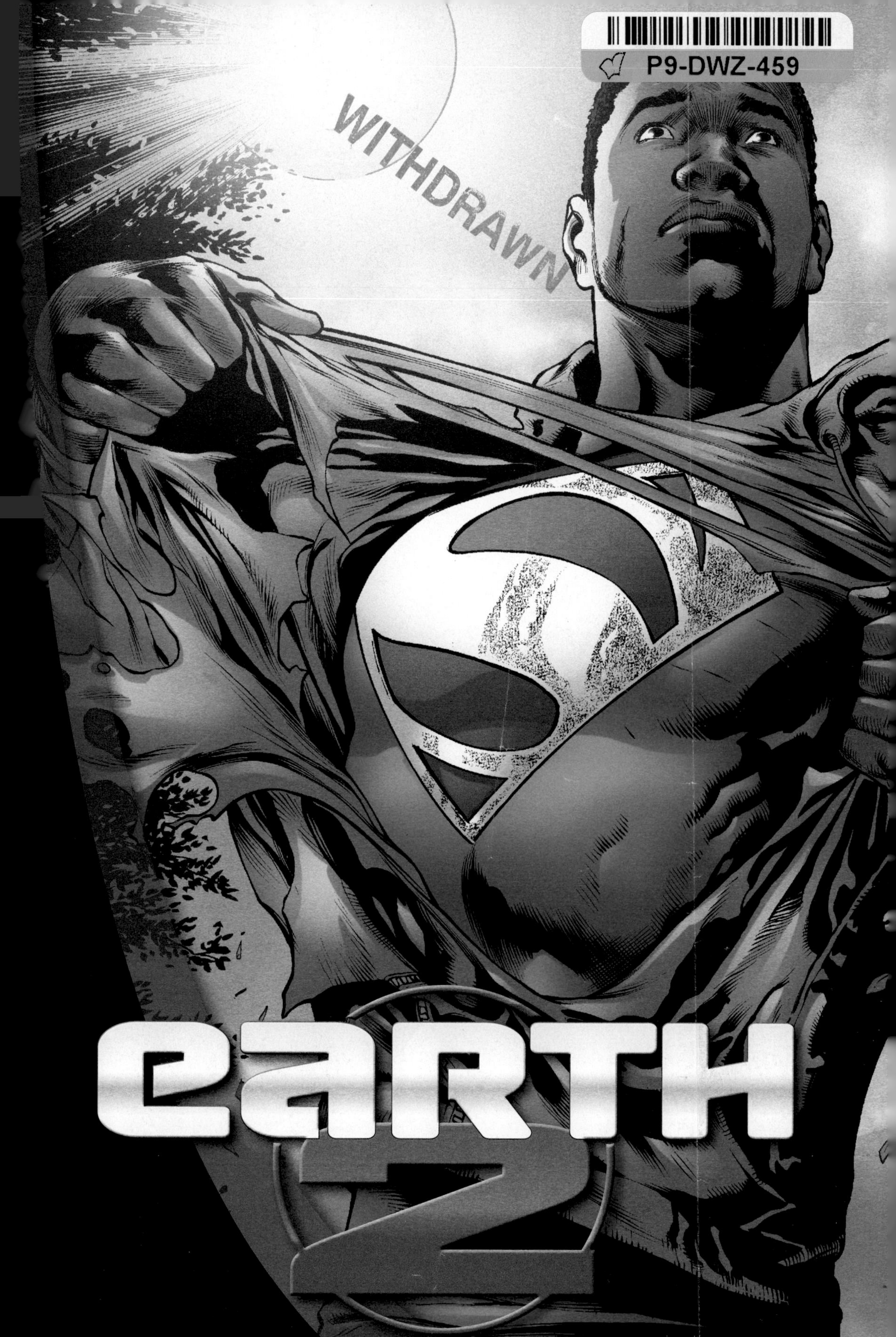

EARTH 2

VOLUME 5 THE KRYPTONIAN

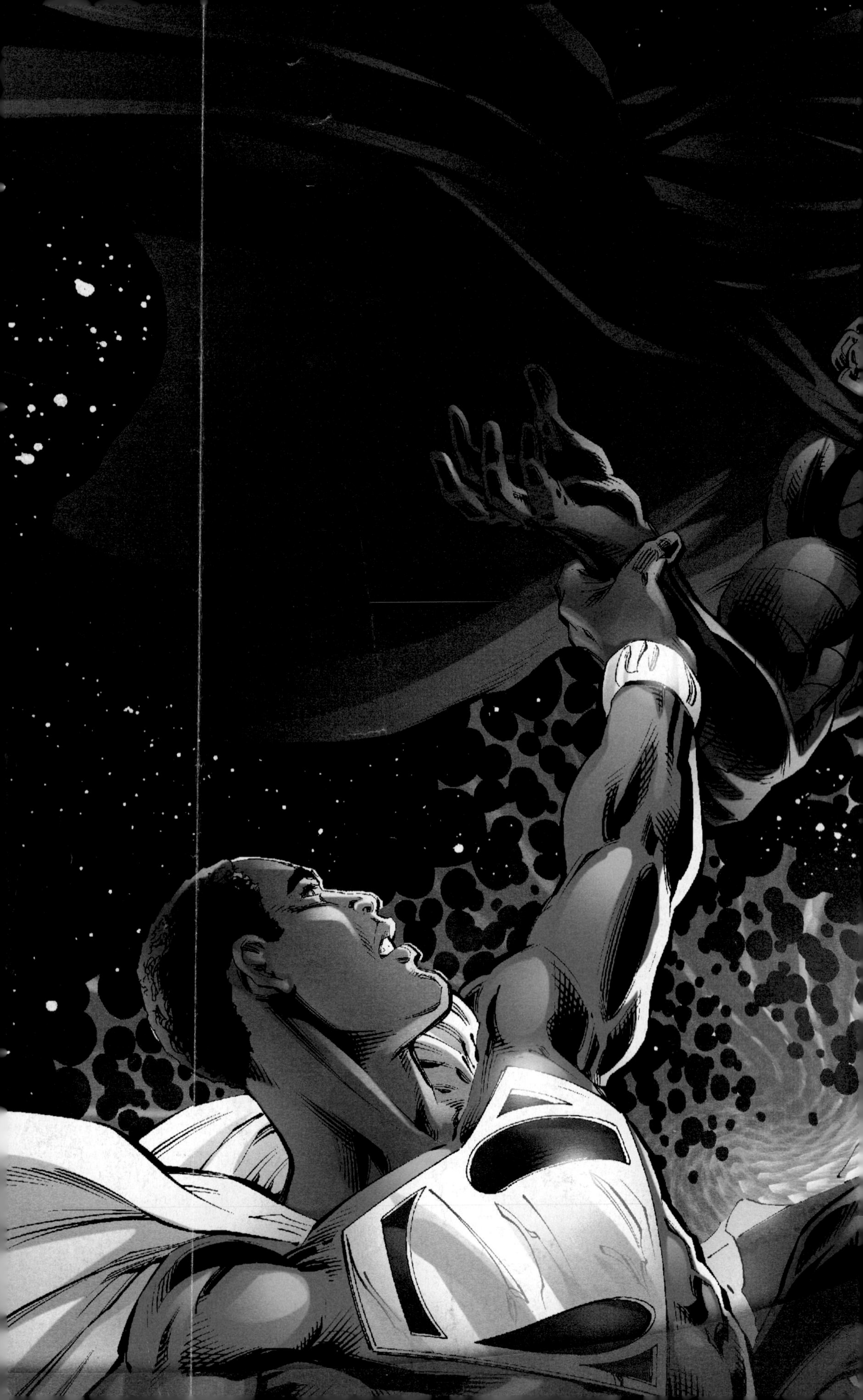

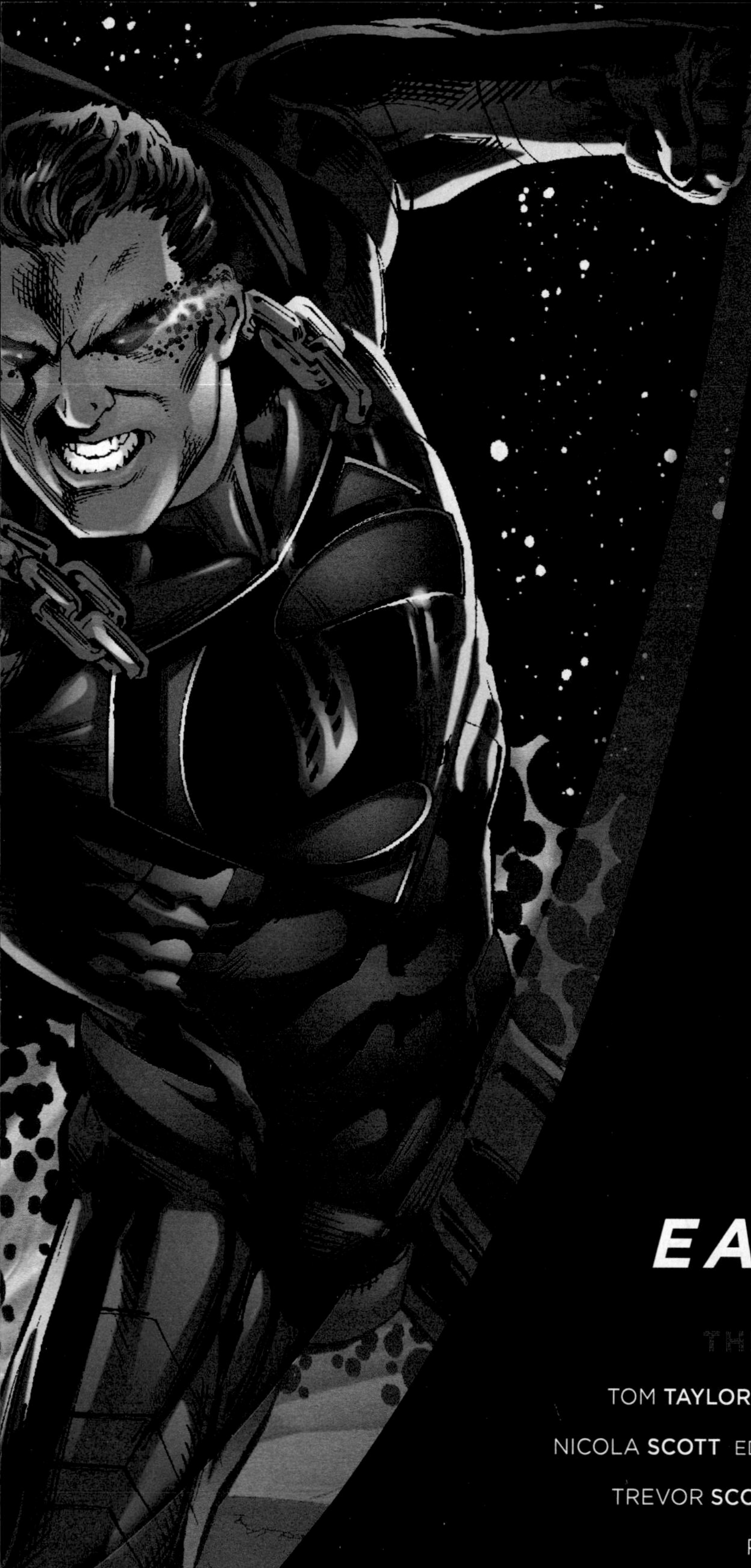

EARTH 2

VOLUME 5
THE KRYPTONIAN

TOM **TAYLOR** DANIEL H. **WILSON** writers

NICOLA **SCOTT** EDDY **BARROWS** pencillers

TREVOR **SCOTT** EBER **FERREIRA** inkers

PETE **PANTAZIS** colorist

DEZI **SIENTY** TAYLOR **ESPOSITO** CARLOS M. **MANGUAL** letterers

J.G. JONES & PAUL MOUNTS collection cover artists

Superman created by JERRY **SIEGEL** and JOE **SHUSTER**
By special arrangement with the Jerry Siegel family

MIKE COTTON Editor – Original Series ANTHONY MARQUES Assistant Editor – Original Series
JEB WOODARD Group Editor – Collected Editions ROBIN WILDMAN Editor – Collected Edition
ROBBIE BIEDERMAN Publication Design

BOB HARRAS Senior VP – Editor-in-Chief, DC Comics

DIANE NELSON President DAN DIDIO and JIM LEE Co-Publishers GEOFF JOHNS Chief Creative Officer
AMIT DESAI Senior VP – Marketing & Global Franchise Management   NAIRI GARDINER Senior VP – Finance
SAM ADES VP – Digital Marketing BOBBIE CHASE VP –Talent Development
MARK CHIARELLO Senior VP – Art, Design & Collected Editions JOHN CUNNINGHAM VP – Content Strategy
ANNE DEPIES VP – Strategy Planning & Reporting DON FALLETTI VP – Manufacturing Operations
LAWRENCE GANEM VP – Editorial Administration & Talent Relations ALISON GILL Senior VP – Manufacturing & Operations
HANK KANALZ Senior VP – Editorial Strategy & Administration JAY KOGAN VP – Legal Affairs
DEREK MADDALENA Senior VP – Sales & Business Development JACK MAHAN VP – Business Affairs
DAN MIRON VP – Sales Planning & Trade Development NICK NAPOLITANO VP – Manufacturing Administration
CAROL ROEDER VP – Marketing EDDIE SCANNELL VP – Mass Account & Digital Sales
COURTNEY SIMMONS Senior VP – Publicity & Communications JIM (SKI) SOKOLOWSKI VP – Comic Book Specialty & Newsstand Sales
SANDY YI Senior VP – Global Franchise Management

EARTH 2 VOLUME 5: THE KRYPTONIAN

DC Comics, 4000 Warner Blvd., Burbank, CA 91522
A Warner Bros. Entertainment Company.
Printed by RR Donnelley, Salem, VA, USA. 10/23/15. First Printing.
ISBN: 978-1-4012-5757-6

Library of Congress Cataloging-in-Publication Data

Taylor, Tom, 1978-
Earth 2. Volume 5, The Kryptonian / Tom Taylor, Nicola Scott, Trevor Scott, Will Blyberg.
pages cm. — (The New 52!)
ISBN 978-1-4012-5757-6
1. Graphic novels. I. Scott, Nicola. II. Scott, Trevor (Comic book artist) III. Blyberg, Will. IV. Title. V. Title: Kryptonian.
PN6727.T293E28 2015
741.5'973—dc23
2014049026

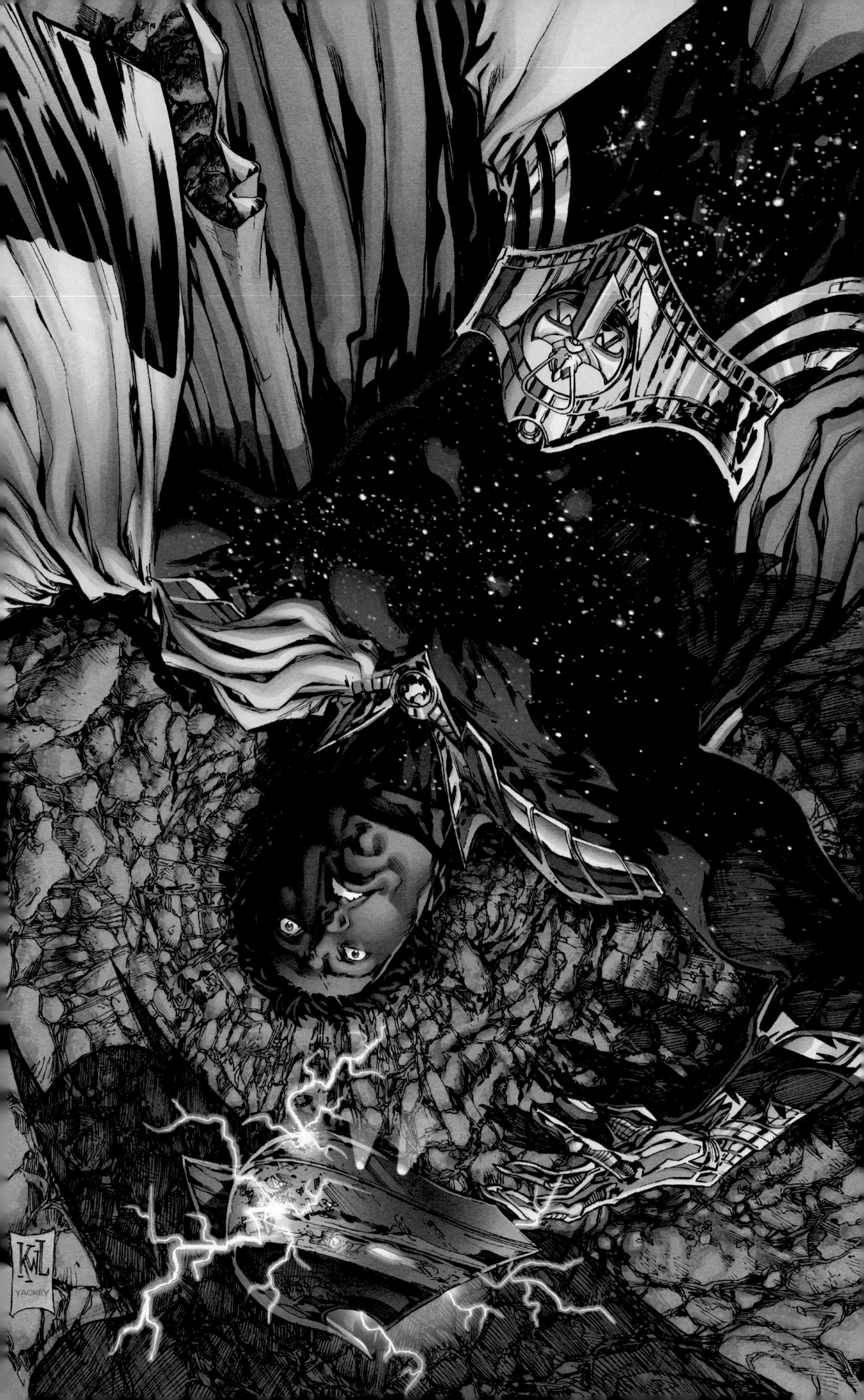
YACKEY

THE KRYPTONIAN PART 1

TOM TAYLOR writer **NICOLA SCOTT** penciller **TREVOR SCOTT** inker **PETE PANTAZIS** colorist cover by **KEN LASHLEY** & **MATT YACKEY**

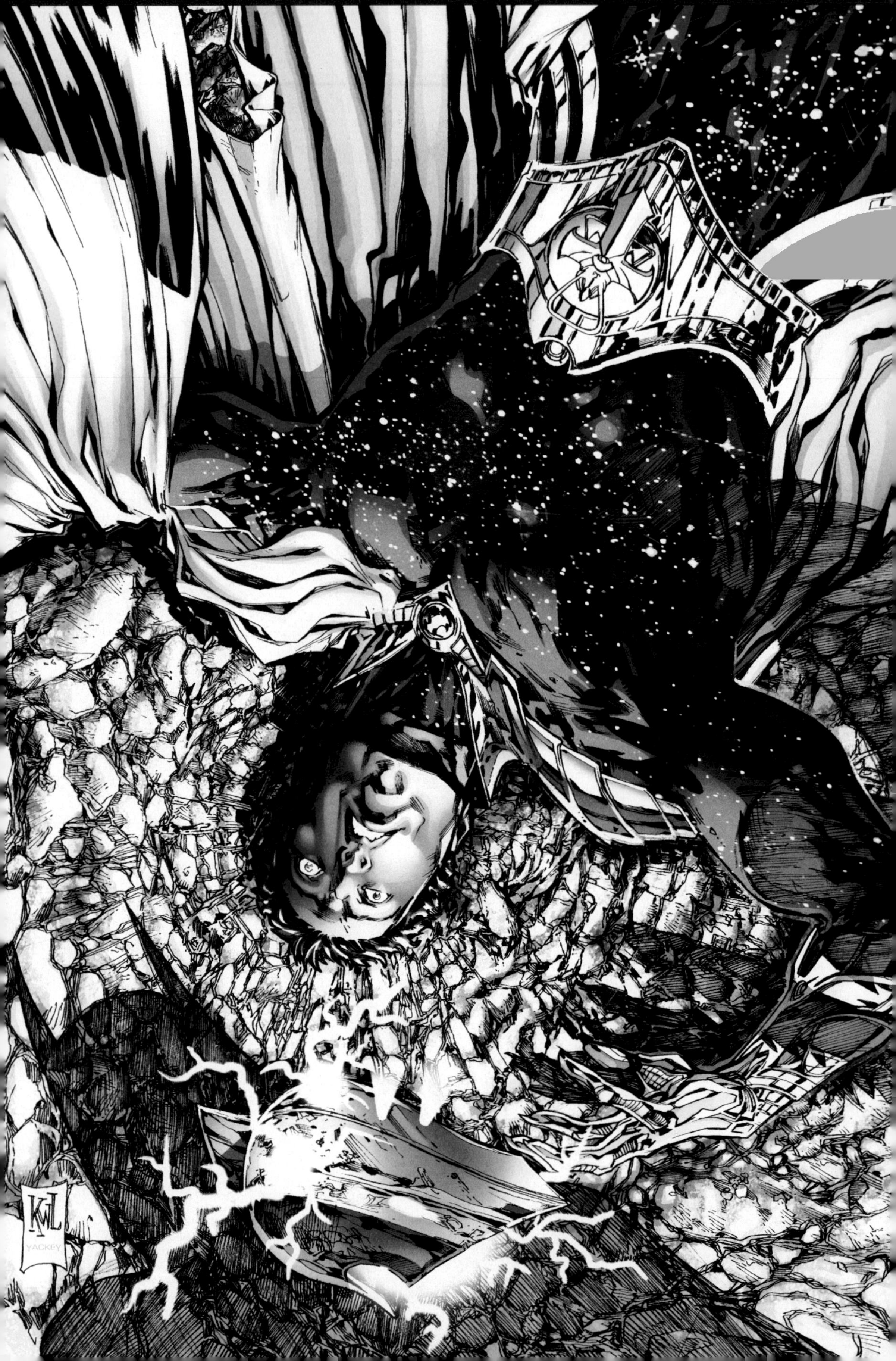

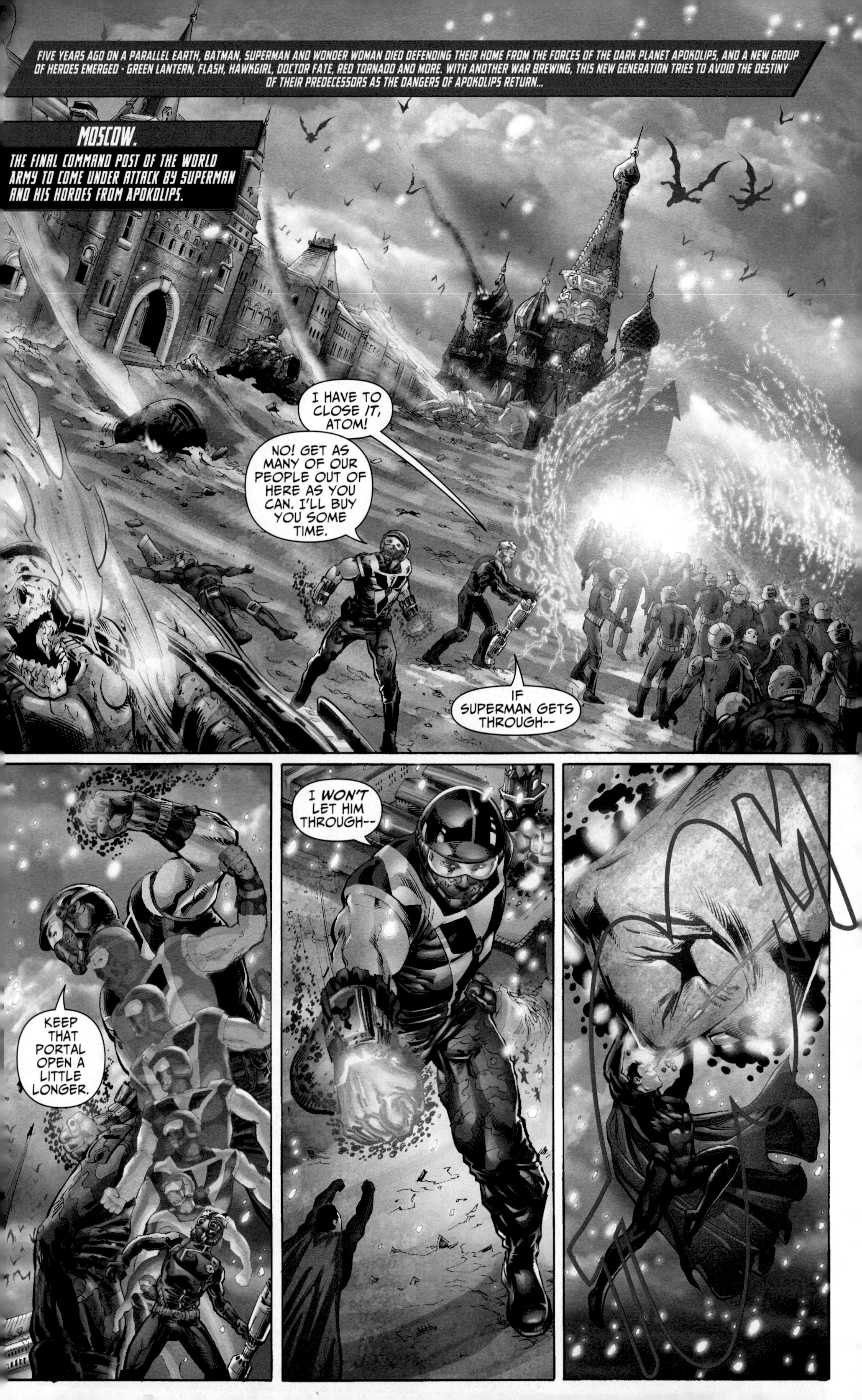
FIVE YEARS AGO ON A PARALLEL EARTH, BATMAN, SUPERMAN AND WONDER WOMAN DIED DEFENDING THEIR HOME FROM THE FORCES OF THE DARK PLANET APOKOLIPS, AND A NEW GROUP OF HEROES EMERGED - GREEN LANTERN, FLASH, HAWKGIRL, DOCTOR FATE, RED TORNADO AND MORE. WITH ANOTHER WAR BREWING, THIS NEW GENERATION TRIES TO AVOID THE DESTINY OF THEIR PREDECESSORS AS THE DANGERS OF APOKOLIPS RETURN...
MOSCOW.
THE FINAL COMMAND POST OF THE WORLD ARMY TO COME UNDER ATTACK BY SUPERMAN AND HIS HORDES FROM APOKOLIPS.
I HAVE TO CLOSE IT, ATOM!
NO! GET AS MANY OF OUR PEOPLE OUT OF HERE AS YOU CAN. I'LL BUY YOU SOME TIME.
IF SUPERMAN GETS THROUGH--
KEEP THAT PORTAL OPEN A LITTLE LONGER.
I *WON'T* LET HIM THROUGH--

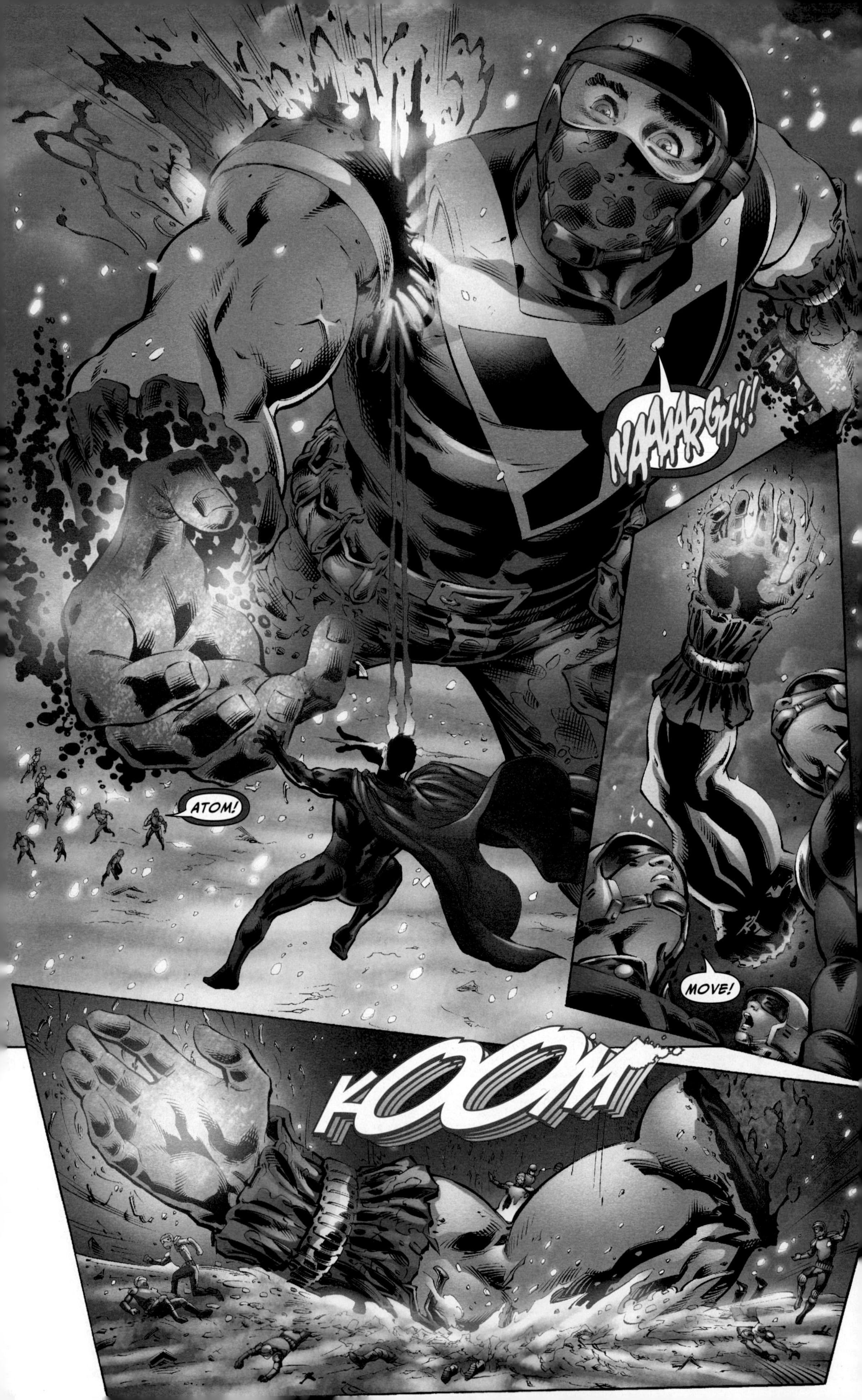
NAAAARGH!!!
ATOM!
MOVE!
KOOM

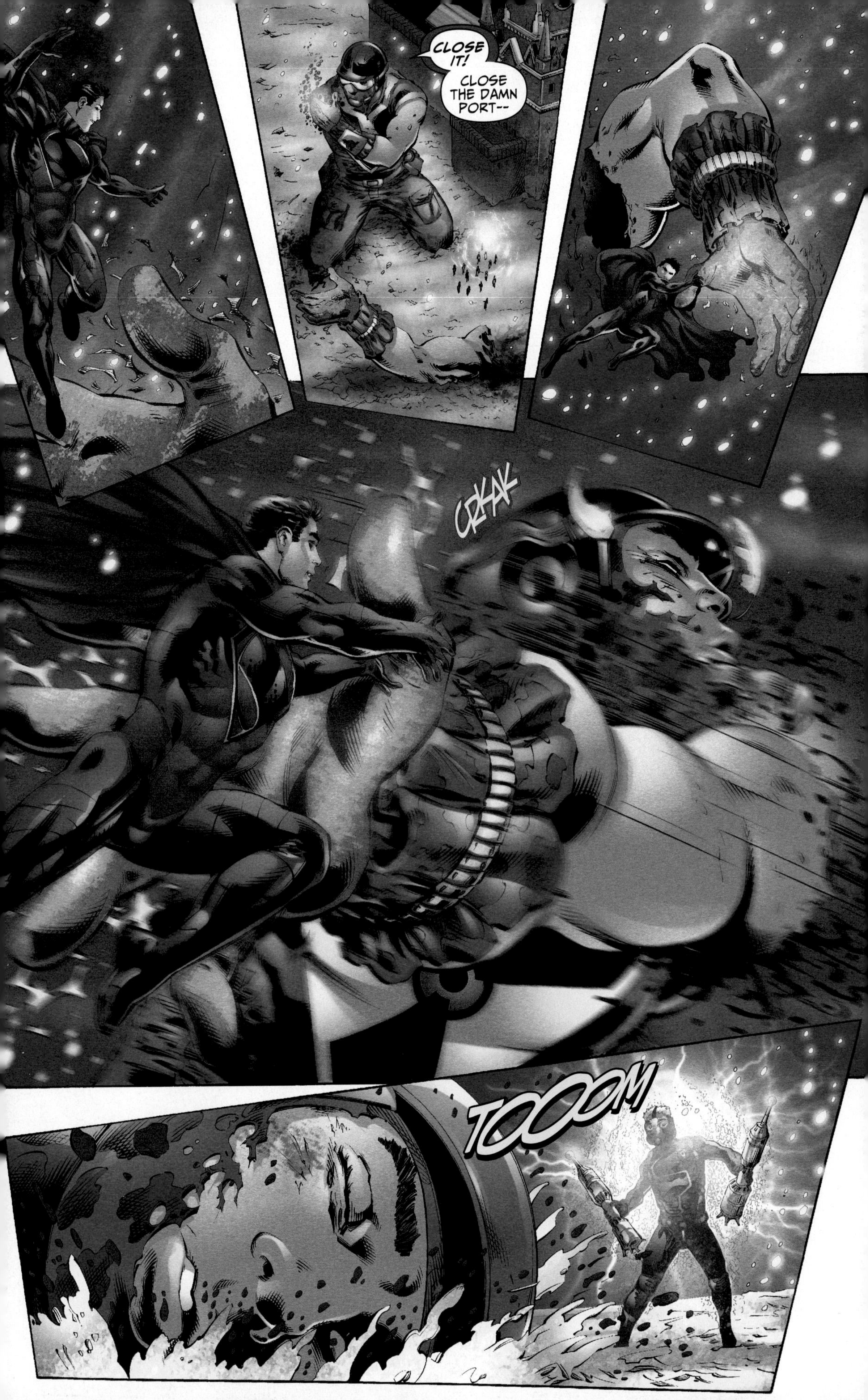
CLOSE IT!
CLOSE THE DAMN PORT--
CRKAK
TOOOOM

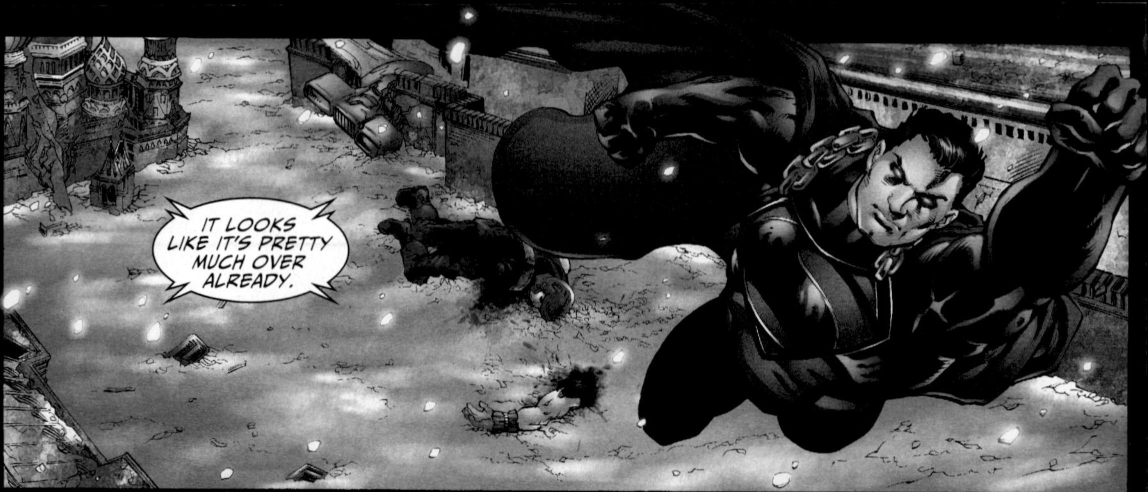
IT LOOKS LIKE IT'S PRETTY MUCH OVER ALREADY.

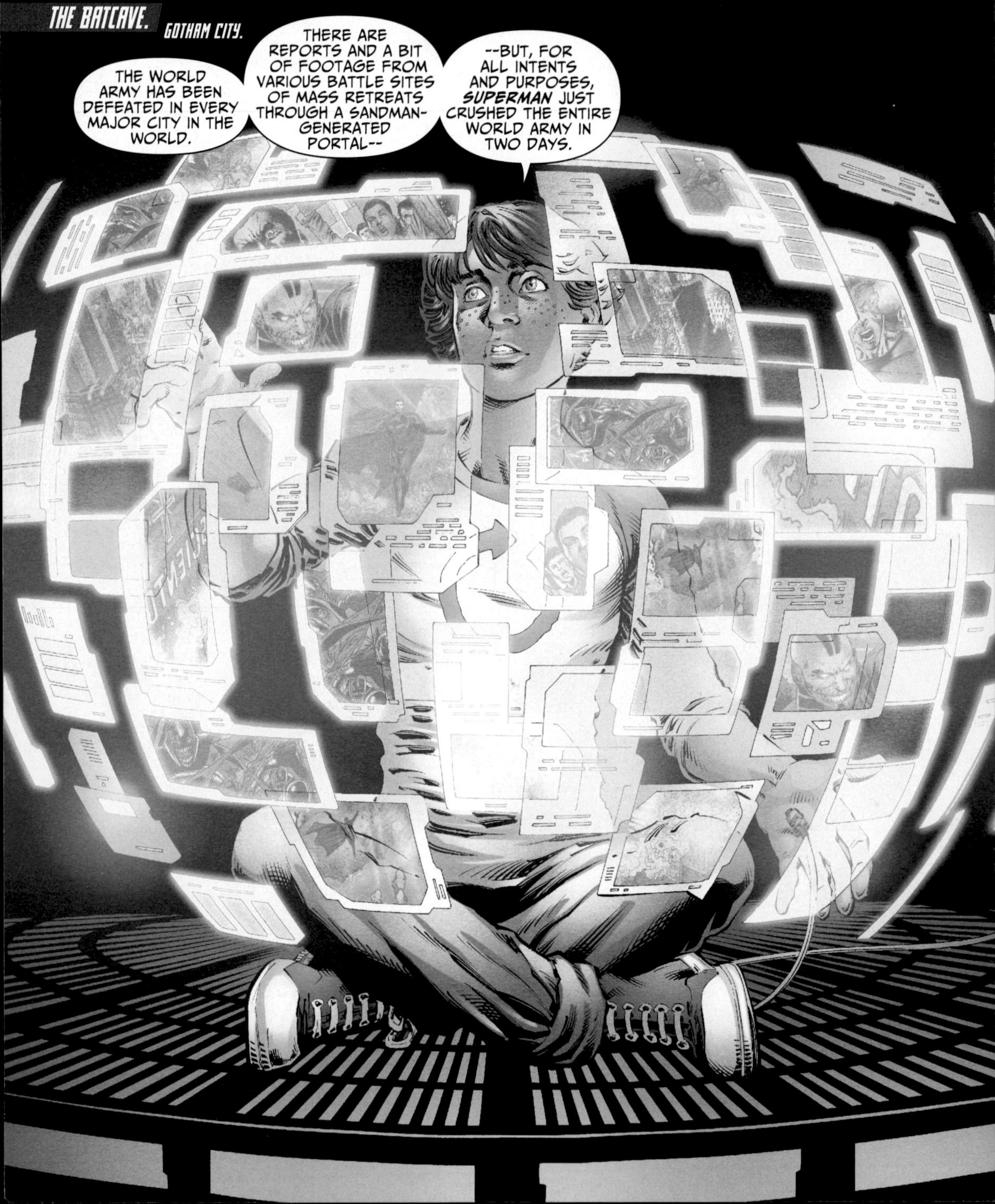
THE BATCAVE.
GOTHAM CITY.
THE WORLD ARMY HAS BEEN DEFEATED IN EVERY MAJOR CITY IN THE WORLD.
THERE ARE REPORTS AND A BIT OF FOOTAGE FROM VARIOUS BATTLE SITES OF MASS RETREATS THROUGH A SANDMAN-GENERATED PORTAL--
--BUT, FOR ALL INTENTS AND PURPOSES, SUPERMAN JUST CRUSHED THE ENTIRE WORLD ARMY IN TWO DAYS.

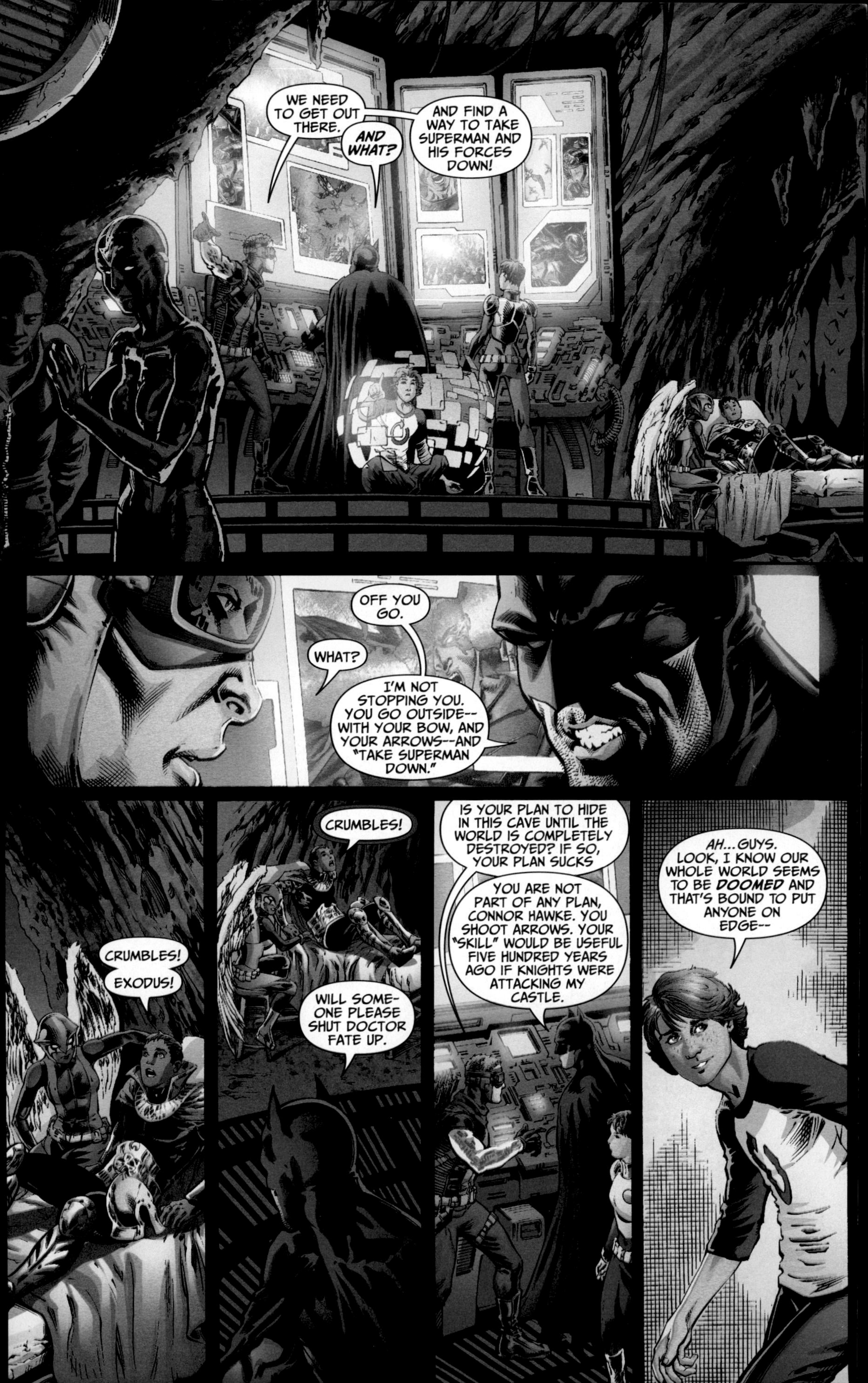
WE NEED TO GET OUT THERE.
AND FIND A WAY TO TAKE SUPERMAN AND HIS FORCES DOWN!
AND WHAT?
OFF YOU GO.
WHAT?
I'M NOT STOPPING YOU. YOU GO OUTSIDE-- WITH YOUR BOW, AND YOUR ARROWS--AND "TAKE SUPERMAN DOWN."
CRUMBLES!
EXODUS!
CRUMBLES!
WILL SOME-ONE PLEASE SHUT DOCTOR FATE UP.
IS YOUR PLAN TO HIDE IN THIS CAVE UNTIL THE WORLD IS COMPLETELY DESTROYED? IF SO, YOUR PLAN SUCKS
YOU ARE NOT PART OF ANY PLAN, CONNOR HAWKE. YOU SHOOT ARROWS. YOUR "SKILL" WOULD BE USEFUL FIVE HUNDRED YEARS AGO IF KNIGHTS WERE ATTACKING MY CASTLE.
AH...GUYS. LOOK, I KNOW OUR WHOLE WORLD SEEMS TO BE DOOMED AND THAT'S BOUND TO PUT ANYONE ON EDGE--

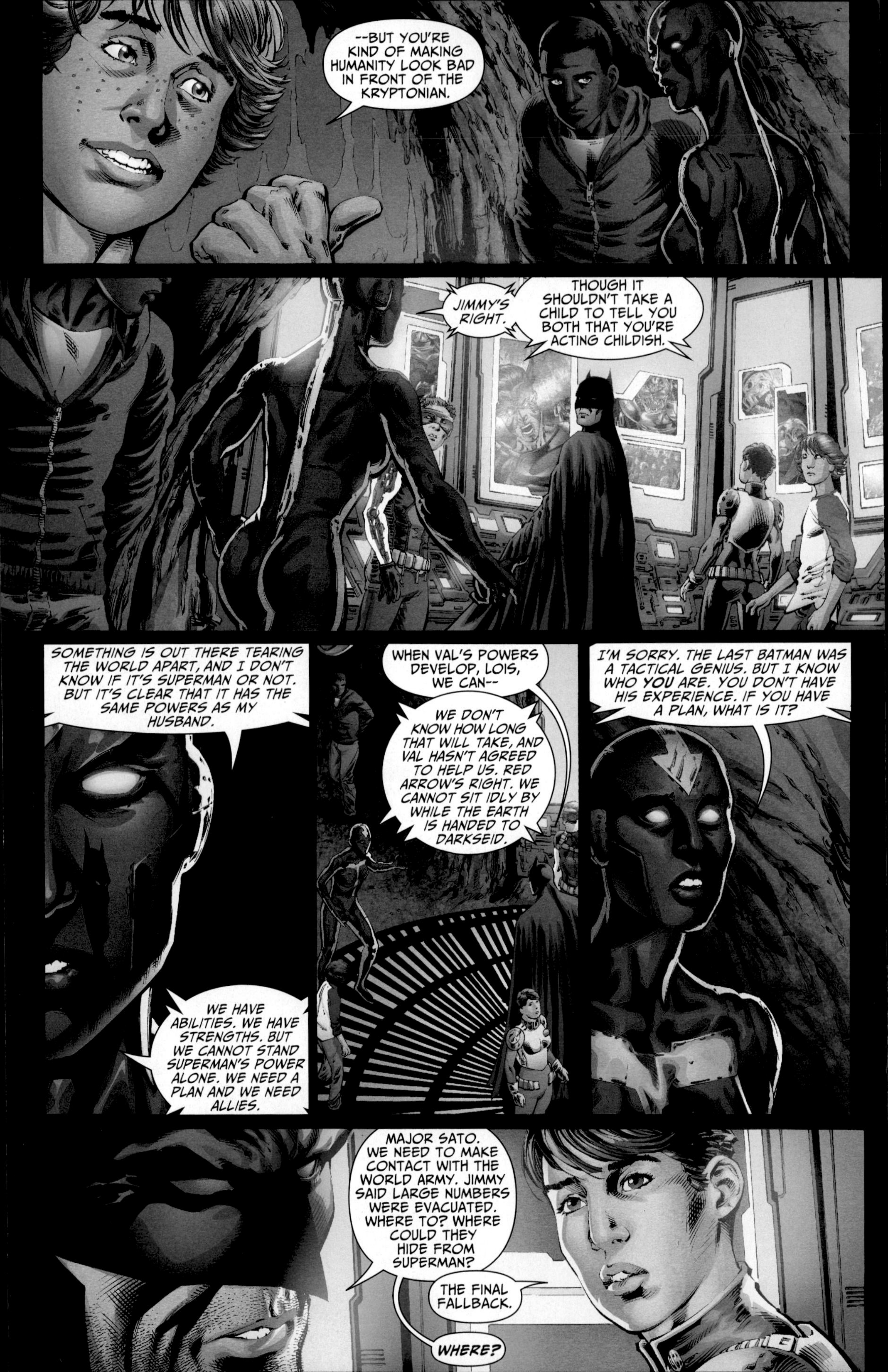
--BUT YOU'RE KIND OF MAKING HUMANITY LOOK BAD IN FRONT OF THE KRYPTONIAN.
JIMMY'S RIGHT.
THOUGH IT SHOULDN'T TAKE A CHILD TO TELL YOU BOTH THAT YOU'RE ACTING CHILDISH.
SOMETHING IS OUT THERE TEARING THE WORLD APART, AND I DON'T KNOW IF IT'S SUPERMAN OR NOT. BUT IT'S CLEAR THAT IT HAS THE SAME POWERS AS MY HUSBAND.
WE HAVE ABILITIES. WE HAVE STRENGTHS. BUT WE CANNOT STAND SUPERMAN'S POWER ALONE. WE NEED A PLAN AND WE NEED ALLIES.
WHEN VAL'S POWERS DEVELOP, LOIS, WE CAN--
WE DON'T KNOW HOW LONG THAT WILL TAKE, AND VAL HASN'T AGREED TO HELP US. RED ARROW'S RIGHT. WE CANNOT SIT IDLY BY WHILE THE EARTH IS HANDED TO DARKSEID.
I'M SORRY. THE LAST BATMAN WAS A TACTICAL GENIUS. BUT I KNOW WHO YOU ARE. YOU DON'T HAVE HIS EXPERIENCE. IF YOU HAVE A PLAN, WHAT IS IT?
MAJOR SATO. WE NEED TO MAKE CONTACT WITH THE WORLD ARMY. JIMMY SAID LARGE NUMBERS WERE EVACUATED. WHERE TO? WHERE COULD THEY HIDE FROM SUPERMAN?
THE FINAL FALLBACK.
WHERE?

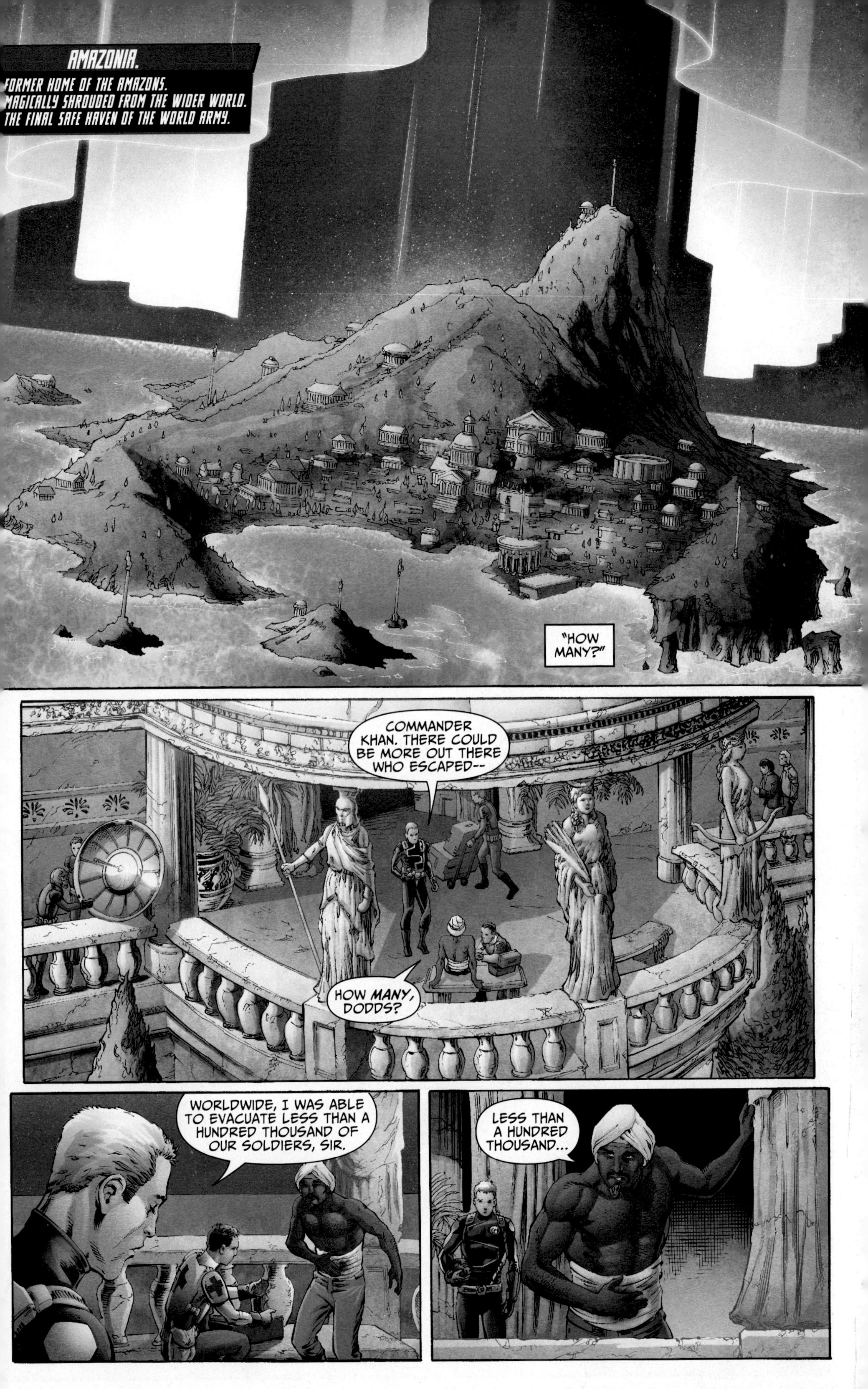
AMAZONIA.
FORMER HOME OF THE AMAZONS.
MAGICALLY SHROUDED FROM THE WIDER WORLD.
THE FINAL SAFE HAVEN OF THE WORLD ARMY.
"HOW MANY?"
COMMANDER KHAN. THERE COULD BE MORE OUT THERE WHO ESCAPED--
HOW MANY, DODDS?
WORLDWIDE, I WAS ABLE TO EVACUATE LESS THAN A HUNDRED THOUSAND OF OUR SOLDIERS, SIR.
LESS THAN A HUNDRED THOUSAND...

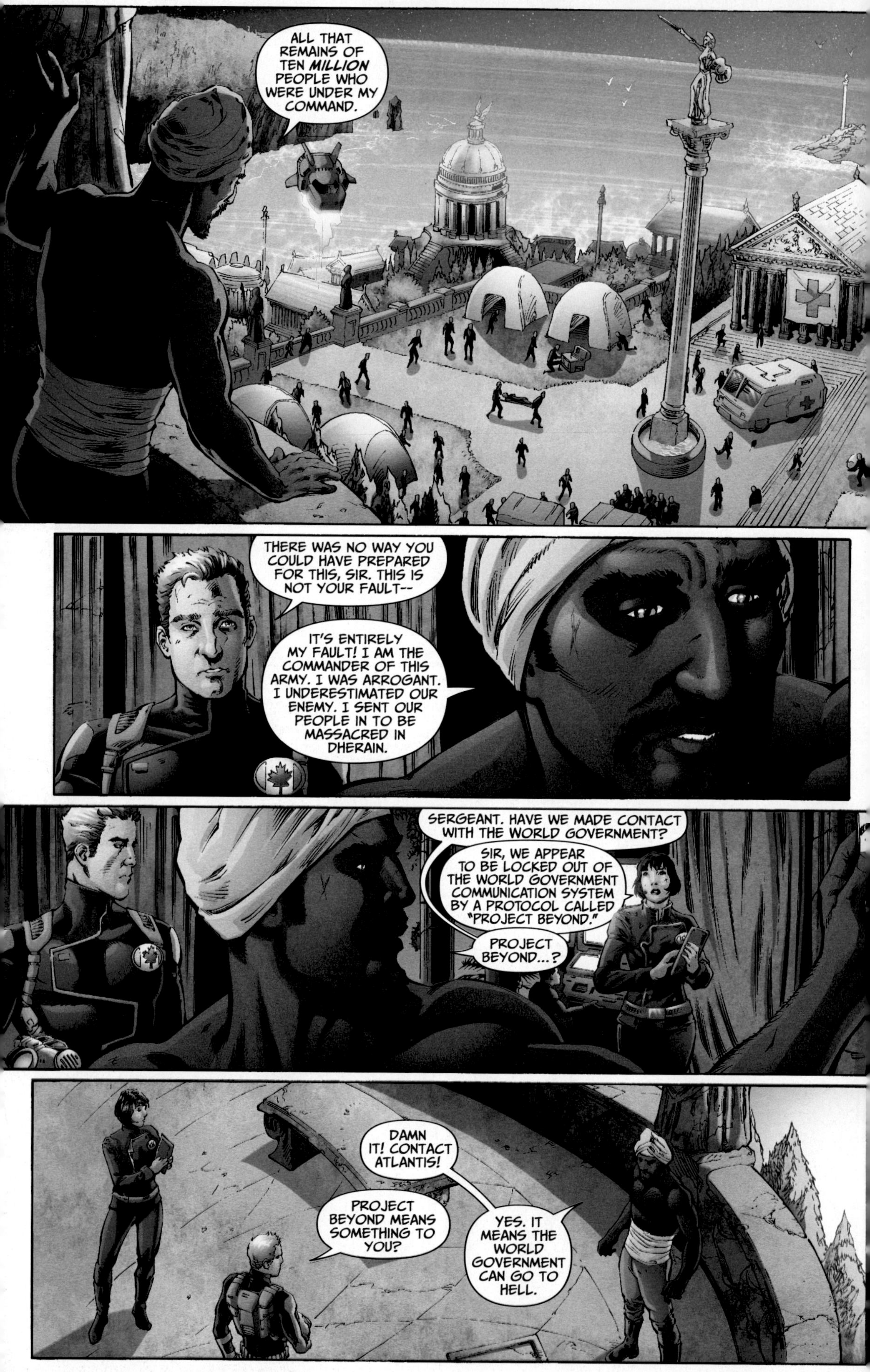
ALL THAT REMAINS OF TEN MILLION PEOPLE WHO WERE UNDER MY COMMAND.
THERE WAS NO WAY YOU COULD HAVE PREPARED FOR THIS, SIR. THIS IS NOT YOUR FAULT--
IT'S ENTIRELY MY FAULT! I AM THE COMMANDER OF THIS ARMY. I WAS ARROGANT. I UNDERESTIMATED OUR ENEMY. I SENT OUR PEOPLE IN TO BE MASSACRED IN DHERAIN.
SERGEANT. HAVE WE MADE CONTACT WITH THE WORLD GOVERNMENT?
SIR, WE APPEAR TO BE LOCKED OUT OF THE WORLD GOVERNMENT COMMUNICATION SYSTEM BY A PROTOCOL CALLED "PROJECT BEYOND."
PROJECT BEYOND...?
DAMN IT! CONTACT ATLANTIS!
PROJECT BEYOND MEANS SOMETHING TO YOU?
YES. IT MEANS THE WORLD GOVERNMENT CAN GO TO HELL.

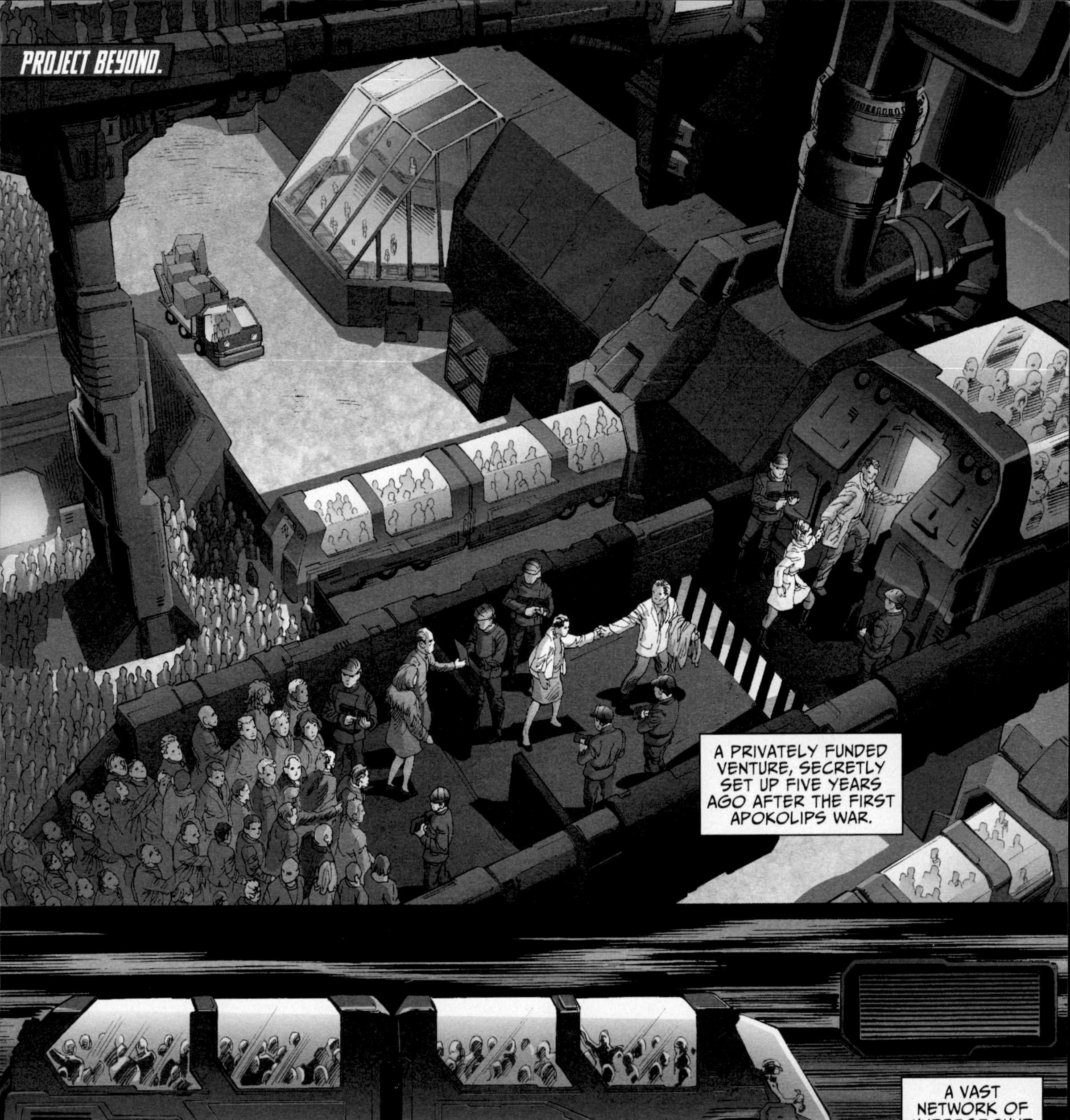
PROJECT BEYOND.
A PRIVATELY FUNDED VENTURE, SECRETLY SET UP FIVE YEARS AGO AFTER THE FIRST APOKOLIPS WAR.

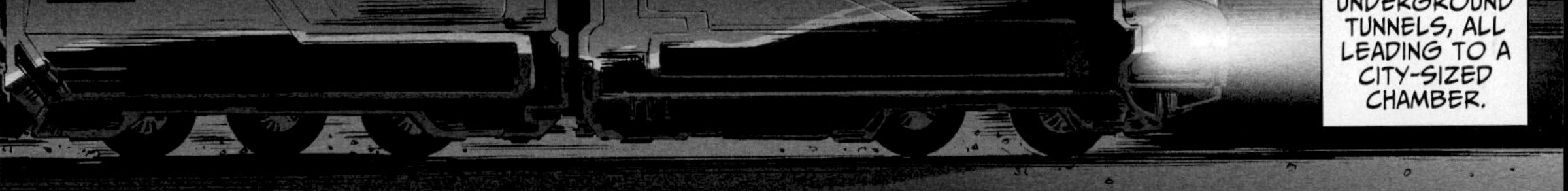
A VAST NETWORK OF UNDERGROUND TUNNELS, ALL LEADING TO A CITY-SIZED CHAMBER.

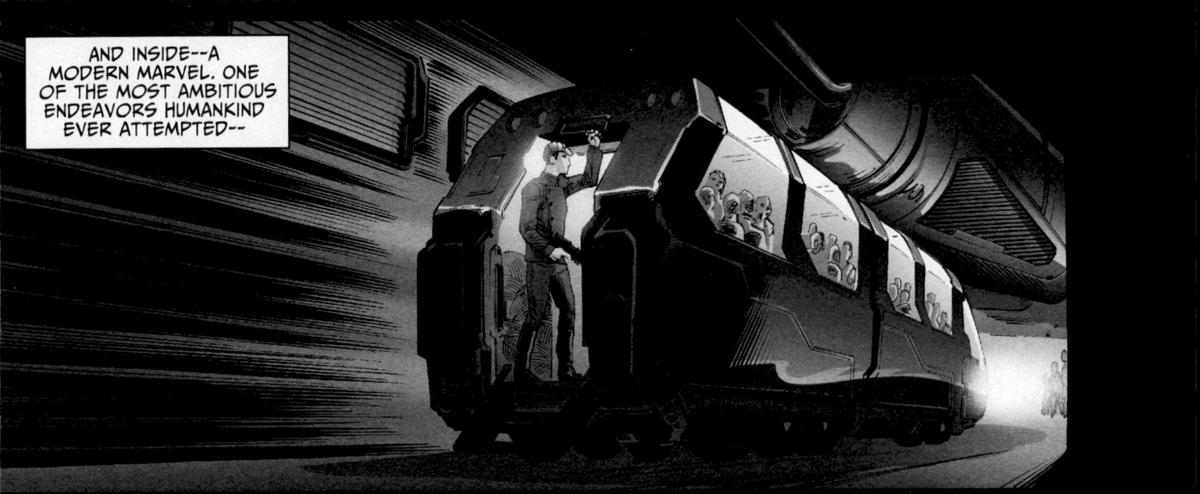
AND INSIDE--A MODERN MARVEL. ONE OF THE MOST AMBITIOUS ENDEAVORS HUMANKIND EVER ATTEMPTED--

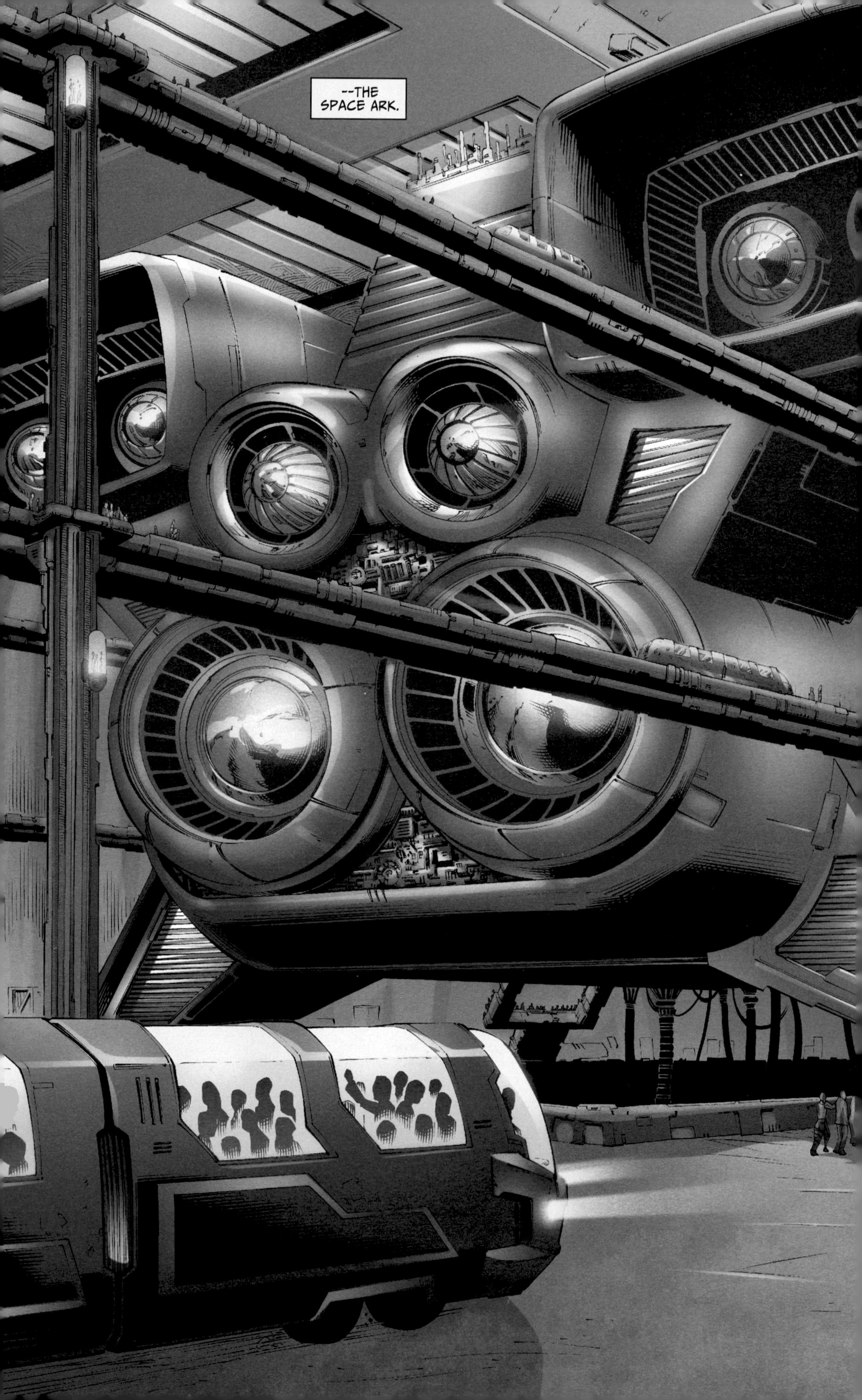
--THE SPACE ARK.

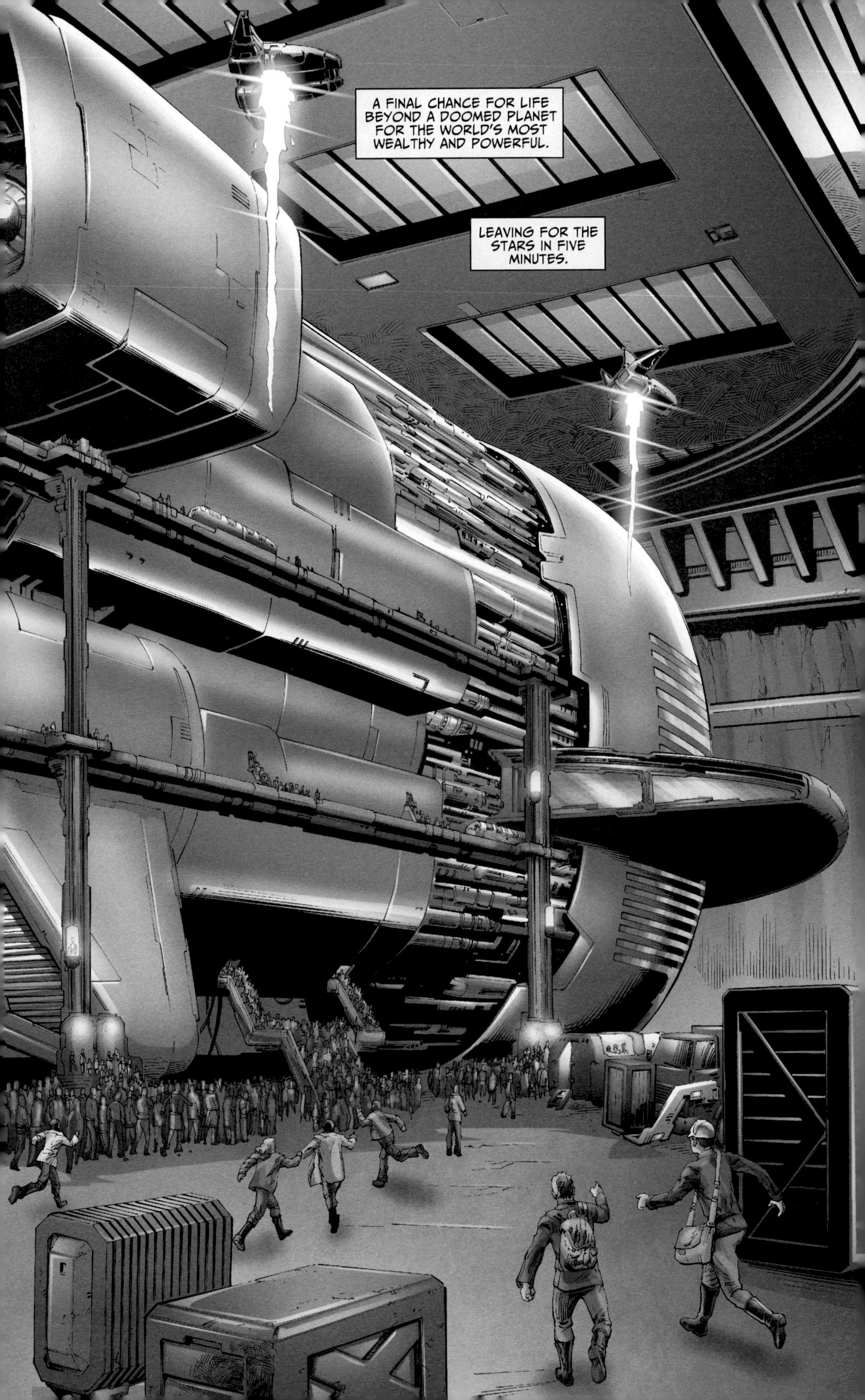
A FINAL CHANCE FOR LIFE BEYOND A DOOMED PLANET FOR THE WORLD'S MOST WEALTHY AND POWERFUL.
LEAVING FOR THE STARS IN FIVE MINUTES.

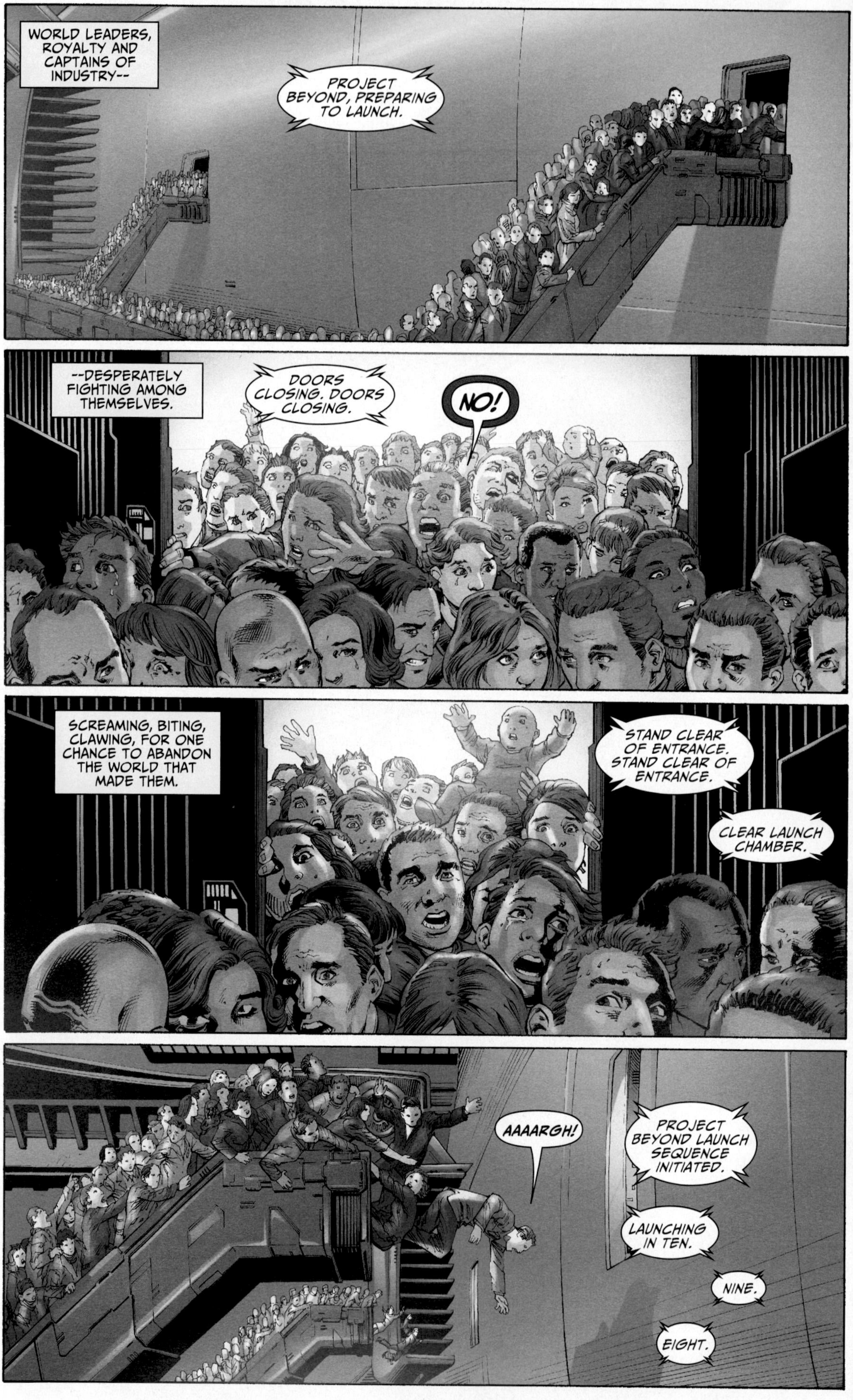

WORLD LEADERS, ROYALTY AND CAPTAINS OF INDUSTRY--
PROJECT BEYOND, PREPARING TO LAUNCH.
--DESPERATELY FIGHTING AMONG THEMSELVES.
DOORS CLOSING. DOORS CLOSING.
NO!
SCREAMING, BITING, CLAWING, FOR ONE CHANCE TO ABANDON THE WORLD THAT MADE THEM.
STAND CLEAR OF ENTRANCE. STAND CLEAR OF ENTRANCE.
CLEAR LAUNCH CHAMBER.
AAAARGH!
PROJECT BEYOND LAUNCH SEQUENCE INITIATED.
LAUNCHING IN TEN.
NINE.
EIGHT.

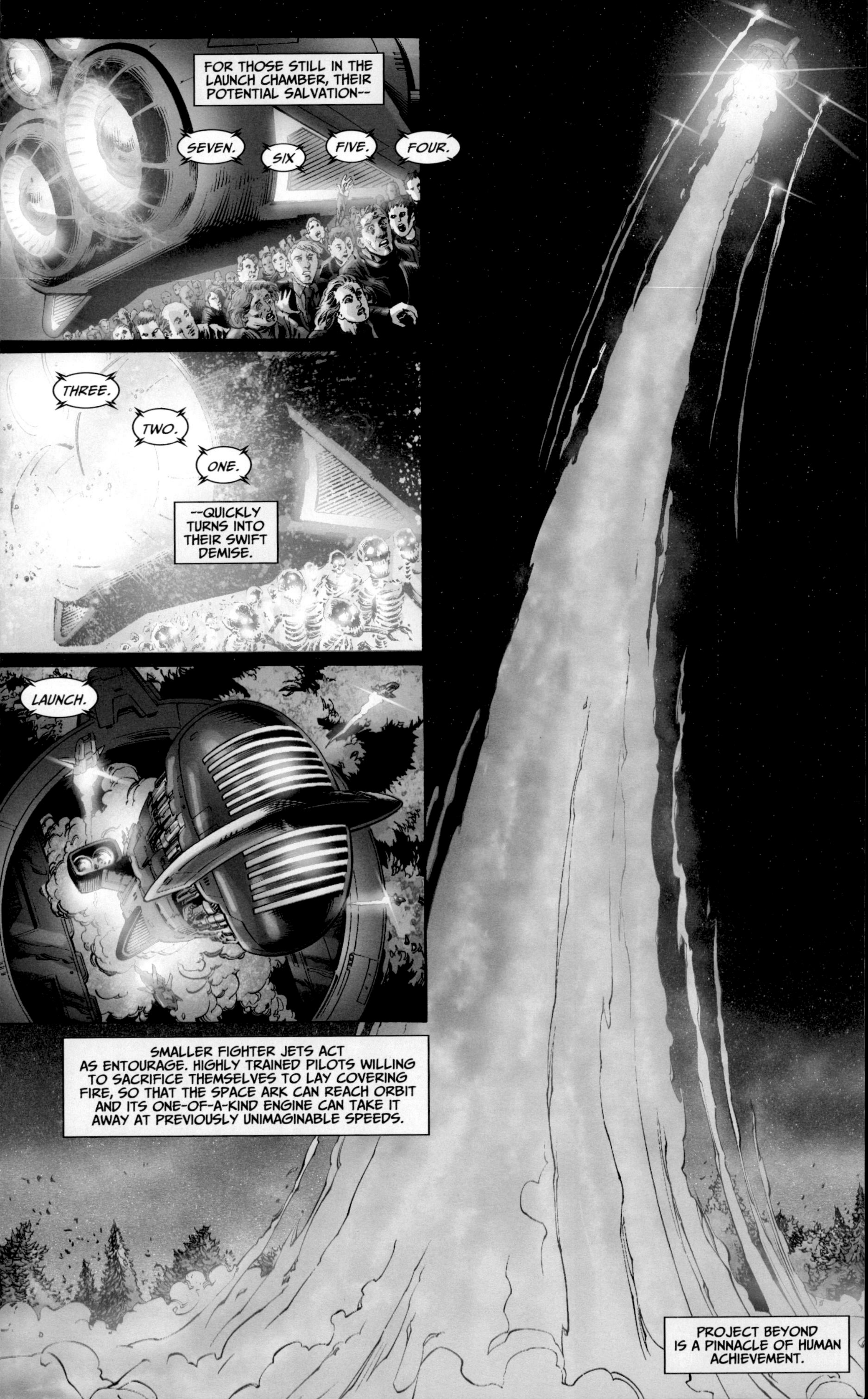

FOR THOSE STILL IN THE LAUNCH CHAMBER, THEIR POTENTIAL SALVATION--
SEVEN.
SIX
FIVE.
FOUR.
THREE.
TWO.
ONE.
--QUICKLY TURNS INTO THEIR SWIFT DEMISE.
LAUNCH.
SMALLER FIGHTER JETS ACT AS ENTOURAGE. HIGHLY TRAINED PILOTS WILLING TO SACRIFICE THEMSELVES TO LAY COVERING FIRE, SO THAT THE SPACE ARK CAN REACH ORBIT AND ITS ONE-OF-A-KIND ENGINE CAN TAKE IT AWAY AT PREVIOUSLY UNIMAGINABLE SPEEDS.
PROJECT BEYOND IS A PINNACLE OF HUMAN ACHIEVEMENT.

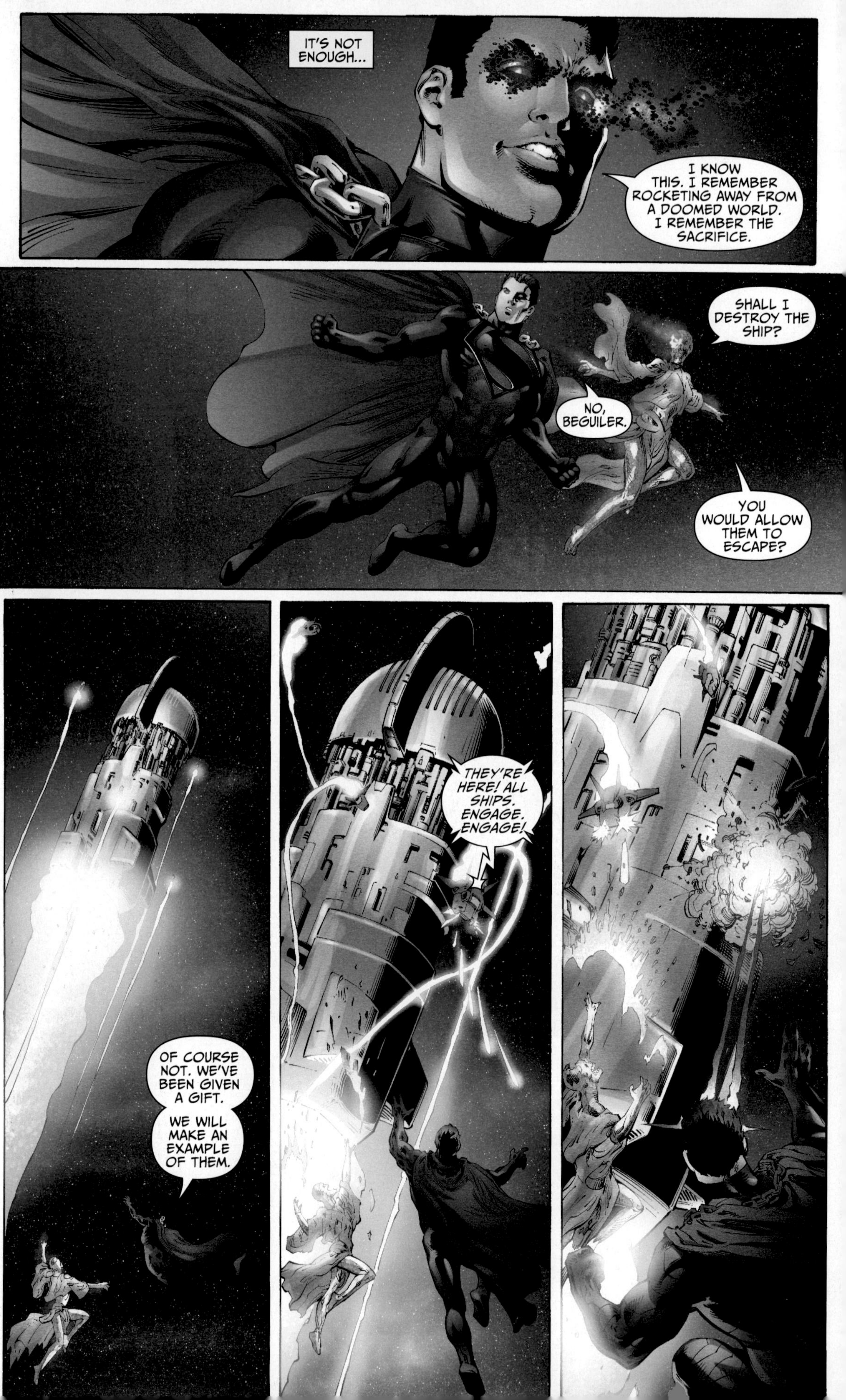
IT'S NOT ENOUGH...
I KNOW THIS. I REMEMBER ROCKETING AWAY FROM A DOOMED WORLD. I REMEMBER THE SACRIFICE.
SHALL I DESTROY THE SHIP?
NO, BEGUILER.
YOU WOULD ALLOW THEM TO ESCAPE?
OF COURSE NOT. WE'VE BEEN GIVEN A GIFT.
WE WILL MAKE AN EXAMPLE OF THEM.
THEY'RE HERE! ALL SHIPS. ENGAGE. ENGAGE!

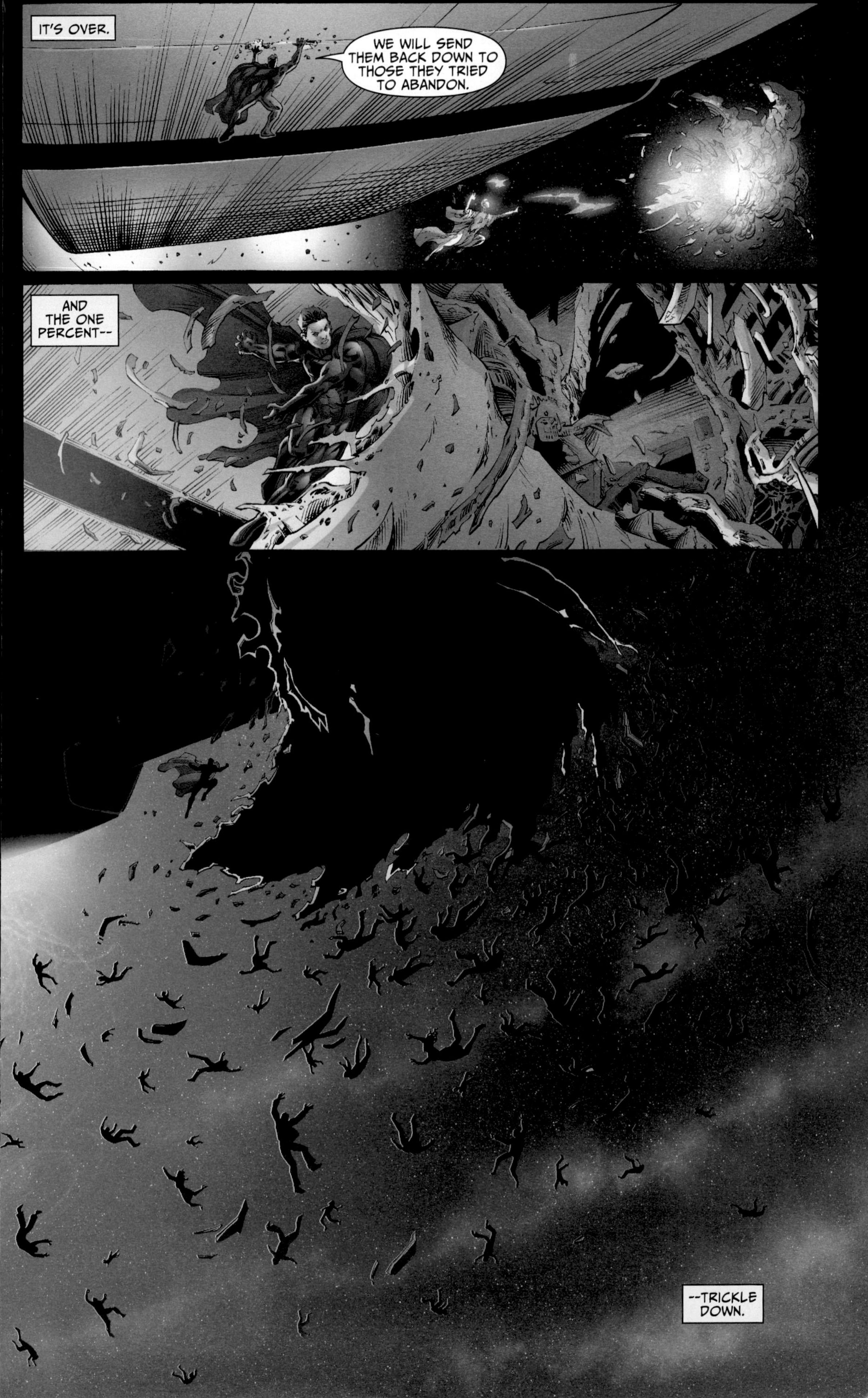
IT'S OVER.
WE WILL SEND THEM BACK DOWN TO THOSE THEY TRIED TO ABANDON.
AND THE ONE PERCENT--
--TRICKLE DOWN.

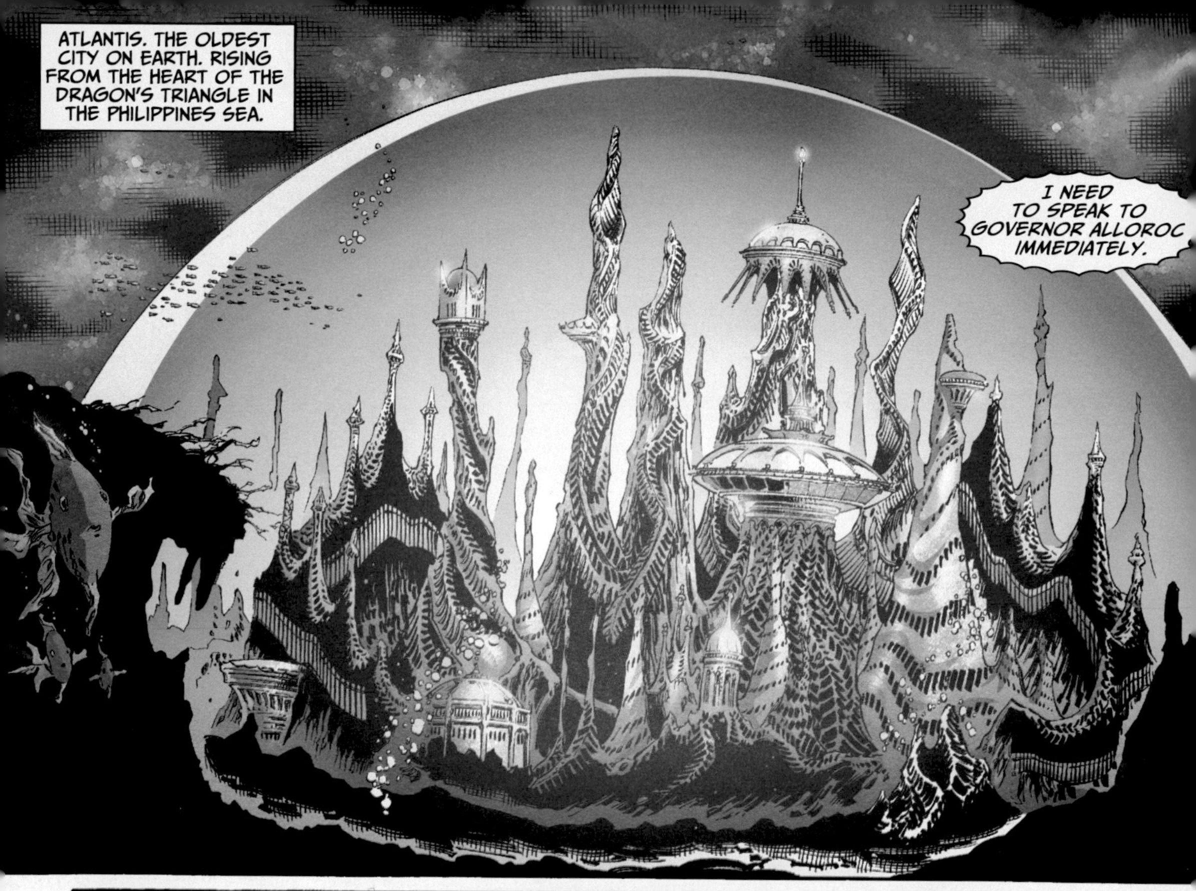
ATLANTIS. THE OLDEST CITY ON EARTH. RISING FROM THE HEART OF THE DRAGON'S TRIANGLE IN THE PHILIPPINES SEA.
I NEED TO SPEAK TO GOVERNOR ALLOROC IMMEDIATELY.

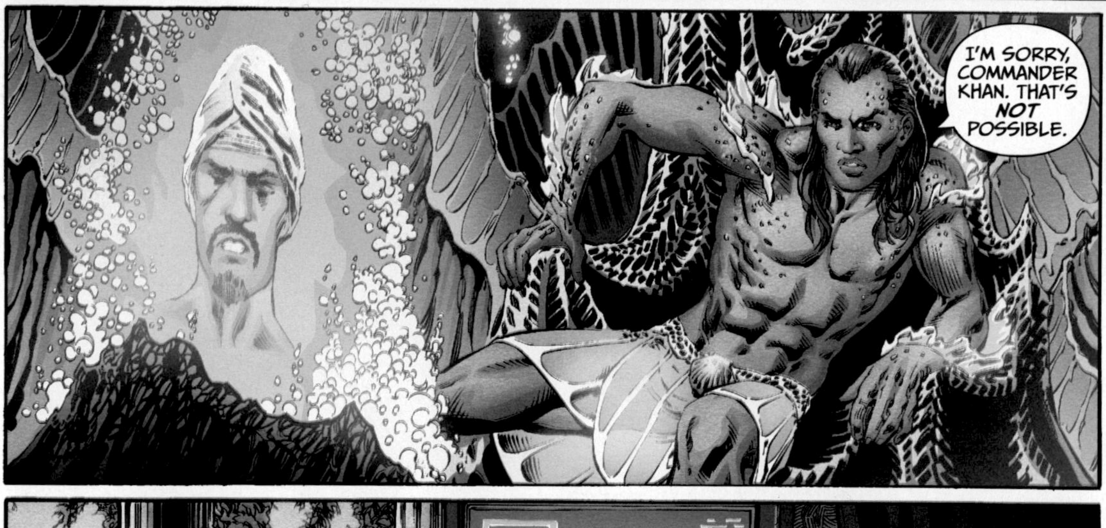
I'M SORRY, COMMANDER KHAN. THAT'S NOT POSSIBLE.

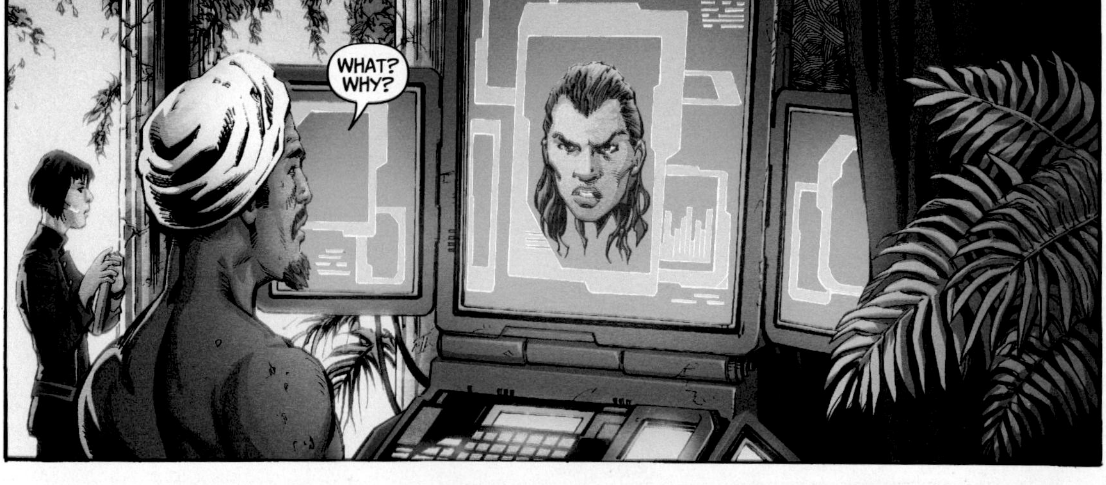
WHAT? WHY?

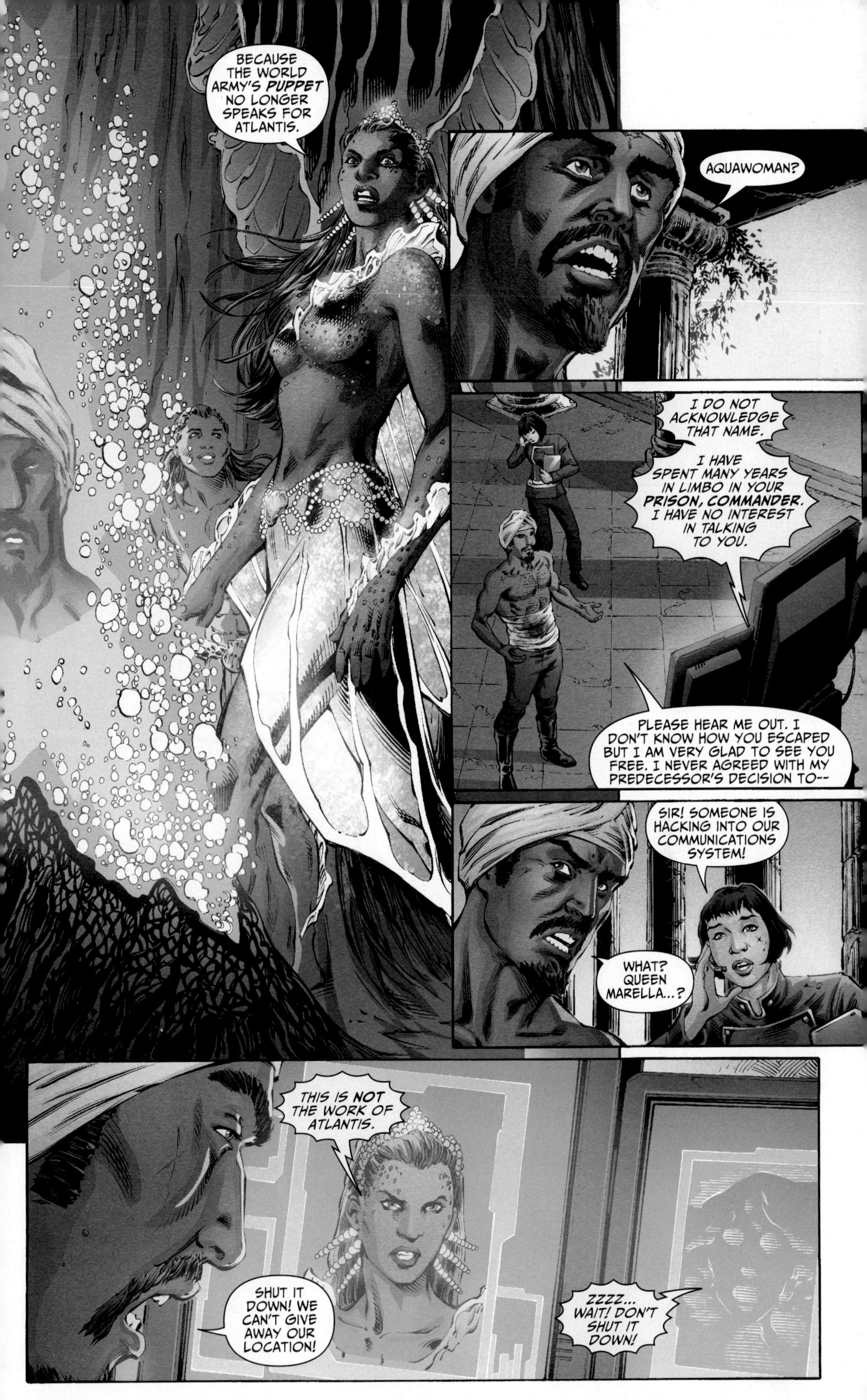
BECAUSE THE WORLD ARMY'S **PUPPET** NO LONGER SPEAKS FOR ATLANTIS.
AQUAWOMAN?
I DO NOT ACKNOWLEDGE THAT NAME.
I HAVE SPENT MANY YEARS IN LIMBO IN YOUR **PRISON, COMMANDER.** I HAVE NO INTEREST IN TALKING TO YOU.
PLEASE HEAR ME OUT. I DON'T KNOW HOW YOU ESCAPED BUT I AM VERY GLAD TO SEE YOU FREE. I NEVER AGREED WITH MY PREDECESSOR'S DECISION TO--
SIR! SOMEONE IS HACKING INTO OUR COMMUNICATIONS SYSTEM!
WHAT? QUEEN MARELLA...?
THIS IS **NOT** THE WORK OF ATLANTIS.
SHUT IT DOWN! WE CAN'T GIVE AWAY OUR LOCATION!
ZZZZ... WAIT! DON'T SHUT IT DOWN!

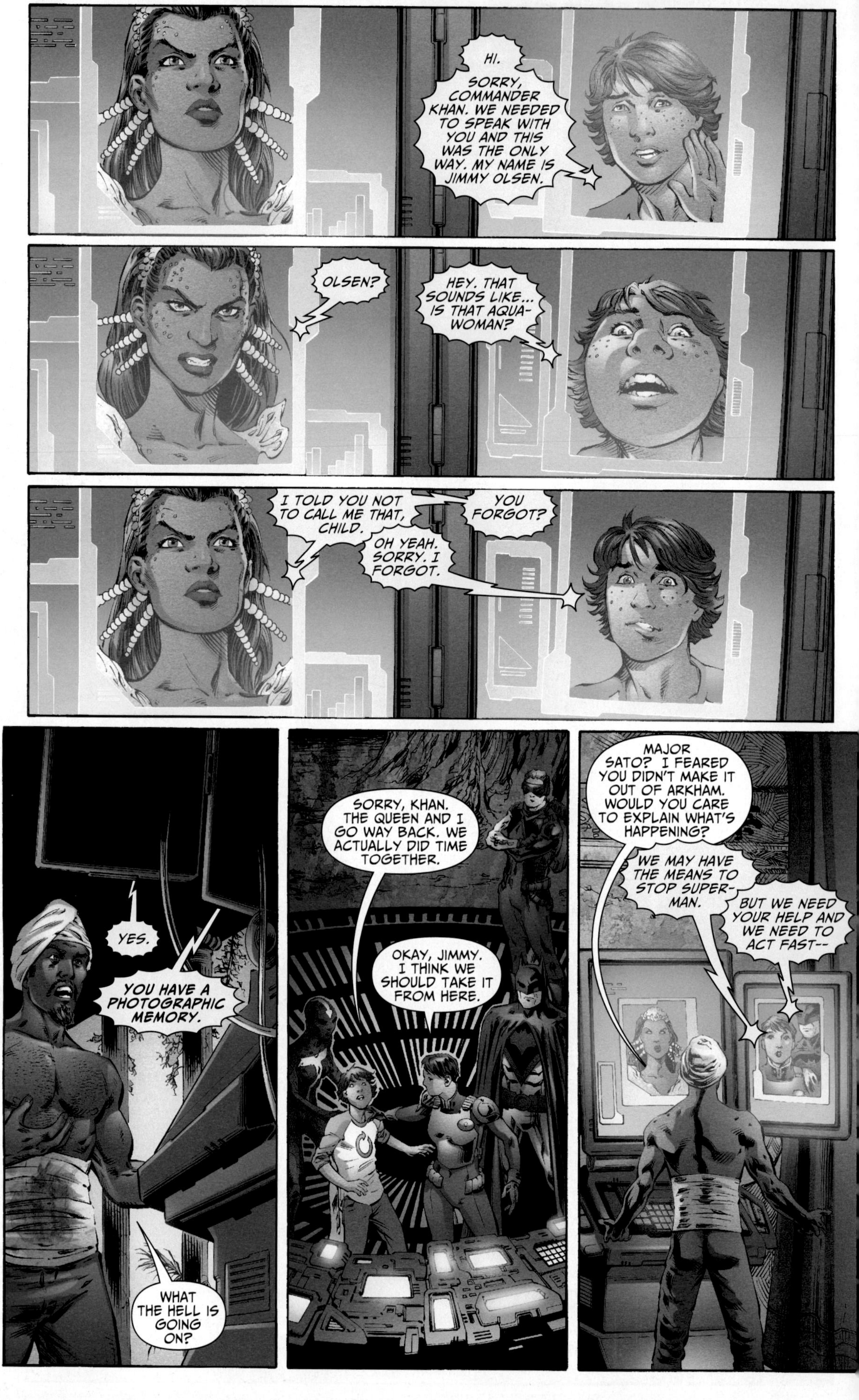
HI.
SORRY, COMMANDER KHAN. WE NEEDED TO SPEAK WITH YOU AND THIS WAS THE ONLY WAY. MY NAME IS JIMMY OLSEN.
OLSEN?
HEY. THAT SOUNDS LIKE... IS THAT AQUA-WOMAN?
I TOLD YOU NOT TO CALL ME THAT, CHILD.
YOU FORGOT?
OH YEAH. SORRY. I FORGOT.
YES.
YOU HAVE A PHOTOGRAPHIC MEMORY.
WHAT THE HELL IS GOING ON?
SORRY, KHAN. THE QUEEN AND I GO WAY BACK. WE ACTUALLY DID TIME TOGETHER.
OKAY, JIMMY. I THINK WE SHOULD TAKE IT FROM HERE.
MAJOR SATO? I FEARED YOU DIDN'T MAKE IT OUT OF ARKHAM. WOULD YOU CARE TO EXPLAIN WHAT'S HAPPENING?
WE MAY HAVE THE MEANS TO STOP SUPER-MAN.
BUT WE NEED YOUR HELP AND WE NEED TO ACT FAST--

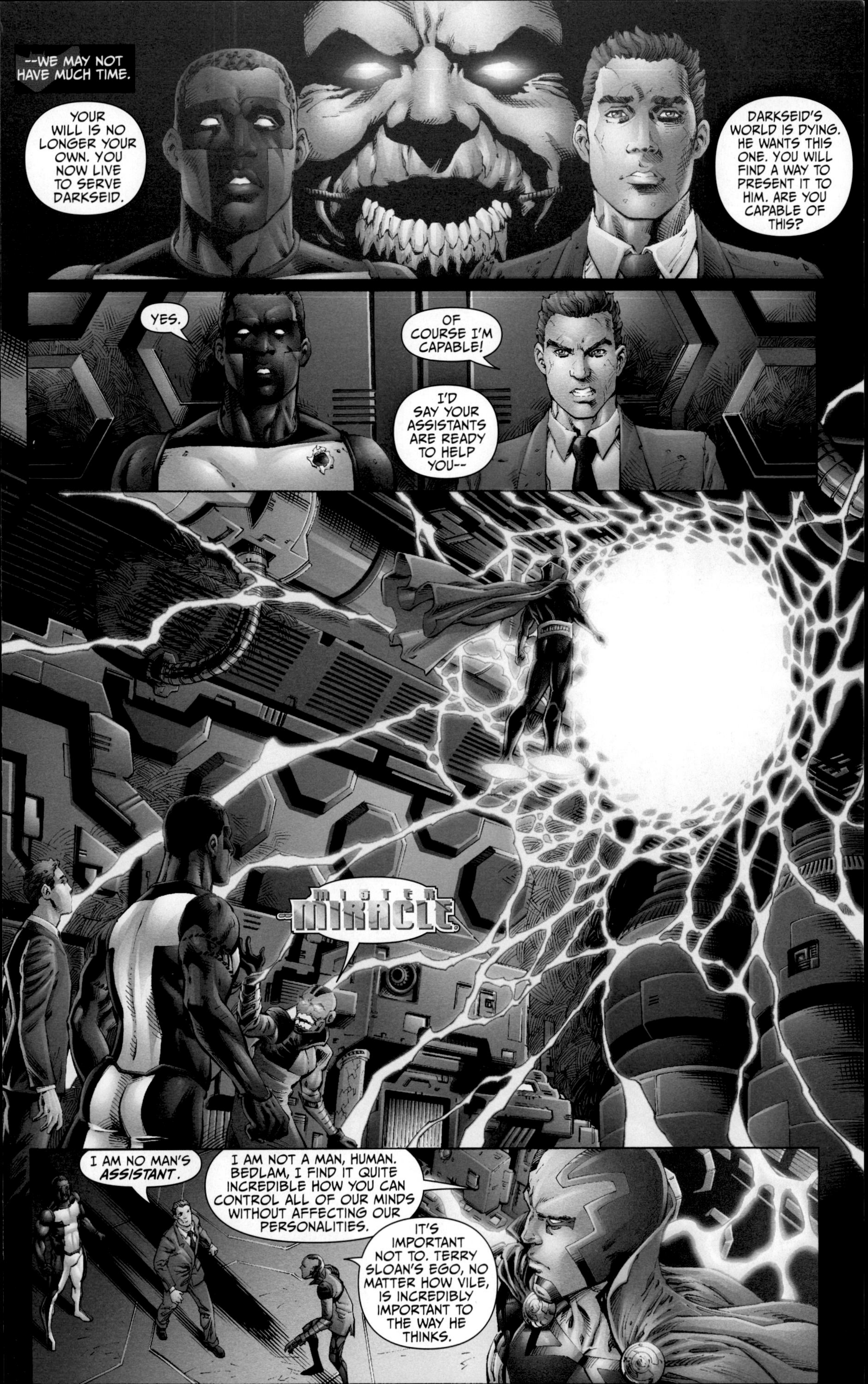
--WE MAY NOT HAVE MUCH TIME.
YOUR WILL IS NO LONGER YOUR OWN. YOU NOW LIVE TO SERVE DARKSEID.
DARKSEID'S WORLD IS DYING. HE WANTS THIS ONE. YOU WILL FIND A WAY TO PRESENT IT TO HIM. ARE YOU CAPABLE OF THIS?
YES.
OF COURSE I'M CAPABLE!
I'D SAY YOUR ASSISTANTS ARE READY TO HELP YOU--
MISTER MIRACLE
I AM NO MAN'S *ASSISTANT*.
I AM NOT A MAN, HUMAN. BEDLAM, I FIND IT QUITE INCREDIBLE HOW YOU CAN CONTROL ALL OF OUR MINDS WITHOUT AFFECTING OUR PERSONALITIES.
IT'S IMPORTANT NOT TO. TERRY SLOAN'S EGO, NO MATTER HOW VILE, IS INCREDIBLY IMPORTANT TO THE WAY HE THINKS.

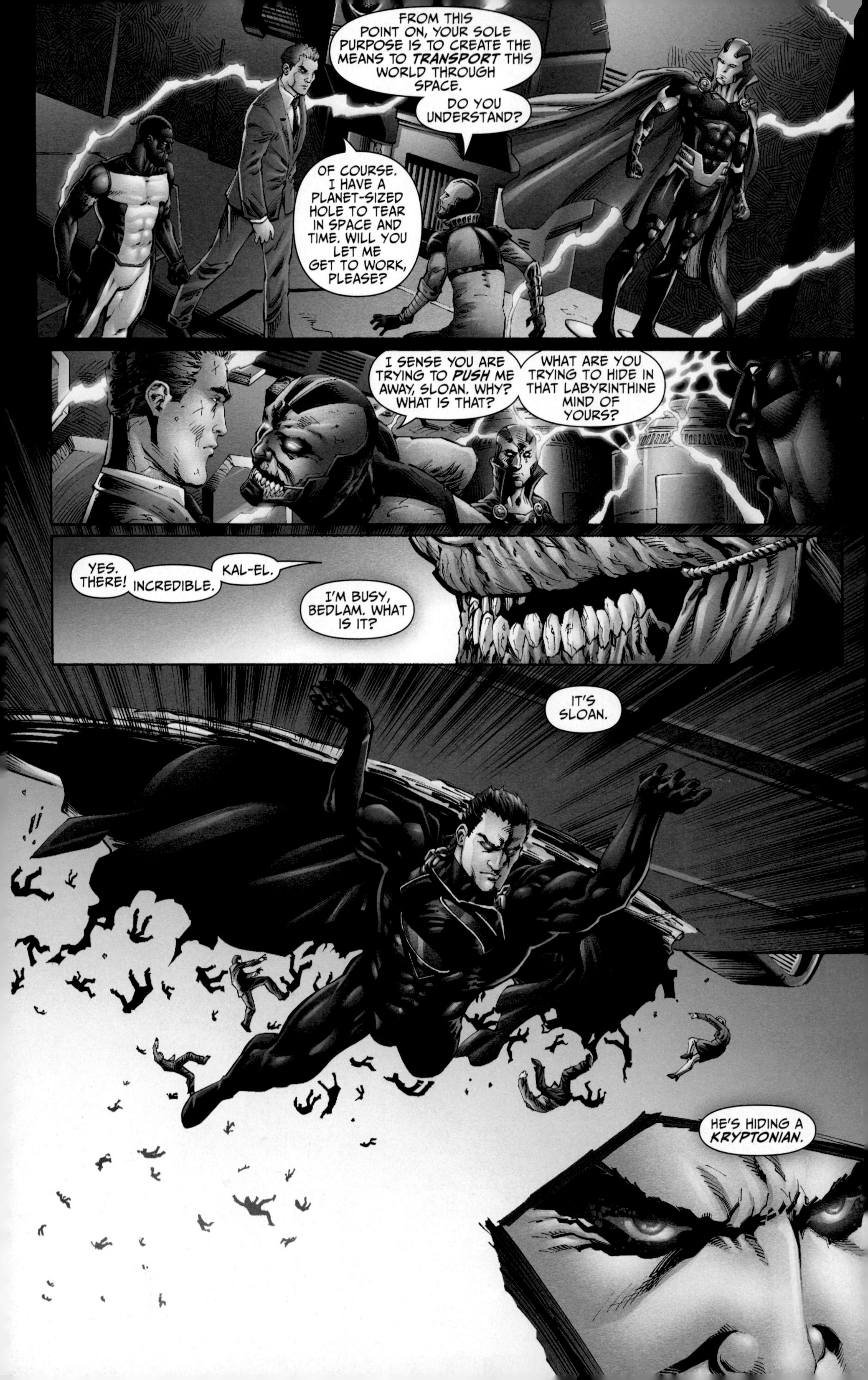

FROM THIS POINT ON, YOUR SOLE PURPOSE IS TO CREATE THE MEANS TO TRANSPORT THIS WORLD THROUGH SPACE.
DO YOU UNDERSTAND?
OF COURSE. I HAVE A PLANET-SIZED HOLE TO TEAR IN SPACE AND TIME. WILL YOU LET ME GET TO WORK, PLEASE?
I SENSE YOU ARE TRYING TO PUSH ME AWAY, SLOAN. WHY? WHAT IS THAT?
WHAT ARE YOU TRYING TO HIDE IN THAT LABYRINTHINE MIND OF YOURS?
YES. THERE!
INCREDIBLE.
KAL-EL.
I'M BUSY, BEDLAM. WHAT IS IT?
IT'S SLOAN.
HE'S HIDING A KRYPTONIAN.

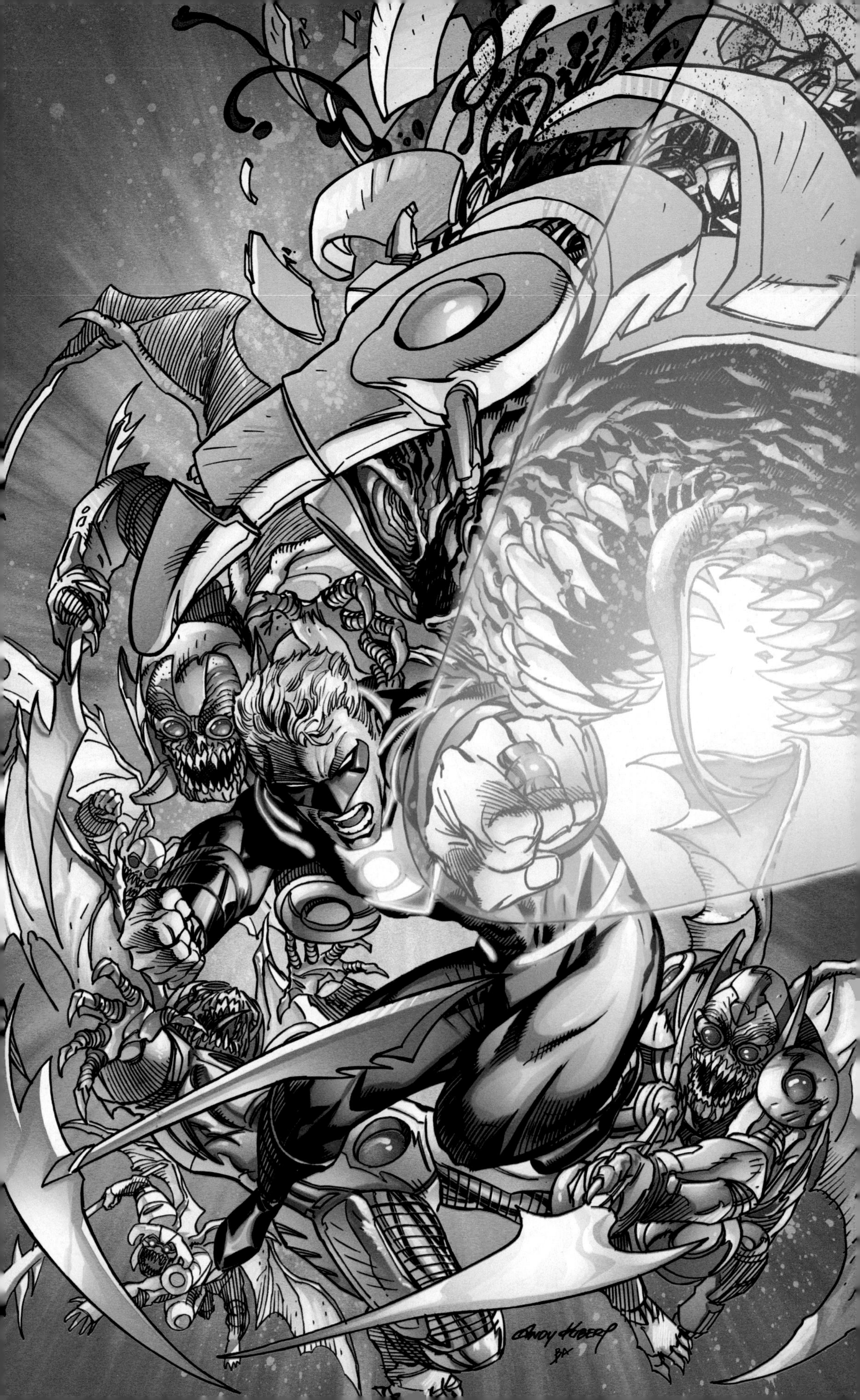

THE KRYPTONIAN PART 2

TOM TAYLOR writer NICOLA SCOTT penciller TREVOR SCOTT inker PETE PANTAZIS colorist cover by ANDY KUBERT & BRAD ANDERSON

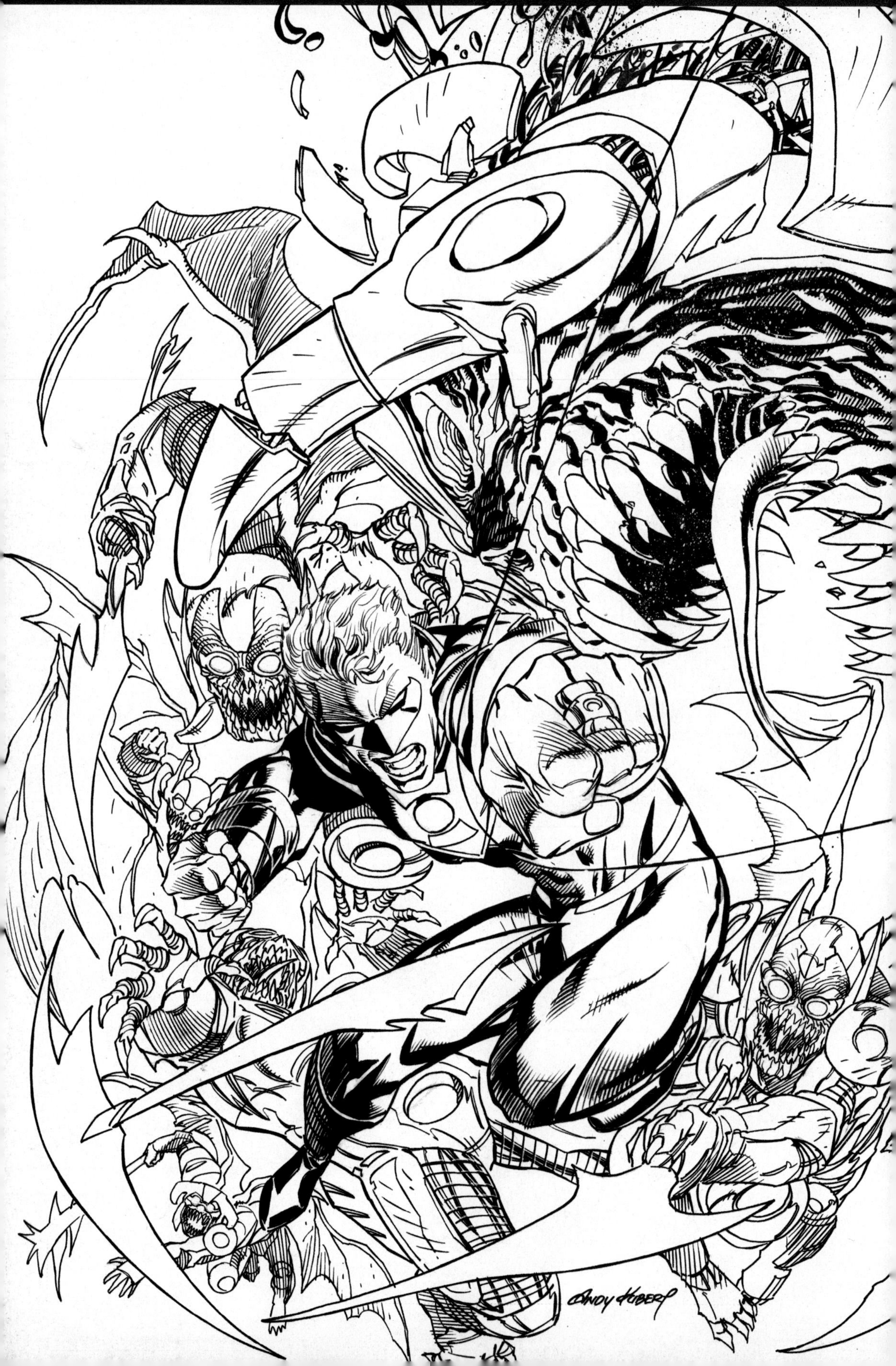
ANDY KUBERT

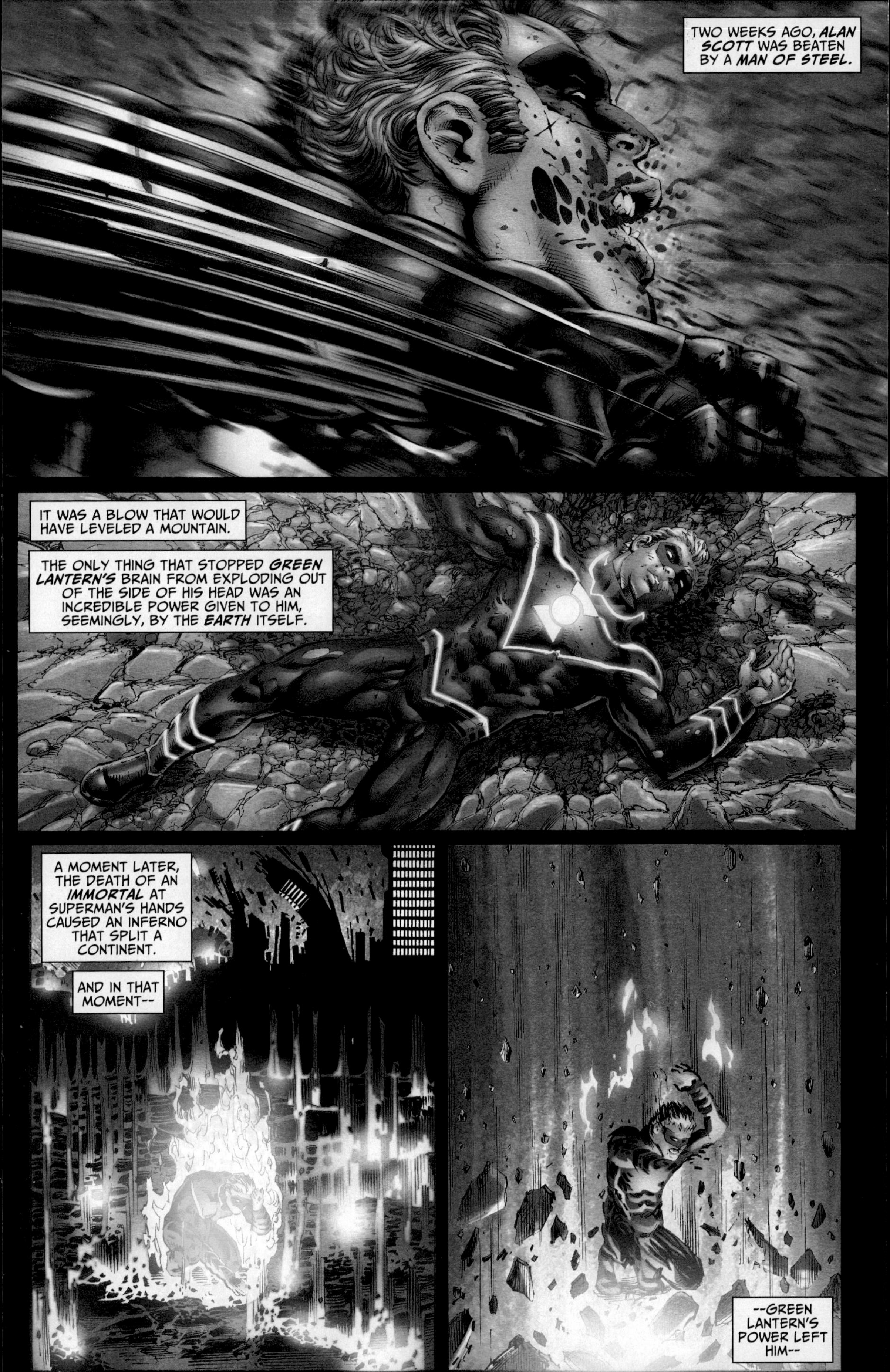
TWO WEEKS AGO, ALAN SCOTT WAS BEATEN BY A MAN OF STEEL.
IT WAS A BLOW THAT WOULD HAVE LEVELED A MOUNTAIN.
THE ONLY THING THAT STOPPED GREEN LANTERN'S BRAIN FROM EXPLODING OUT OF THE SIDE OF HIS HEAD WAS AN INCREDIBLE POWER GIVEN TO HIM, SEEMINGLY, BY THE EARTH ITSELF.
A MOMENT LATER, THE DEATH OF AN IMMORTAL AT SUPERMAN'S HANDS CAUSED AN INFERNO THAT SPLIT A CONTINENT.
AND IN THAT MOMENT--
--GREEN LANTERN'S POWER LEFT HIM--

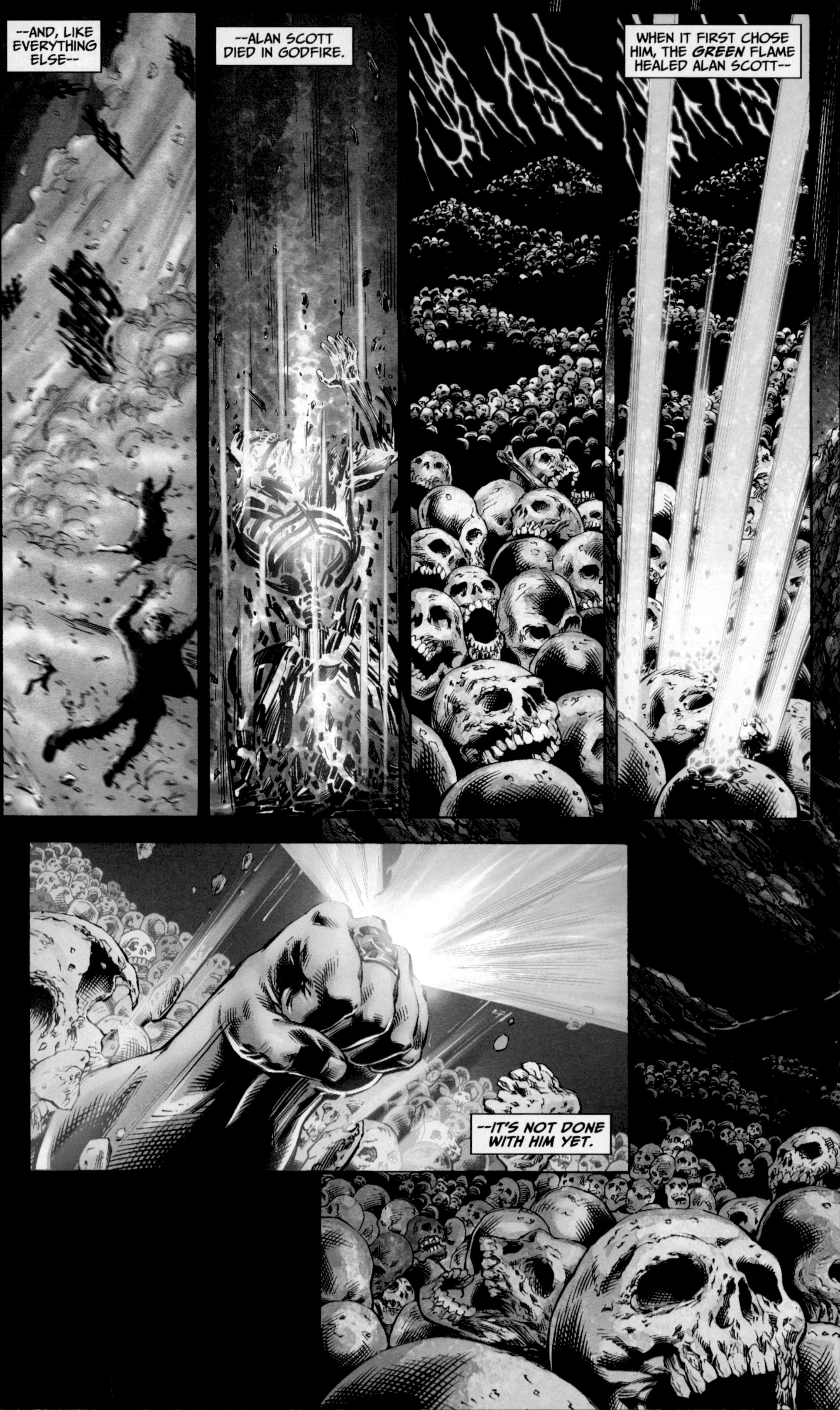
--AND, LIKE EVERYTHING ELSE--
--ALAN SCOTT DIED IN GODFIRE.
WHEN IT FIRST CHOSE HIM, THE GREEN FLAME HEALED ALAN SCOTT--
--IT'S NOT DONE WITH HIM YET.

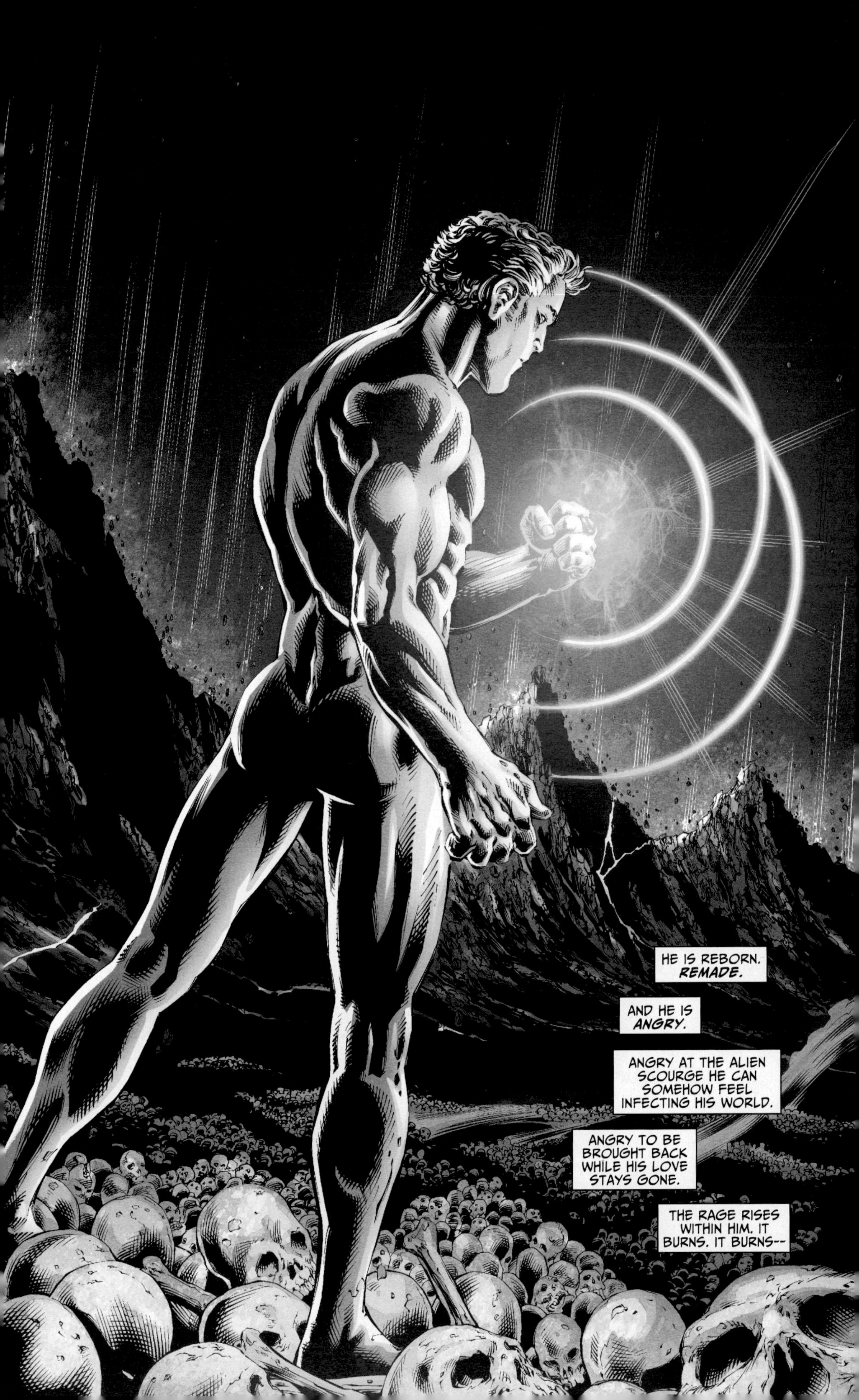
HE IS REBORN. *REMADE.*
AND HE IS *ANGRY.*
ANGRY AT THE ALIEN SCOURGE HE CAN SOMEHOW FEEL INFECTING HIS WORLD.
ANGRY TO BE BROUGHT BACK WHILE HIS LOVE STAYS GONE.
THE RAGE RISES WITHIN HIM. IT BURNS. IT BURNS--

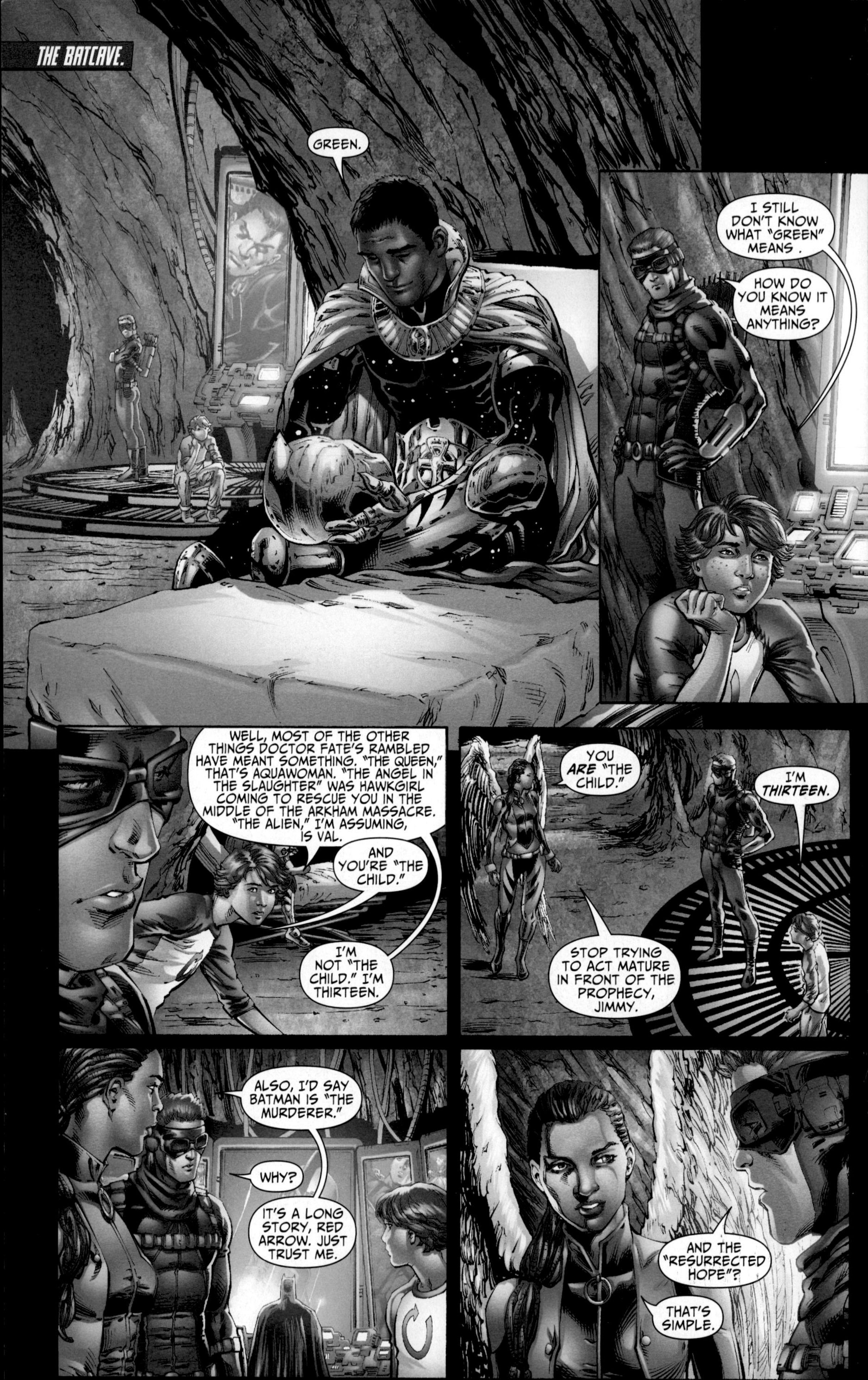
THE BATCAVE.
GREEN.
I STILL DON'T KNOW WHAT "GREEN" MEANS .
HOW DO YOU KNOW IT MEANS ANYTHING?
WELL, MOST OF THE OTHER THINGS DOCTOR FATE'S RAMBLED HAVE MEANT SOMETHING. "THE QUEEN," THAT'S AQUAWOMAN. "THE ANGEL IN THE SLAUGHTER" WAS HAWKGIRL COMING TO RESCUE YOU IN THE MIDDLE OF THE ARKHAM MASSACRE. "THE ALIEN," I'M ASSUMING, IS VAL.
AND YOU'RE "THE CHILD."
I'M NOT "THE CHILD." I'M THIRTEEN.
YOU ARE "THE CHILD."
I'M THIRTEEN.
STOP TRYING TO ACT MATURE IN FRONT OF THE PROPHECY, JIMMY.
ALSO, I'D SAY BATMAN IS "THE MURDERER."
WHY?
IT'S A LONG STORY, RED ARROW. JUST TRUST ME.
AND THE "RESURRECTED HOPE"?
THAT'S SIMPLE.

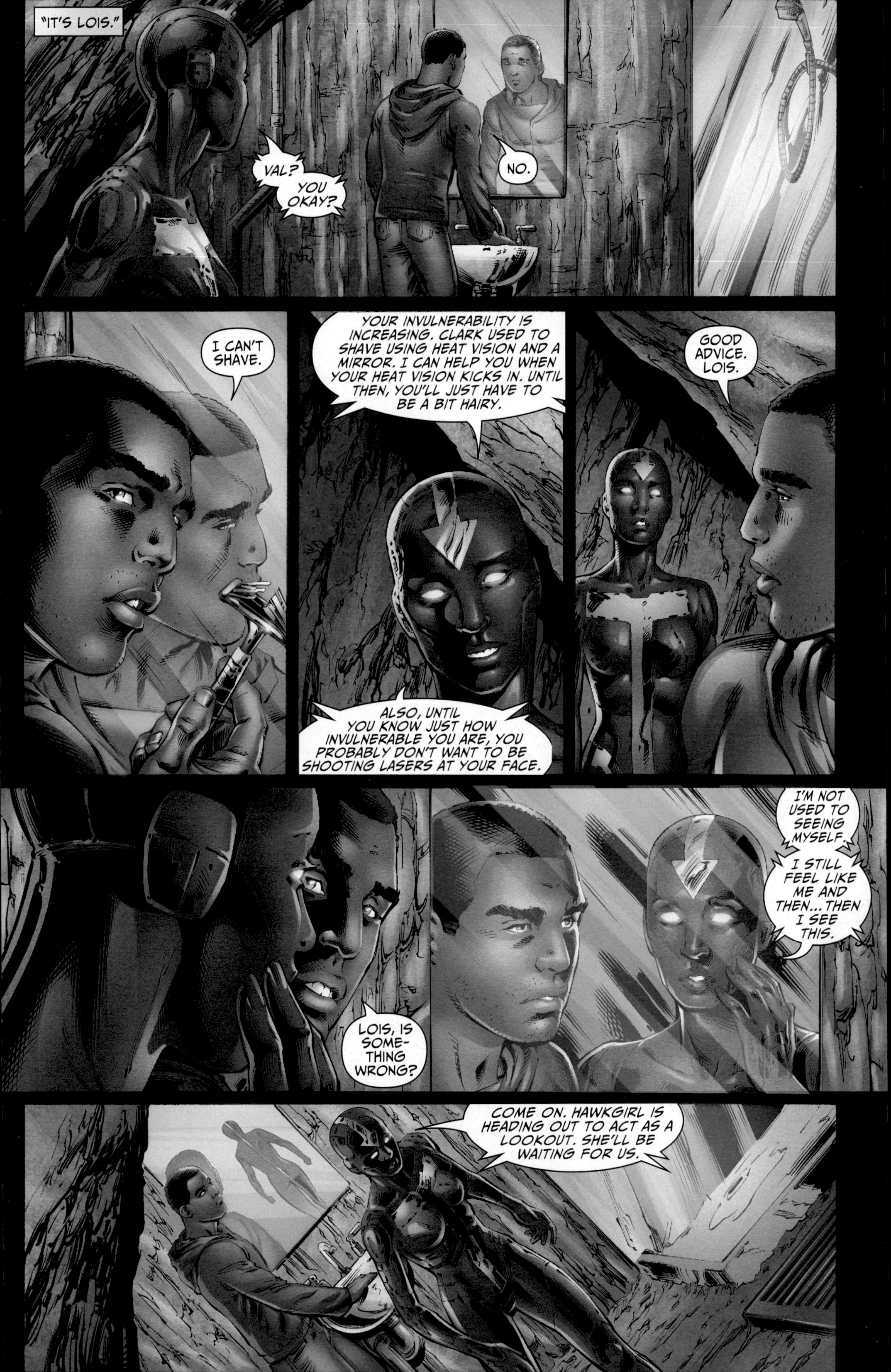
"IT'S LOIS."
VAL?
YOU OKAY?
NO.
I CAN'T SHAVE.
YOUR INVULNERABILITY IS INCREASING. CLARK USED TO SHAVE USING HEAT VISION AND A MIRROR. I CAN HELP YOU WHEN YOUR HEAT VISION KICKS IN. UNTIL THEN, YOU'LL JUST HAVE TO BE A BIT HAIRY.
ALSO, UNTIL YOU KNOW JUST HOW INVULNERABLE YOU ARE, YOU PROBABLY DON'T WANT TO BE SHOOTING LASERS AT YOUR FACE.
GOOD ADVICE. LOIS.
LOIS, IS SOME-THING WRONG?
I'M NOT USED TO SEEING MYSELF.
I STILL FEEL LIKE ME AND THEN... THEN I SEE THIS.
COME ON. HAWKGIRL IS HEADING OUT TO ACT AS A LOOKOUT. SHE'LL BE WAITING FOR US.

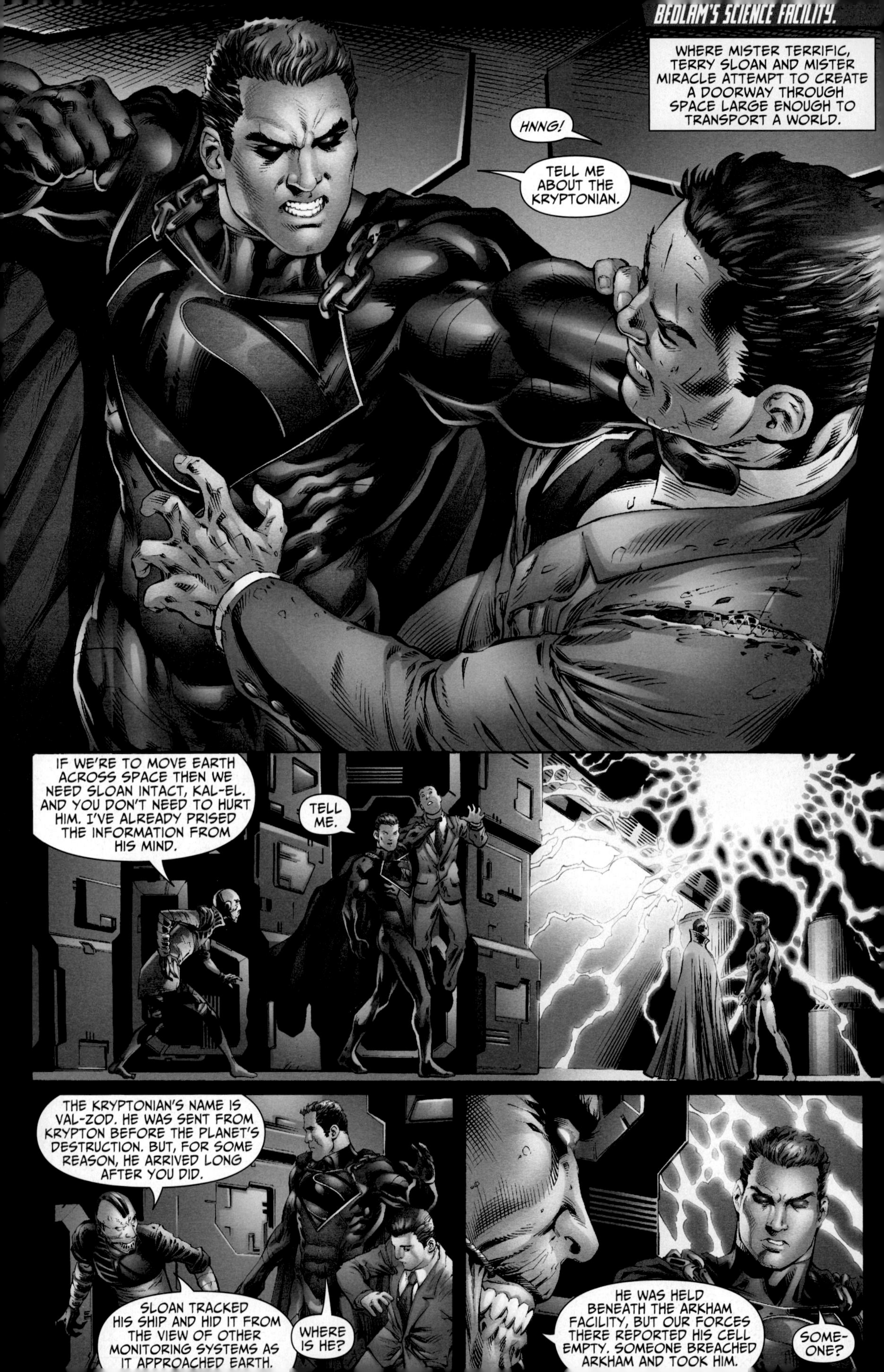
BEDLAM'S SCIENCE FACILITY.
WHERE MISTER TERRIFIC, TERRY SLOAN AND MISTER MIRACLE ATTEMPT TO CREATE A DOORWAY THROUGH SPACE LARGE ENOUGH TO TRANSPORT A WORLD.
HNNG!
TELL ME ABOUT THE KRYPTONIAN.
IF WE'RE TO MOVE EARTH ACROSS SPACE THEN WE NEED SLOAN INTACT, KAL-EL. AND YOU DON'T NEED TO HURT HIM. I'VE ALREADY PRISED THE INFORMATION FROM HIS MIND.
TELL ME.
THE KRYPTONIAN'S NAME IS VAL-ZOD. HE WAS SENT FROM KRYPTON BEFORE THE PLANET'S DESTRUCTION. BUT, FOR SOME REASON, HE ARRIVED LONG AFTER YOU DID.
SLOAN TRACKED HIS SHIP AND HID IT FROM THE VIEW OF OTHER MONITORING SYSTEMS AS IT APPROACHED EARTH.
WHERE IS HE?
HE WAS HELD BENEATH THE ARKHAM FACILITY, BUT OUR FORCES THERE REPORTED HIS CELL EMPTY. SOMEONE BREACHED ARKHAM AND TOOK HIM.
SOME-ONE?

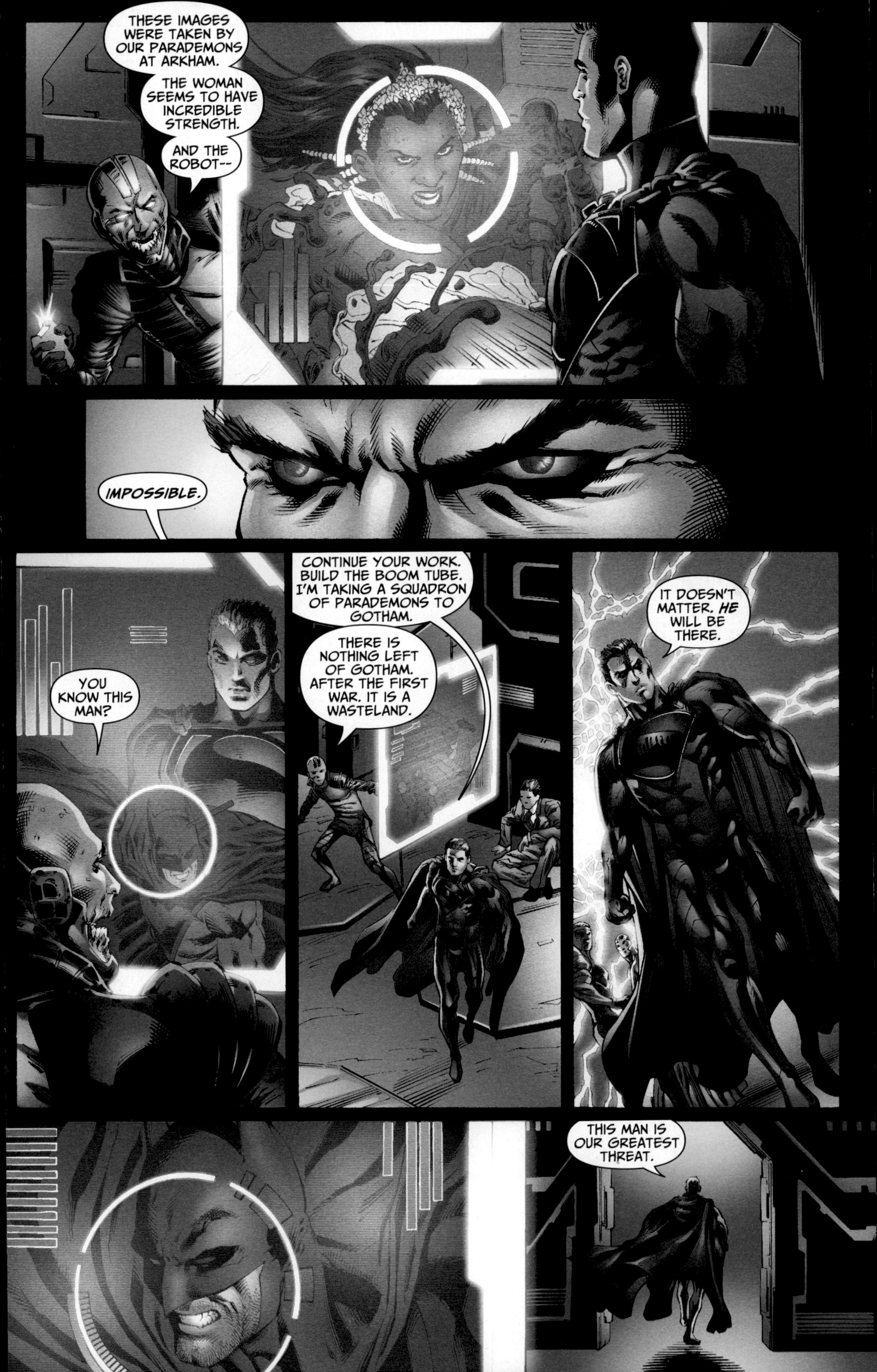
THESE IMAGES WERE TAKEN BY OUR PARADEMONS AT ARKHAM.
THE WOMAN SEEMS TO HAVE INCREDIBLE STRENGTH.
AND THE ROBOT--
IMPOSSIBLE.
YOU KNOW THIS MAN?
CONTINUE YOUR WORK. BUILD THE BOOM TUBE. I'M TAKING A SQUADRON OF PARADEMONS TO GOTHAM.
THERE IS NOTHING LEFT OF GOTHAM. AFTER THE FIRST WAR. IT IS A WASTELAND.
IT DOESN'T MATTER. *HE* WILL BE THERE.
THIS MAN IS OUR GREATEST THREAT.

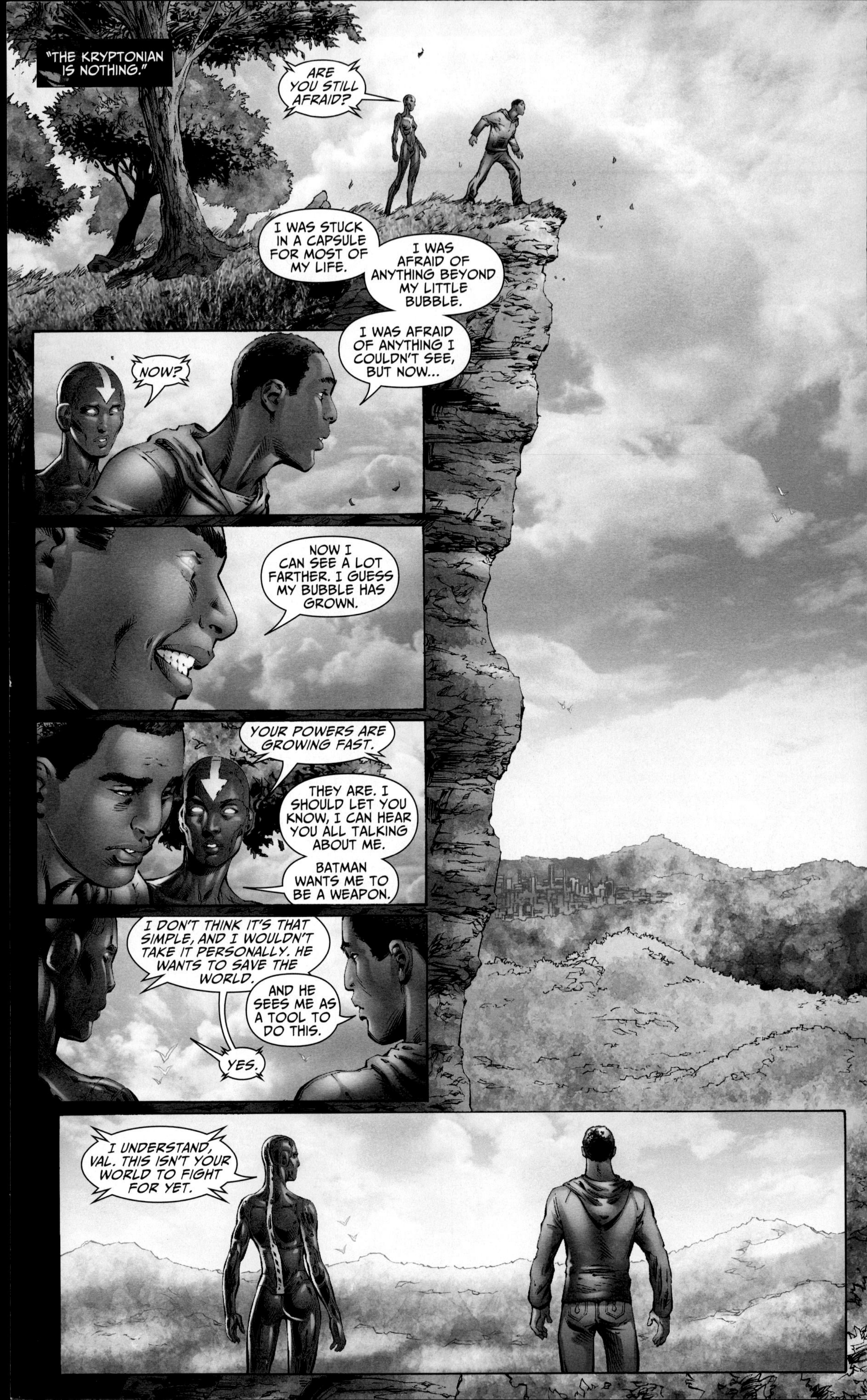
"THE KRYPTONIAN IS NOTHING."
ARE YOU STILL AFRAID?
I WAS STUCK IN A CAPSULE FOR MOST OF MY LIFE.
I WAS AFRAID OF ANYTHING BEYOND MY LITTLE BUBBLE.
I WAS AFRAID OF ANYTHING I COULDN'T SEE, BUT NOW...
NOW?
NOW I CAN SEE A LOT FARTHER. I GUESS MY BUBBLE HAS GROWN.
YOUR POWERS ARE GROWING FAST.
THEY ARE. I SHOULD LET YOU KNOW, I CAN HEAR YOU ALL TALKING ABOUT ME.
BATMAN WANTS ME TO BE A WEAPON.
I DON'T THINK IT'S THAT SIMPLE, AND I WOULDN'T TAKE IT PERSONALLY. HE WANTS TO SAVE THE WORLD.
AND HE SEES ME AS A TOOL TO DO THIS.
YES.
I UNDERSTAND, VAL. THIS ISN'T YOUR WORLD TO FIGHT FOR YET.

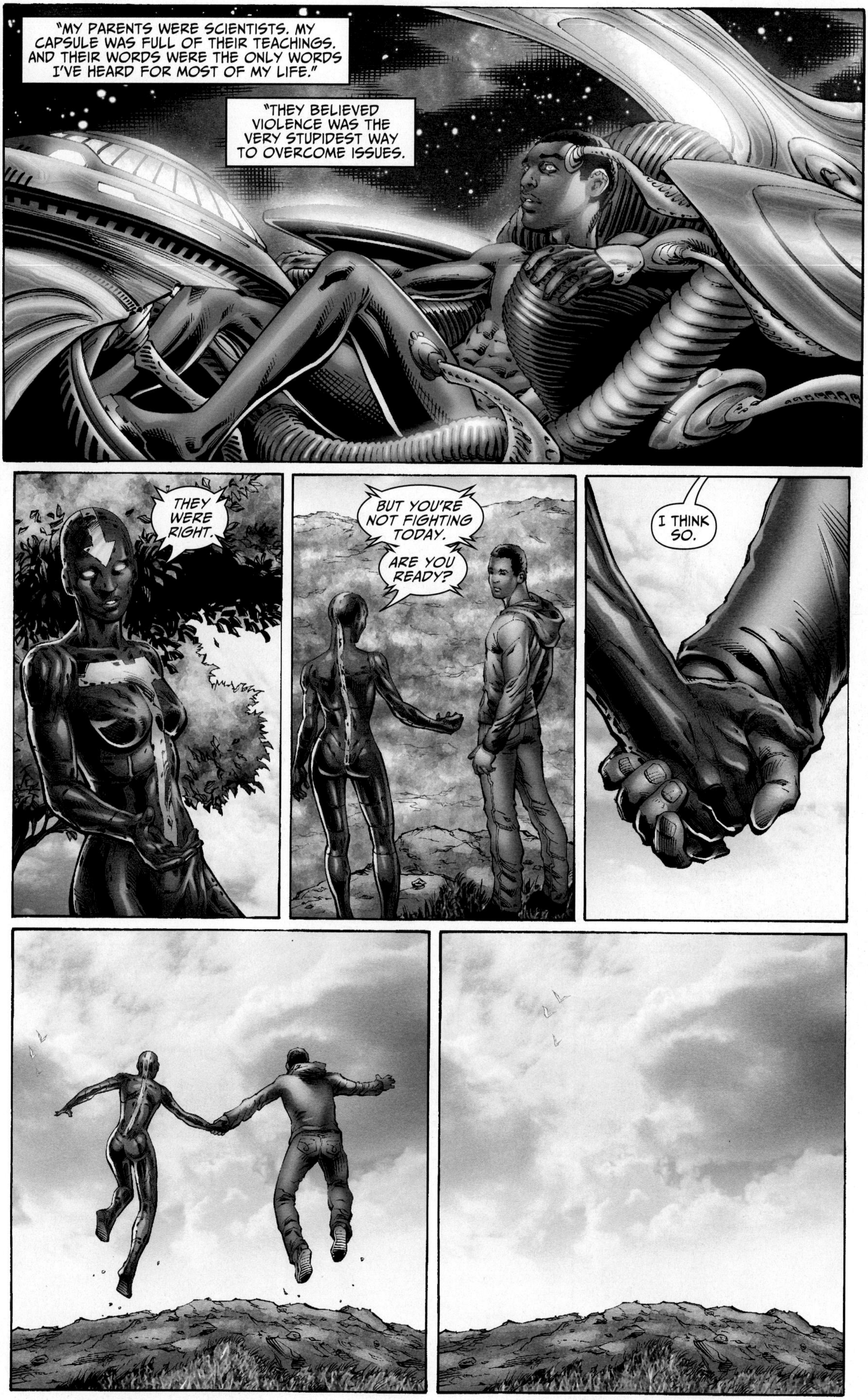
"MY PARENTS WERE SCIENTISTS. MY CAPSULE WAS FULL OF THEIR TEACHINGS. AND THEIR WORDS WERE THE ONLY WORDS I'VE HEARD FOR MOST OF MY LIFE."
"THEY BELIEVED VIOLENCE WAS THE VERY STUPIDEST WAY TO OVERCOME ISSUES.
THEY WERE RIGHT.
BUT YOU'RE NOT FIGHTING TODAY.
ARE YOU READY?
I THINK SO.

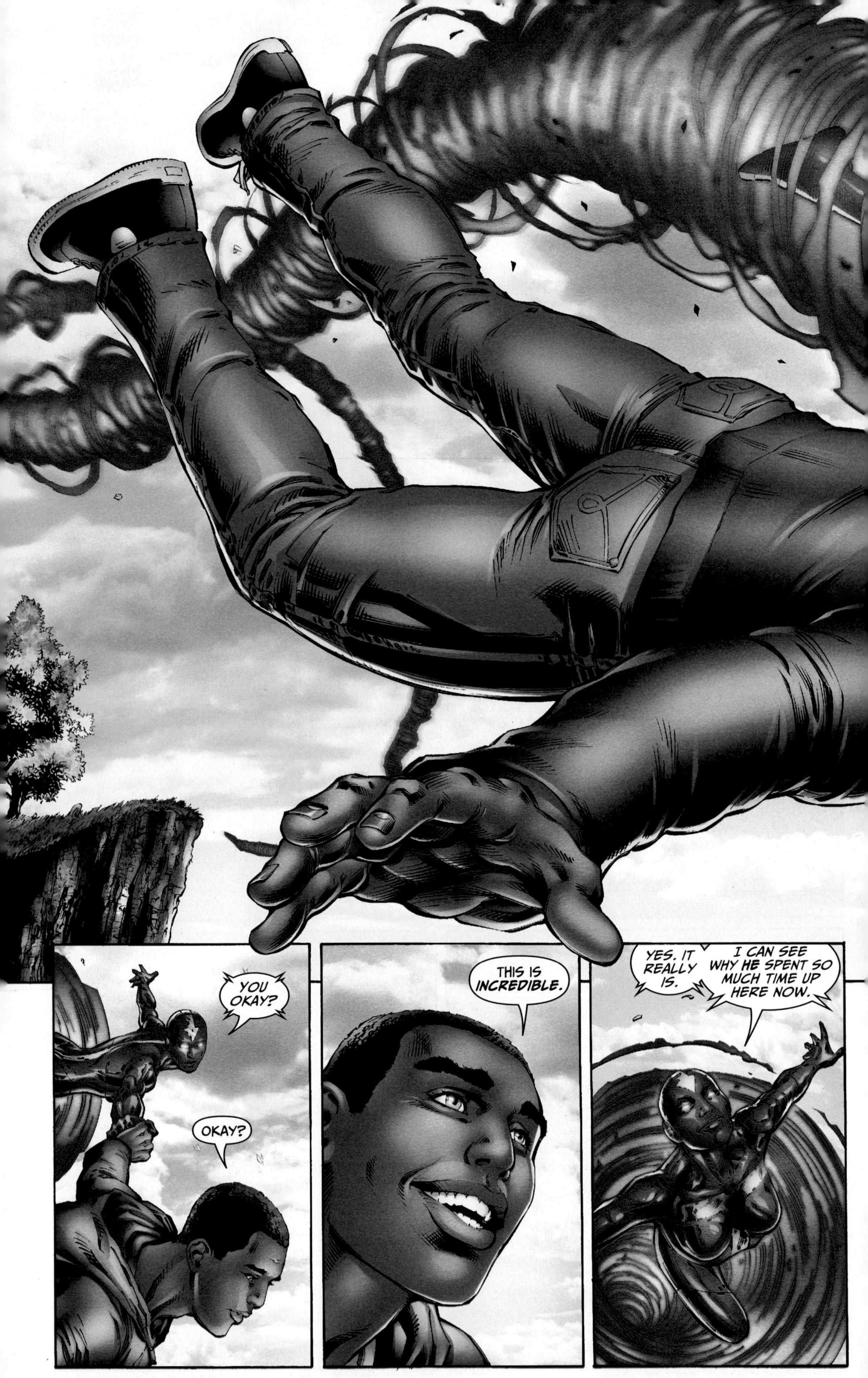
YOU OKAY?
OKAY?
THIS IS INCREDIBLE.
YES. IT REALLY IS.
I CAN SEE WHY HE SPENT SO MUCH TIME UP HERE NOW.

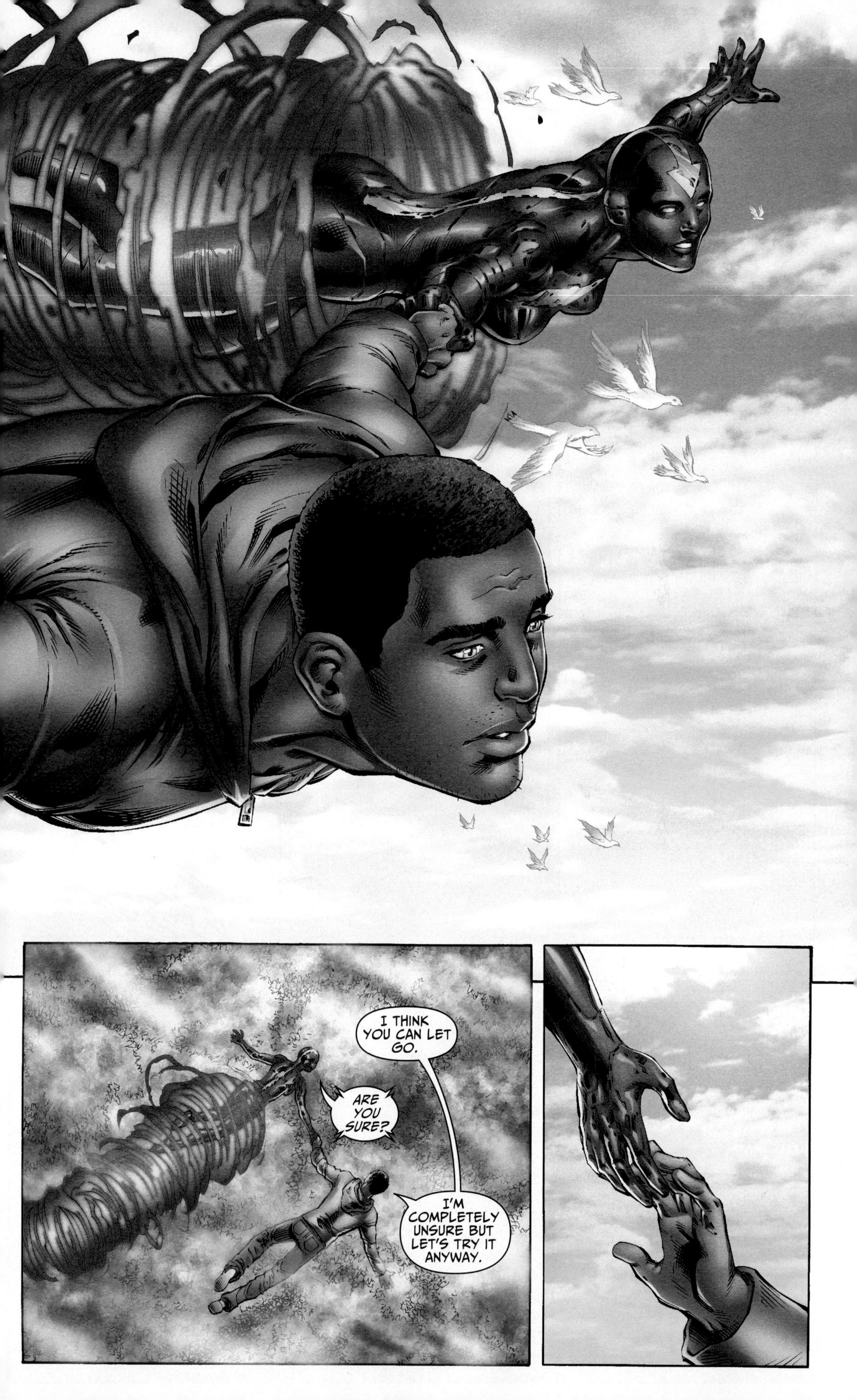
I THINK YOU CAN LET GO.
ARE YOU SURE?
I'M COMPLETELY UNSURE BUT LET'S TRY IT ANYWAY.

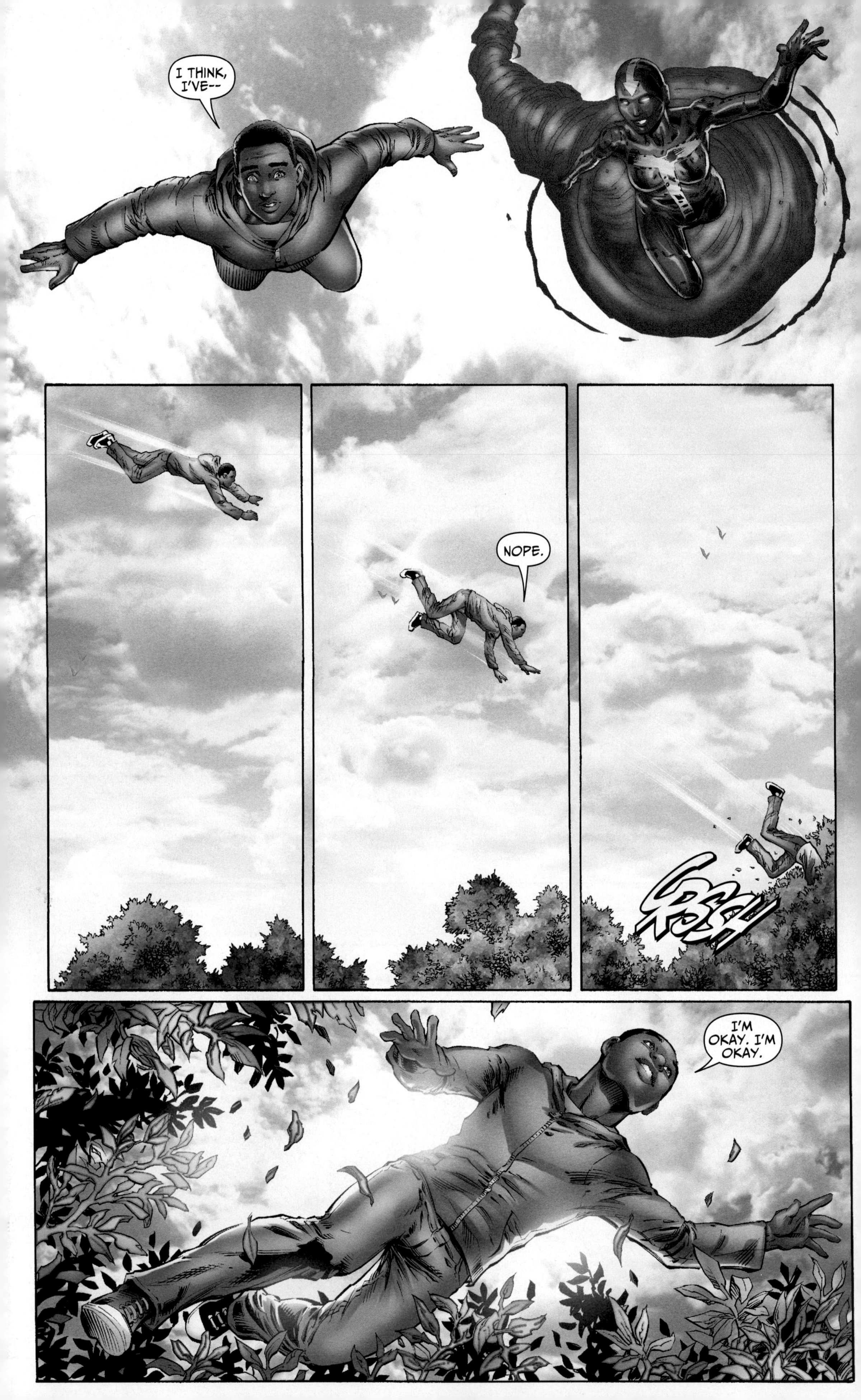
I THINK, I'VE--
NOPE.
KRSSH
I'M OKAY. I'M OKAY.

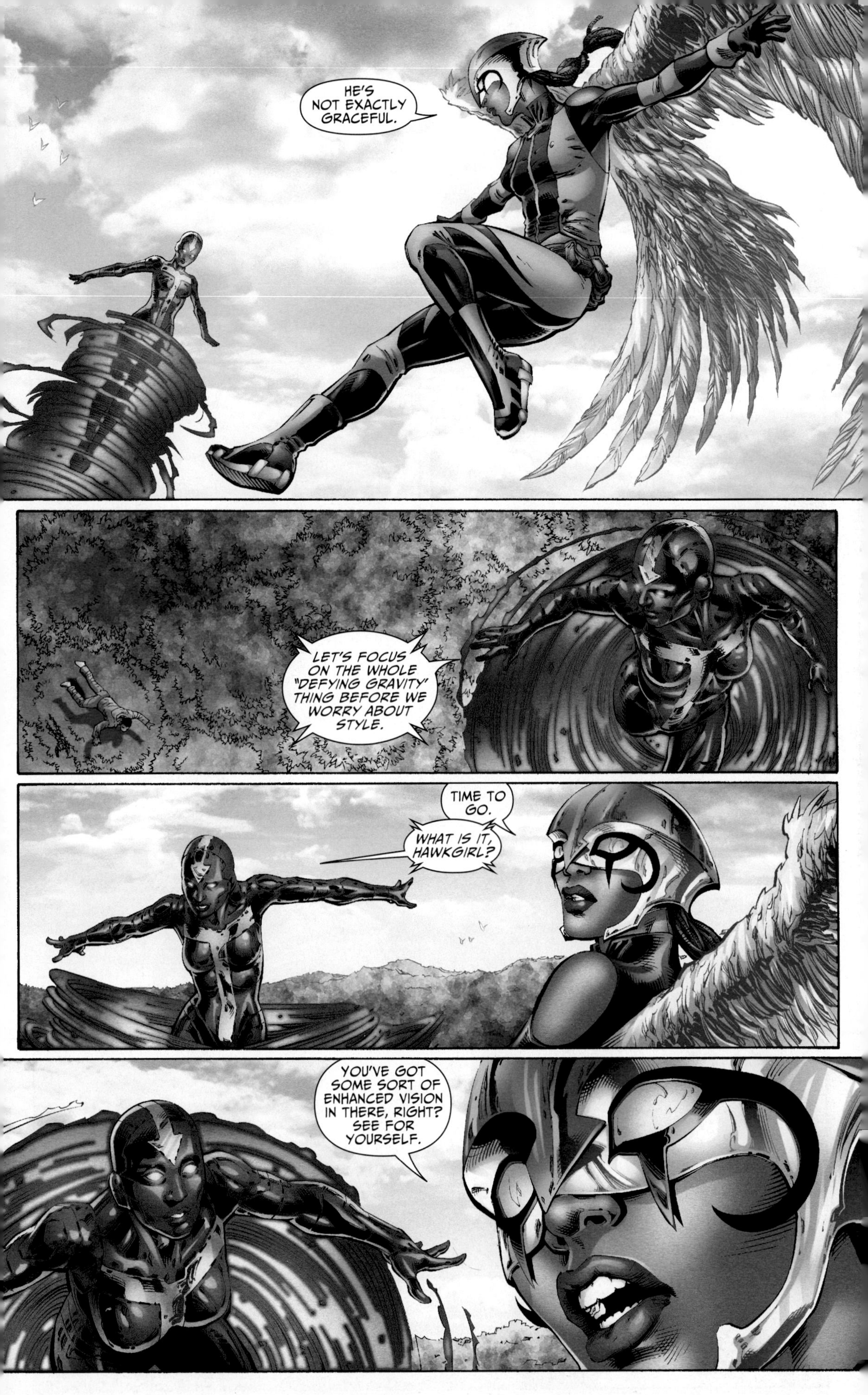
HE'S NOT EXACTLY GRACEFUL.
LET'S FOCUS ON THE WHOLE "DEFYING GRAVITY" THING BEFORE WE WORRY ABOUT STYLE.
TIME TO GO.
WHAT IS IT, HAWKGIRL?
YOU'VE GOT SOME SORT OF ENHANCED VISION IN THERE, RIGHT? SEE FOR YOURSELF.

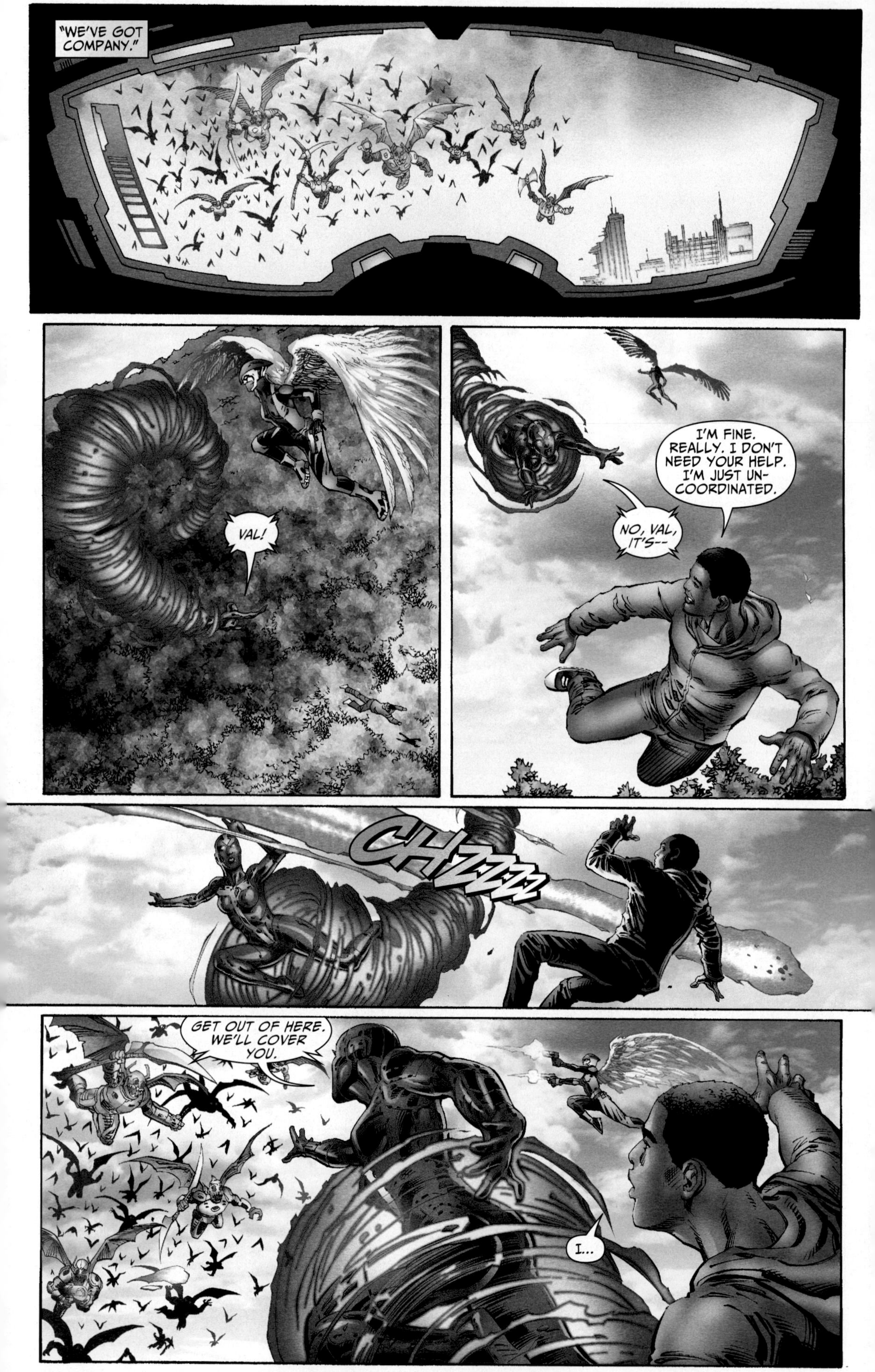
"WE'VE GOT COMPANY."
VAL!
I'M FINE. REALLY. I DON'T NEED YOUR HELP. I'M JUST UN-COORDINATED.
NO, VAL, IT'S--
CHZZZZ
GET OUT OF HERE. WE'LL COVER YOU.
I...

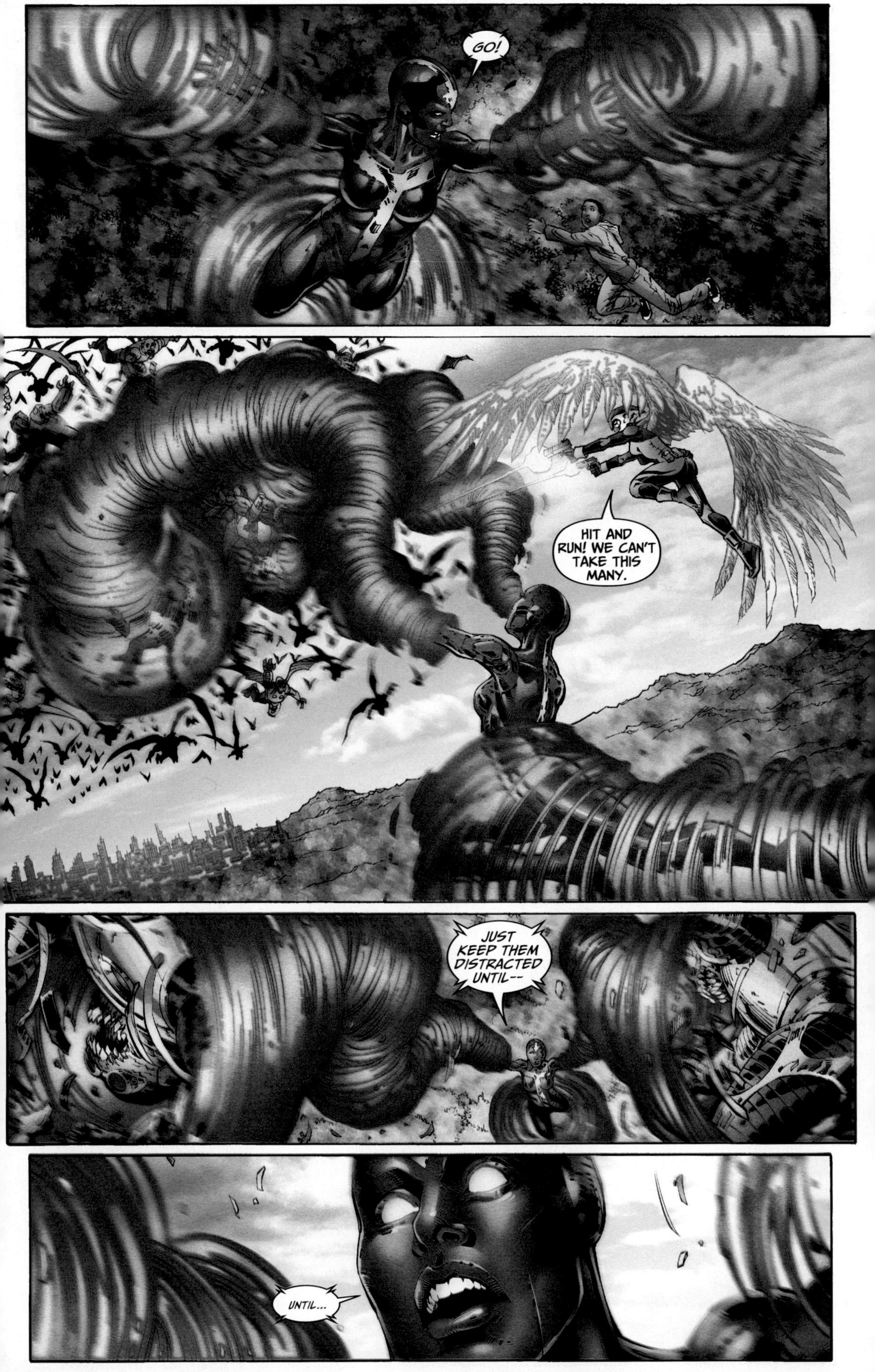
GO!
HIT AND RUN! WE CAN'T TAKE THIS MANY.
JUST KEEP THEM DISTRACTED UNTIL--
UNTIL...

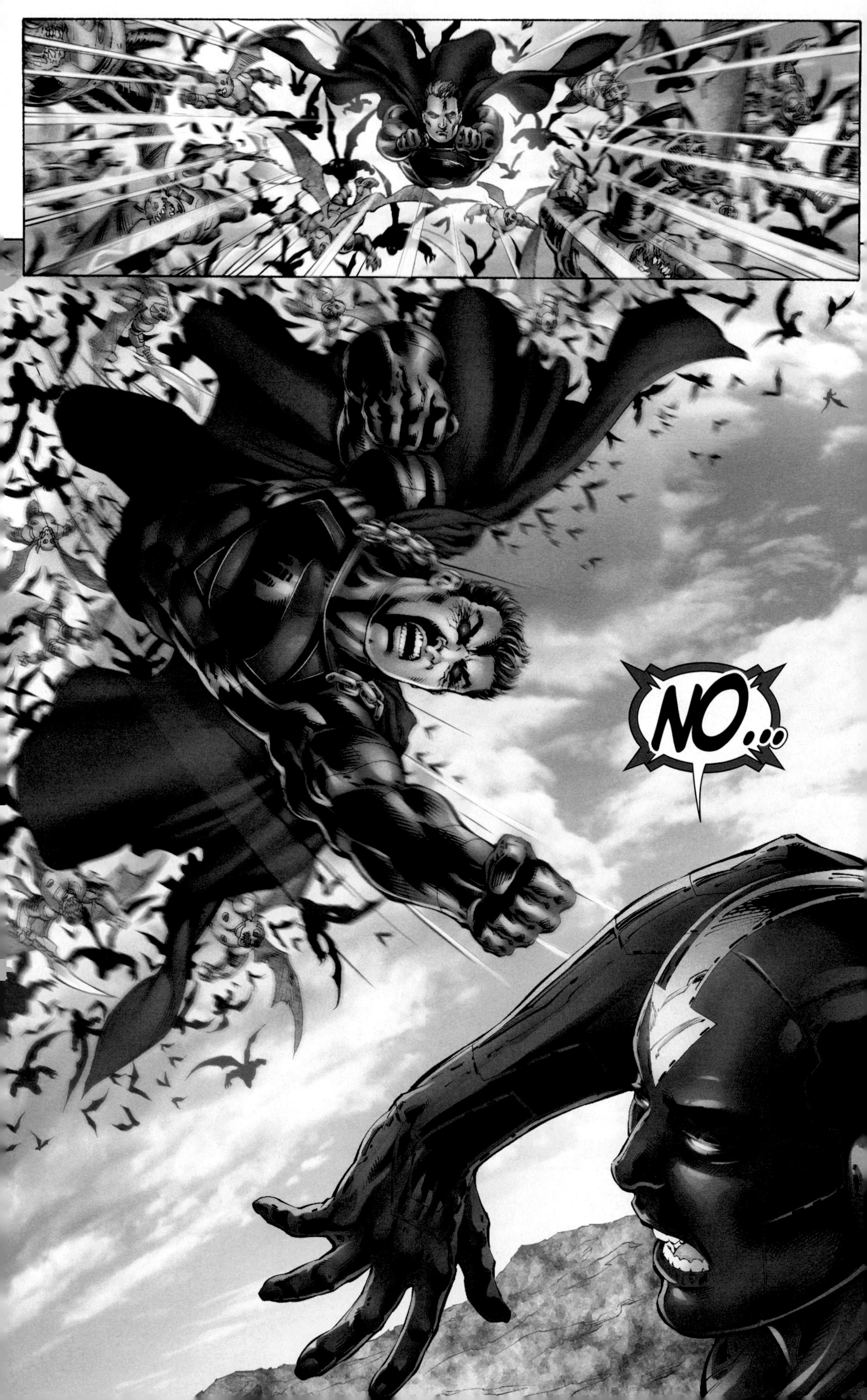
NO...

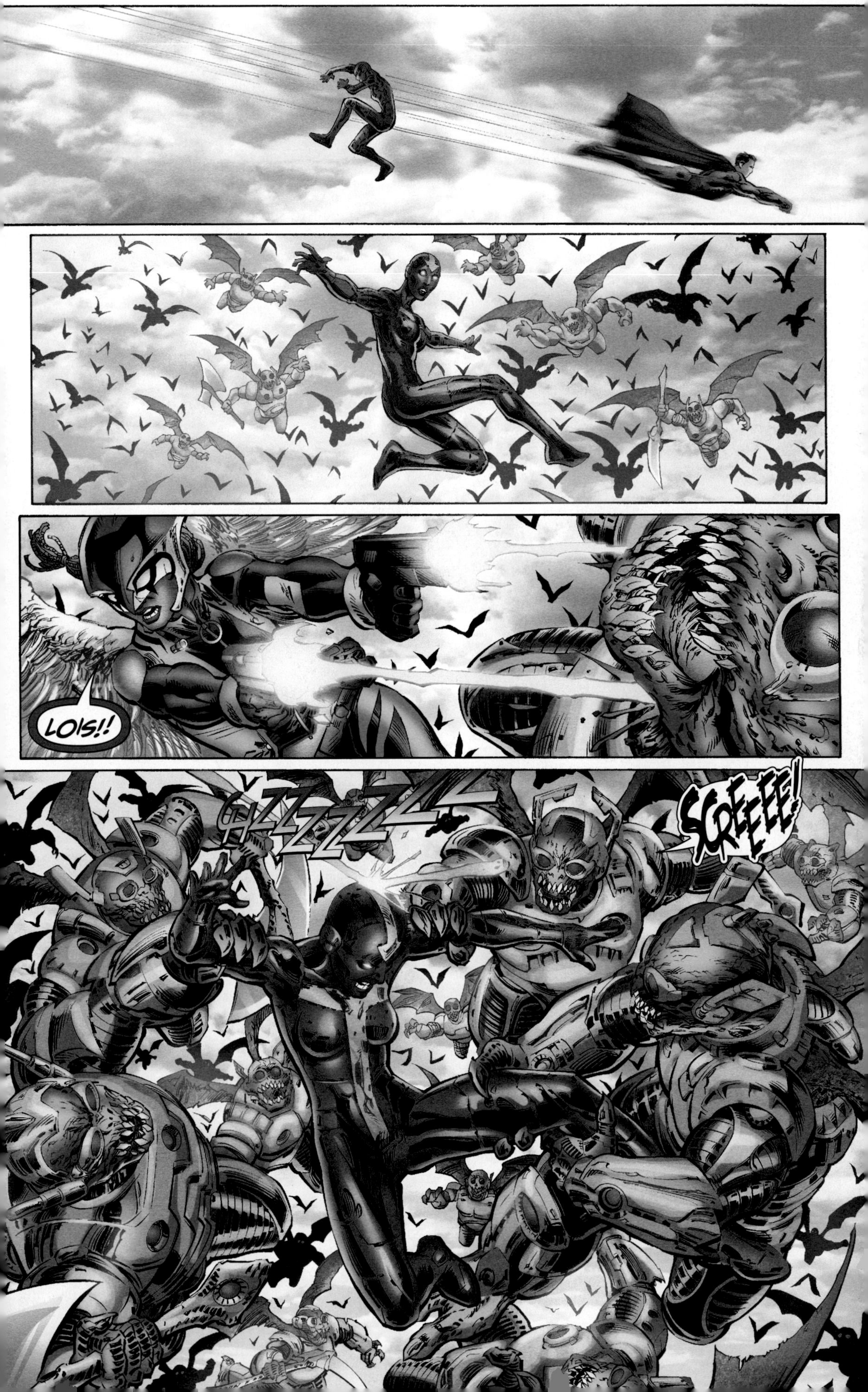
LOIS!!
ZZZZZZZZ
SCREEEEE!

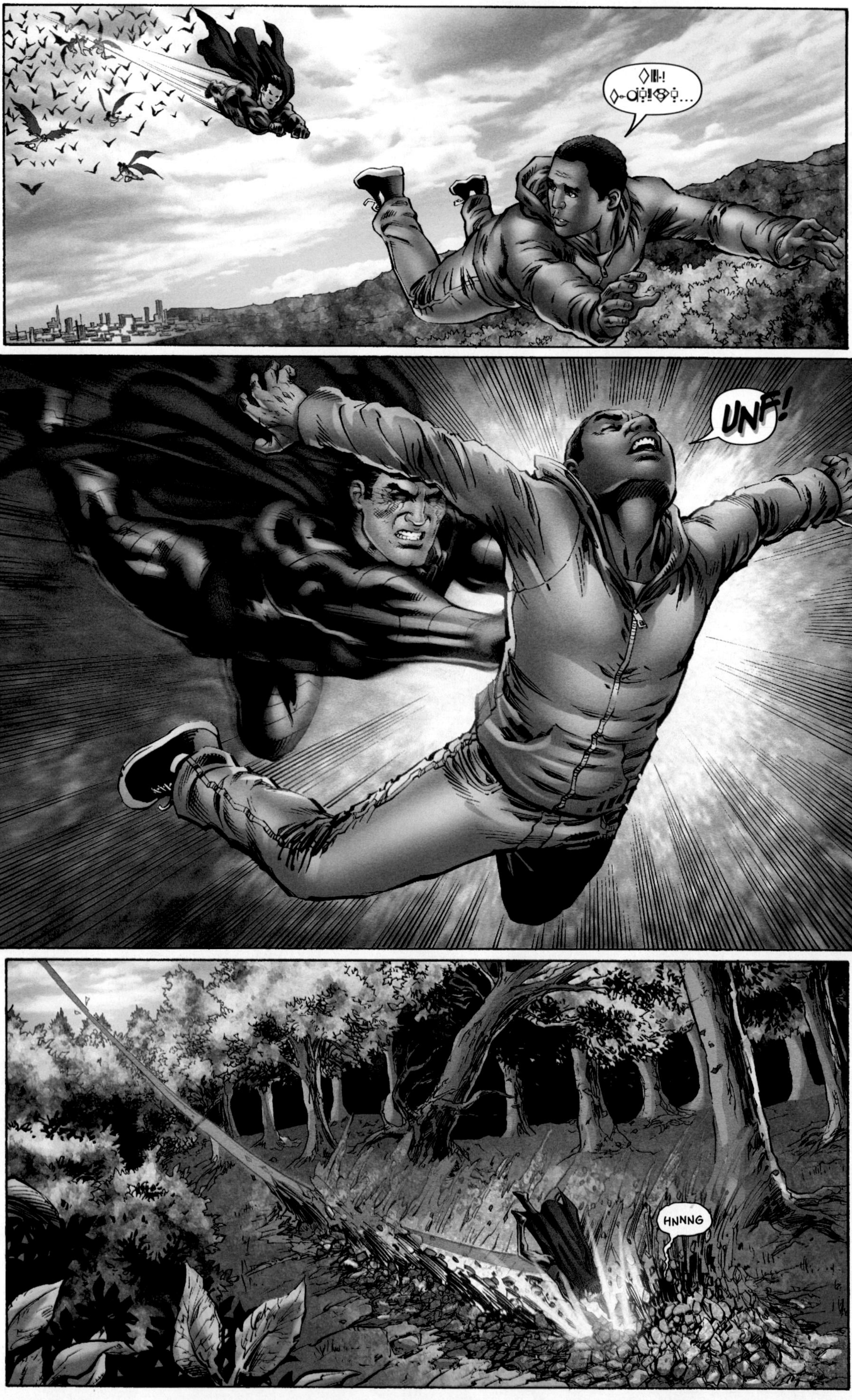
UNF!
HNNNG

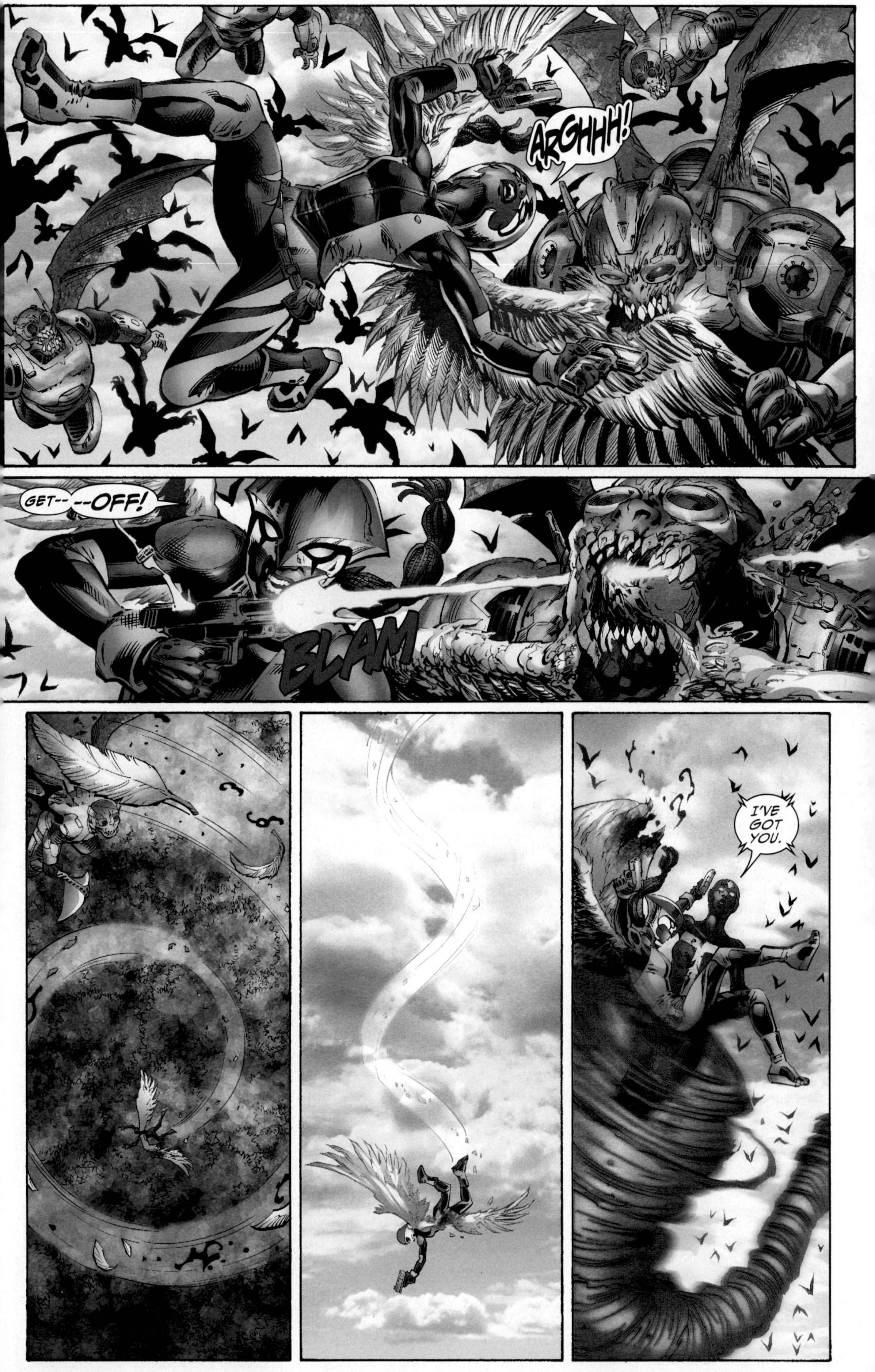
ARGHHH!
GET--
--OFF!
BLAM
I'VE GOT YOU.

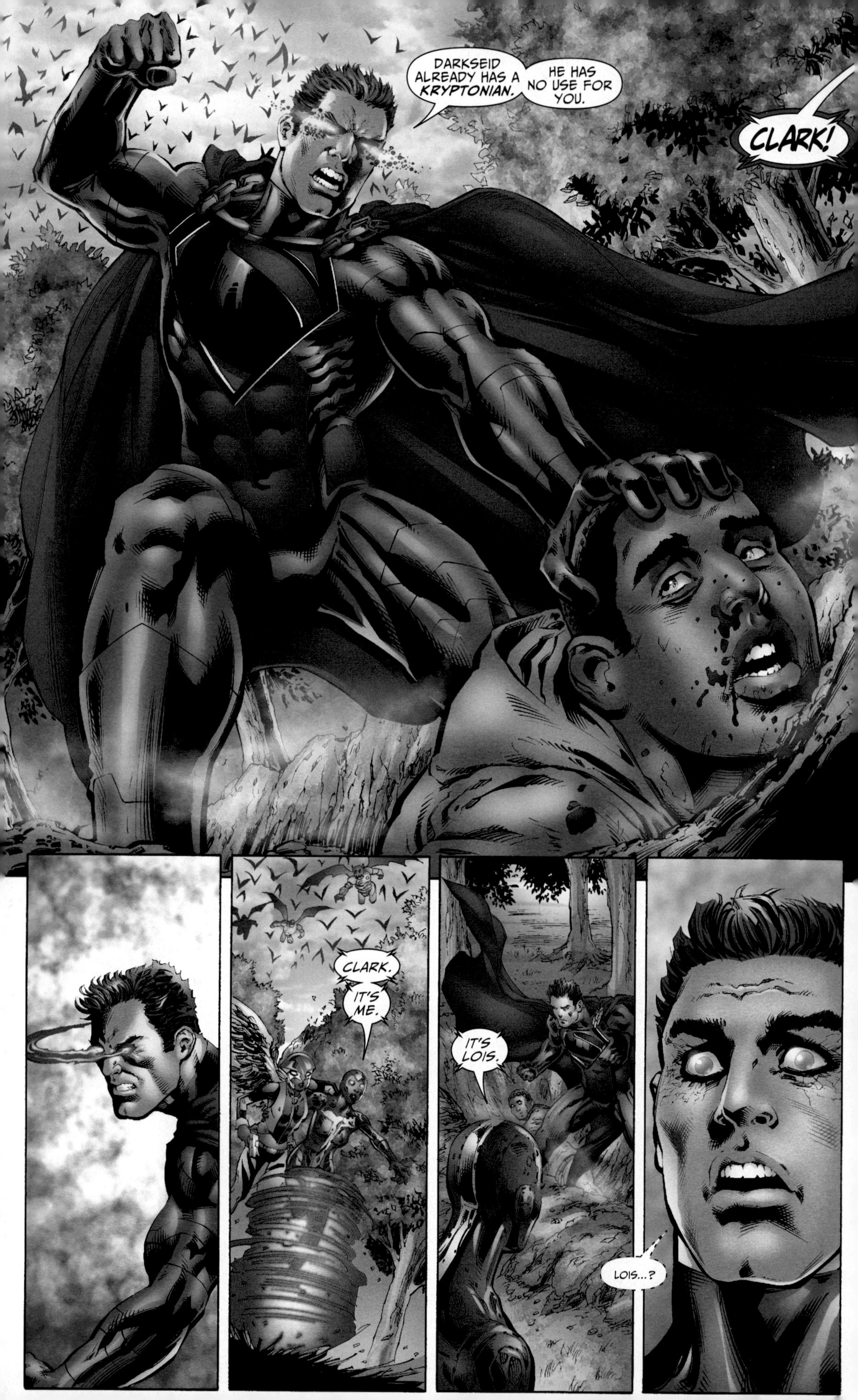
DARKSEID ALREADY HAS A KRYPTONIAN.
HE HAS NO USE FOR YOU.
CLARK!
CLARK.
IT'S ME.
IT'S LOIS.
LOIS...?

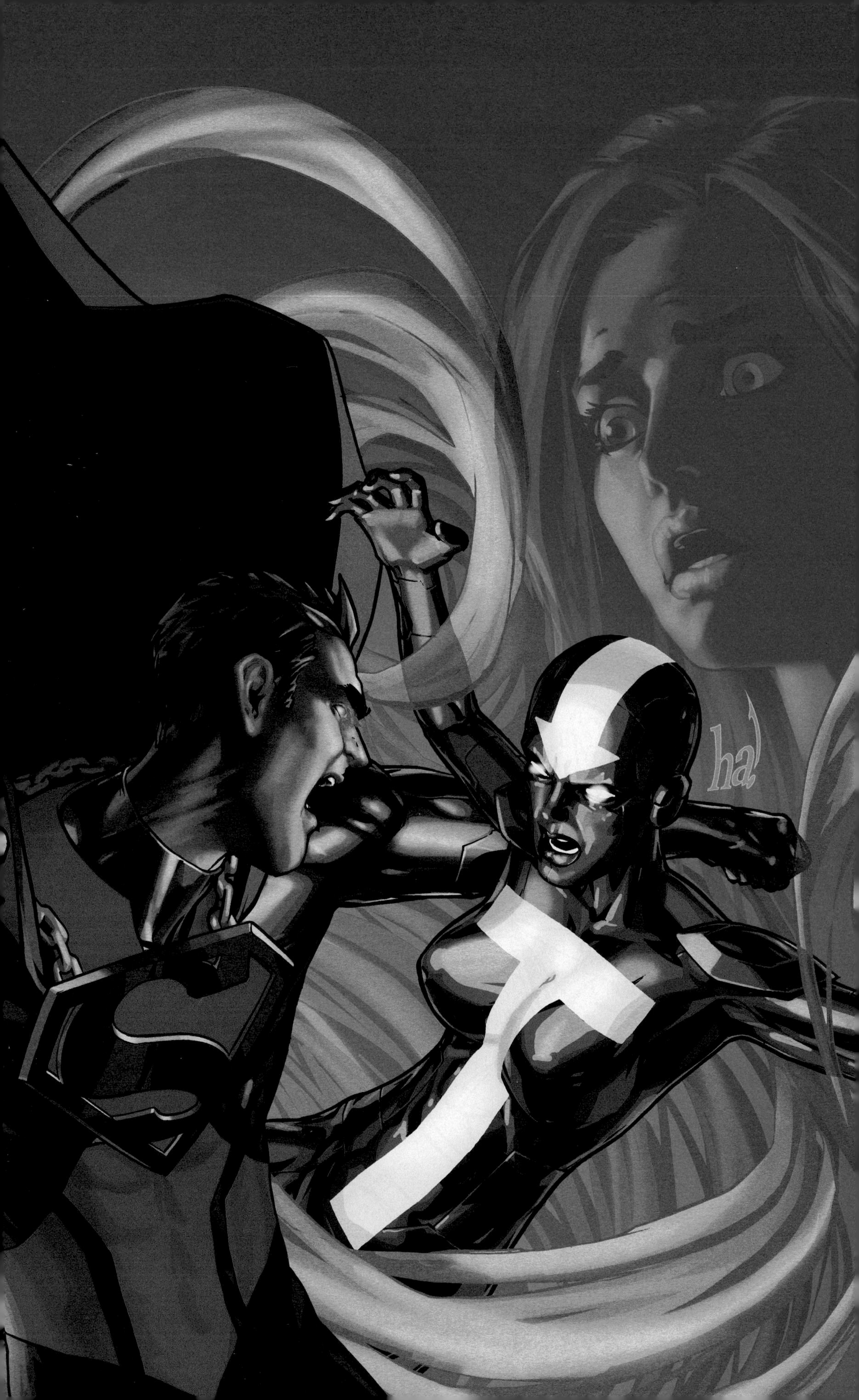
ha!

THE KRYPTONIAN PART 3

TOM TAYLOR writer **NICOLA SCOTT** penciller **TREVOR SCOTT** inker **PETE PANTAZIS** colorist cover by **GENE HA**

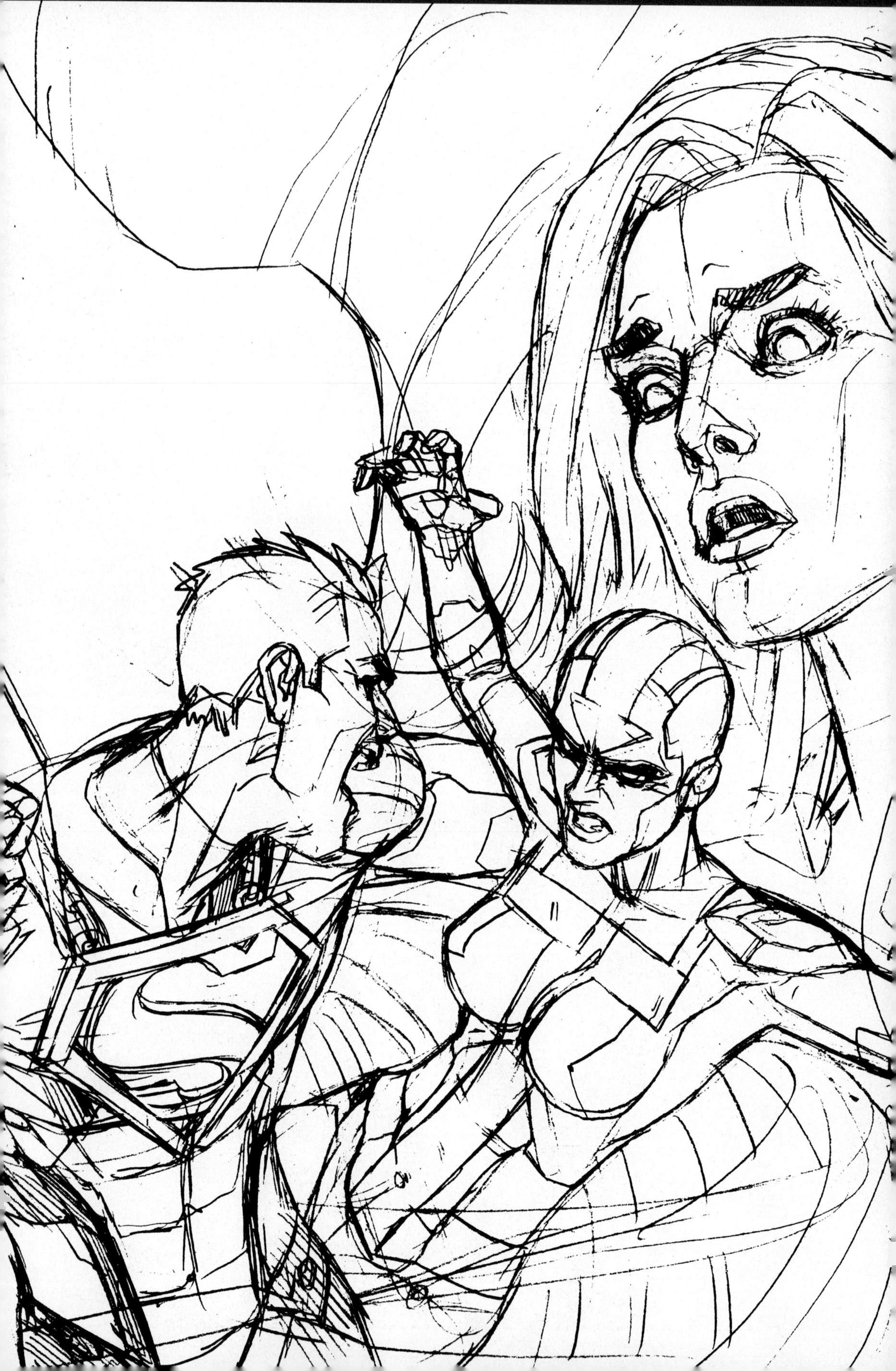

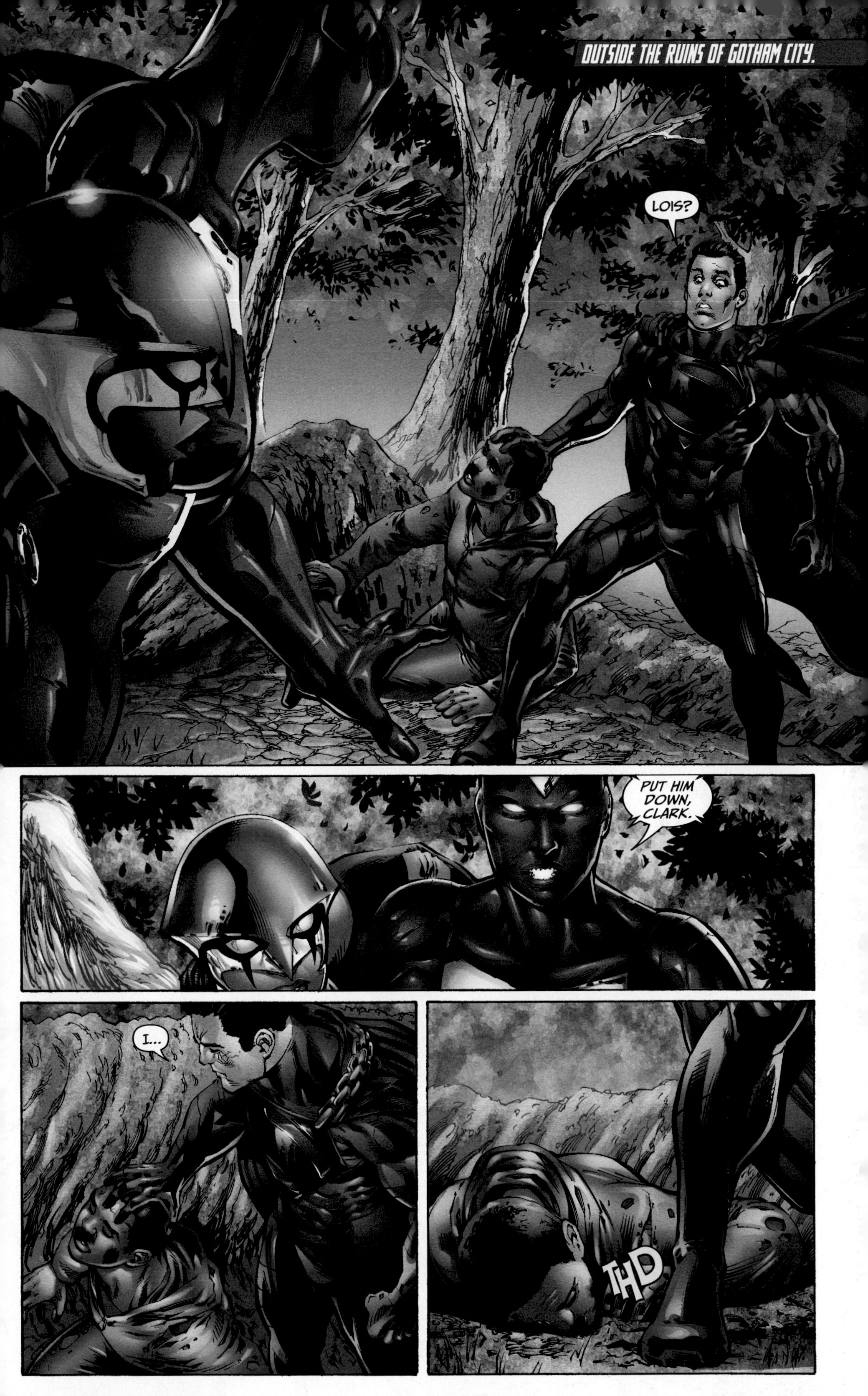
OUTSIDE THE RUINS OF GOTHAM CITY.
LOIS?
PUT HIM DOWN, CLARK.
I...
THD

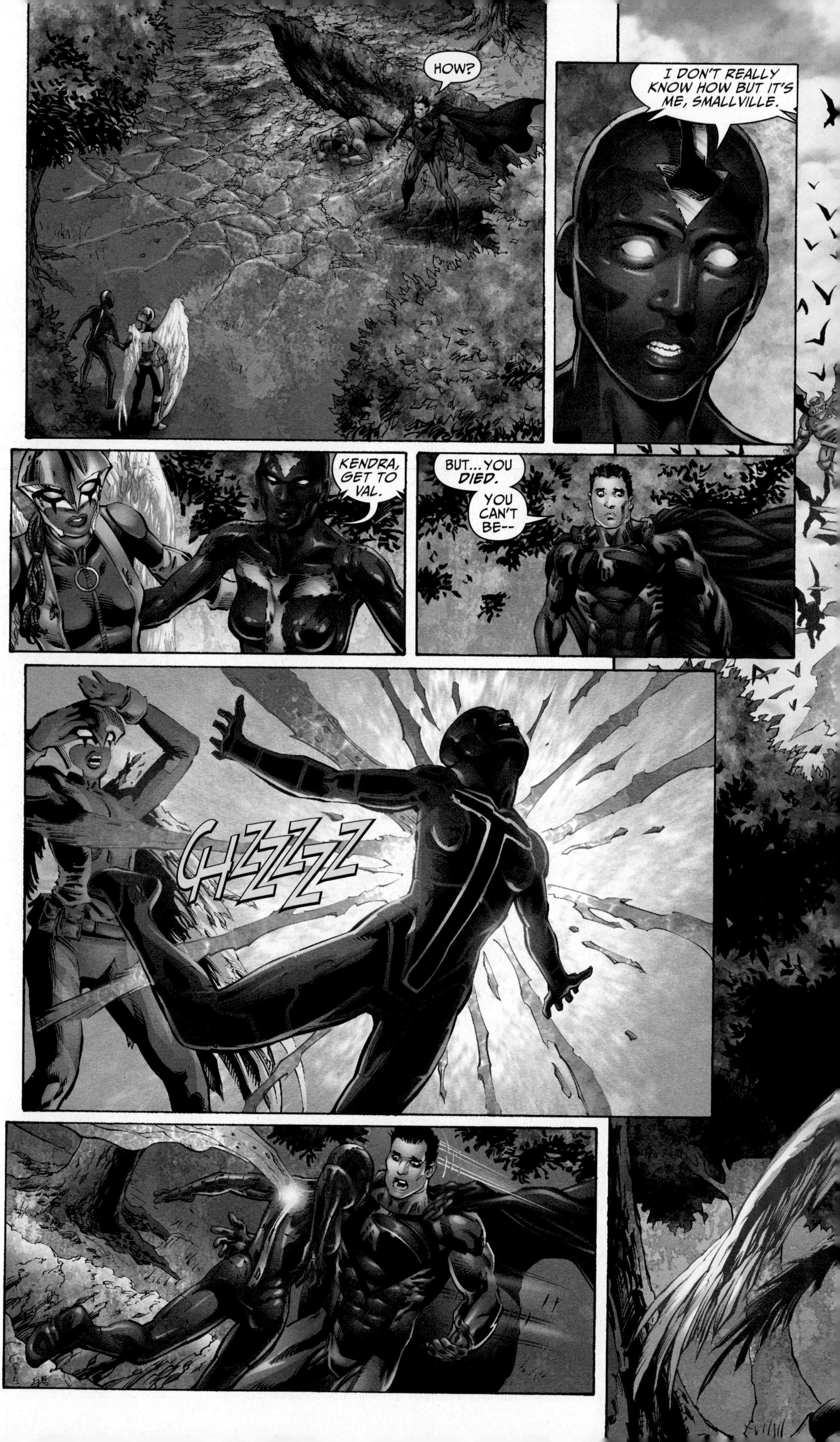
HOW?
I DON'T REALLY KNOW HOW BUT IT'S ME, SMALLVILLE.
KENDRA, GET TO VAL.
BUT...YOU DIED.
YOU CAN'T BE--
CHZZZZ

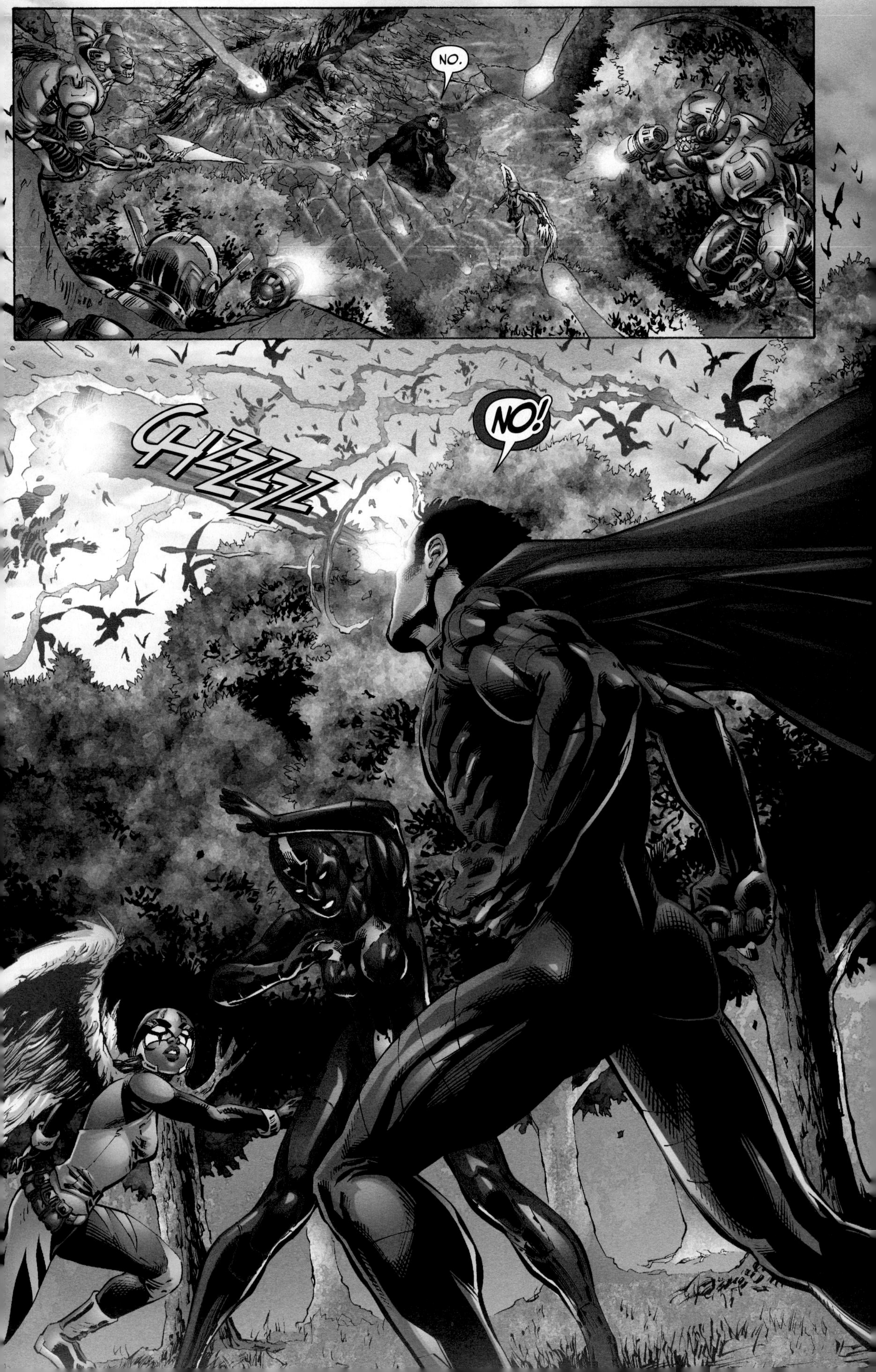
NO.
CHZZZZ
NO!

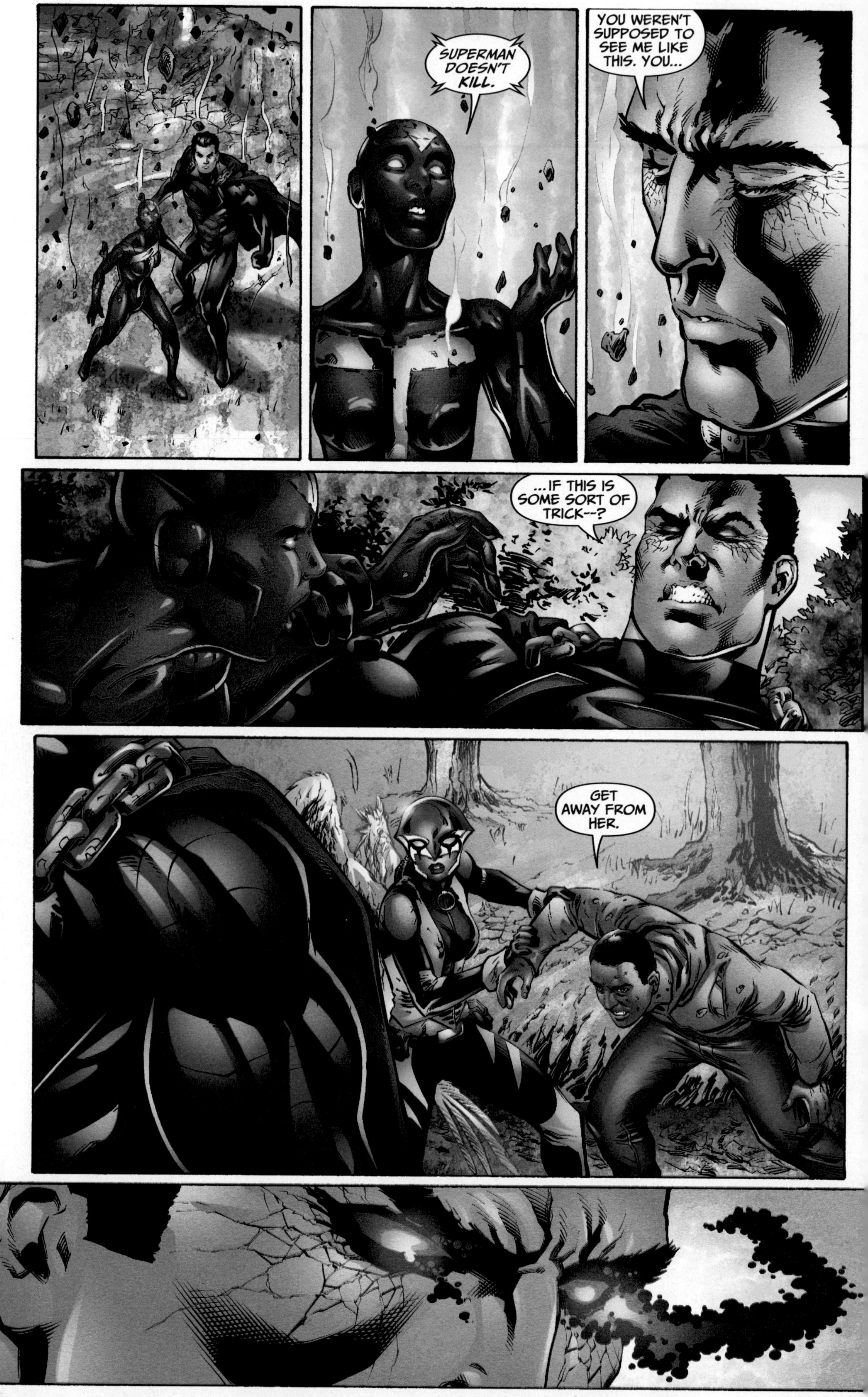
SUPERMAN DOESN'T KILL.
YOU WEREN'T SUPPOSED TO SEE ME LIKE THIS. YOU...
...IF THIS IS SOME SORT OF TRICK--?
GET AWAY FROM HER.

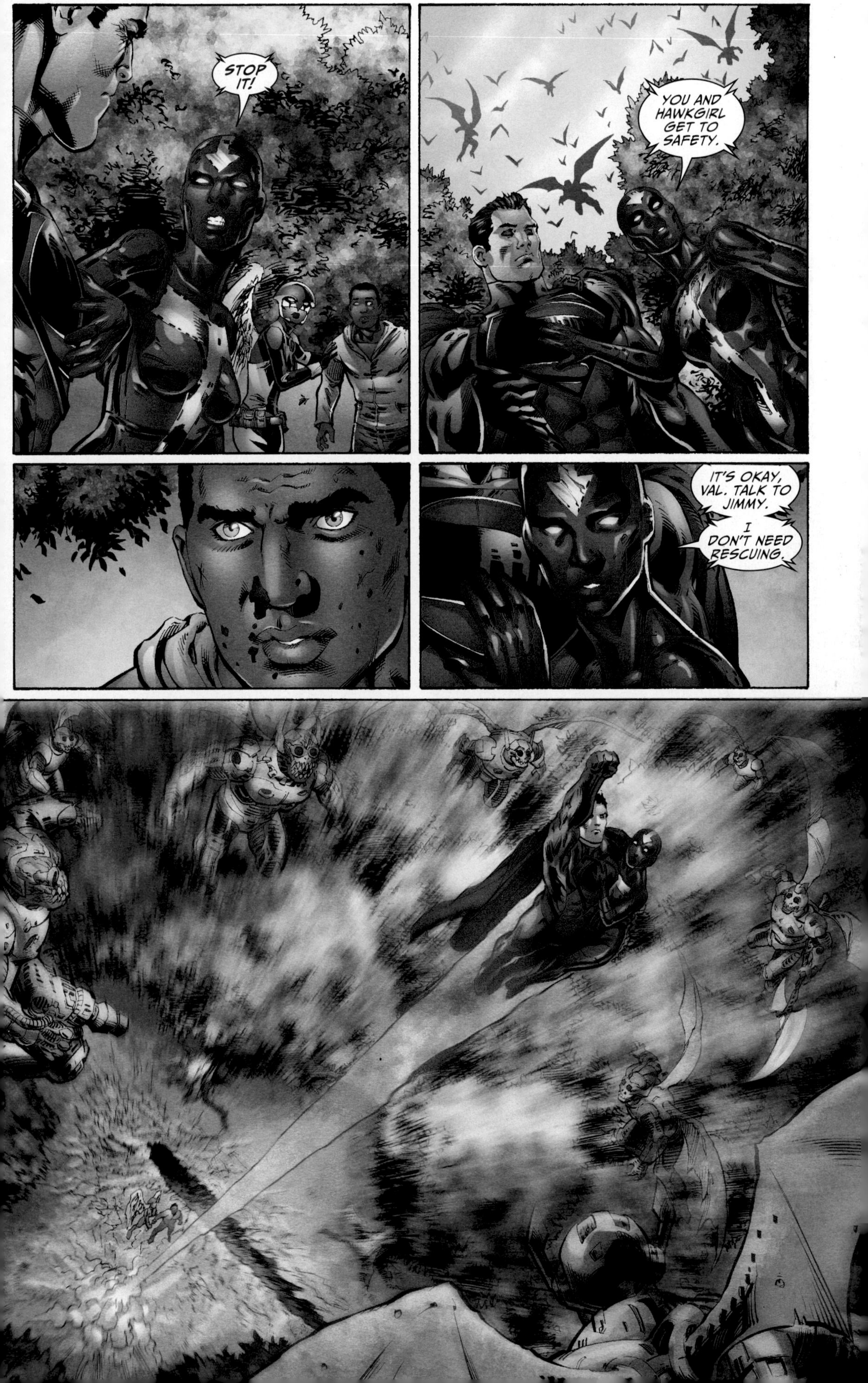
STOP IT!
YOU AND HAWKGIRL GET TO SAFETY.
IT'S OKAY, VAL. TALK TO JIMMY.
I DON'T NEED RESCUING.

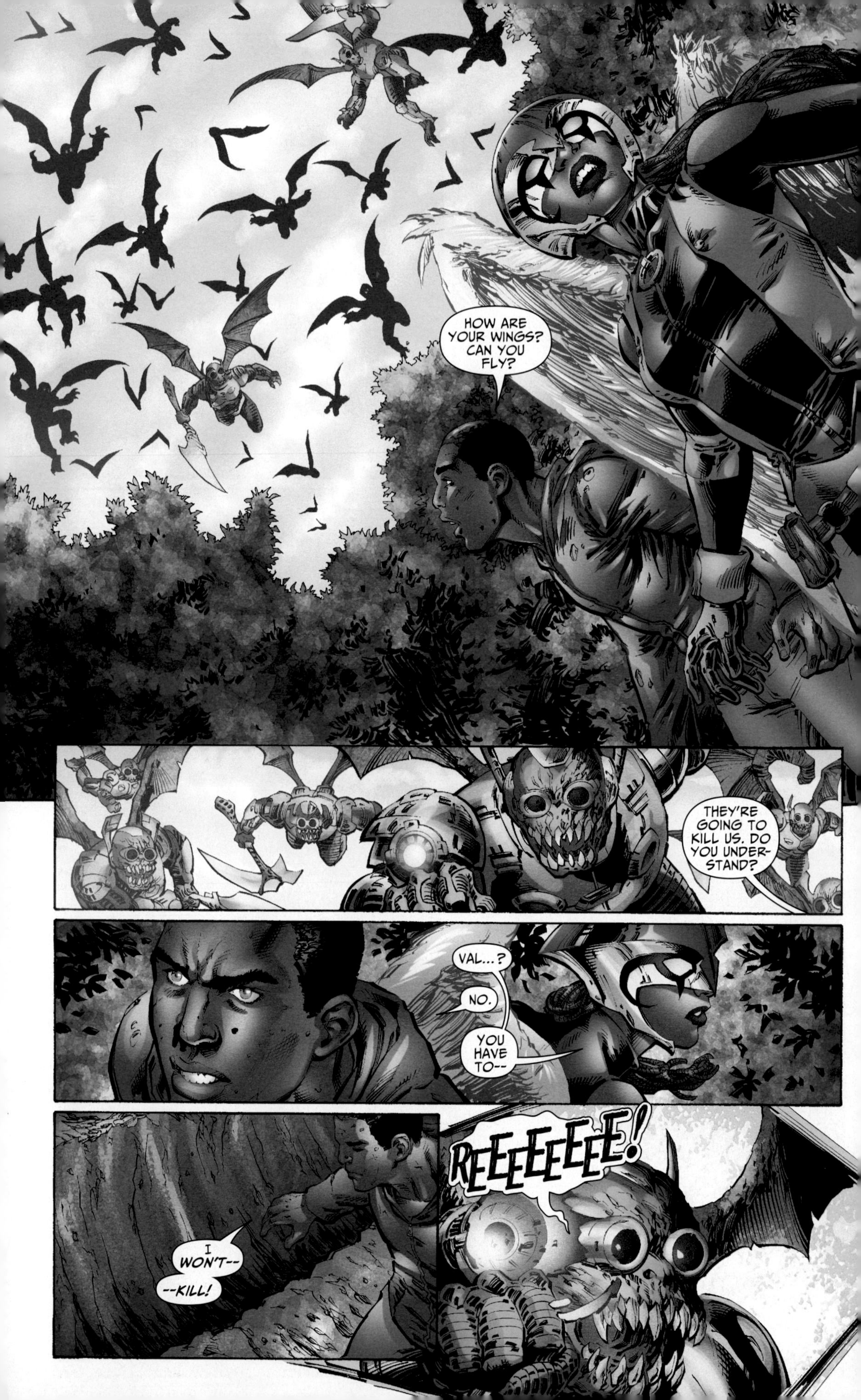
HOW ARE YOUR WINGS? CAN YOU FLY?
THEY'RE GOING TO KILL US. DO YOU UNDERSTAND?
VAL...?
NO.
YOU HAVE TO--
I WON'T--
--KILL!
REEEEEEEEE!

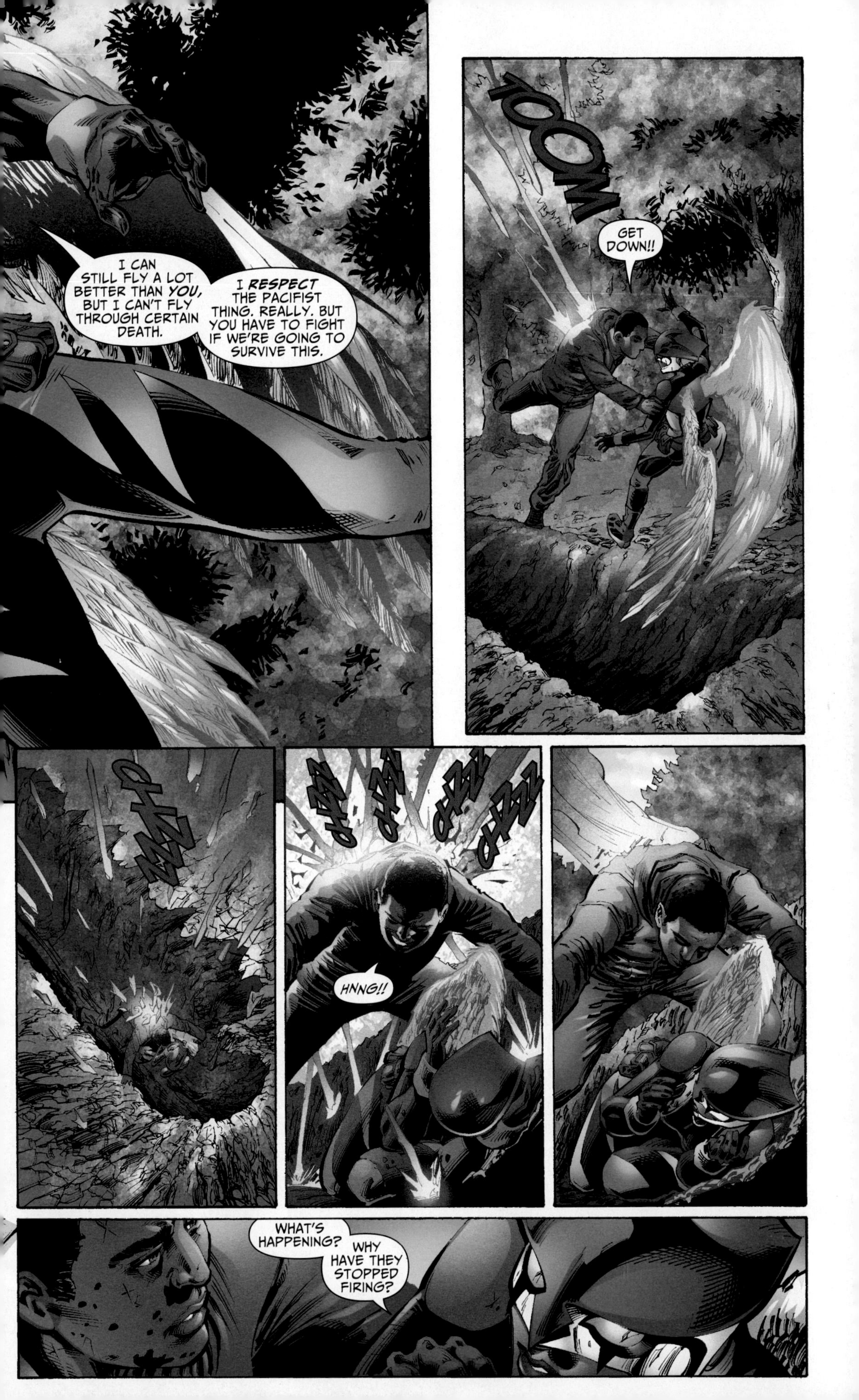
I CAN STILL FLY A LOT BETTER THAN *YOU*, BUT I CAN'T FLY THROUGH CERTAIN DEATH.
I *RESPECT* THE PACIFIST THING. REALLY. BUT YOU HAVE TO FIGHT IF WE'RE GOING TO SURVIVE THIS.
TOOOM
GET DOWN!!
CHZZZ
ZZZIP
ZZZIP
ZZZIP
ZZZIP
HNNG!!
WHAT'S HAPPENING?
WHY HAVE THEY STOPPED FIRING?

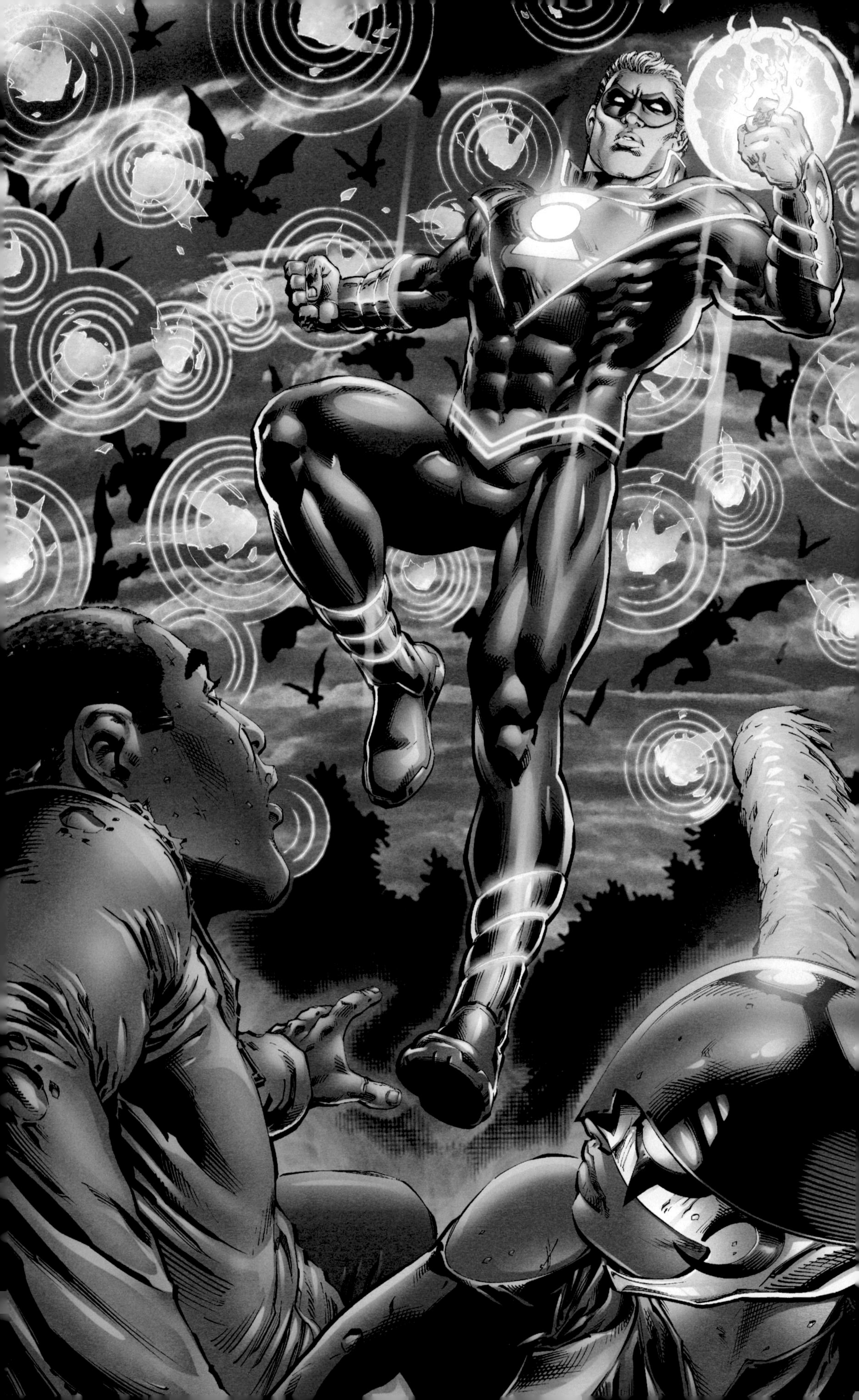

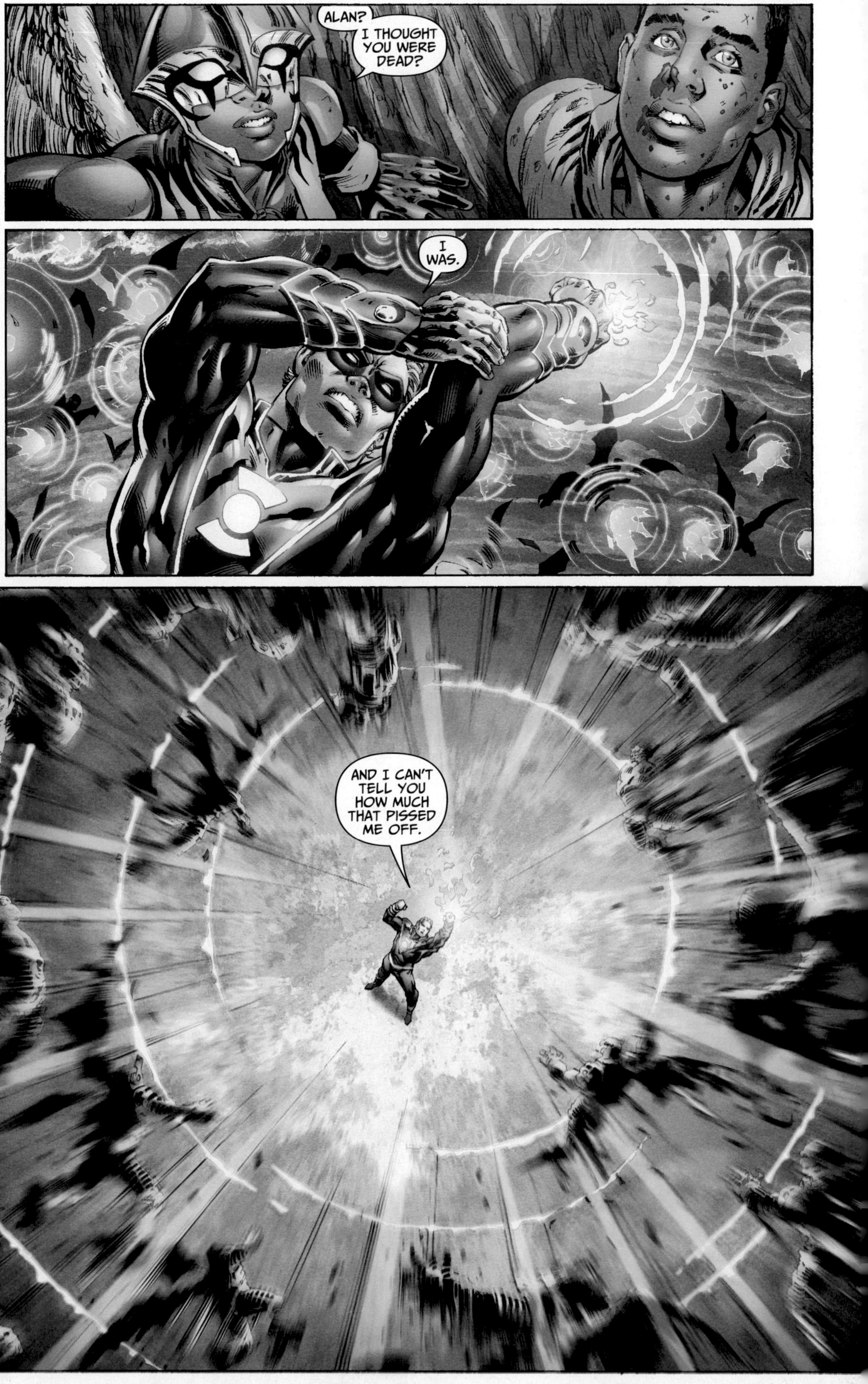
ALAN? I THOUGHT YOU WERE DEAD?
I WAS.
AND I CAN'T TELL YOU HOW MUCH THAT PISSED ME OFF.

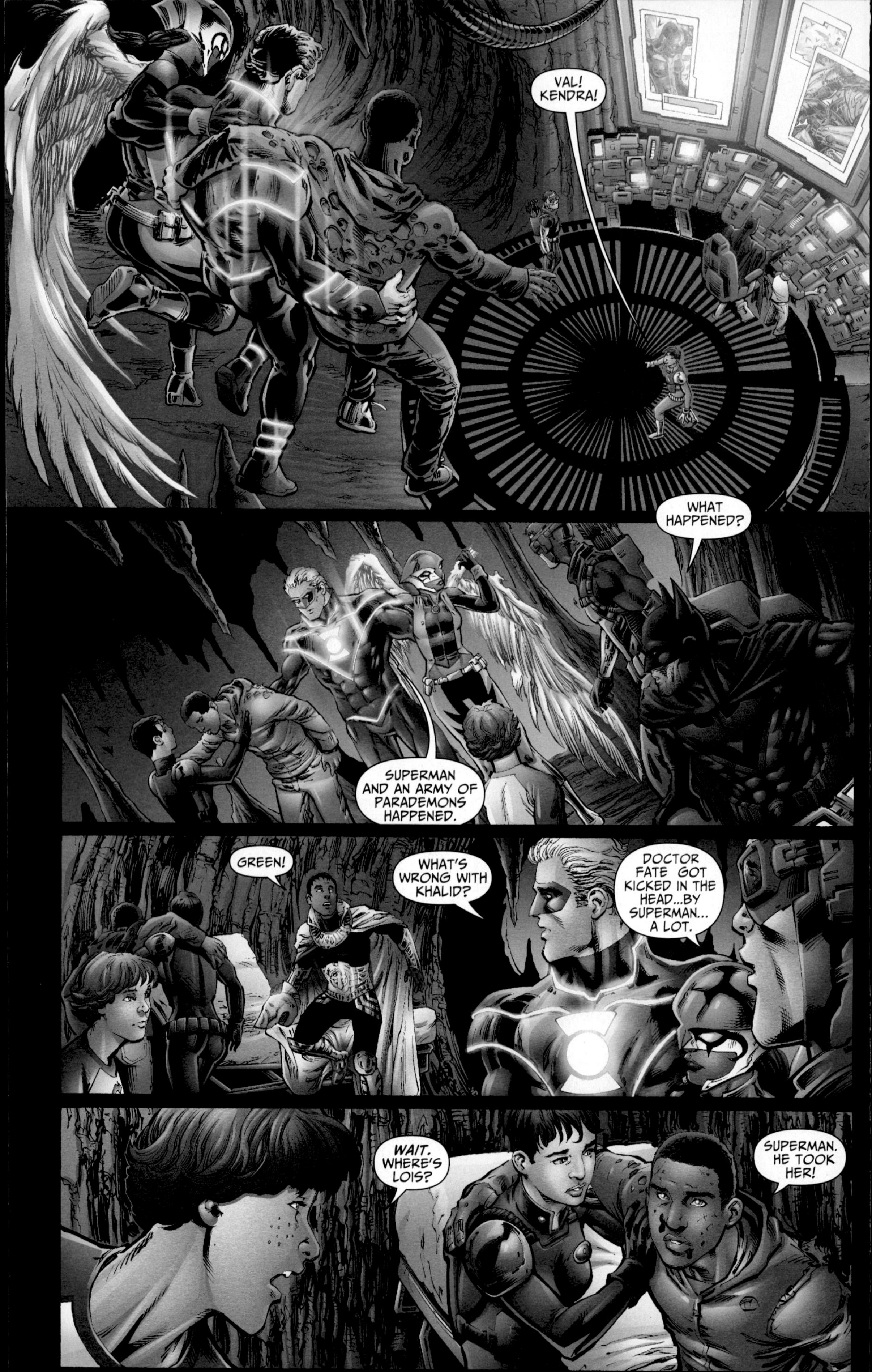
VAL! KENDRA!
WHAT HAPPENED?
SUPERMAN AND AN ARMY OF PARADEMONS HAPPENED.
GREEN!
WHAT'S WRONG WITH KHALID?
DOCTOR FATE GOT KICKED IN THE HEAD...BY SUPERMAN... A LOT.
WAIT. WHERE'S LOIS?
SUPERMAN. HE TOOK HER!

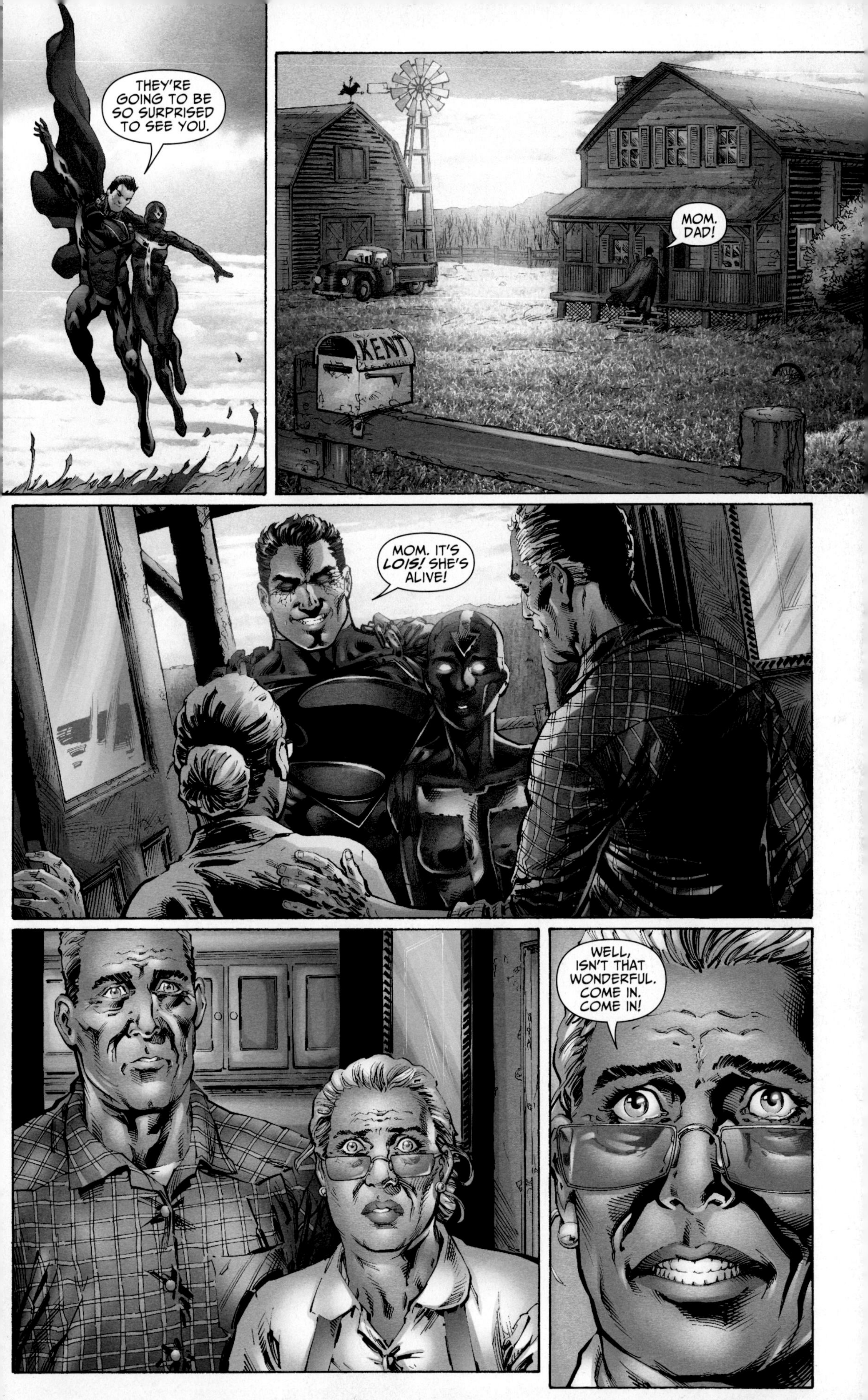
THEY'RE GOING TO BE SO SURPRISED TO SEE YOU.
KENT
MOM. DAD!
MOM. IT'S *LOIS!* SHE'S ALIVE!
WELL, ISN'T THAT WONDERFUL. COME IN. COME IN!

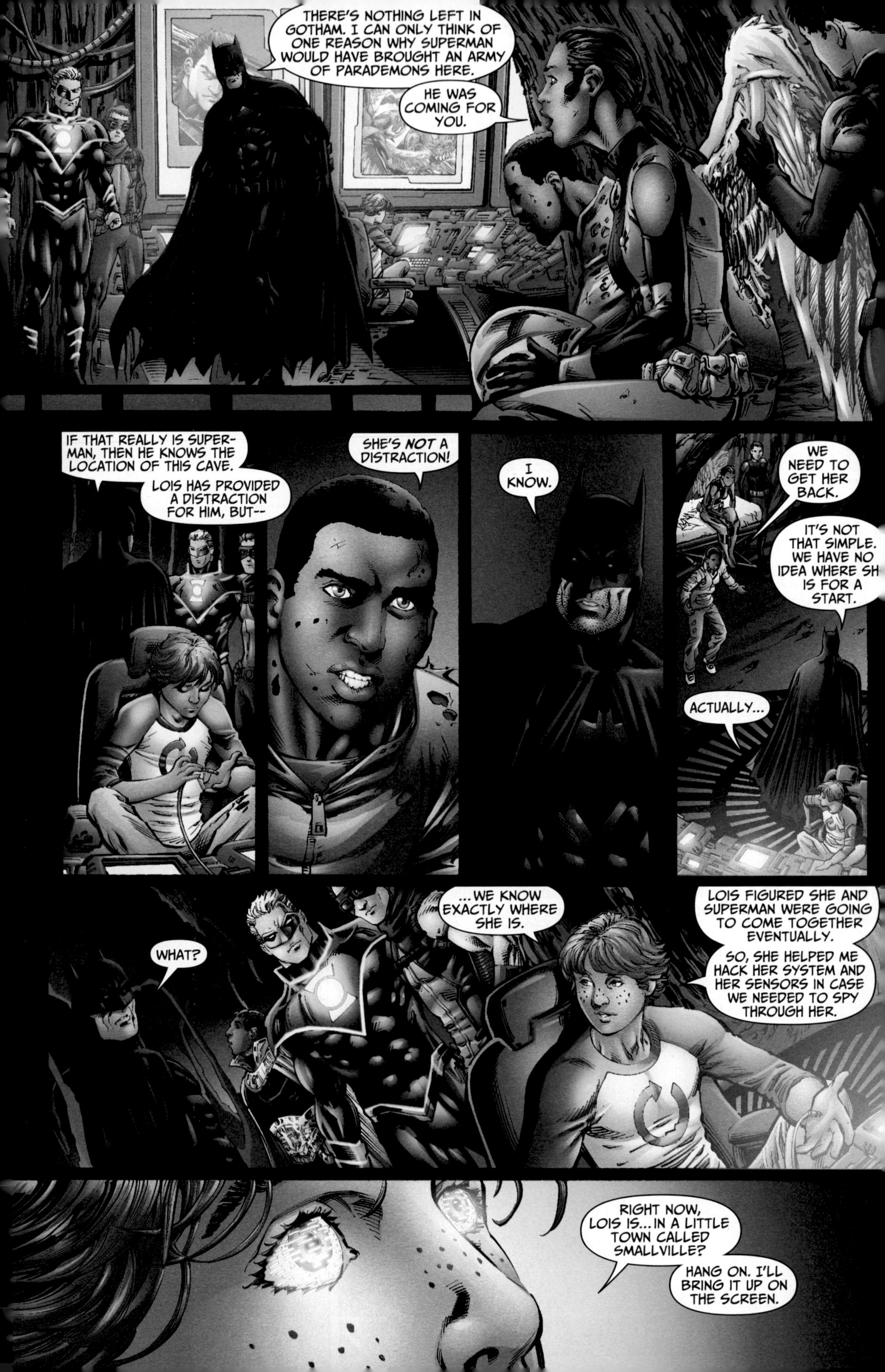
THERE'S NOTHING LEFT IN GOTHAM. I CAN ONLY THINK OF ONE REASON WHY SUPERMAN WOULD HAVE BROUGHT AN ARMY OF PARADEMONS HERE.
HE WAS COMING FOR YOU.
IF THAT REALLY IS SUPER-MAN, THEN HE KNOWS THE LOCATION OF THIS CAVE.
LOIS HAS PROVIDED A DISTRACTION FOR HIM, BUT--
SHE'S NOT A DISTRACTION!
I KNOW.
WE NEED TO GET HER BACK.
IT'S NOT THAT SIMPLE. WE HAVE NO IDEA WHERE SH IS FOR A START.
ACTUALLY...
...WE KNOW EXACTLY WHERE SHE IS.
WHAT?
LOIS FIGURED SHE AND SUPERMAN WERE GOING TO COME TOGETHER EVENTUALLY.
SO, SHE HELPED ME HACK HER SYSTEM AND HER SENSORS IN CASE WE NEEDED TO SPY THROUGH HER.
RIGHT NOW, LOIS IS...IN A LITTLE TOWN CALLED SMALLVILLE?
HANG ON. I'LL BRING IT UP ON THE SCREEN.

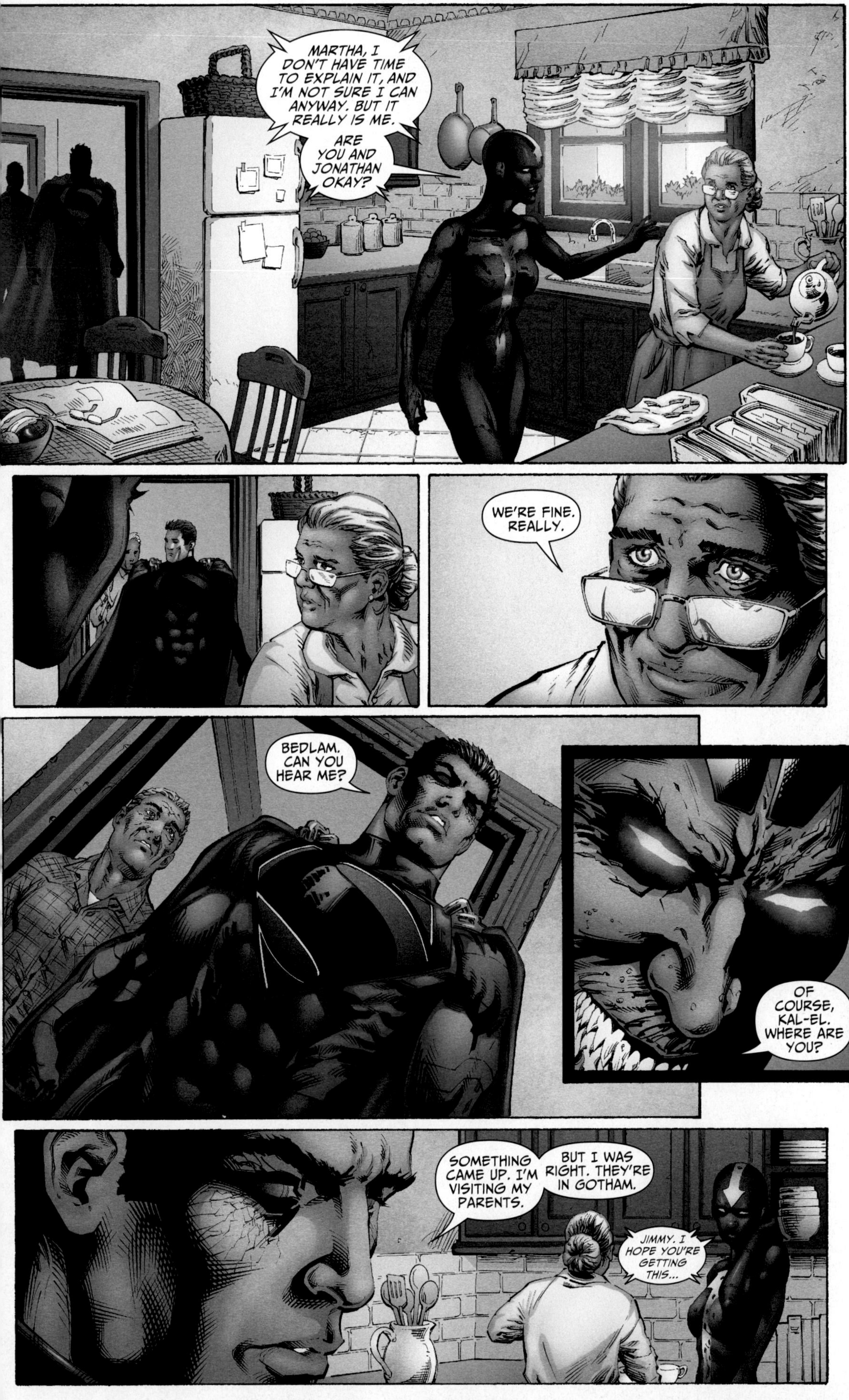
MARTHA, I DON'T HAVE TIME TO EXPLAIN IT, AND I'M NOT SURE I CAN ANYWAY. BUT IT REALLY IS ME.
ARE YOU AND JONATHAN OKAY?
WE'RE FINE. REALLY.
BEDLAM. CAN YOU HEAR ME?
OF COURSE, KAL-EL. WHERE ARE YOU?
SOMETHING CAME UP. I'M VISITING MY PARENTS.
BUT I WAS RIGHT. THEY'RE IN GOTHAM.
JIMMY. I HOPE YOU'RE GETTING THIS...

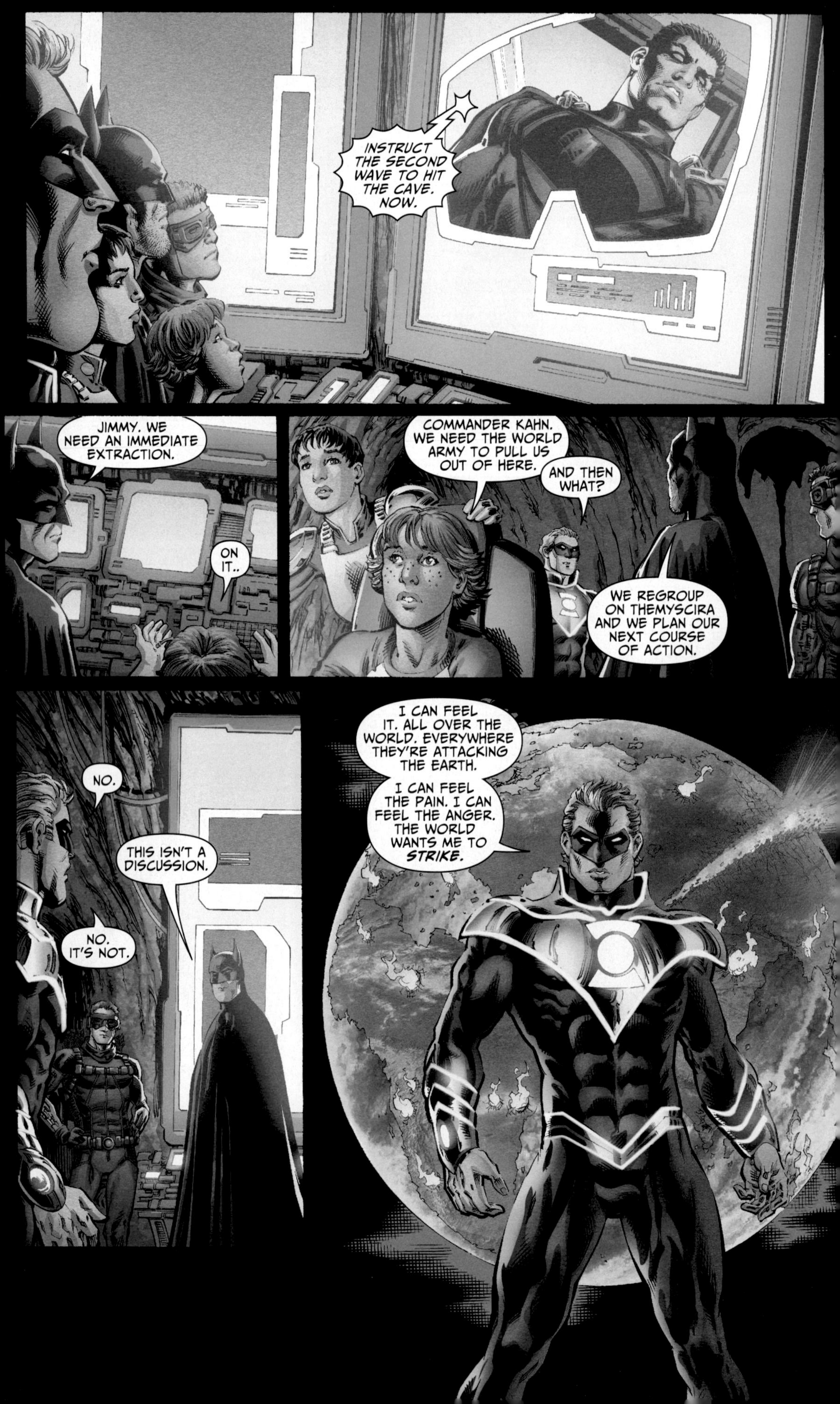
INSTRUCT THE SECOND WAVE TO HIT THE CAVE. NOW.
JIMMY. WE NEED AN IMMEDIATE EXTRACTION.
ON IT..
COMMANDER KAHN. WE NEED THE WORLD ARMY TO PULL US OUT OF HERE.
AND THEN WHAT?
WE REGROUP ON THEMYSCIRA AND WE PLAN OUR NEXT COURSE OF ACTION.
NO.
THIS ISN'T A DISCUSSION.
NO. IT'S NOT.
I CAN FEEL IT. ALL OVER THE WORLD. EVERYWHERE THEY'RE ATTACKING THE EARTH.
I CAN FEEL THE PAIN. I CAN FEEL THE ANGER. THE WORLD WANTS ME TO STRIKE.

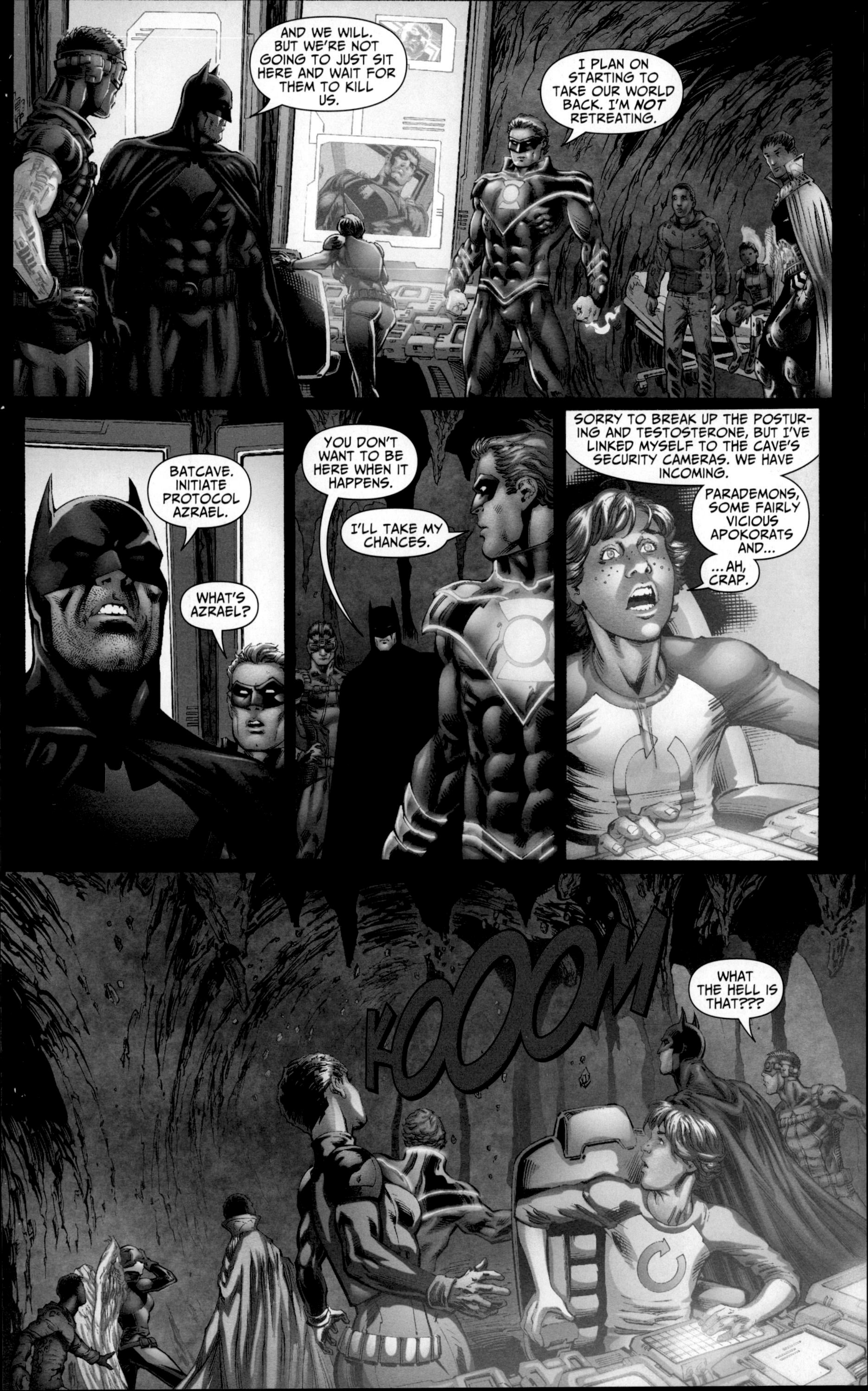
AND WE WILL. BUT WE'RE NOT GOING TO JUST SIT HERE AND WAIT FOR THEM TO KILL US.
I PLAN ON STARTING TO TAKE OUR WORLD BACK. I'M *NOT* RETREATING.
BATCAVE. INITIATE PROTOCOL AZRAEL.
WHAT'S AZRAEL?
YOU DON'T WANT TO BE HERE WHEN IT HAPPENS.
I'LL TAKE MY CHANCES.
SORRY TO BREAK UP THE POSTURING AND TESTOSTERONE, BUT I'VE LINKED MYSELF TO THE CAVE'S SECURITY CAMERAS. WE HAVE INCOMING.
PARADEMONS, SOME FAIRLY VICIOUS APOKORATS AND...
...AH, CRAP.
KOOOOM
WHAT THE HELL IS THAT???

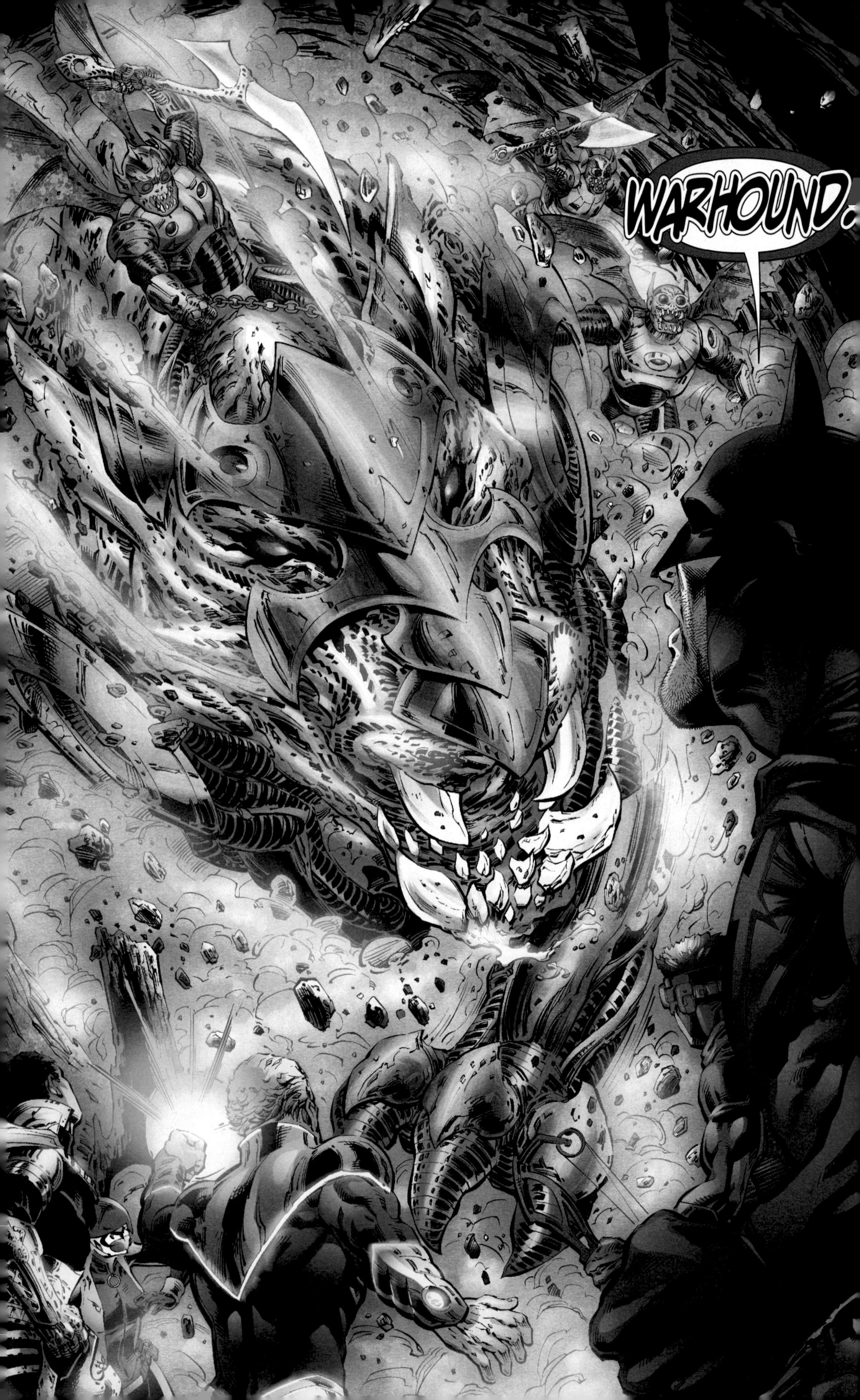
WARHOUND.

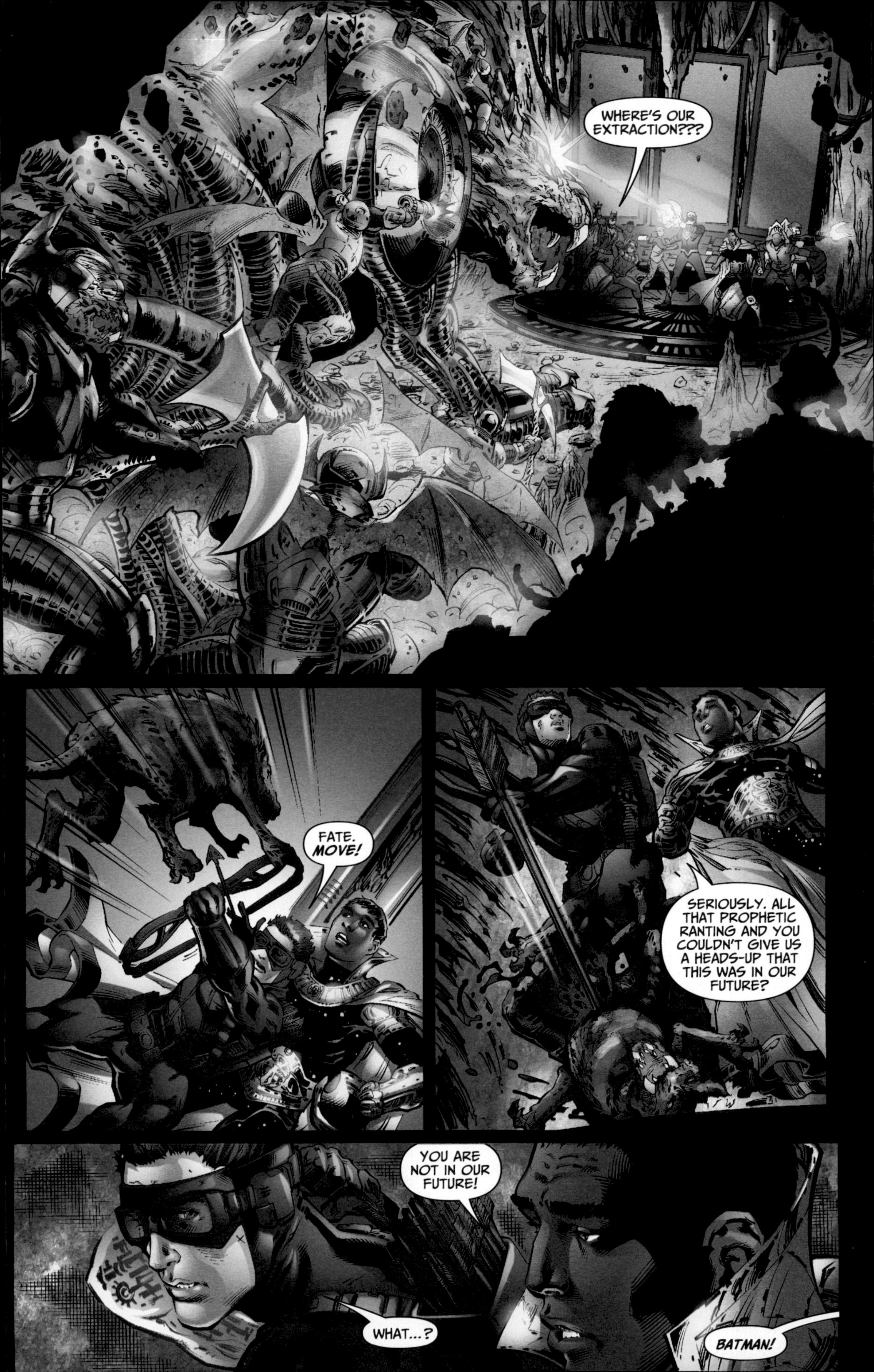
WHERE'S OUR EXTRACTION???
FATE. MOVE!
SERIOUSLY. ALL THAT PROPHETIC RANTING AND YOU COULDN'T GIVE US A HEADS-UP THAT THIS WAS IN OUR FUTURE?
YOU ARE NOT IN OUR FUTURE!
WHAT...?
BATMAN!

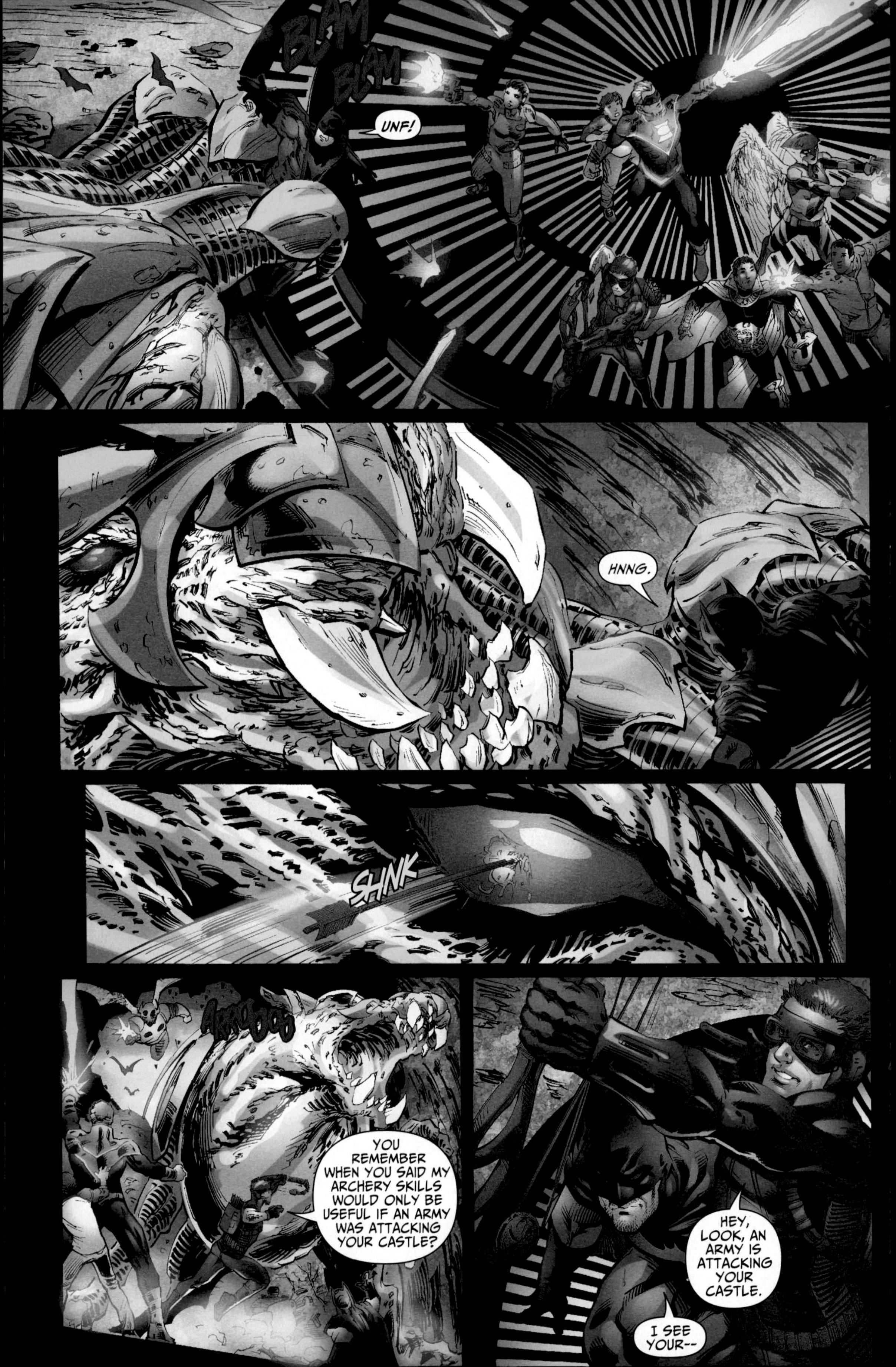
BLAM
BLAM
UNF!
HNNG.
SHNK
YOU REMEMBER WHEN YOU SAID MY ARCHERY SKILLS WOULD ONLY BE USEFUL IF AN ARMY WAS ATTACKING YOUR CASTLE?
HEY, LOOK, AN ARMY IS ATTACKING YOUR CASTLE.
I SEE YOUR--

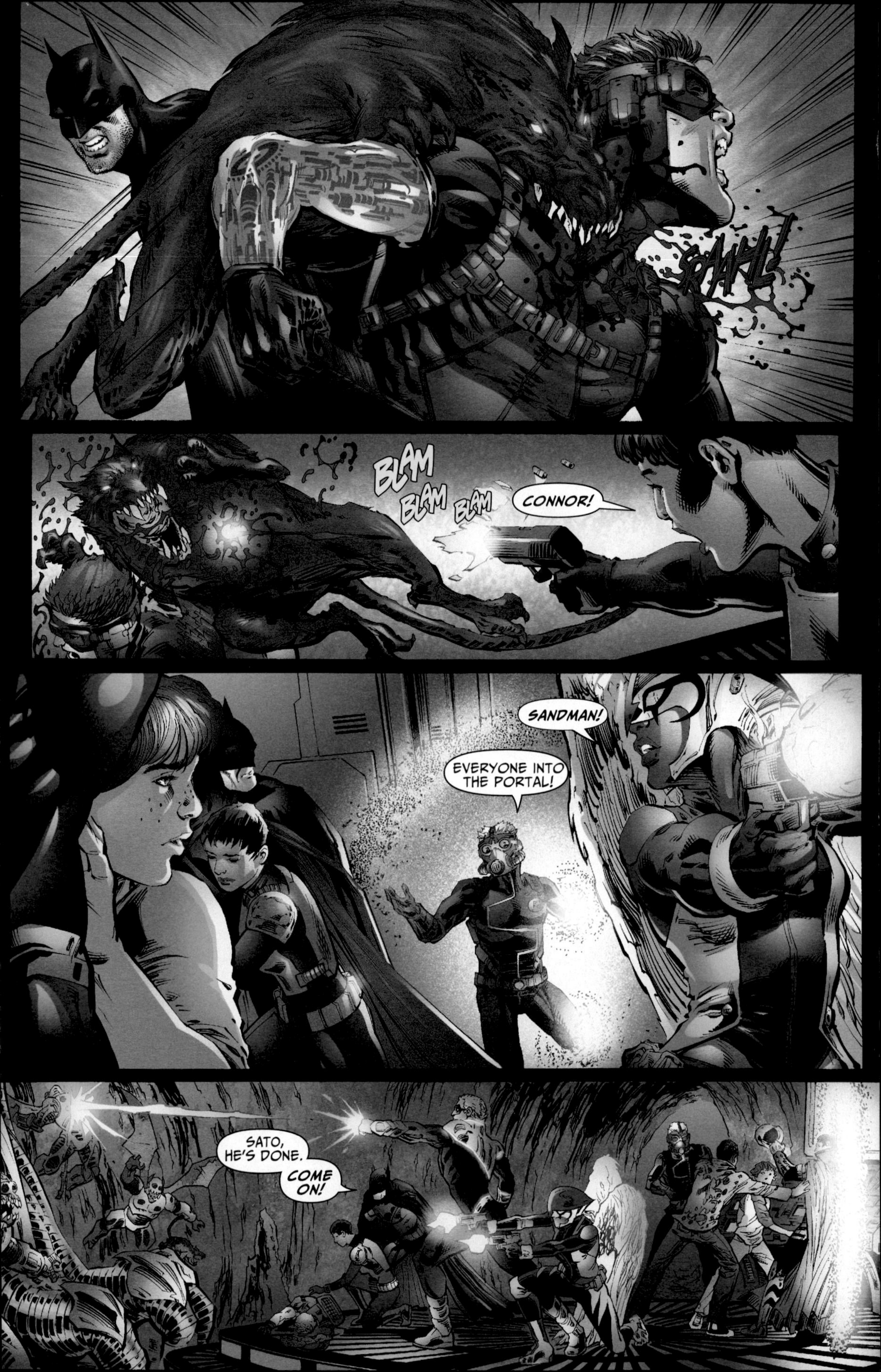
SRAAHL!
BLAM
BLAM
BLAM
CONNOR!
SANDMAN!
EVERYONE INTO THE PORTAL!
SATO, HE'S DONE.
COME ON!

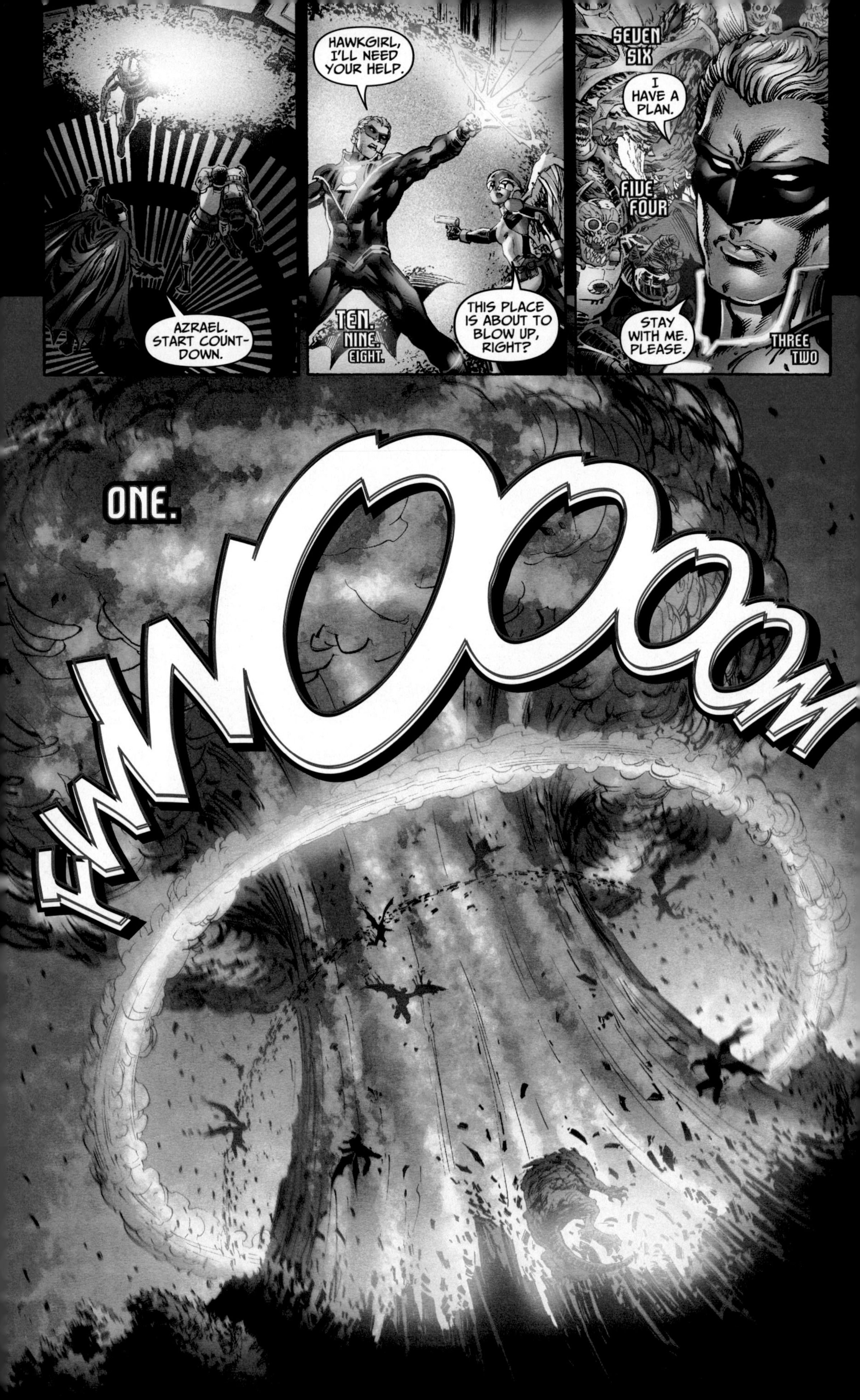
AZRAEL. START COUNT-DOWN.
HAWKGIRL, I'LL NEED YOUR HELP.
TEN. NINE. EIGHT.
THIS PLACE IS ABOUT TO BLOW UP, RIGHT?
SEVEN SIX
I HAVE A PLAN.
FIVE. FOUR
STAY WITH ME. PLEASE.
THREE TWO
ONE.
FWOOOoom

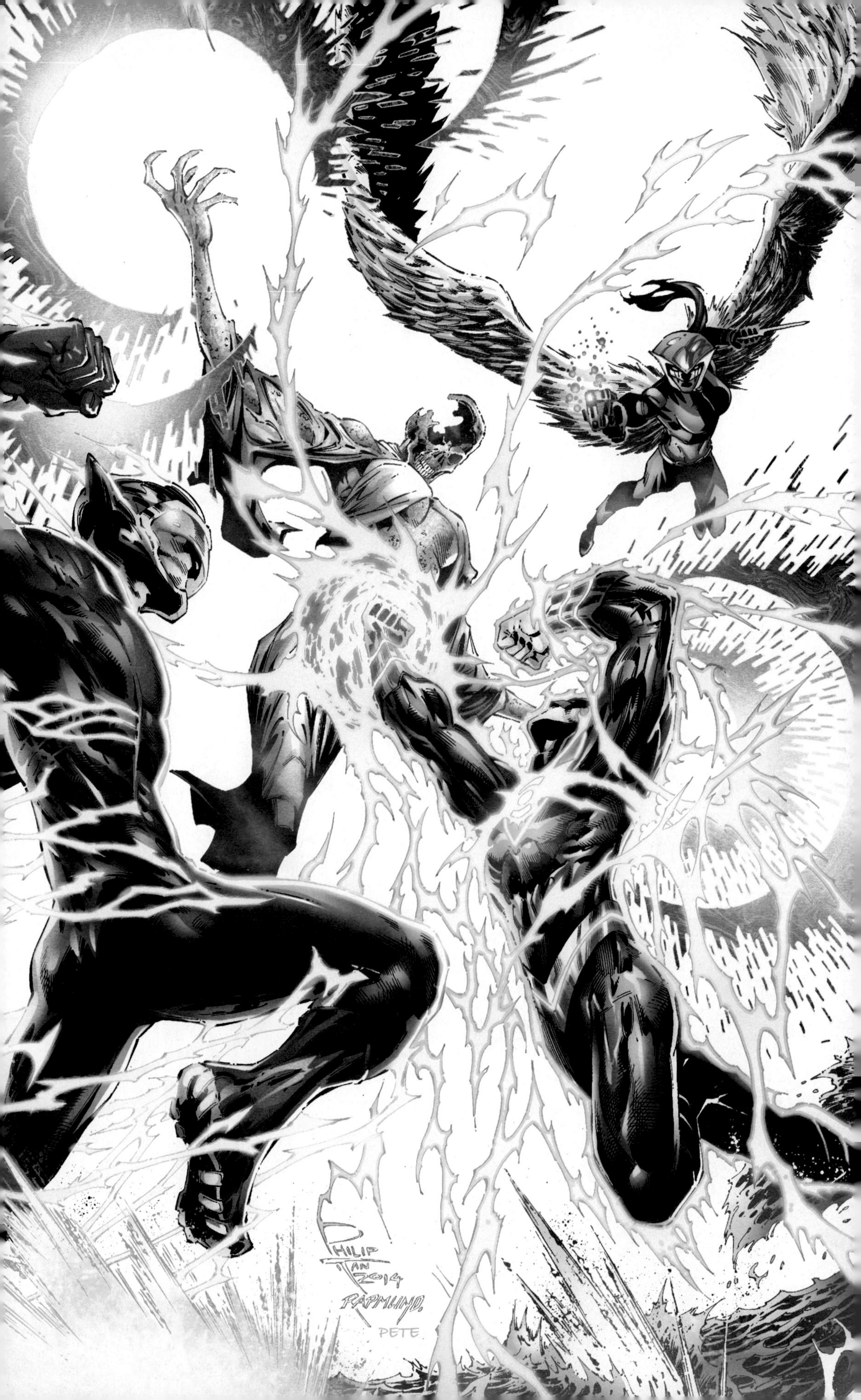
PHILIP TAN 2014
RAPMUND.
PETE

THE KRYPTONIAN PART 4

TOM TAYLOR writer EDDY BARROWS penciller EBER FERREIRA inker PETE PANTAZIS colorist cover by PHILIP TAN, NORM RAPMUND & PETE PANTAZIS

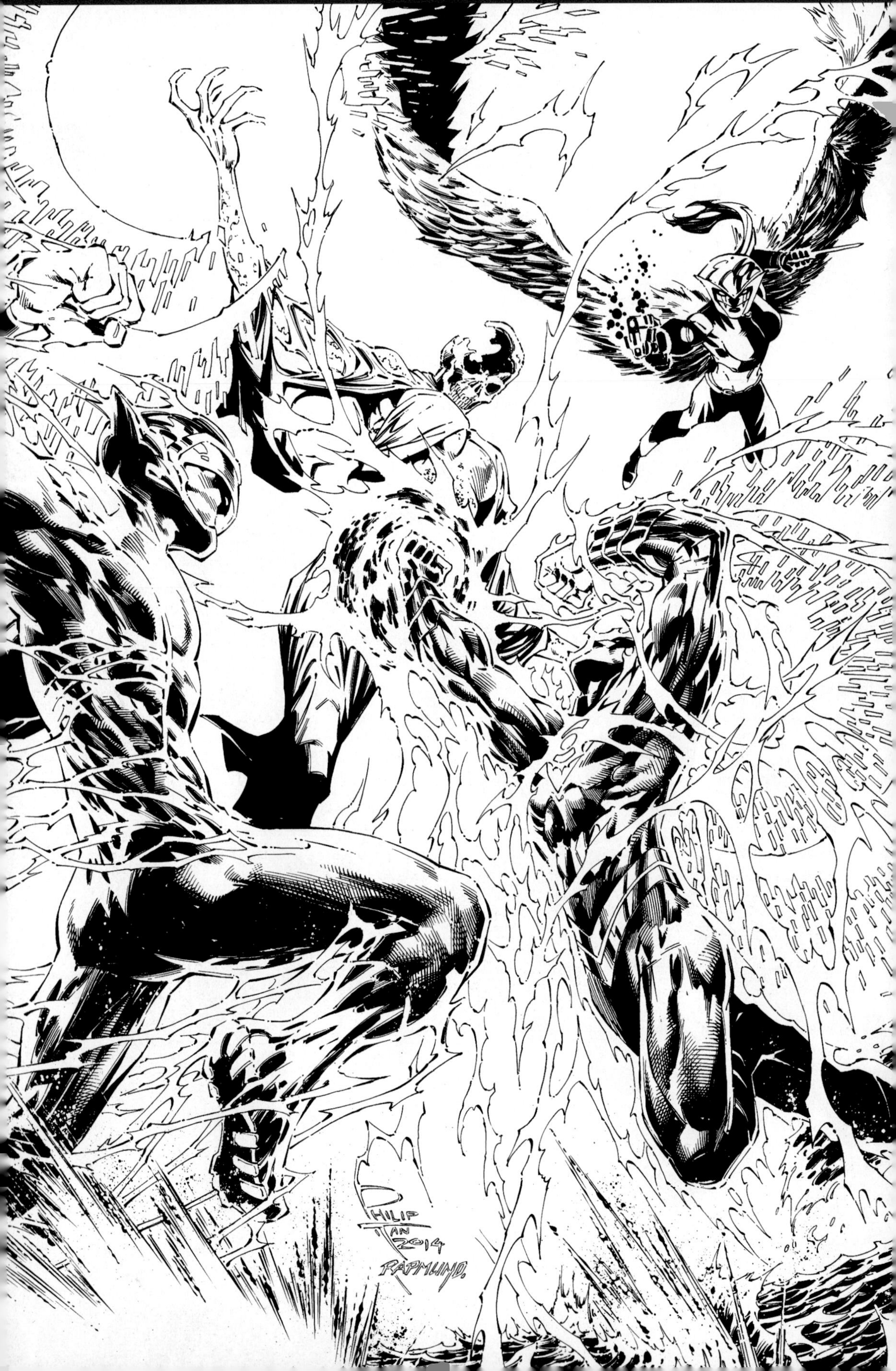
PHILIP TAN 2014
RAPMUND.

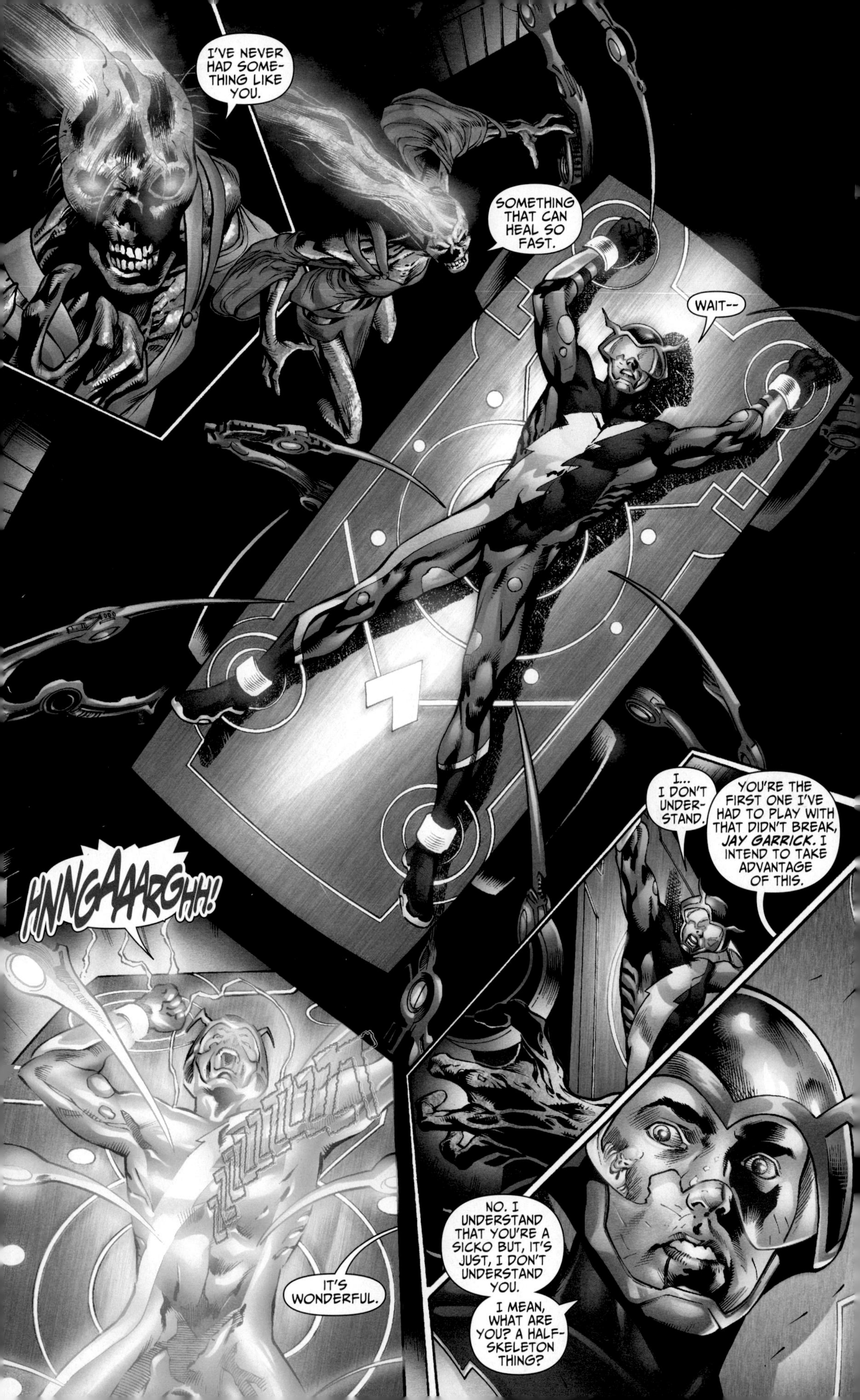
I'VE NEVER HAD SOME-THING LIKE YOU.
SOMETHING THAT CAN HEAL SO FAST.
WAIT--
I... I DON'T UNDER-STAND.
YOU'RE THE FIRST ONE I'VE HAD TO PLAY WITH THAT DIDN'T BREAK, JAY GARRICK. I INTEND TO TAKE ADVANTAGE OF THIS.
HNNGAAARGHH!
IT'S WONDERFUL.
NO. I UNDERSTAND THAT YOU'RE A SICKO BUT, IT'S JUST, I DON'T UNDERSTAND YOU.
I MEAN, WHAT ARE YOU? A HALF-SKELETON THING?

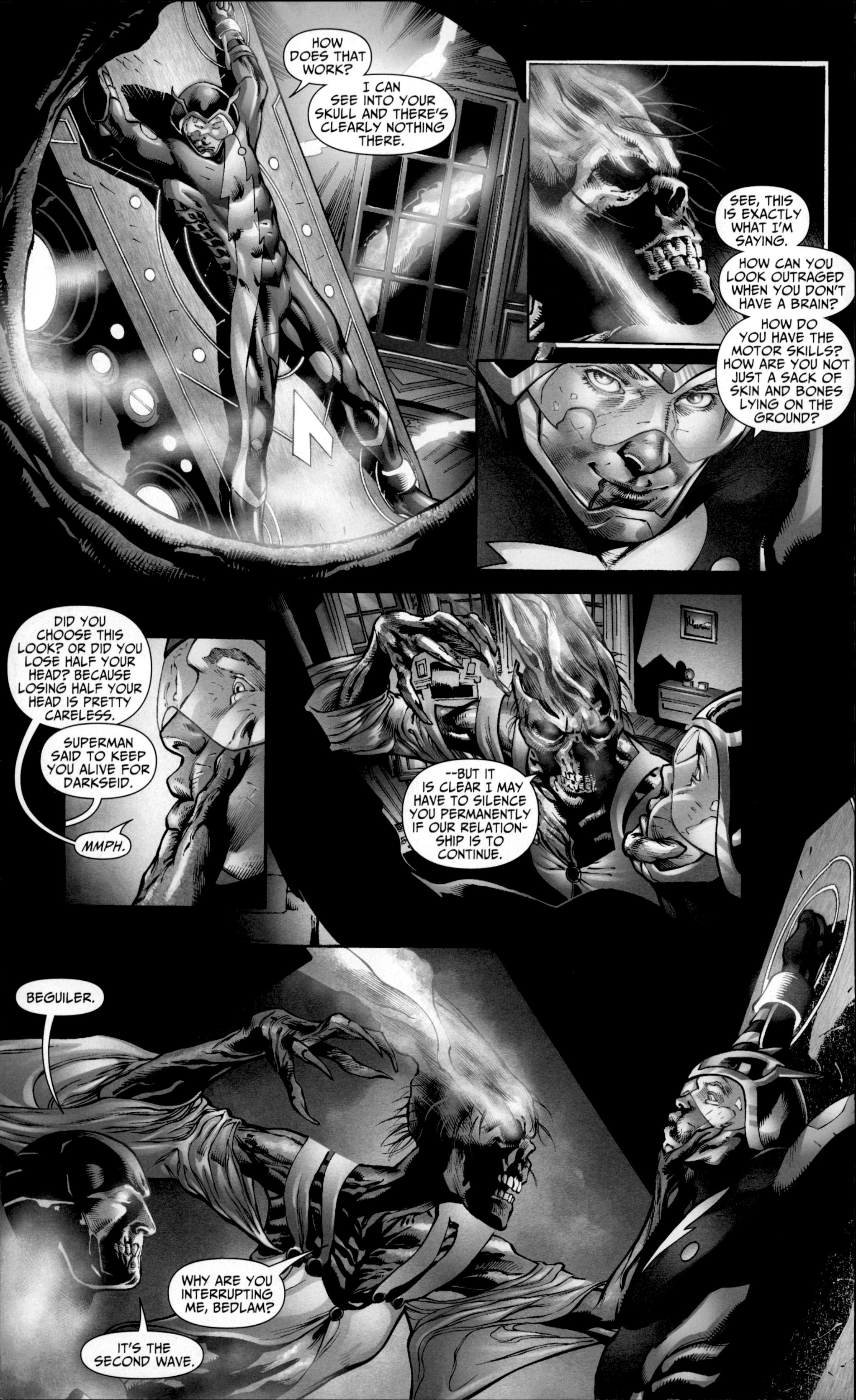
HOW DOES THAT WORK?
I CAN SEE INTO YOUR SKULL AND THERE'S CLEARLY NOTHING THERE.
SEE, THIS IS EXACTLY WHAT I'M SAYING.
HOW CAN YOU LOOK OUTRAGED WHEN YOU DON'T HAVE A BRAIN?
HOW DO YOU HAVE THE MOTOR SKILLS? HOW ARE YOU NOT JUST A SACK OF SKIN AND BONES LYING ON THE GROUND?
DID YOU CHOOSE THIS LOOK? OR DID YOU LOSE HALF YOUR HEAD? BECAUSE LOSING HALF YOUR HEAD IS PRETTY CARELESS.
SUPERMAN SAID TO KEEP YOU ALIVE FOR DARKSEID.
MMPH.
--BUT IT IS CLEAR I MAY HAVE TO SILENCE YOU PERMANENTLY IF OUR RELATION-SHIP IS TO CONTINUE.
BEGUILER.
WHY ARE YOU INTERRUPTING ME, BEDLAM?
IT'S THE SECOND WAVE.

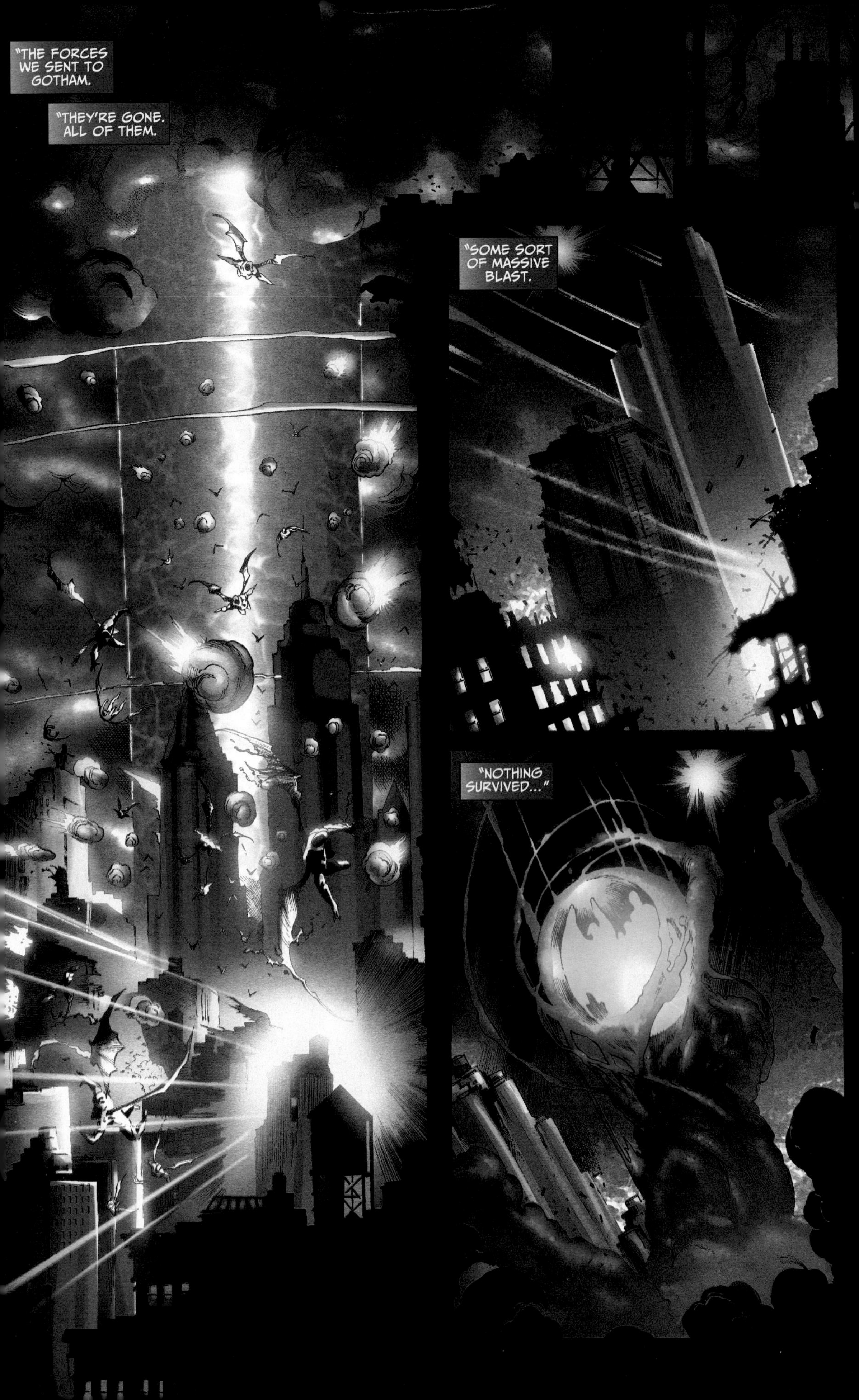
"THE FORCES WE SENT TO GOTHAM.
"THEY'RE GONE. ALL OF THEM.
"SOME SORT OF MASSIVE BLAST.
"NOTHING SURVIVED..."

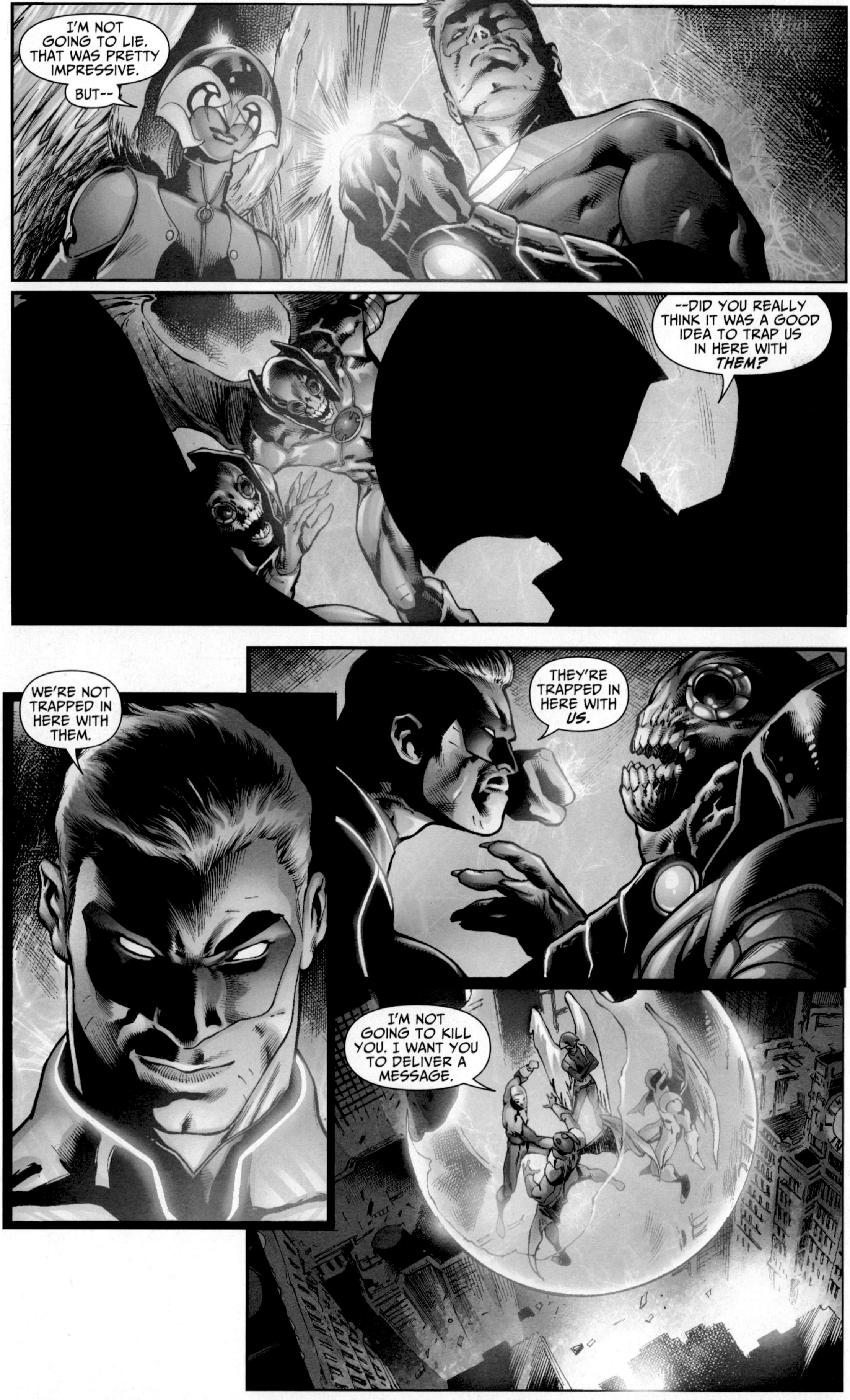
I'M NOT GOING TO LIE. THAT WAS PRETTY IMPRESSIVE.
BUT--
--DID YOU REALLY THINK IT WAS A GOOD IDEA TO TRAP US IN HERE WITH *THEM?*
WE'RE NOT TRAPPED IN HERE WITH THEM.
THEY'RE TRAPPED IN HERE WITH *US.*
I'M NOT GOING TO KILL YOU. I WANT YOU TO DELIVER A MESSAGE.

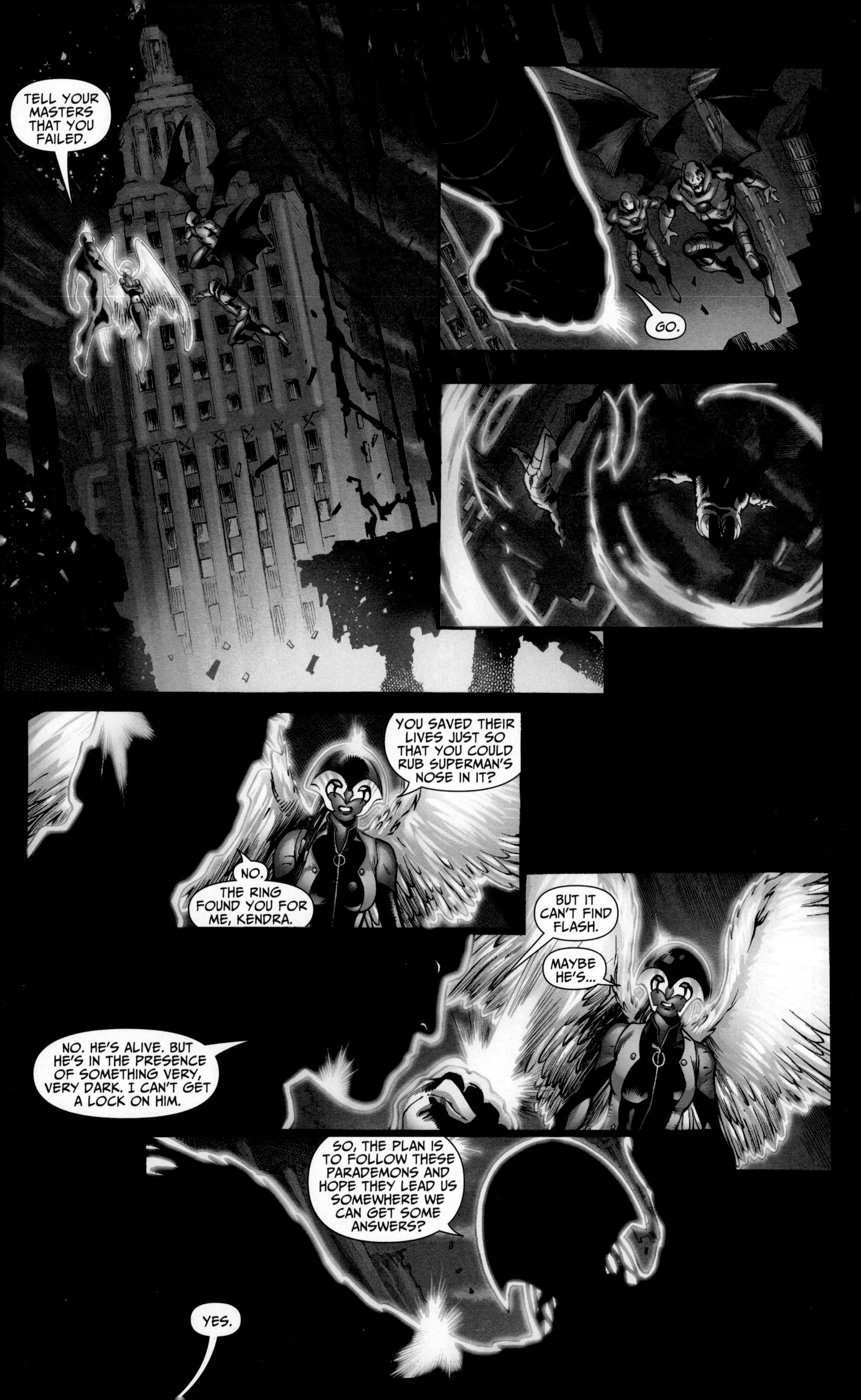
TELL YOUR MASTERS THAT YOU FAILED.
GO.
YOU SAVED THEIR LIVES JUST SO THAT YOU COULD RUB SUPERMAN'S NOSE IN IT?
NO.
THE RING FOUND YOU FOR ME, KENDRA.
BUT IT CAN'T FIND FLASH.
MAYBE HE'S...
NO. HE'S ALIVE. BUT HE'S IN THE PRESENCE OF SOMETHING VERY, VERY DARK. I CAN'T GET A LOCK ON HIM.
SO, THE PLAN IS TO FOLLOW THESE PARADEMONS AND HOPE THEY LEAD US SOMEWHERE WE CAN GET SOME ANSWERS?
YES.

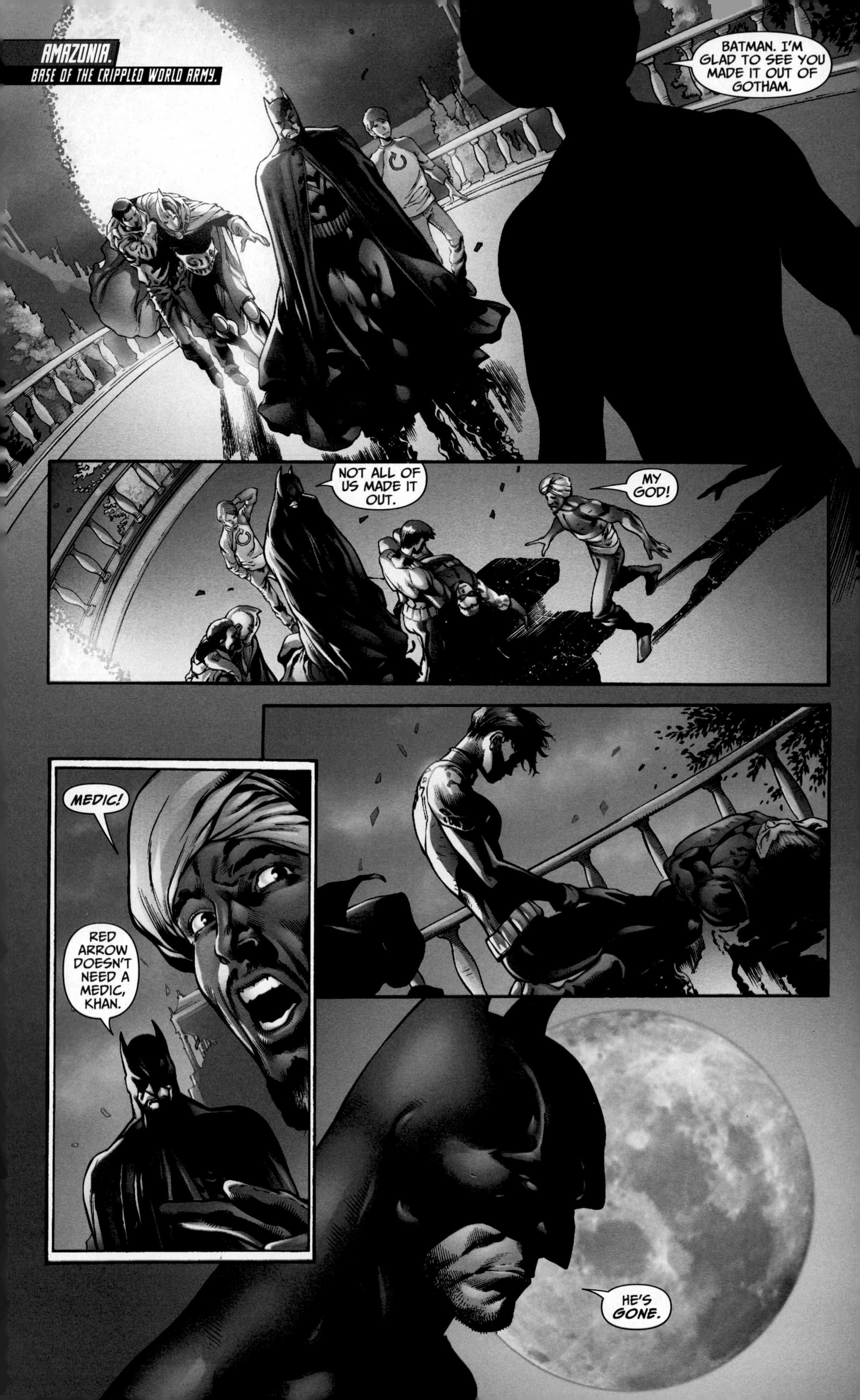
AMAZONIA.
BASE OF THE CRIPPLED WORLD ARMY.
BATMAN. I'M GLAD TO SEE YOU MADE IT OUT OF GOTHAM.
NOT ALL OF US MADE IT OUT.
MY GOD!
MEDIC!
RED ARROW DOESN'T NEED A MEDIC, KHAN.
HE'S GONE.

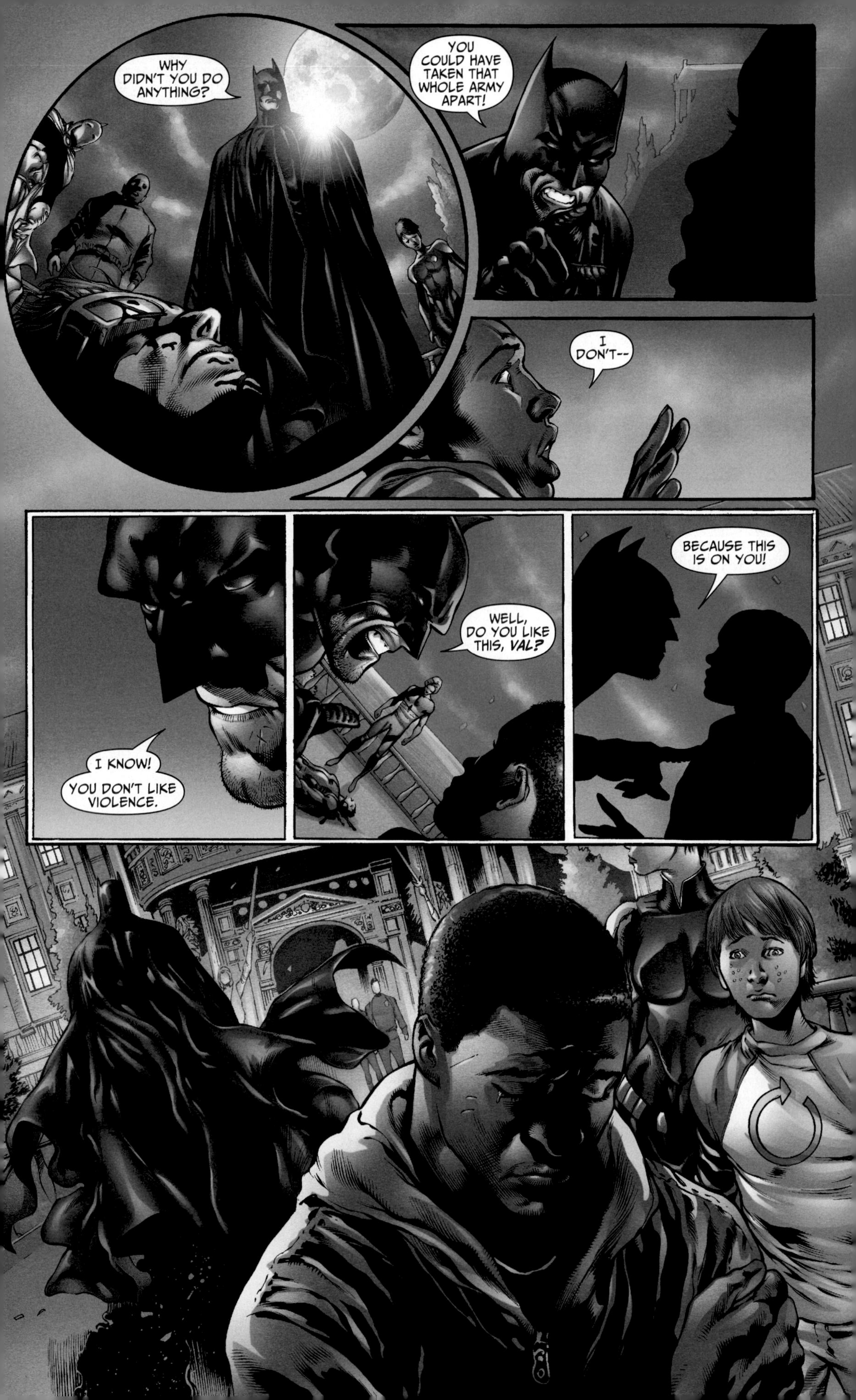
WHY DIDN'T YOU DO ANYTHING?
YOU COULD HAVE TAKEN THAT WHOLE ARMY APART!
I DON'T--
I KNOW!
YOU DON'T LIKE VIOLENCE.
WELL, DO YOU LIKE THIS, *VAL?*
BECAUSE THIS IS ON YOU!

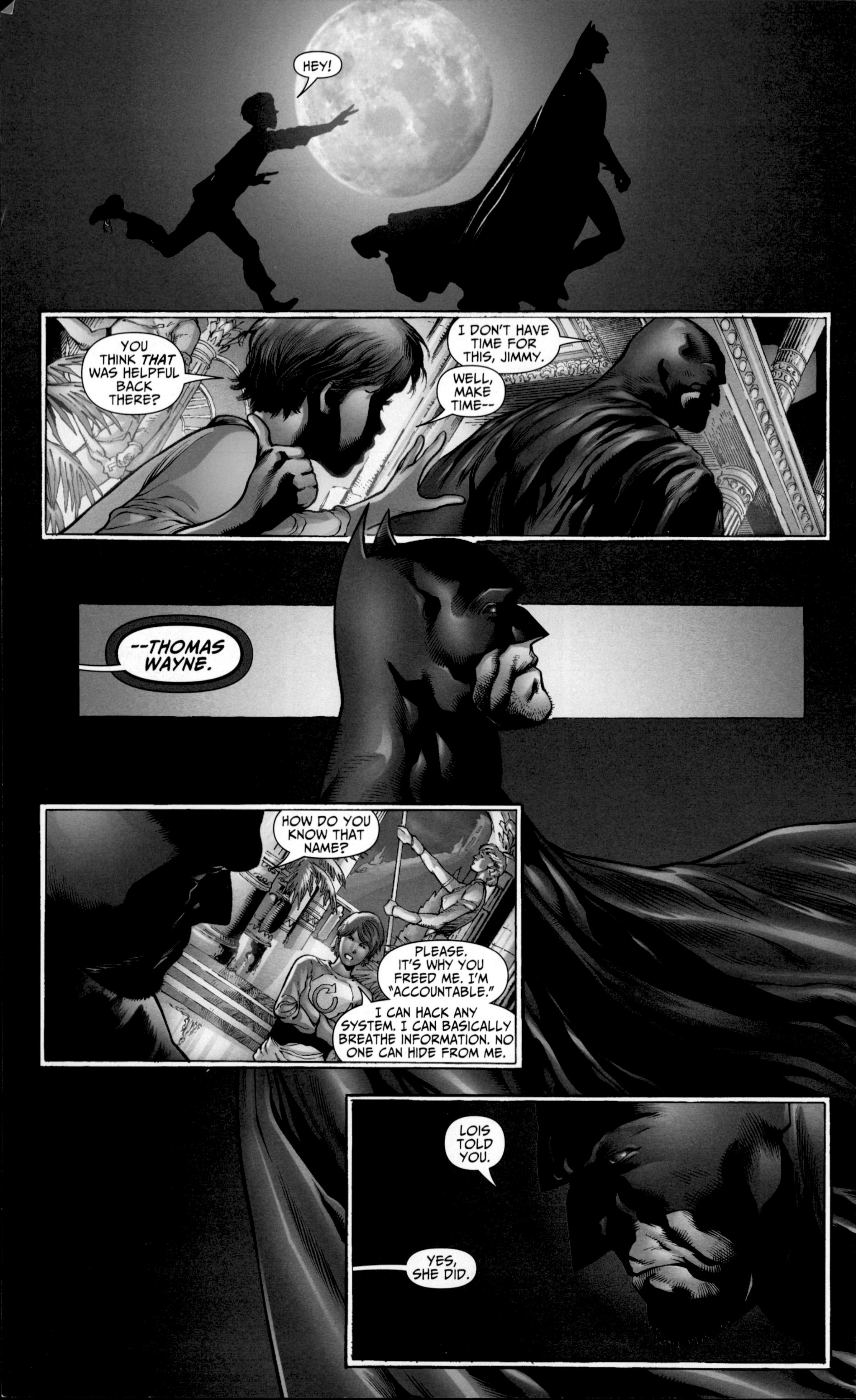
HEY!
YOU THINK *THAT* WAS HELPFUL BACK THERE?
I DON'T HAVE TIME FOR THIS, JIMMY.
WELL, MAKE TIME--
--THOMAS WAYNE.
HOW DO YOU KNOW THAT NAME?
PLEASE. IT'S WHY YOU FREED ME. I'M "ACCOUNTABLE."
I CAN HACK ANY SYSTEM. I CAN BASICALLY BREATHE INFORMATION. NO ONE CAN HIDE FROM ME.
LOIS TOLD YOU.
YES, SHE DID.

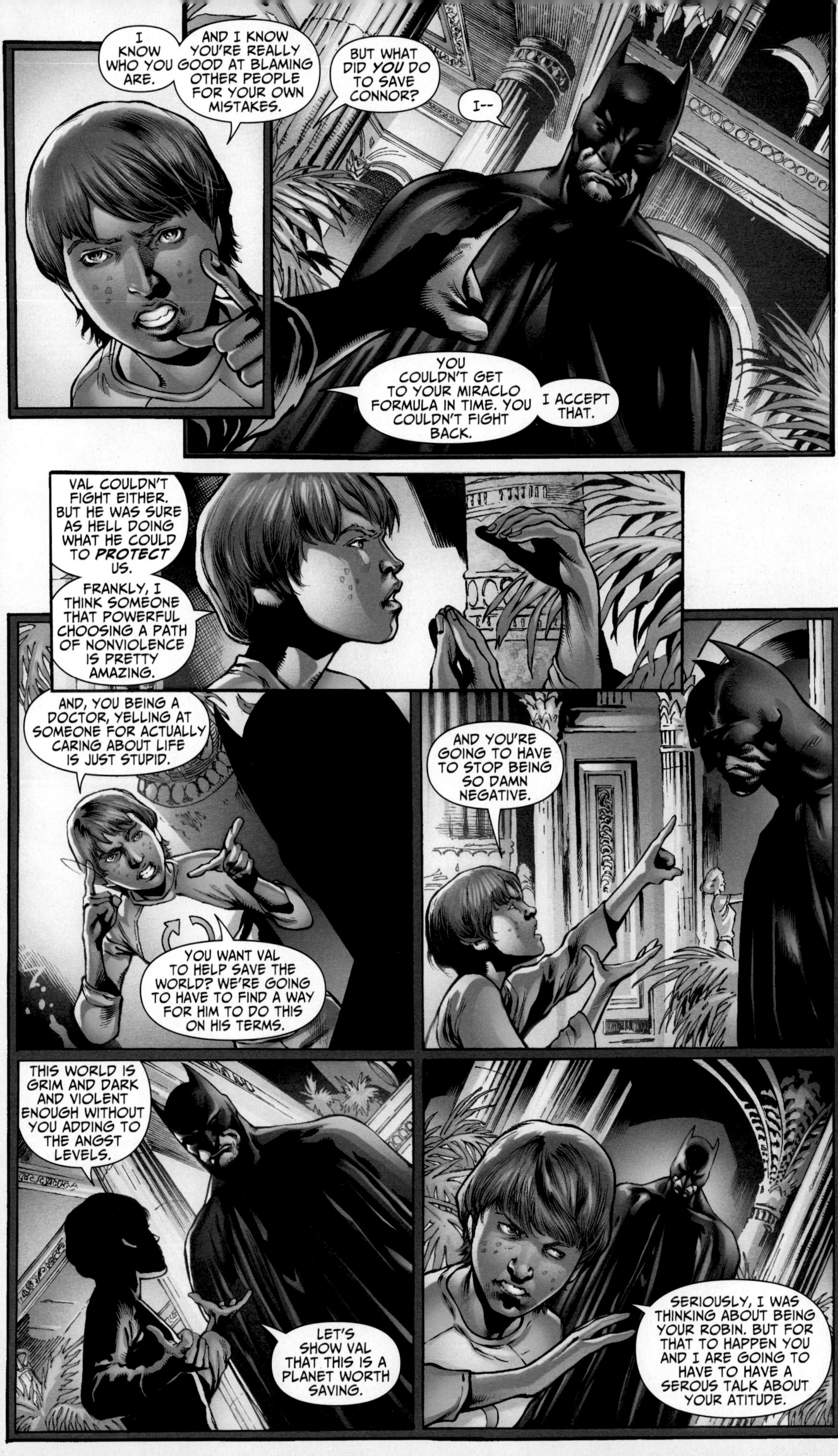
I KNOW WHO YOU ARE.
AND I KNOW YOU'RE REALLY GOOD AT BLAMING OTHER PEOPLE FOR YOUR OWN MISTAKES.
BUT WHAT DID *YOU* DO TO SAVE CONNOR?
I--
YOU COULDN'T GET TO YOUR MIRACLO FORMULA IN TIME. YOU COULDN'T FIGHT BACK.
I ACCEPT THAT.
VAL COULDN'T FIGHT EITHER. BUT HE WAS SURE AS HELL DOING WHAT HE COULD TO **PROTECT** US.
FRANKLY, I THINK SOMEONE THAT POWERFUL CHOOSING A PATH OF NONVIOLENCE IS PRETTY AMAZING.
AND, YOU BEING A DOCTOR, YELLING AT SOMEONE FOR ACTUALLY CARING ABOUT LIFE IS JUST STUPID.
YOU WANT VAL TO HELP SAVE THE WORLD? WE'RE GOING TO HAVE TO FIND A WAY FOR HIM TO DO THIS ON HIS TERMS.
AND YOU'RE GOING TO HAVE TO STOP BEING SO DAMN NEGATIVE.
THIS WORLD IS GRIM AND DARK AND VIOLENT ENOUGH WITHOUT YOU ADDING TO THE ANGST LEVELS.
LET'S SHOW VAL THAT THIS IS A PLANET WORTH SAVING.
SERIOUSLY, I WAS THINKING ABOUT BEING YOUR ROBIN. BUT FOR THAT TO HAPPEN YOU AND I ARE GOING TO HAVE TO HAVE A SEROUS TALK ABOUT YOUR ATITUDE.

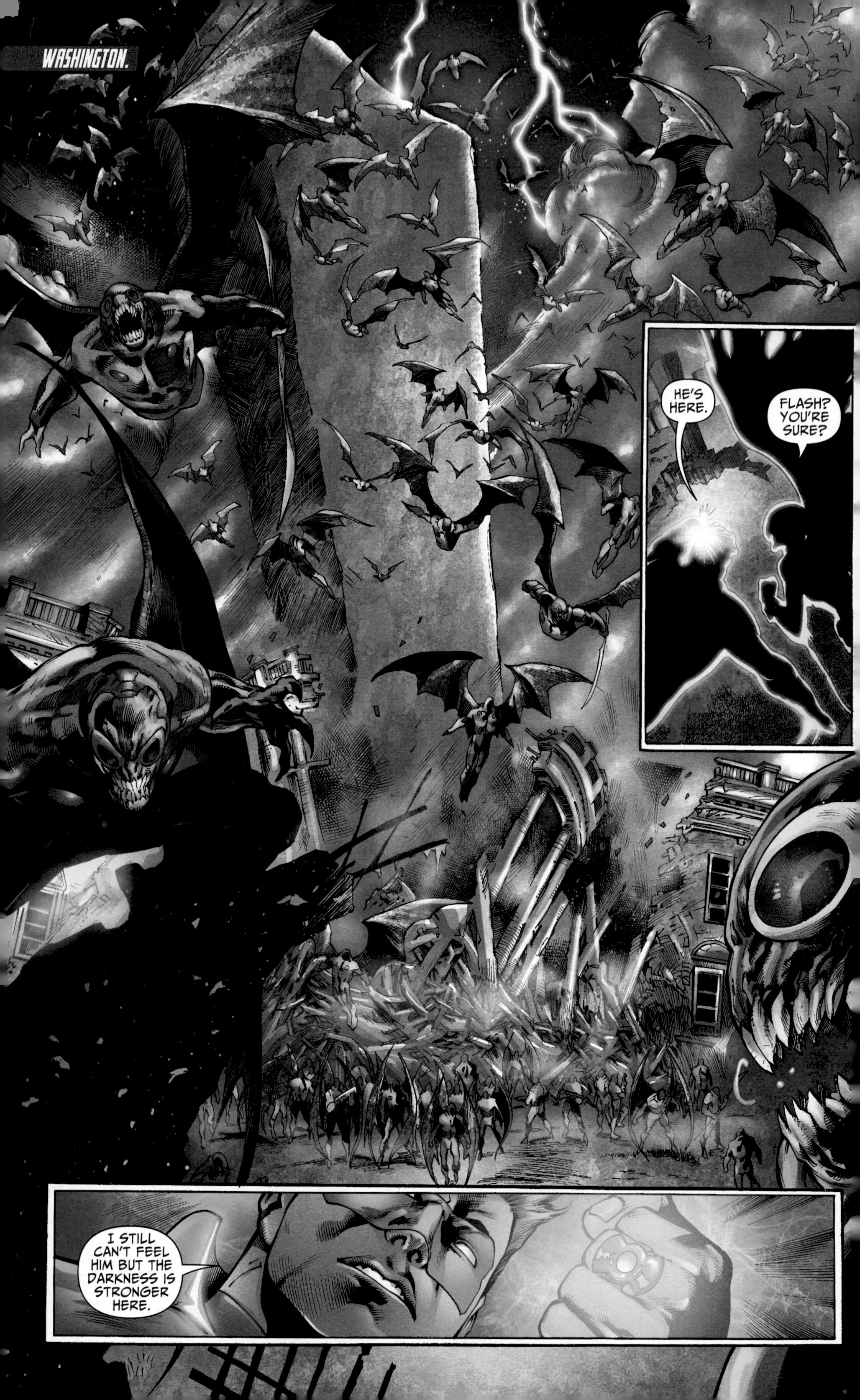
WASHINGTON.
HE'S HERE.
FLASH? YOU'RE SURE?
I STILL CAN'T FEEL HIM BUT THE DARKNESS IS STRONGER HERE.

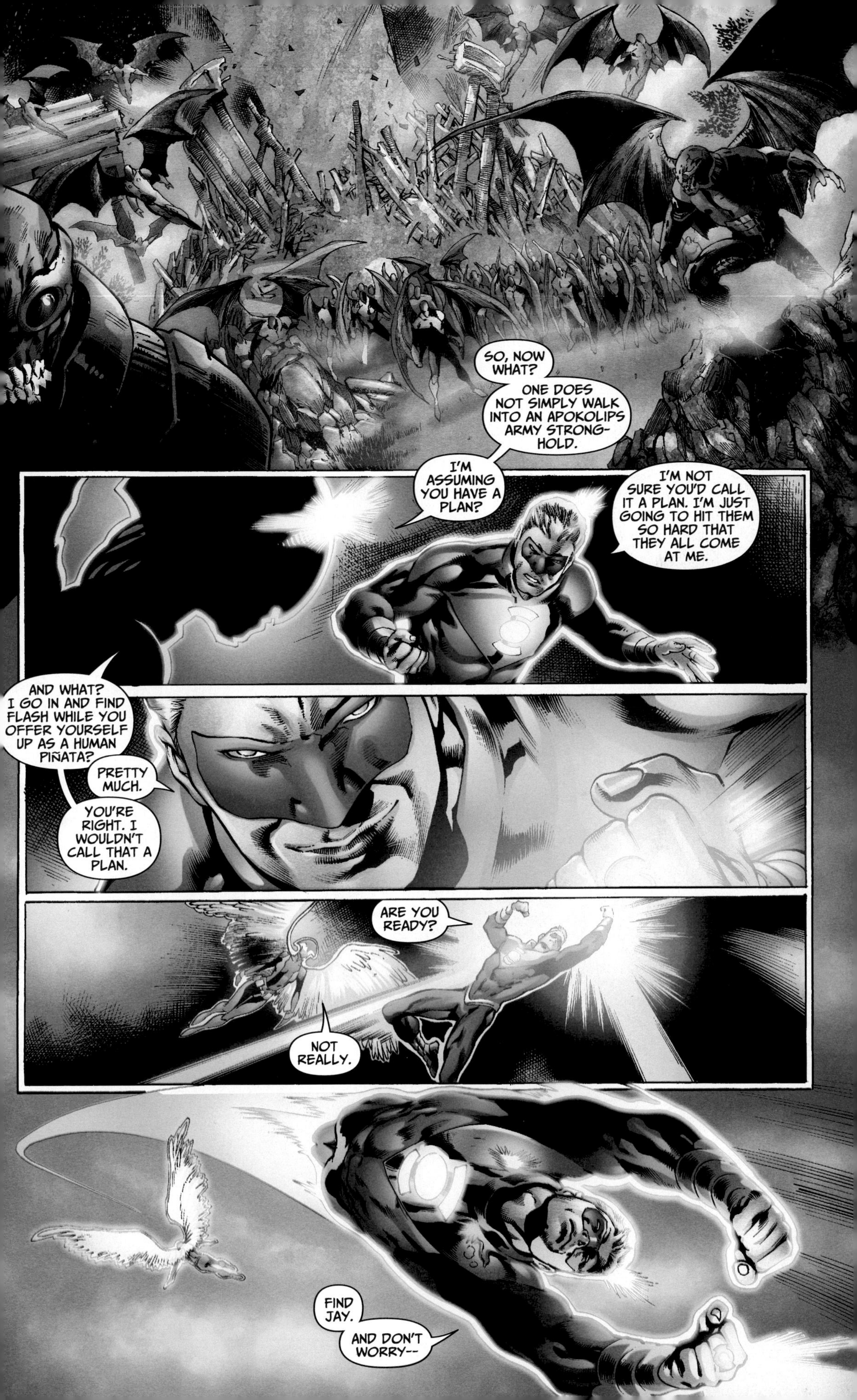
SO, NOW WHAT?
ONE DOES NOT SIMPLY WALK INTO AN APOKOLIPS ARMY STRONG-HOLD.
I'M ASSUMING YOU HAVE A PLAN?
I'M NOT SURE YOU'D CALL IT A PLAN. I'M JUST GOING TO HIT THEM SO HARD THAT THEY ALL COME AT ME.
AND WHAT? I GO IN AND FIND FLASH WHILE YOU OFFER YOURSELF UP AS A HUMAN PIÑATA?
PRETTY MUCH.
YOU'RE RIGHT. I WOULDN'T CALL THAT A PLAN.
ARE YOU READY?
NOT REALLY.
FIND JAY.
AND DON'T WORRY--

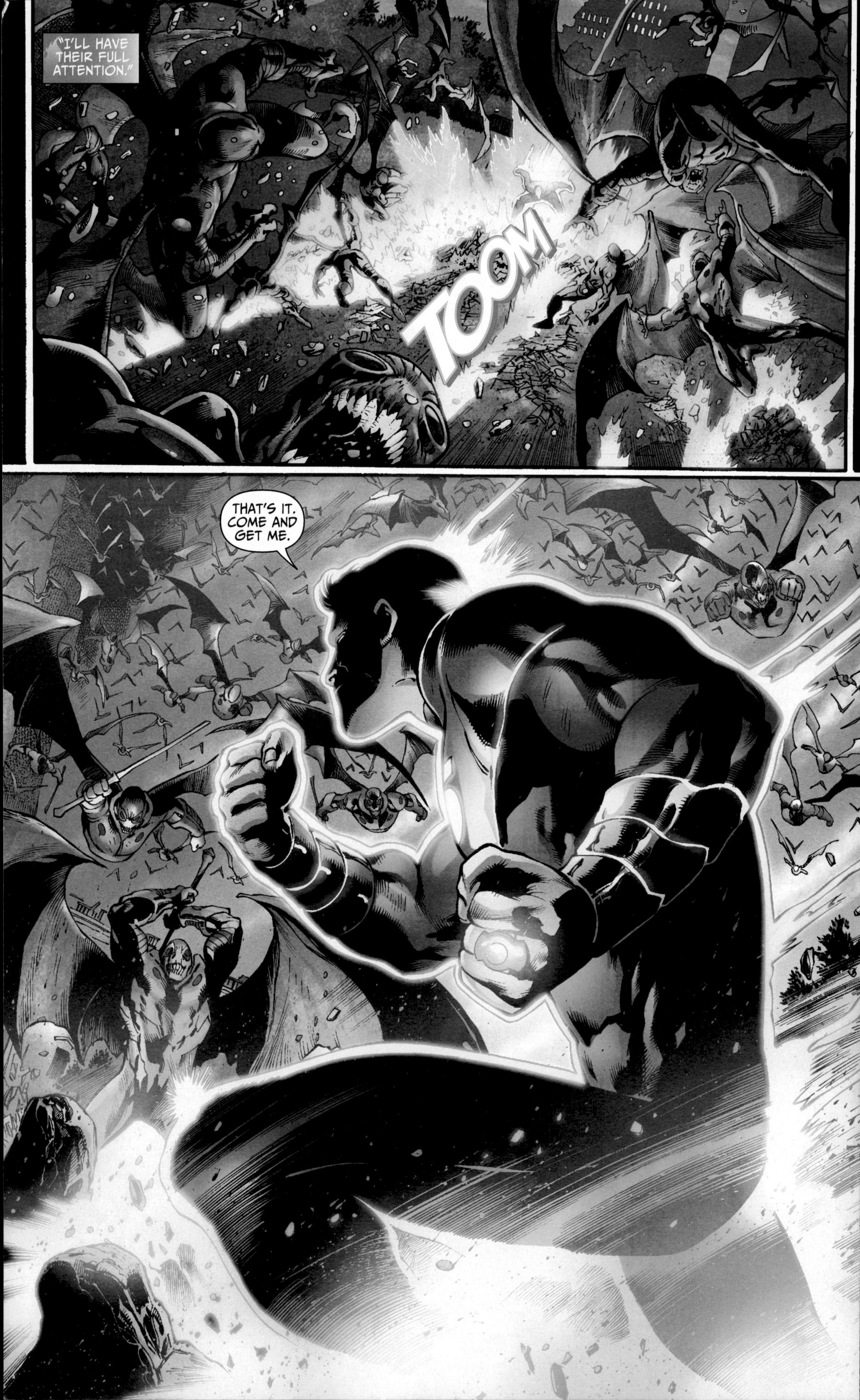
"I'LL HAVE THEIR FULL ATTENTION."
TOOM
THAT'S IT. COME AND GET ME.

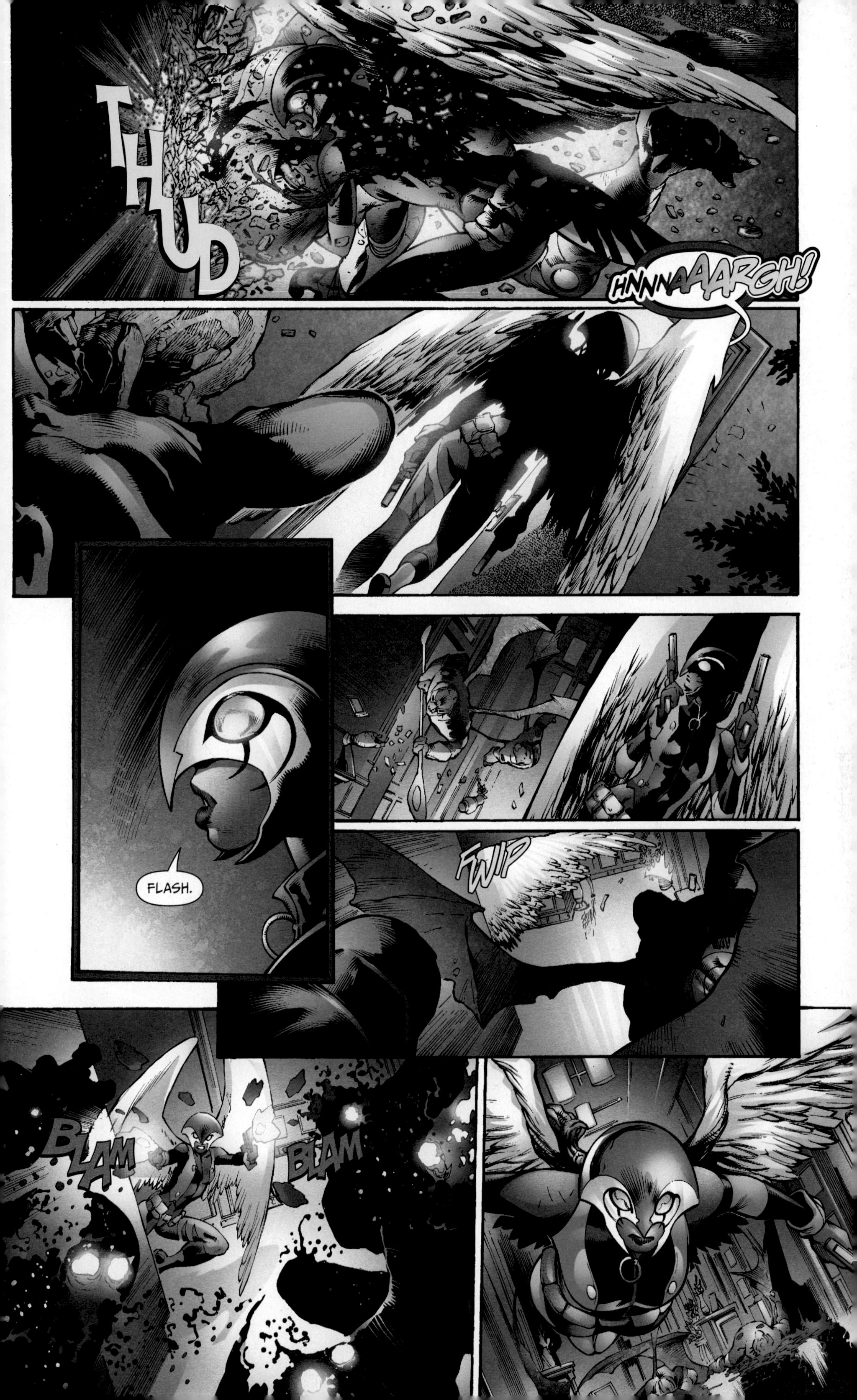
THUD
HNNNAAARGH!
FLASH.
FWIP
BLAM
BLAM

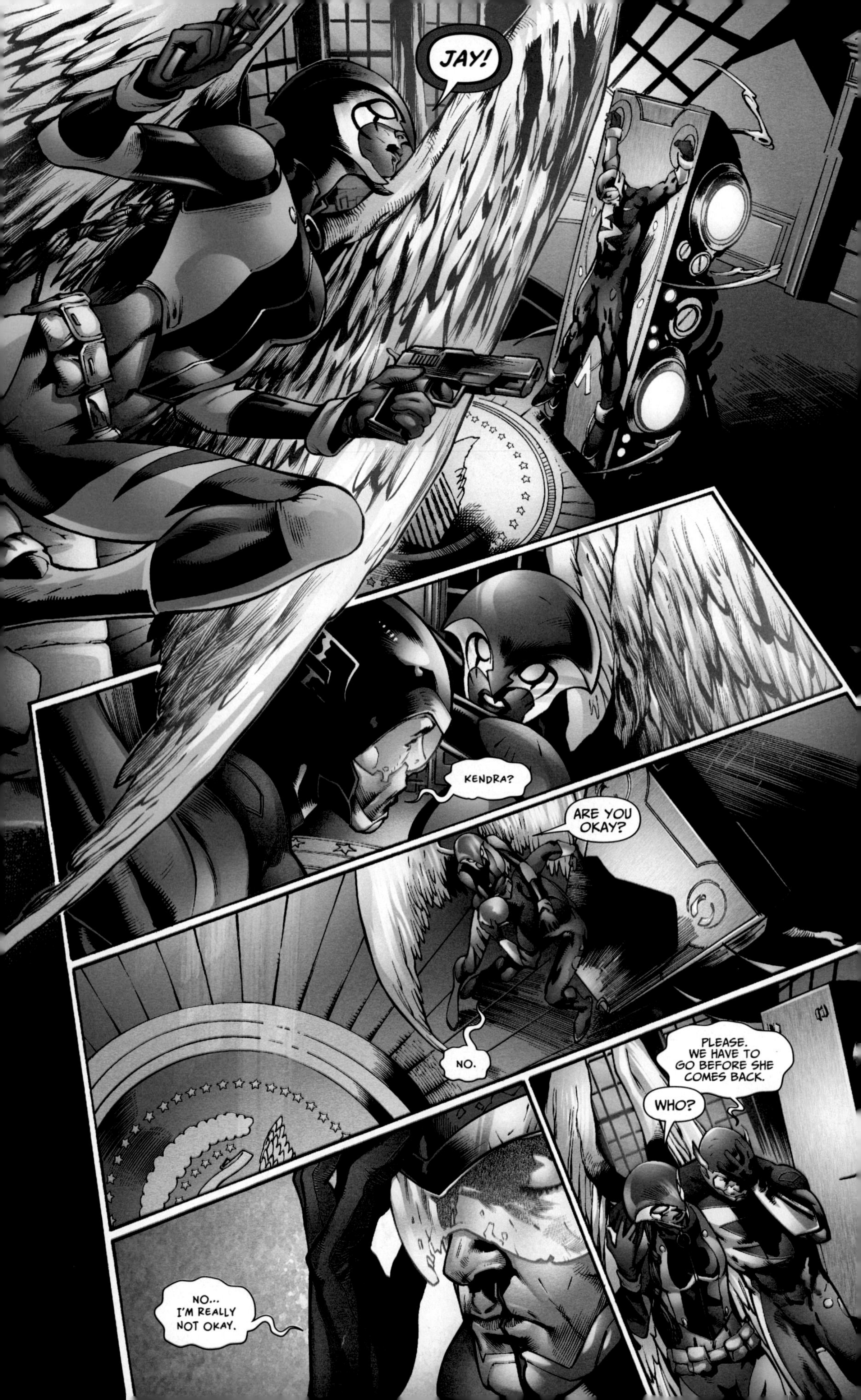
JAY!
KENDRA?
ARE YOU OKAY?
NO.
PLEASE. WE HAVE TO GO BEFORE SHE COMES BACK.
WHO?
NO... I'M REALLY NOT OKAY.

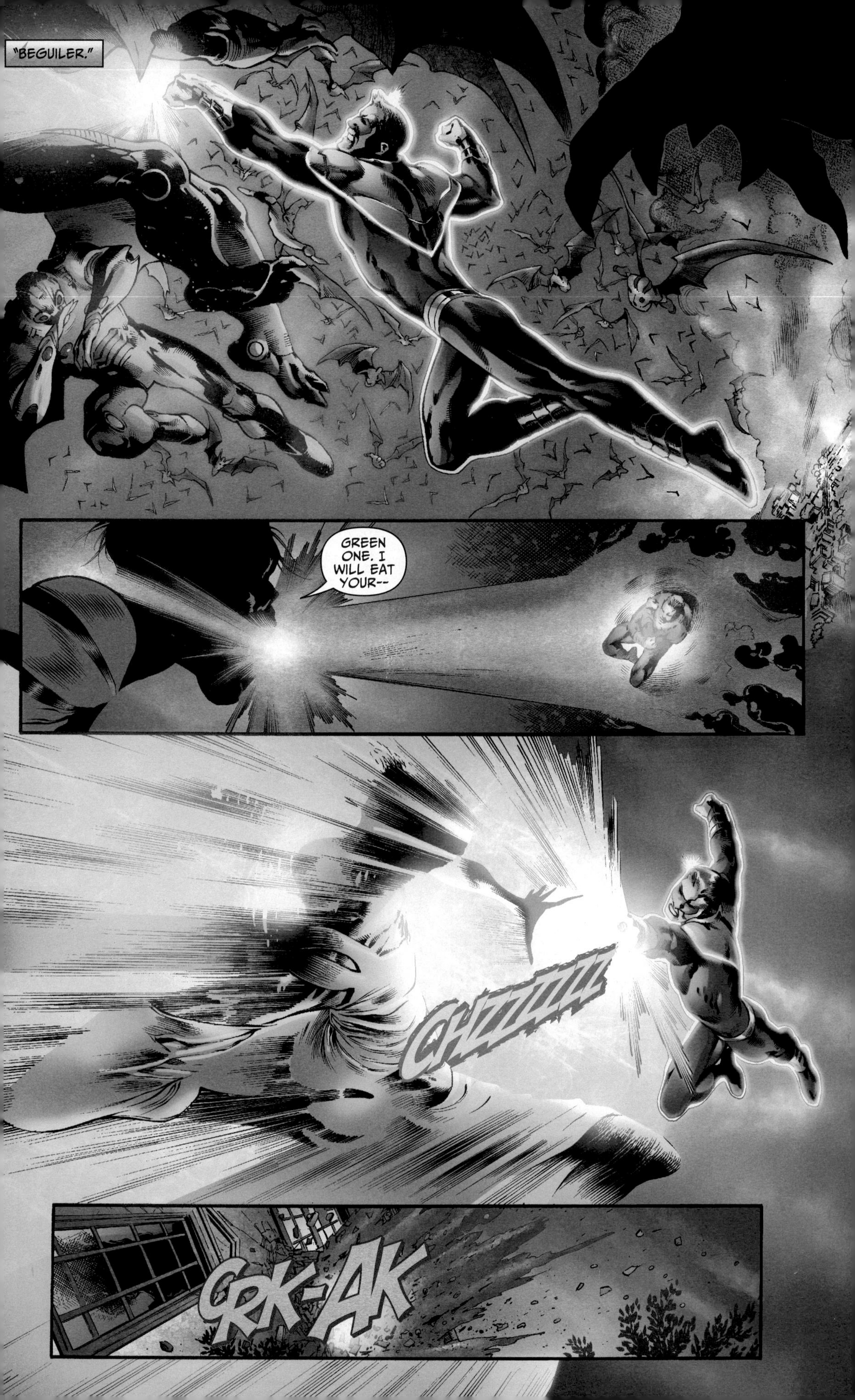
"BEGUILER."
GREEN ONE. I WILL EAT YOUR--
CHZZZZZZ
CRK-AK

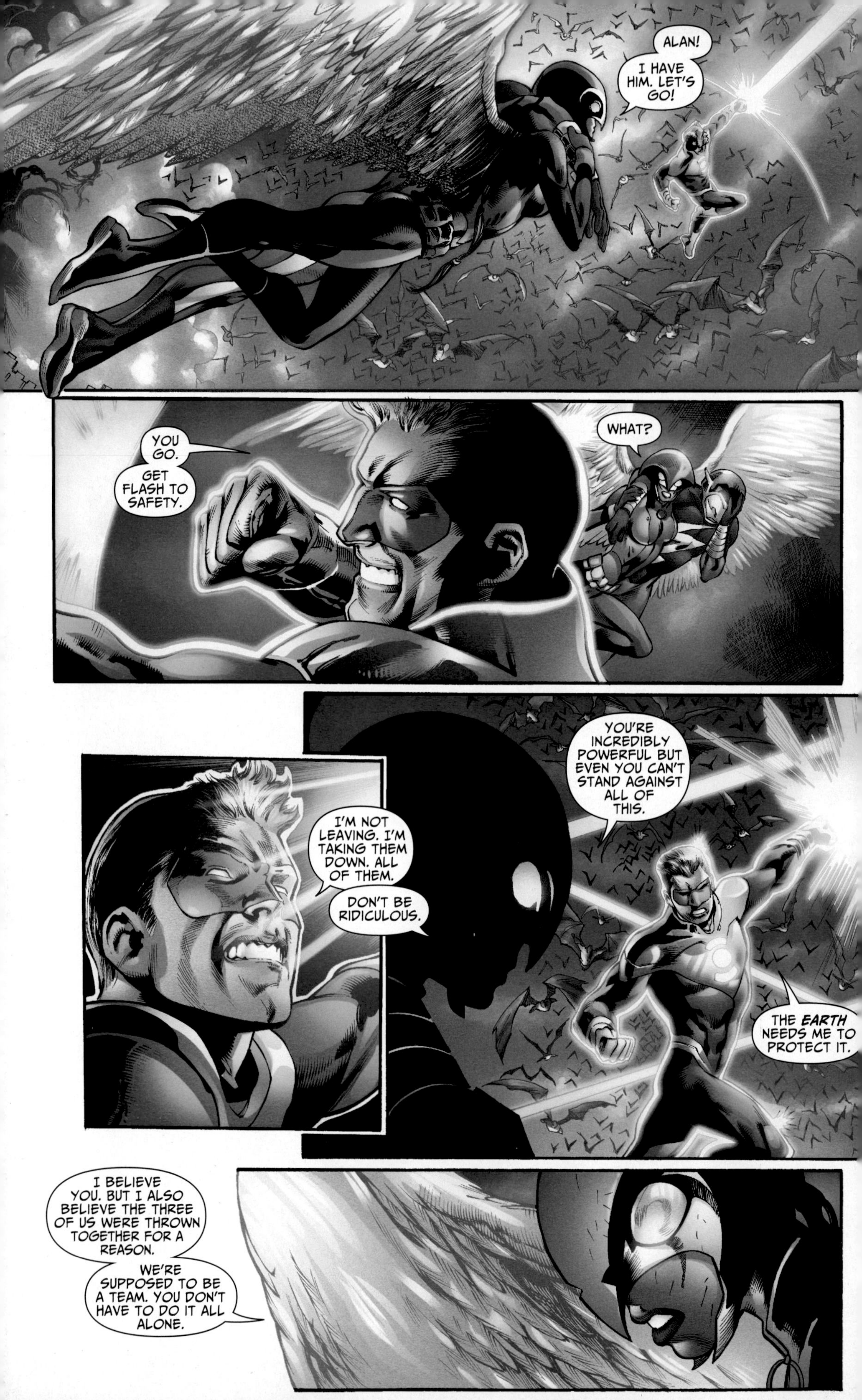
ALAN!
I HAVE HIM. LET'S GO!
YOU GO.
GET FLASH TO SAFETY.
WHAT?
I'M NOT LEAVING. I'M TAKING THEM DOWN. ALL OF THEM.
DON'T BE RIDICULOUS.
YOU'RE INCREDIBLY POWERFUL BUT EVEN YOU CAN'T STAND AGAINST ALL OF THIS.
THE *EARTH* NEEDS ME TO PROTECT IT.
I BELIEVE YOU. BUT I ALSO BELIEVE THE THREE OF US WERE THROWN TOGETHER FOR A REASON.
WE'RE SUPPOSED TO BE A TEAM. YOU DON'T HAVE TO DO IT ALL ALONE.

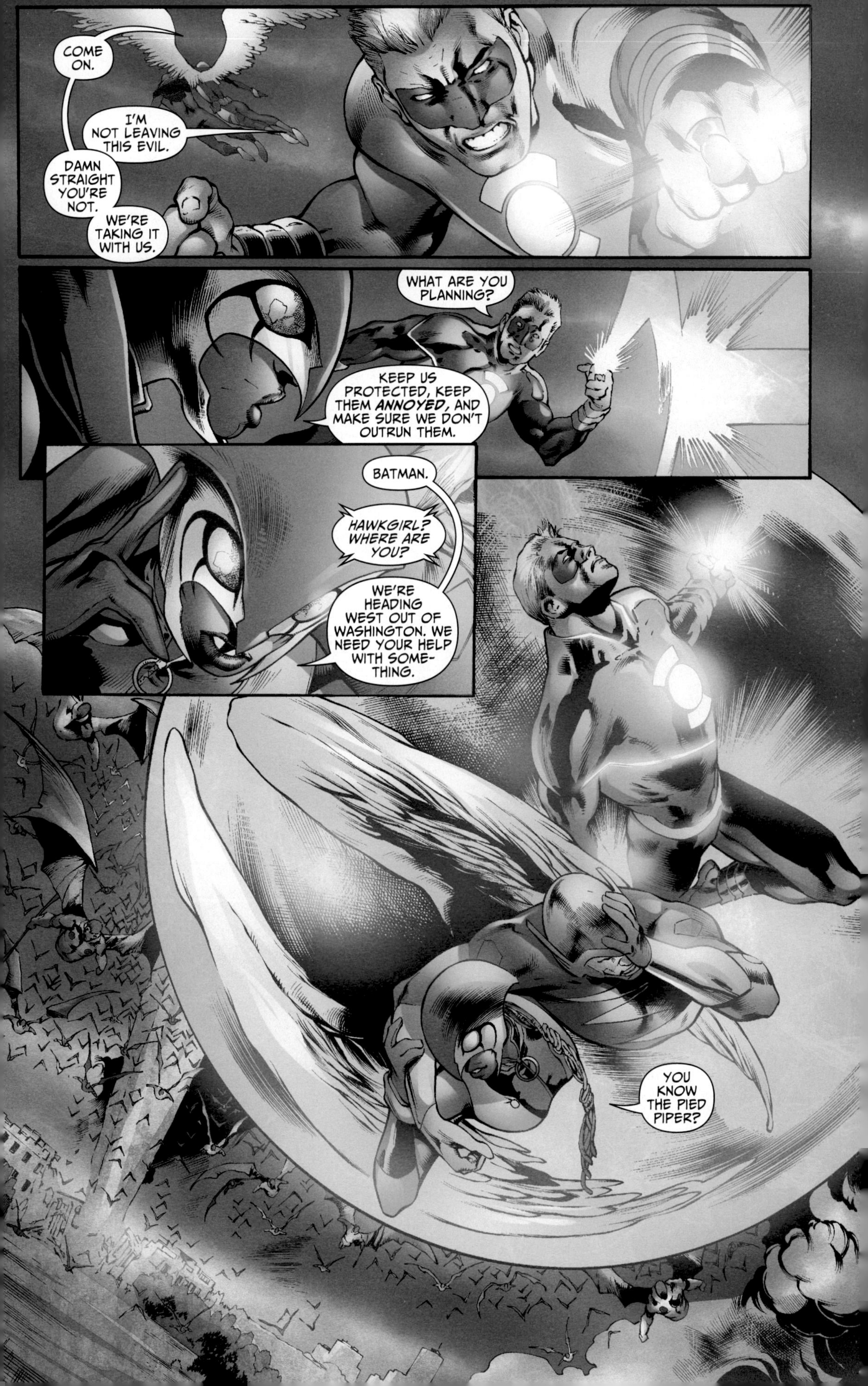
COME ON.
I'M NOT LEAVING THIS EVIL.
DAMN STRAIGHT YOU'RE NOT.
WE'RE TAKING IT WITH US.
WHAT ARE YOU PLANNING?
KEEP US PROTECTED, KEEP THEM *ANNOYED*, AND MAKE SURE WE DON'T OUTRUN THEM.
BATMAN.
HAWKGIRL? WHERE ARE YOU?
WE'RE HEADING WEST OUT OF WASHINGTON. WE NEED YOUR HELP WITH SOME-THING.
YOU KNOW THE PIED PIPER?

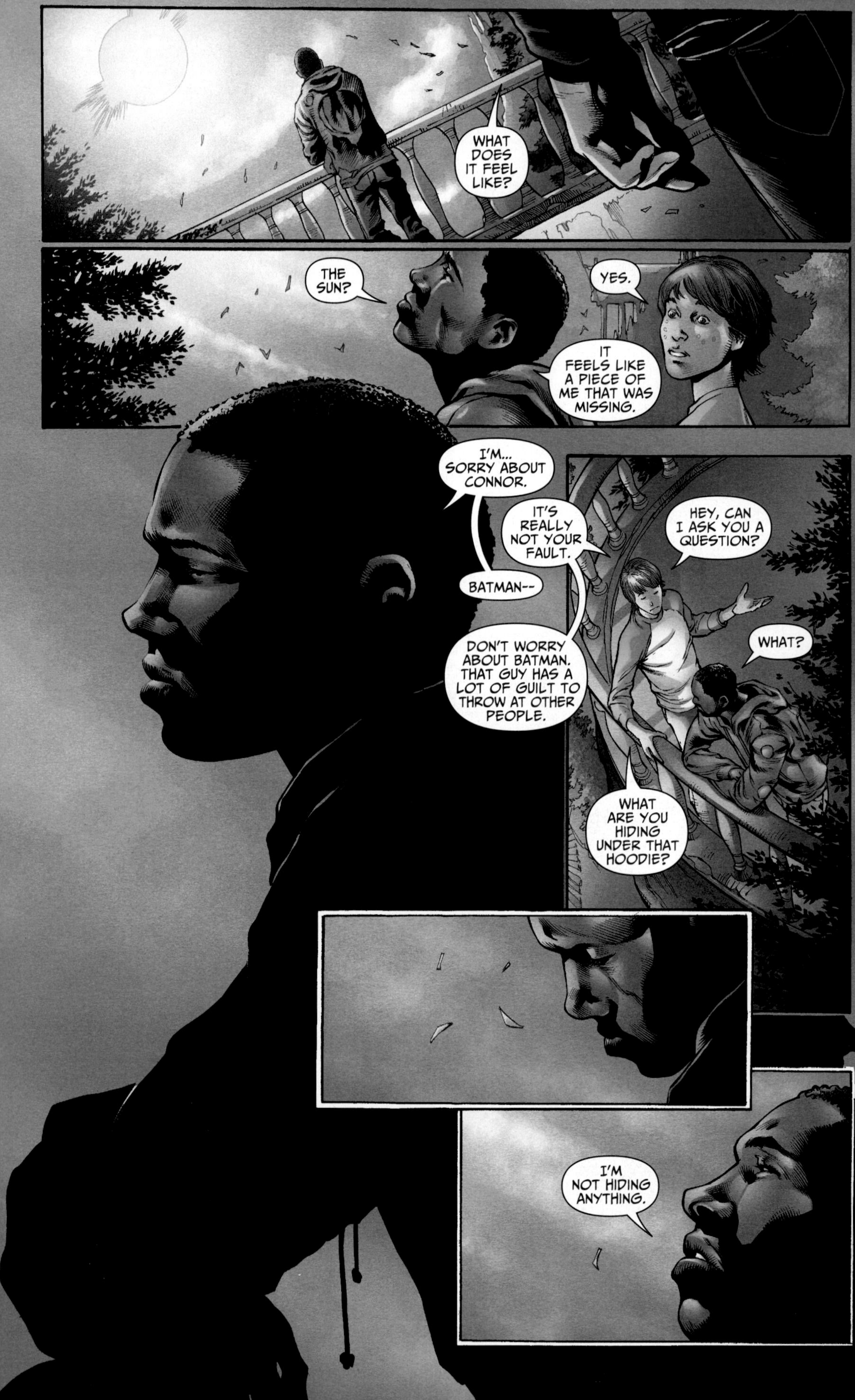

WHAT DOES IT FEEL LIKE?
THE SUN?
YES.
IT FEELS LIKE A PIECE OF ME THAT WAS MISSING.
I'M... SORRY ABOUT CONNOR.
IT'S REALLY NOT YOUR FAULT.
BATMAN--
DON'T WORRY ABOUT BATMAN. THAT GUY HAS A LOT OF GUILT TO THROW AT OTHER PEOPLE.
HEY, CAN I ASK YOU A QUESTION?
WHAT?
WHAT ARE YOU HIDING UNDER THAT HOODIE?
I'M NOT HIDING ANYTHING.

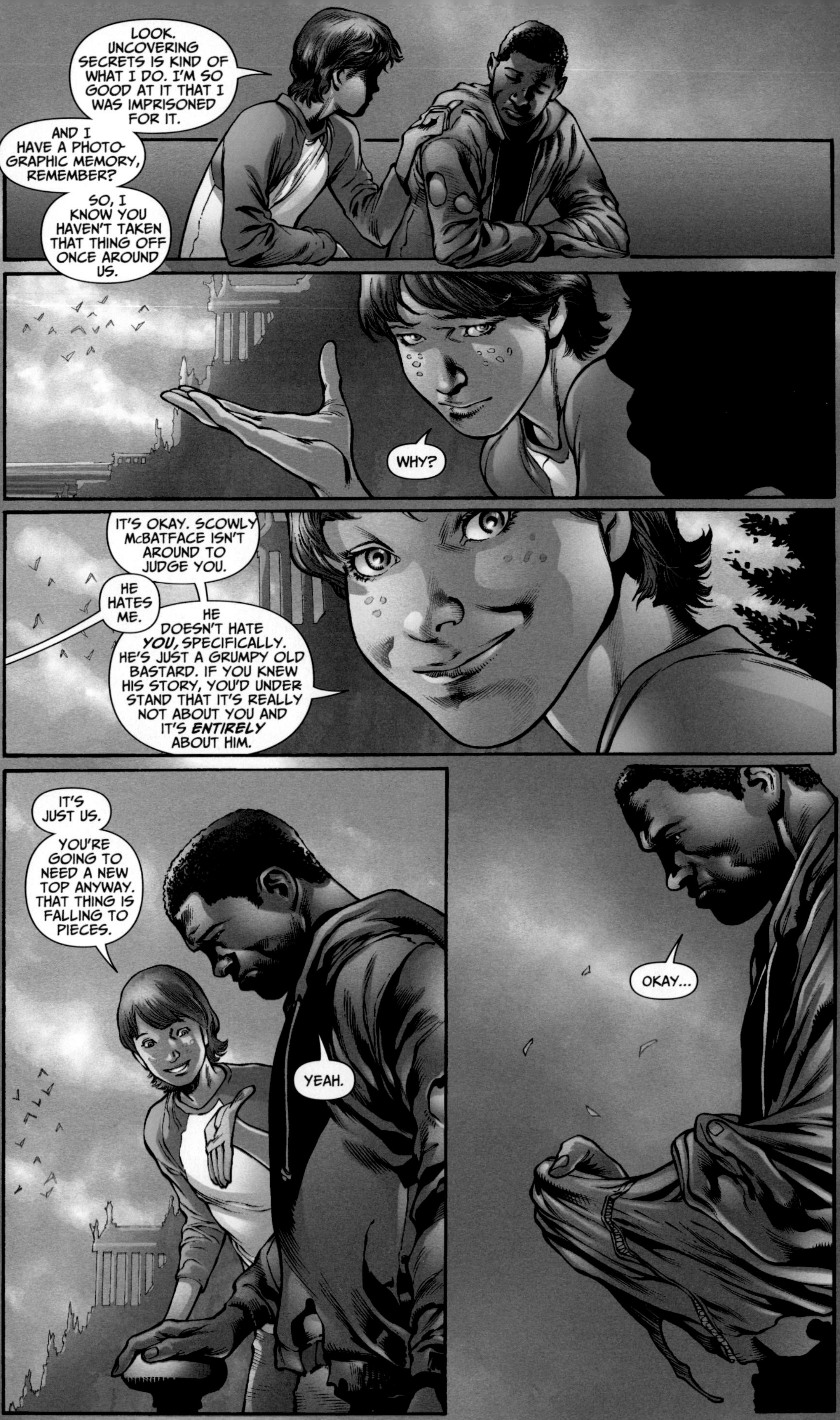
LOOK. UNCOVERING SECRETS IS KIND OF WHAT I DO. I'M SO GOOD AT IT THAT I WAS IMPRISONED FOR IT.
AND I HAVE A PHOTO-GRAPHIC MEMORY, REMEMBER?
SO, I KNOW YOU HAVEN'T TAKEN THAT THING OFF ONCE AROUND US.
WHY?
IT'S OKAY. SCOWLY McBATFACE ISN'T AROUND TO JUDGE YOU.
HE HATES ME.
HE DOESN'T HATE *YOU,* SPECIFICALLY. HE'S JUST A GRUMPY OLD BASTARD. IF YOU KNEW HIS STORY, YOU'D UNDER STAND THAT IT'S REALLY NOT ABOUT YOU AND IT'S *ENTIRELY* ABOUT HIM.
IT'S JUST US.
YOU'RE GOING TO NEED A NEW TOP ANYWAY. THAT THING IS FALLING TO PIECES.
YEAH.
OKAY...

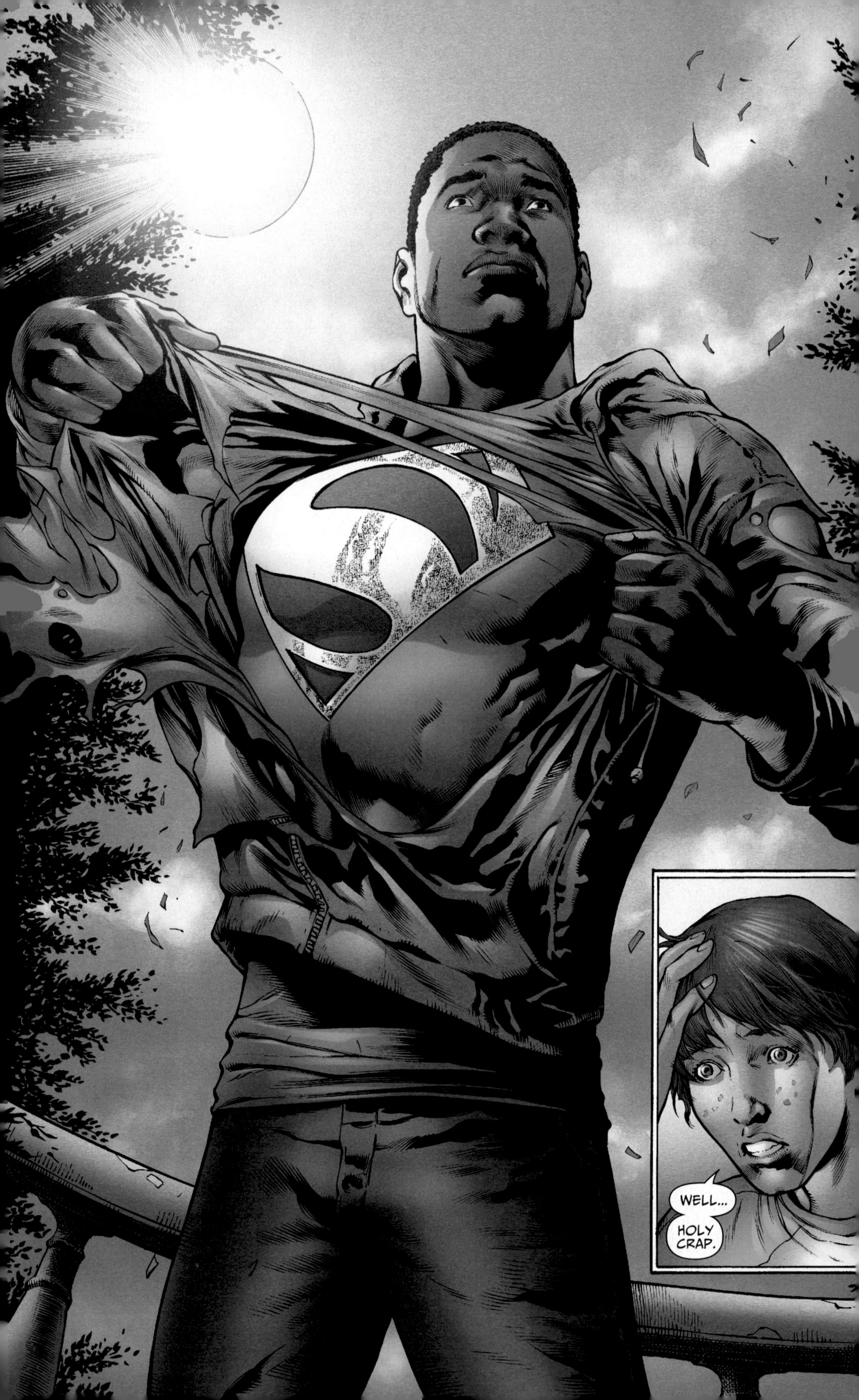
WELL...
HOLY CRAP.

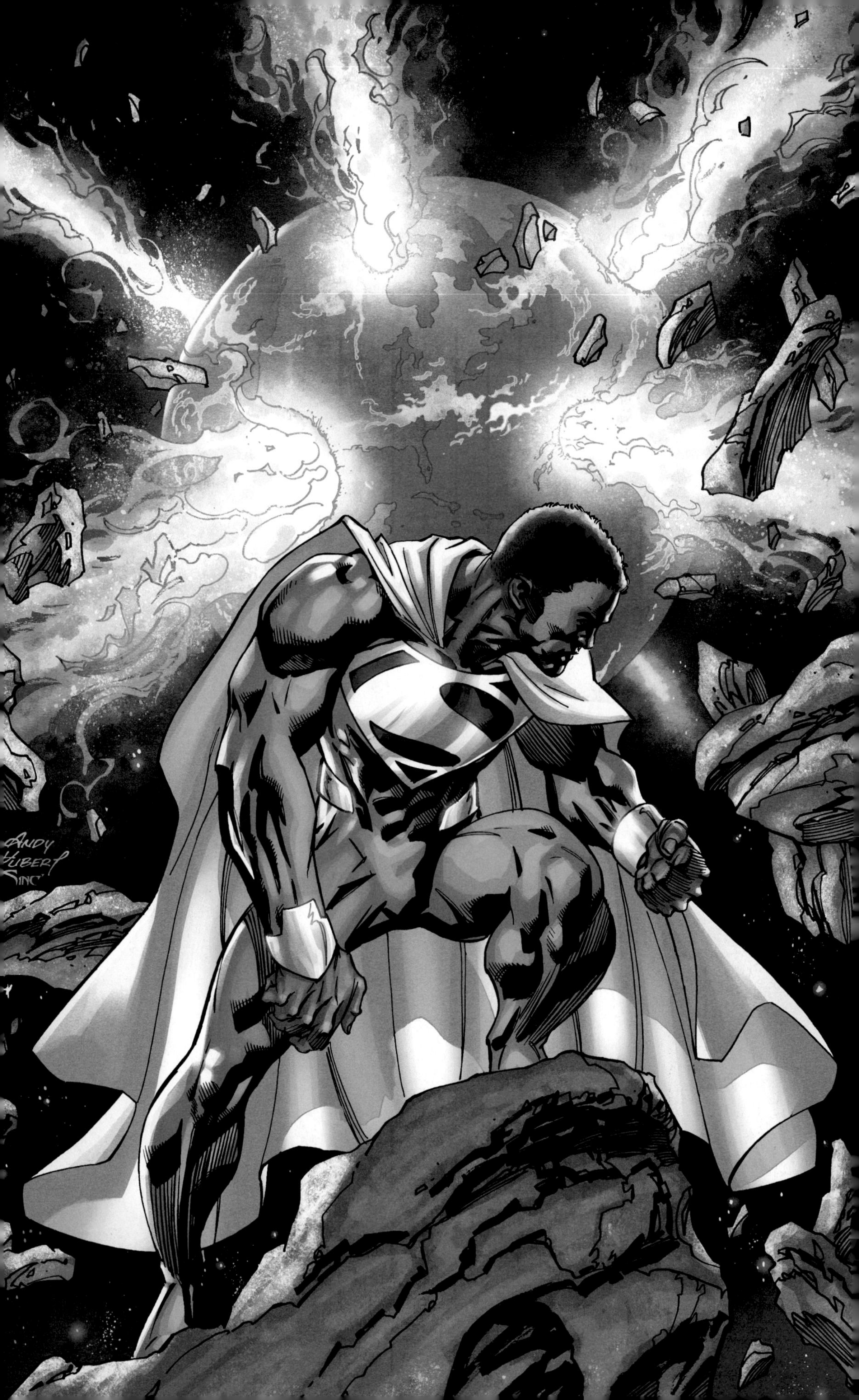

THE KRYPTONIAN PART 5

TOM TAYLOR writer **NICOLA SCOTT** penciller **TREVOR SCOTT** inker **PETE PANTAZIS** colorist cover by **ANDY KUBERT** & **ALEX SINCLAIR**

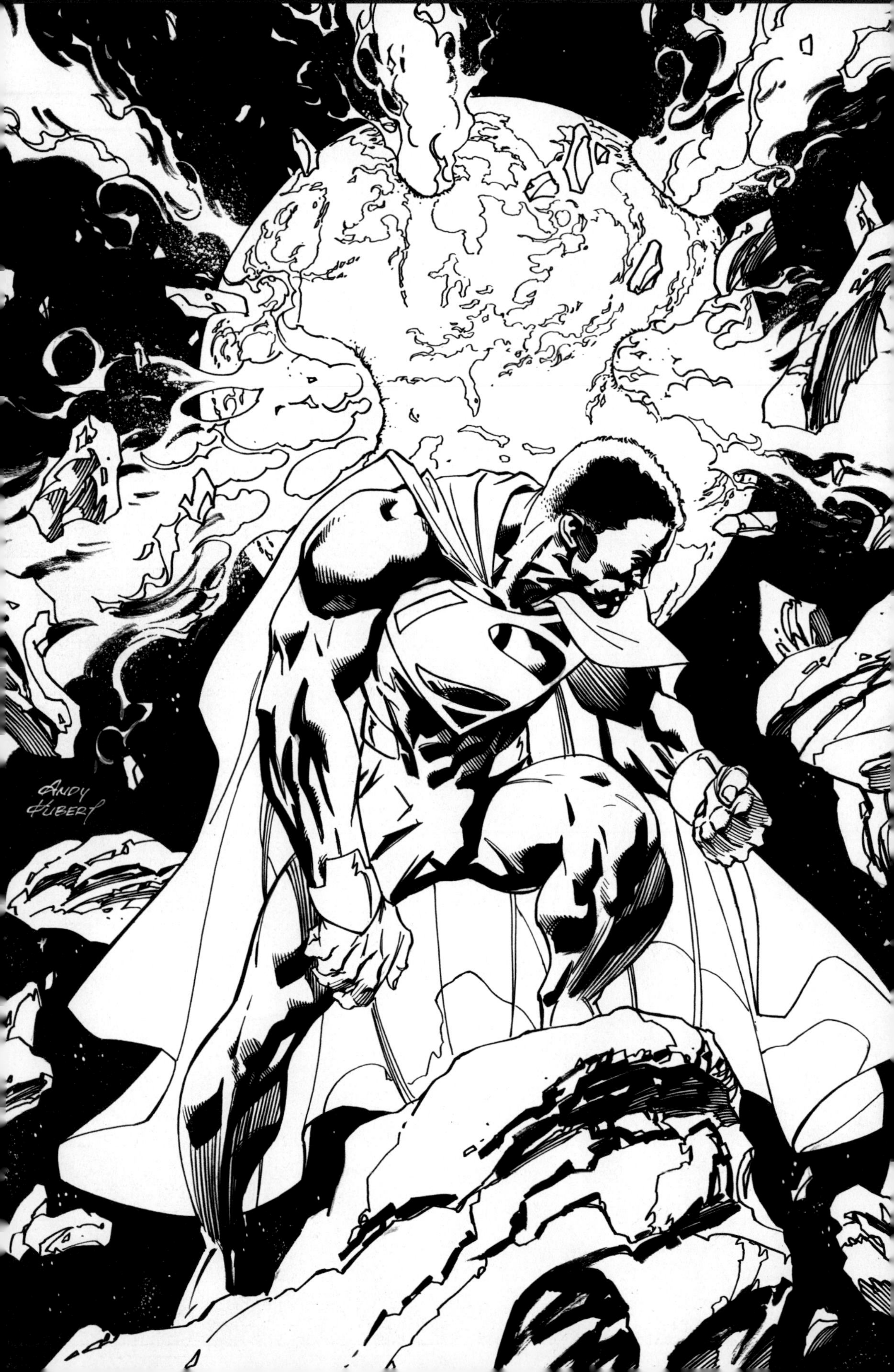
ANDY KUBERT

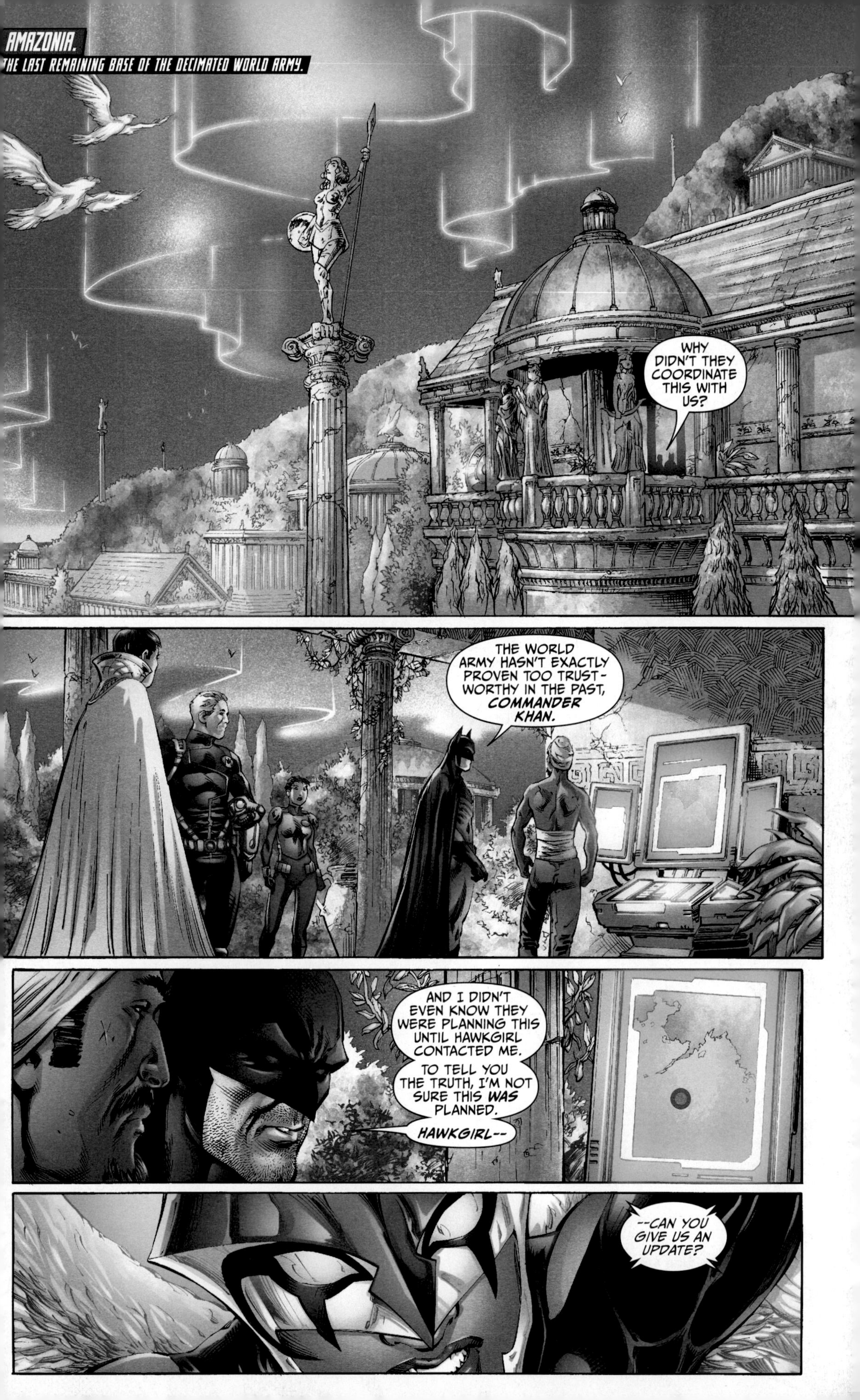
AMAZONIA.
THE LAST REMAINING BASE OF THE DECIMATED WORLD ARMY.
WHY DIDN'T THEY COORDINATE THIS WITH US?
THE WORLD ARMY HASN'T EXACTLY PROVEN TOO TRUST-WORTHY IN THE PAST, COMMANDER KHAN.
AND I DIDN'T EVEN KNOW THEY WERE PLANNING THIS UNTIL HAWKGIRL CONTACTED ME.
TO TELL YOU THE TRUTH, I'M NOT SURE THIS WAS PLANNED.
HAWKGIRL--
--CAN YOU GIVE US AN UPDATE?

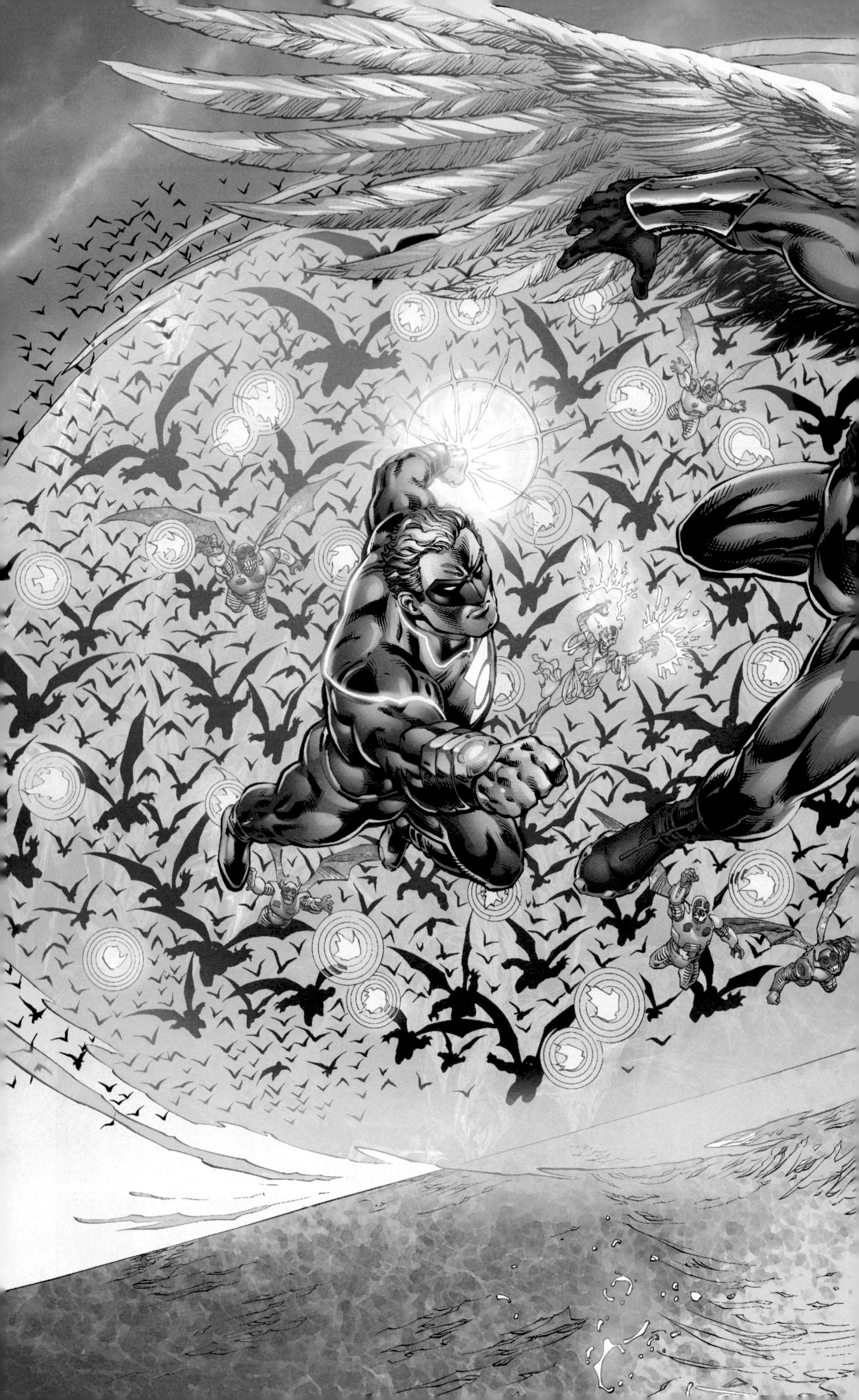

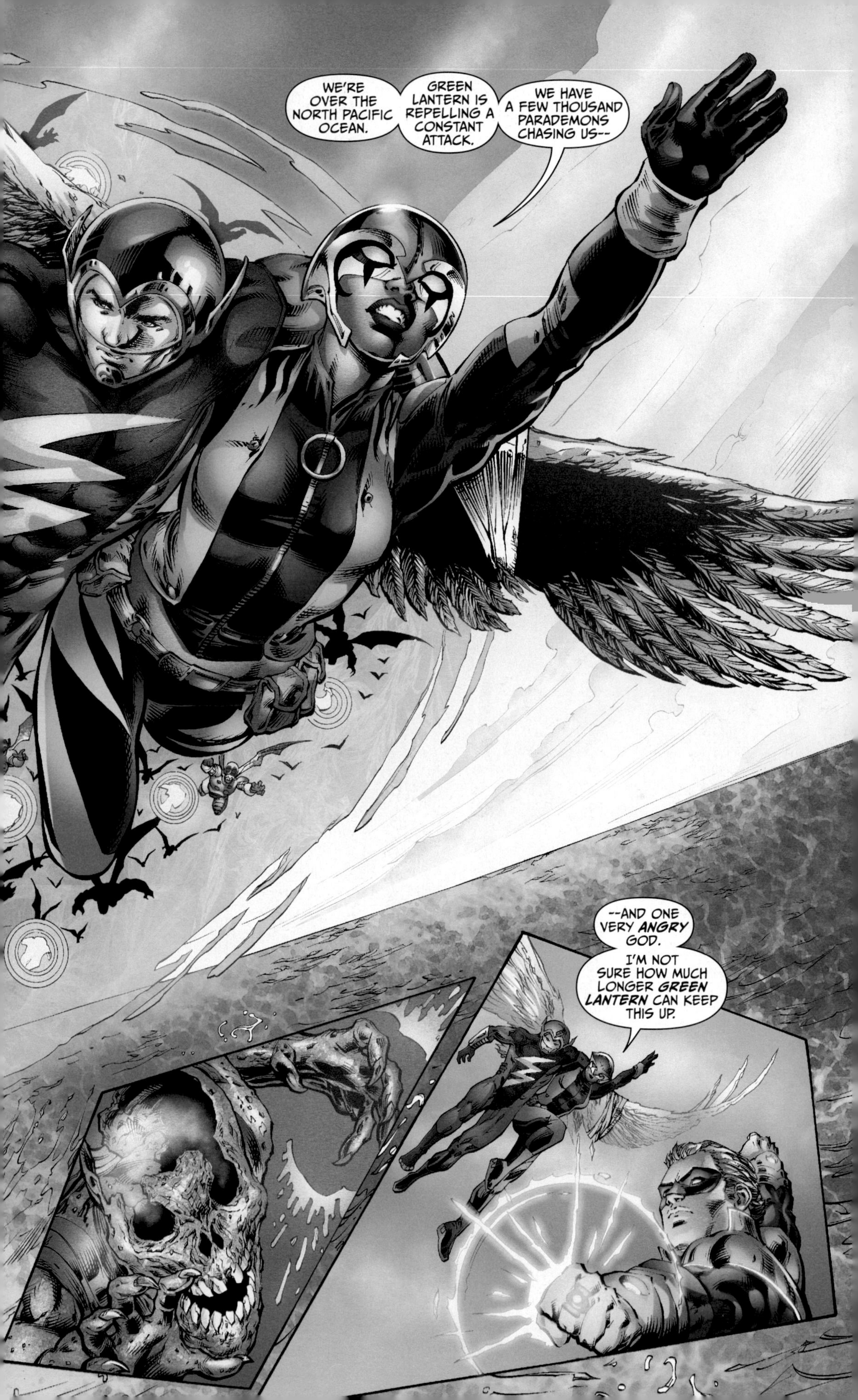
WE'RE OVER THE NORTH PACIFIC OCEAN.
GREEN LANTERN IS REPELLING A CONSTANT ATTACK.
WE HAVE A FEW THOUSAND PARADEMONS CHASING US--
--AND ONE VERY ANGRY GOD.
I'M NOT SURE HOW MUCH LONGER GREEN LANTERN CAN KEEP THIS UP.

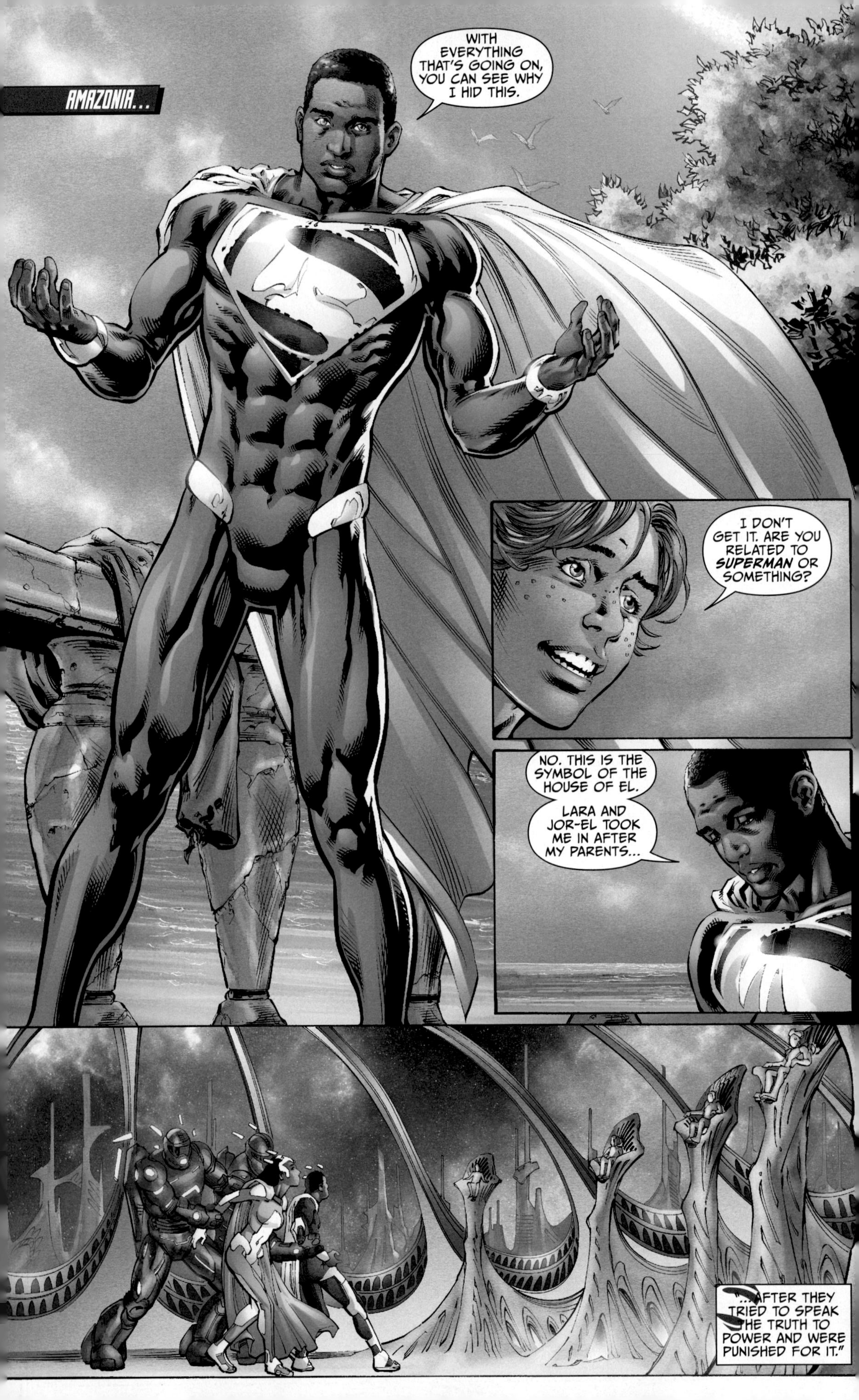
AMAZONIA...
WITH EVERYTHING THAT'S GOING ON, YOU CAN SEE WHY I HID THIS.
I DON'T GET IT. ARE YOU RELATED TO SUPERMAN OR SOMETHING?
NO. THIS IS THE SYMBOL OF THE HOUSE OF EL.
LARA AND JOR-EL TOOK ME IN AFTER MY PARENTS...
"...AFTER THEY TRIED TO SPEAK THE TRUTH TO POWER AND WERE PUNISHED FOR IT."

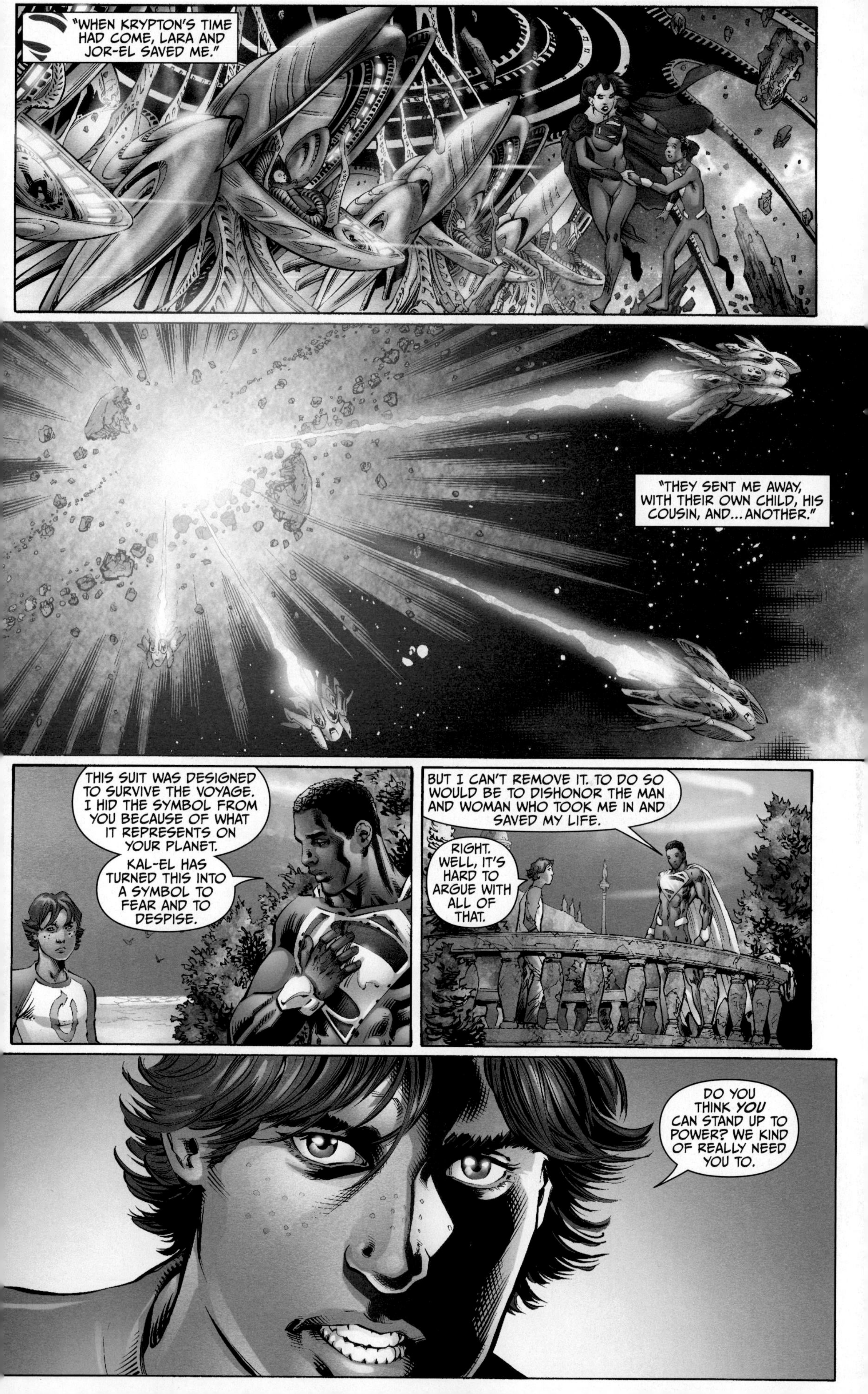
"WHEN KRYPTON'S TIME HAD COME, LARA AND JOR-EL SAVED ME."
"THEY SENT ME AWAY, WITH THEIR OWN CHILD, HIS COUSIN, AND... ANOTHER."
THIS SUIT WAS DESIGNED TO SURVIVE THE VOYAGE. I HID THE SYMBOL FROM YOU BECAUSE OF WHAT IT REPRESENTS ON YOUR PLANET.
KAL-EL HAS TURNED THIS INTO A SYMBOL TO FEAR AND TO DESPISE.
BUT I CAN'T REMOVE IT. TO DO SO WOULD BE TO DISHONOR THE MAN AND WOMAN WHO TOOK ME IN AND SAVED MY LIFE.
RIGHT. WELL, IT'S HARD TO ARGUE WITH ALL OF THAT.
DO YOU THINK *YOU* CAN STAND UP TO POWER? WE KIND OF REALLY NEED YOU TO.

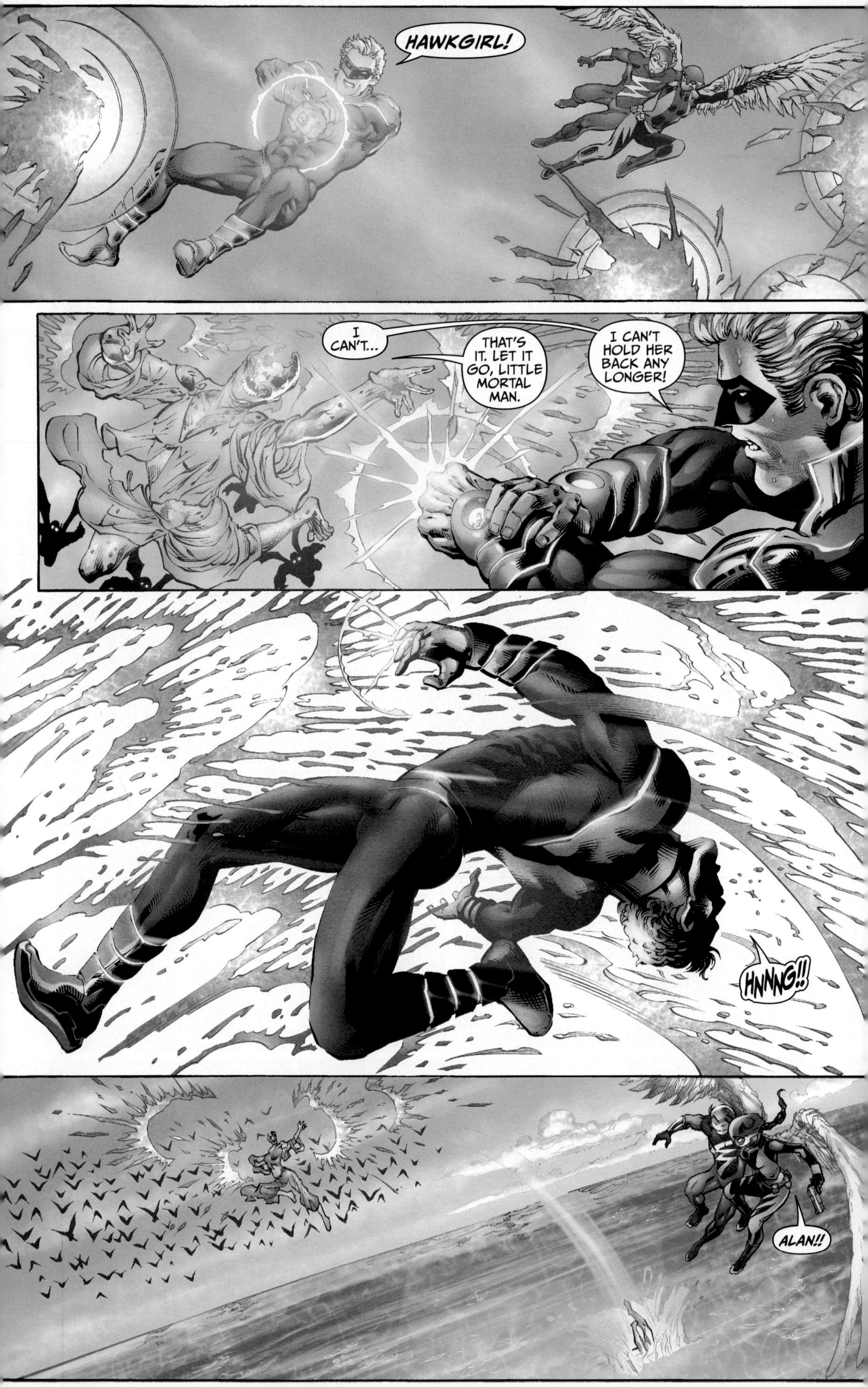
HAWKGIRL!
I CAN'T...
THAT'S IT. LET IT GO, LITTLE MORTAL MAN.
I CAN'T HOLD HER BACK ANY LONGER!
HNNNG!!
ALAN!!

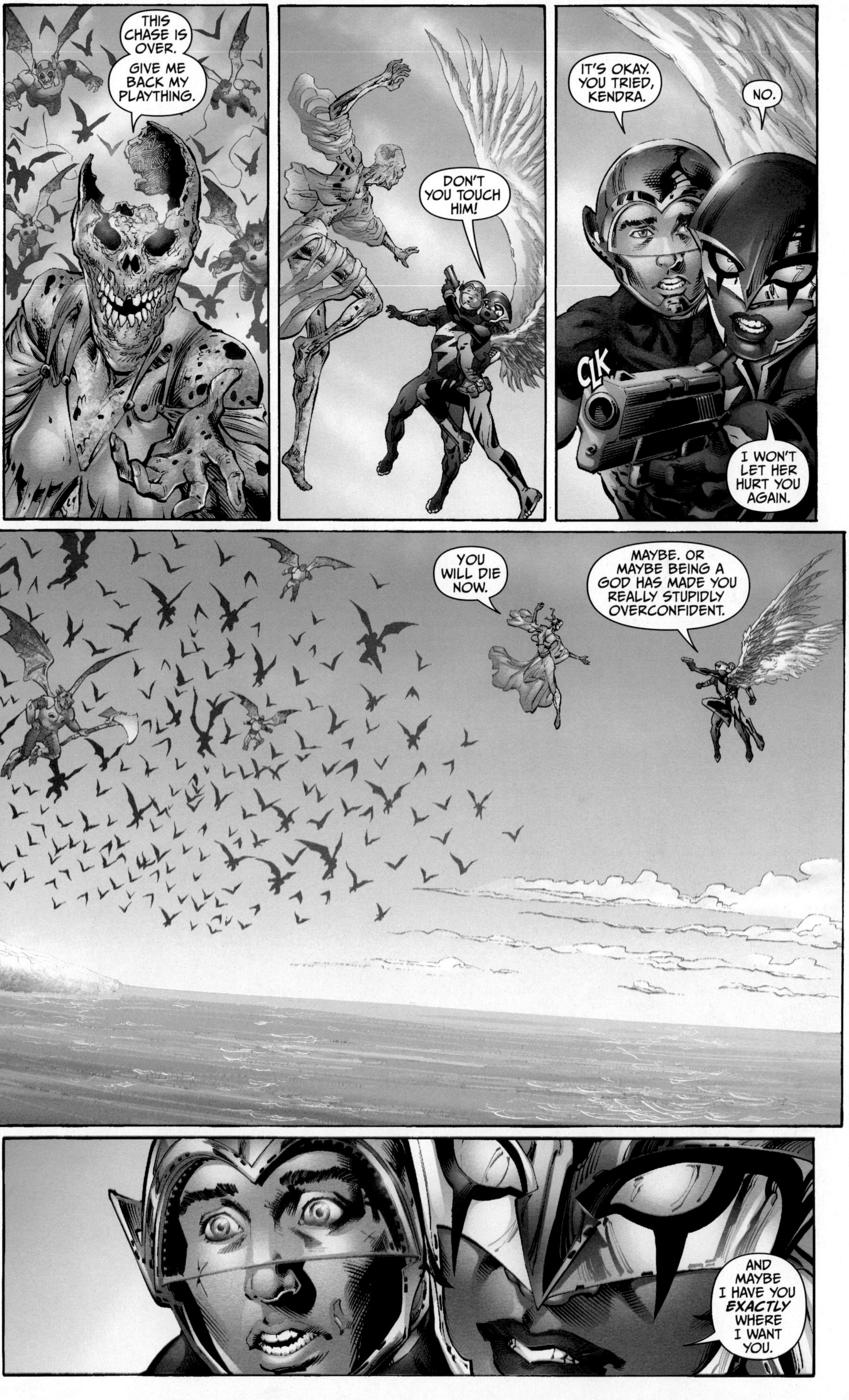
THIS CHASE IS OVER.
GIVE ME BACK MY PLAYTHING.
DON'T YOU TOUCH HIM!
IT'S OKAY. YOU TRIED, KENDRA.
NO.
CLK
I WON'T LET HER HURT YOU AGAIN.
YOU WILL DIE NOW.
MAYBE. OR MAYBE BEING A GOD HAS MADE YOU REALLY STUPIDLY OVERCONFIDENT.
AND MAYBE I HAVE YOU *EXACTLY* WHERE I WANT YOU.

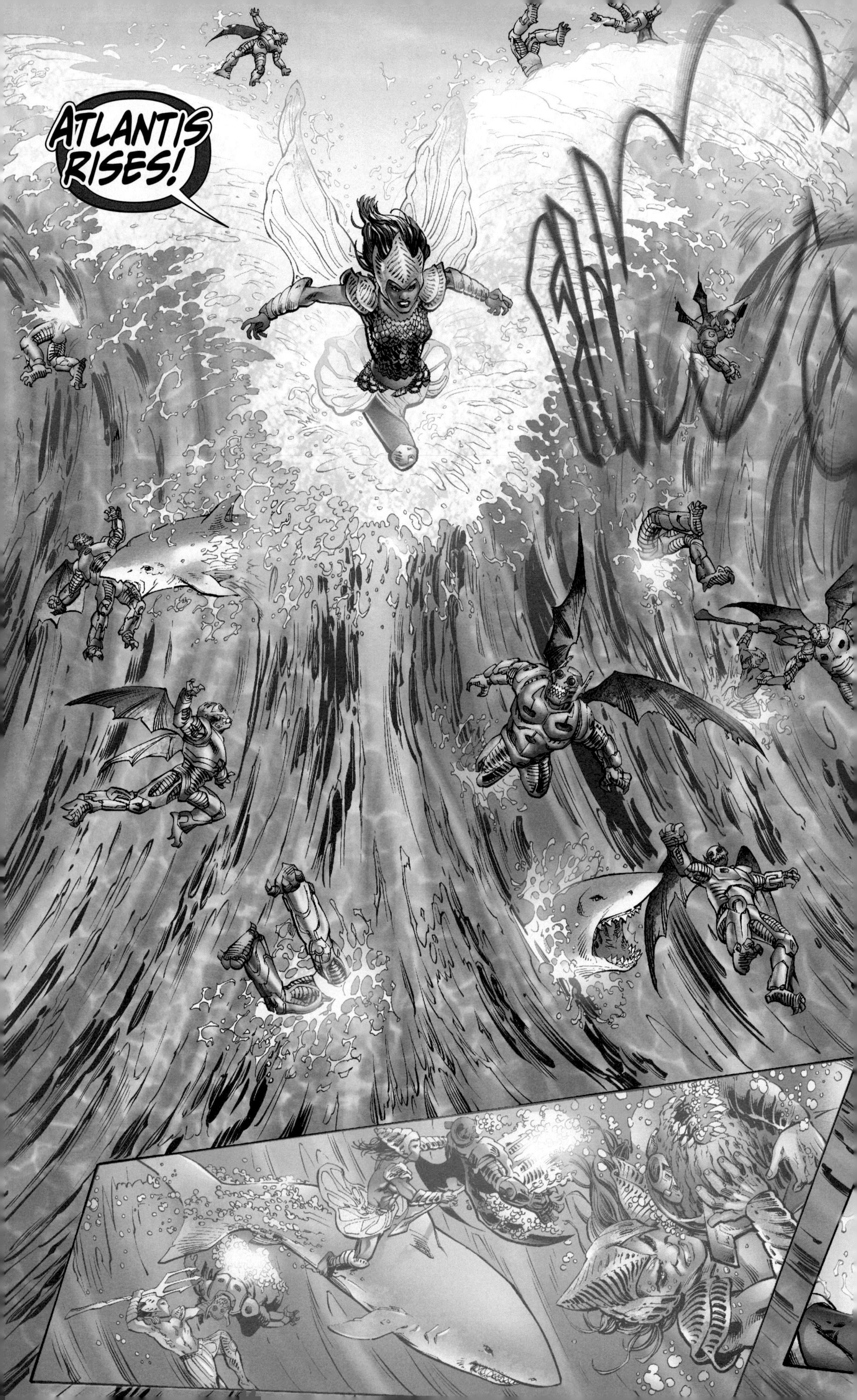
ATLANTIS RISES!

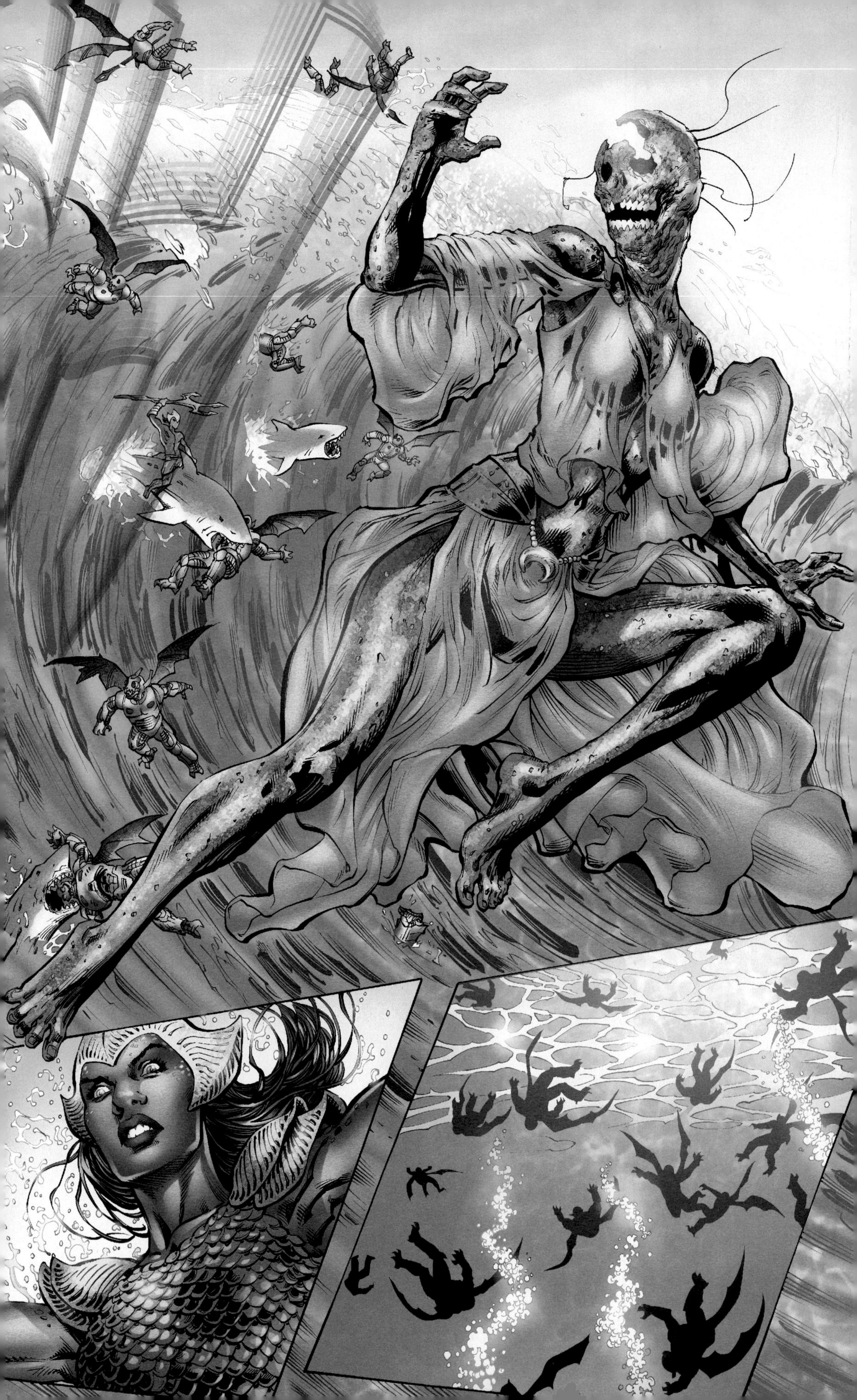

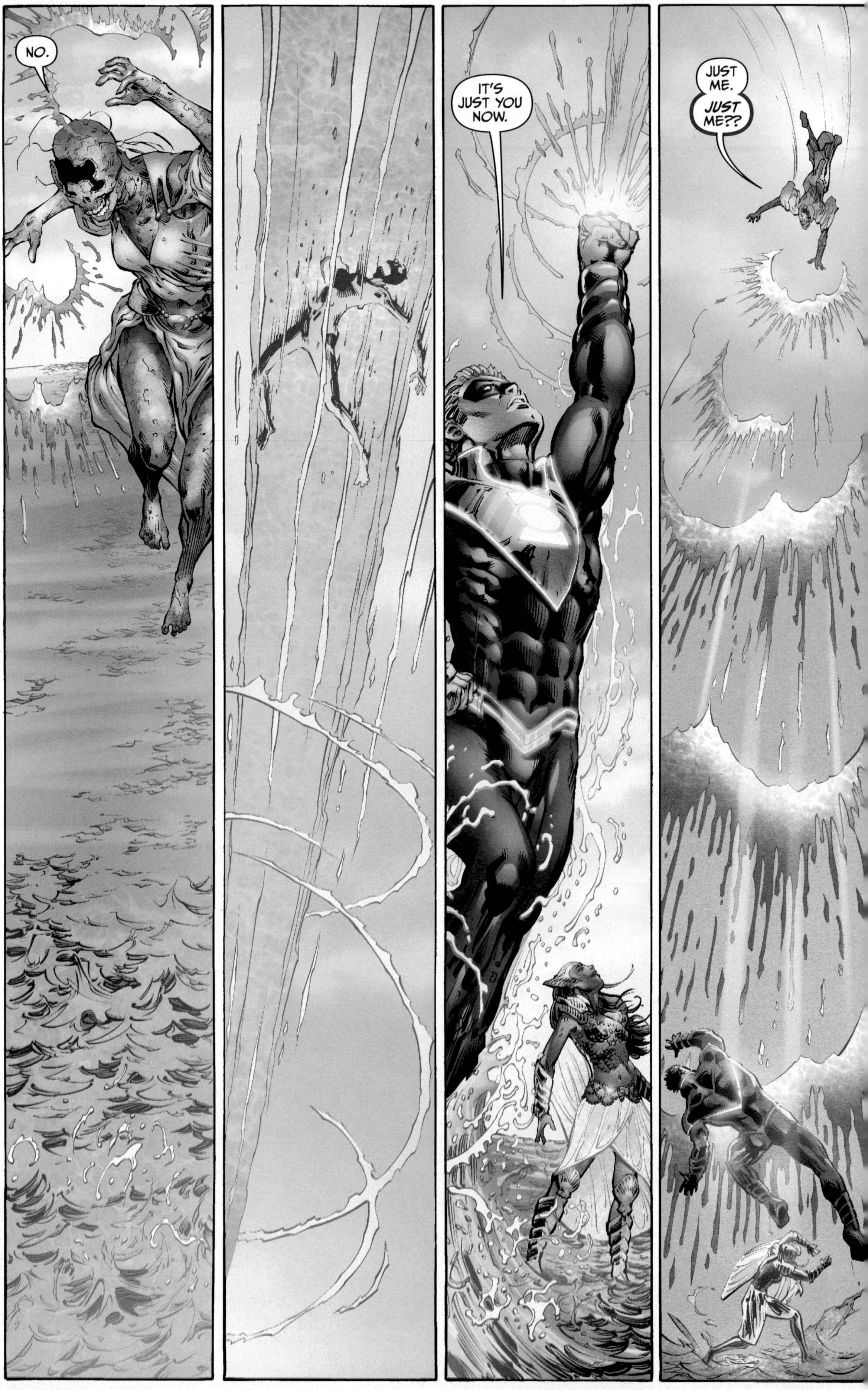
NO.
IT'S JUST YOU NOW.
JUST ME. JUST ME??

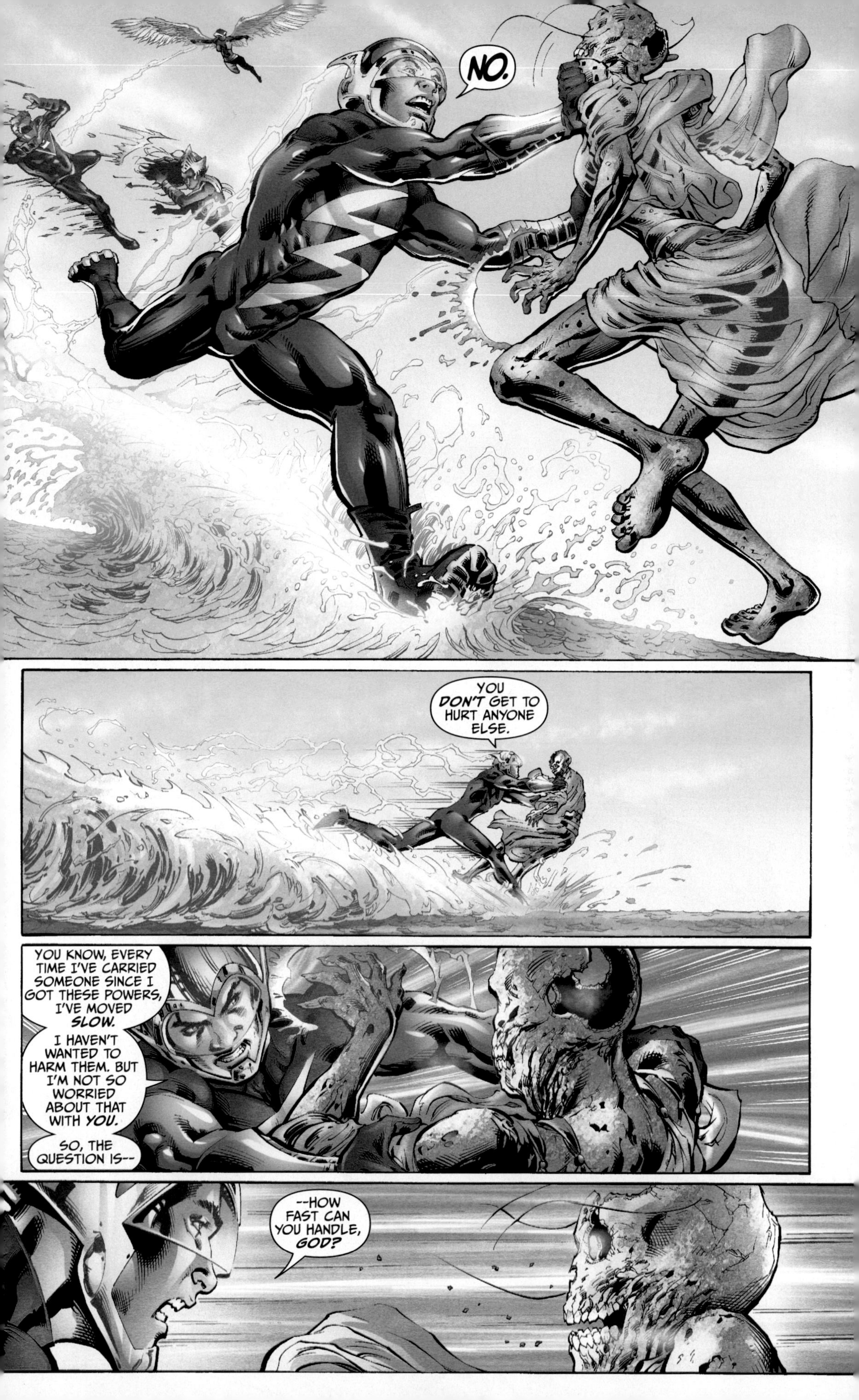
NO.
YOU DON'T GET TO HURT ANYONE ELSE.
YOU KNOW, EVERY TIME I'VE CARRIED SOMEONE SINCE I GOT THESE POWERS, I'VE MOVED SLOW.
I HAVEN'T WANTED TO HARM THEM. BUT I'M NOT SO WORRIED ABOUT THAT WITH YOU.
SO, THE QUESTION IS--
--HOW FAST CAN YOU HANDLE, GOD?

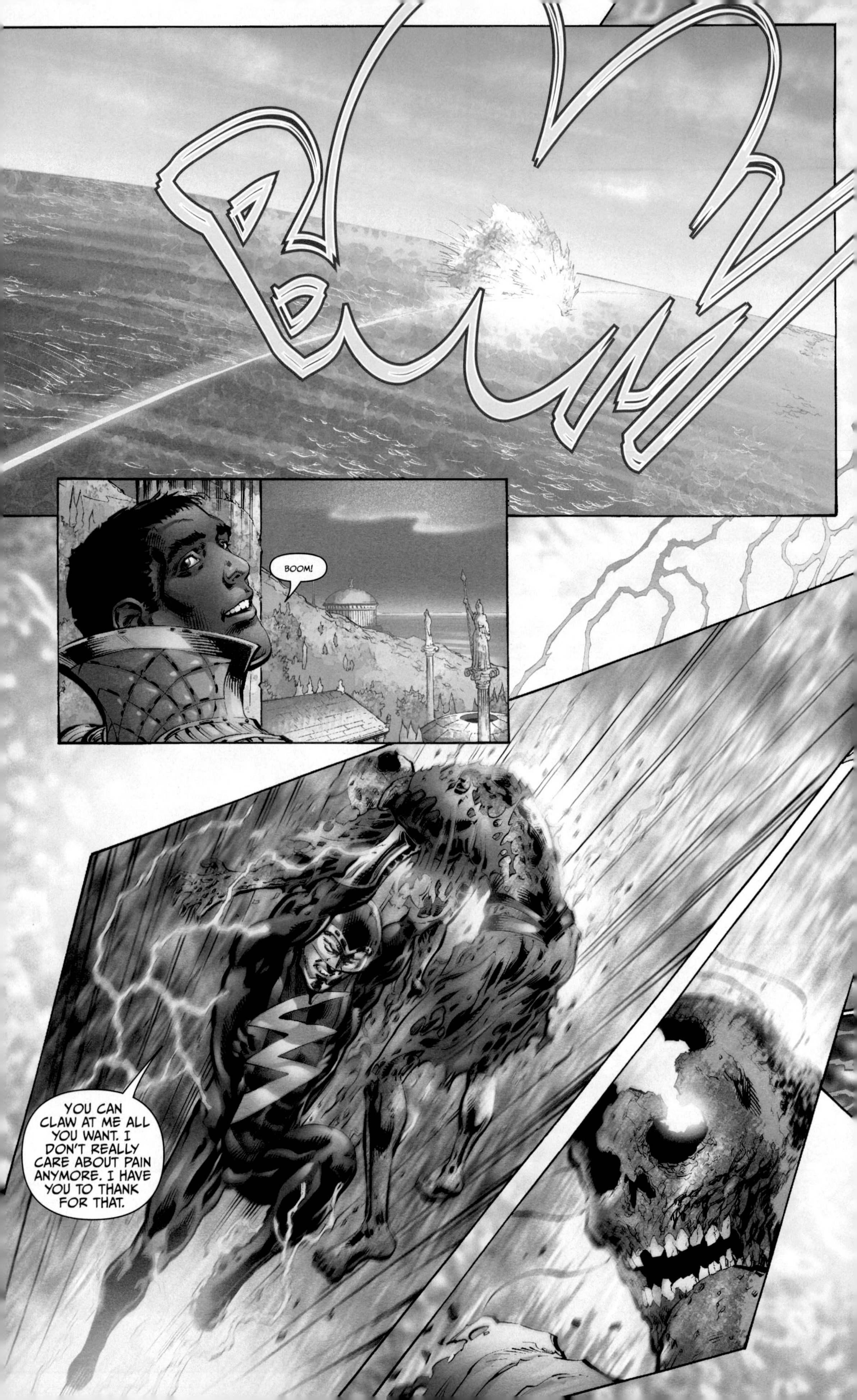
BAMM
BOOM!
YOU CAN CLAW AT ME ALL YOU WANT. I DON'T REALLY CARE ABOUT PAIN ANYMORE. I HAVE YOU TO THANK FOR THAT.

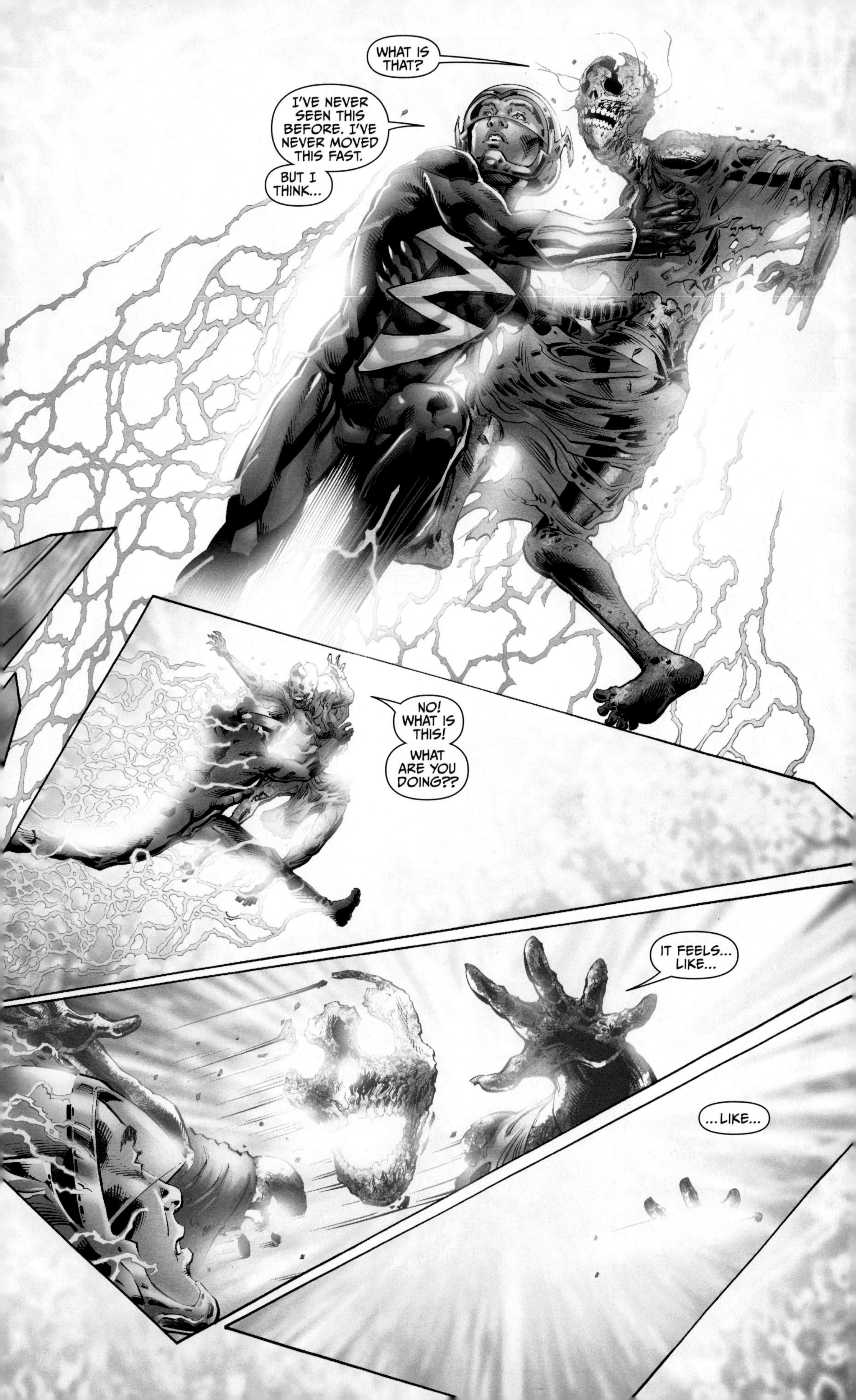
WHAT IS THAT?
I'VE NEVER SEEN THIS BEFORE. I'VE NEVER MOVED THIS FAST.
BUT I THINK...
NO! WHAT IS THIS!
WHAT ARE YOU DOING??
IT FEELS... LIKE...
...LIKE...

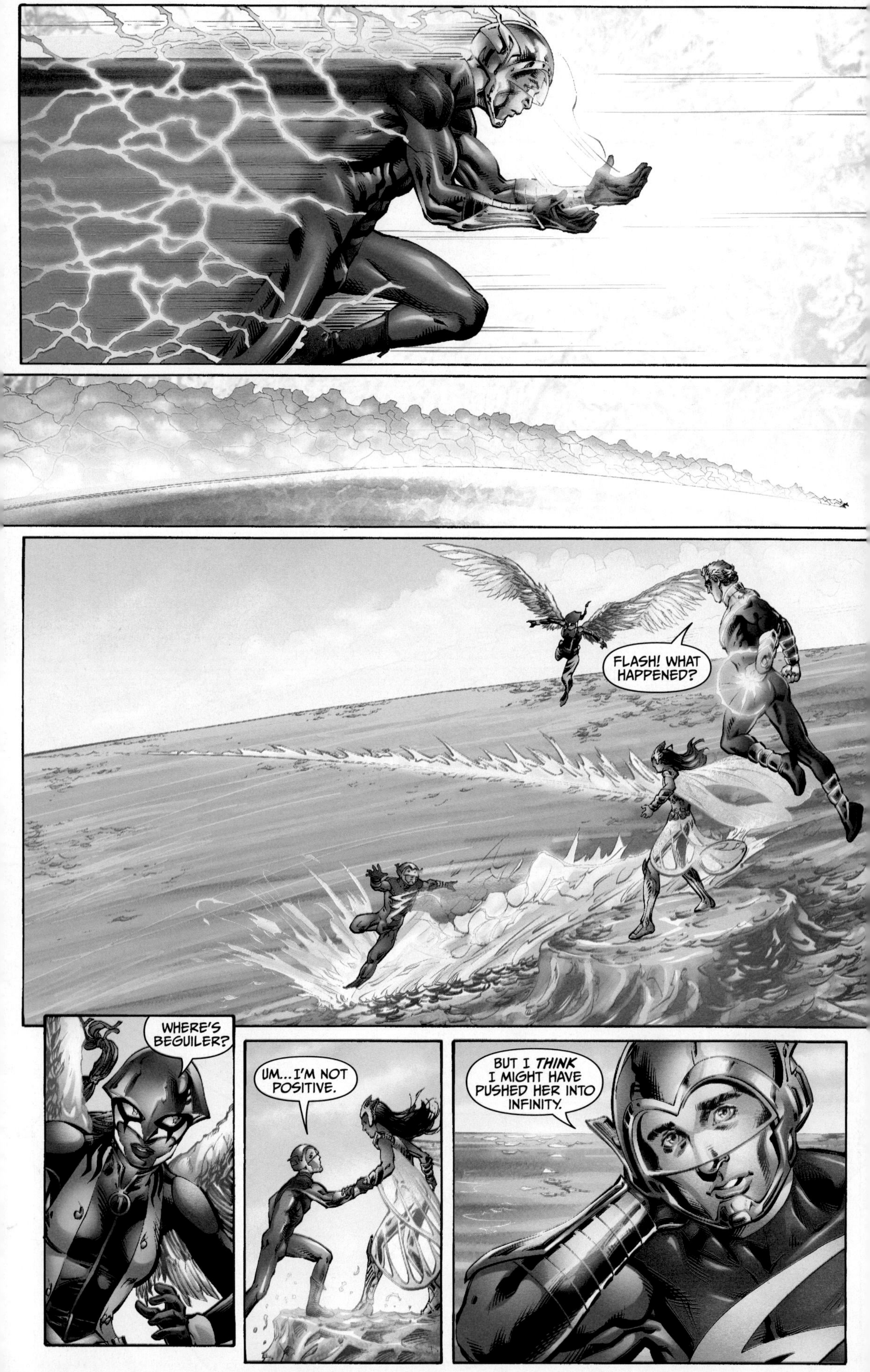
FLASH! WHAT HAPPENED?
WHERE'S BEGUILER?
UM...I'M NOT POSITIVE.
BUT I *THINK* I MIGHT HAVE PUSHED HER INTO INFINITY.

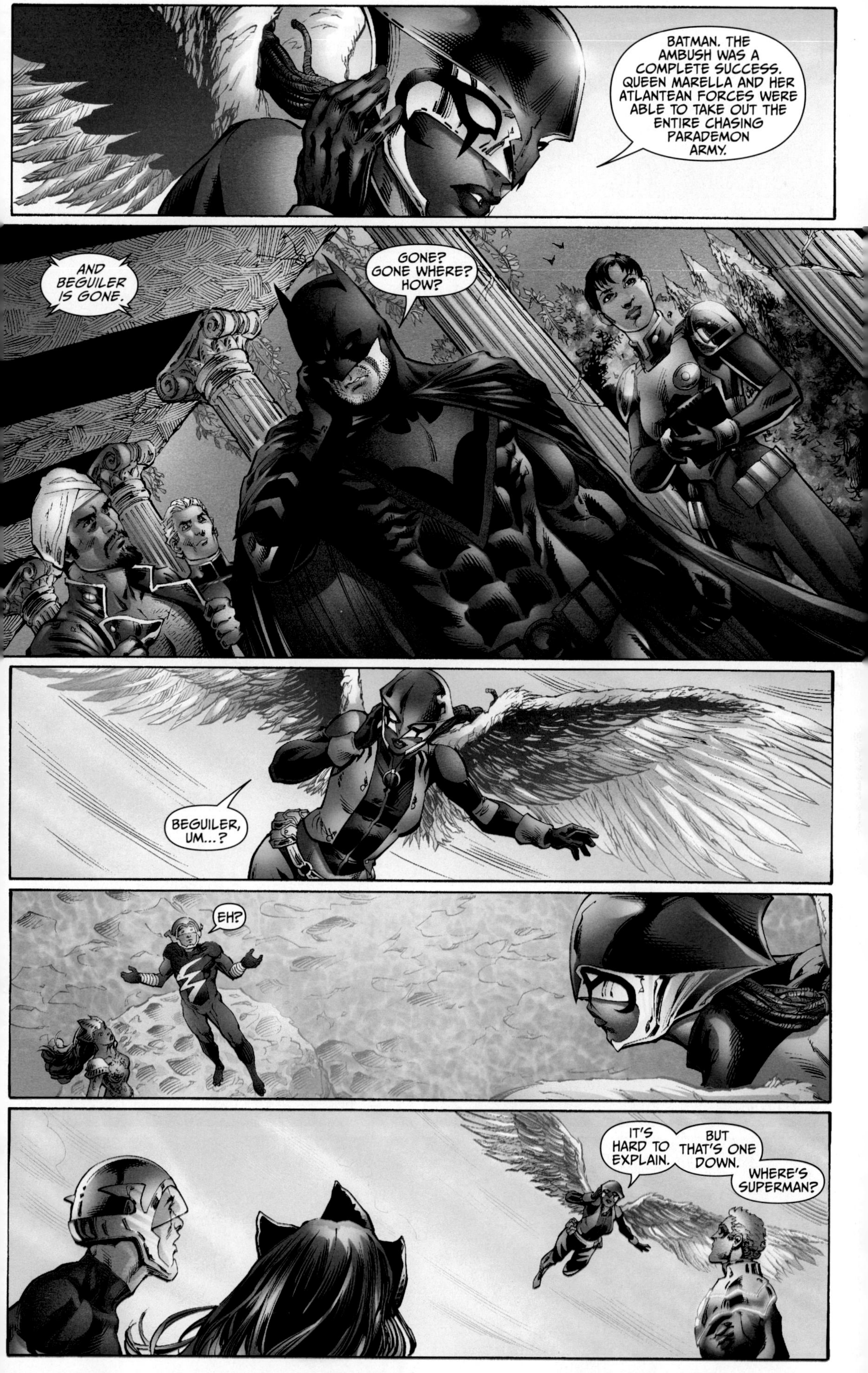
BATMAN. THE AMBUSH WAS A COMPLETE SUCCESS. QUEEN MARELLA AND HER ATLANTEAN FORCES WERE ABLE TO TAKE OUT THE ENTIRE CHASING PARADEMON ARMY.
AND BEGUILER IS GONE.
GONE? GONE WHERE? HOW?
BEGUILER, UM...?
EH?
IT'S HARD TO EXPLAIN.
BUT THAT'S ONE DOWN.
WHERE'S SUPERMAN?

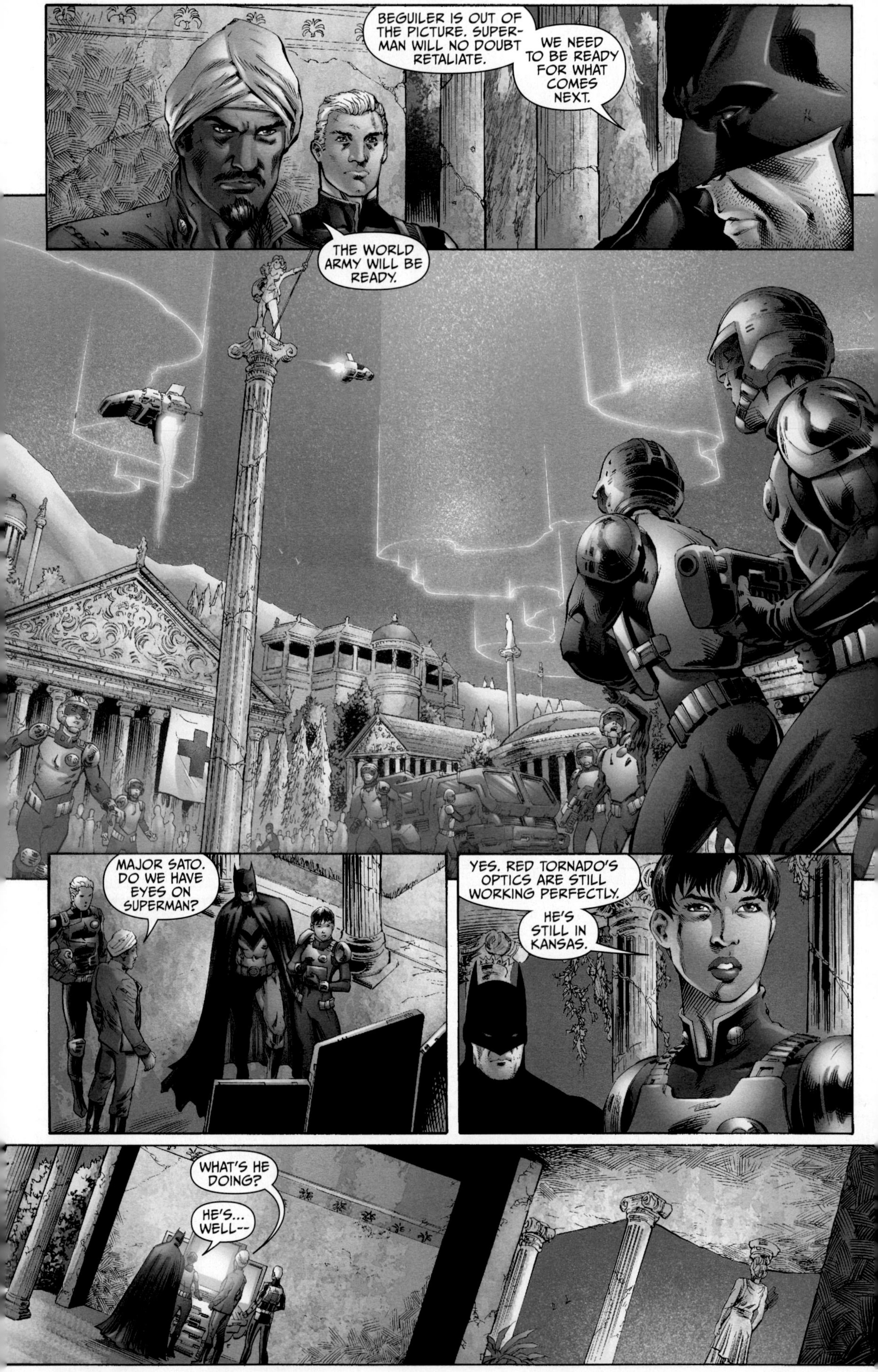
BEGUILER IS OUT OF THE PICTURE. SUPERMAN WILL NO DOUBT RETALIATE.
WE NEED TO BE READY FOR WHAT COMES NEXT.
THE WORLD ARMY WILL BE READY.
MAJOR SATO. DO WE HAVE EYES ON SUPERMAN?
YES. RED TORNADO'S OPTICS ARE STILL WORKING PERFECTLY.
HE'S STILL IN KANSAS.
WHAT'S HE DOING?
HE'S... WELL--

"—HE'S SITTING DOWN TO DINNER WITH HIS PARENTS."

I'LL SET THE TABLE.

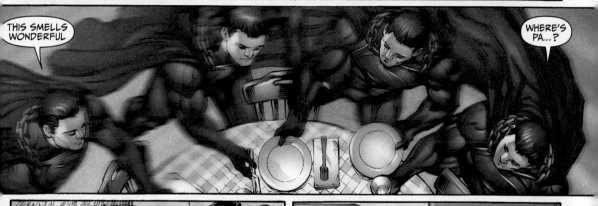

THIS SMELLS WONDERFUL

WHERE'S PA...?

AH. I CAN SEE HIM. HE'S IN THE BARN.

MARTHA. WHAT IS GOING ON?

PLEASE, LOIS. DON'T MAKE TROUBLE. HE CAN HEAR US!

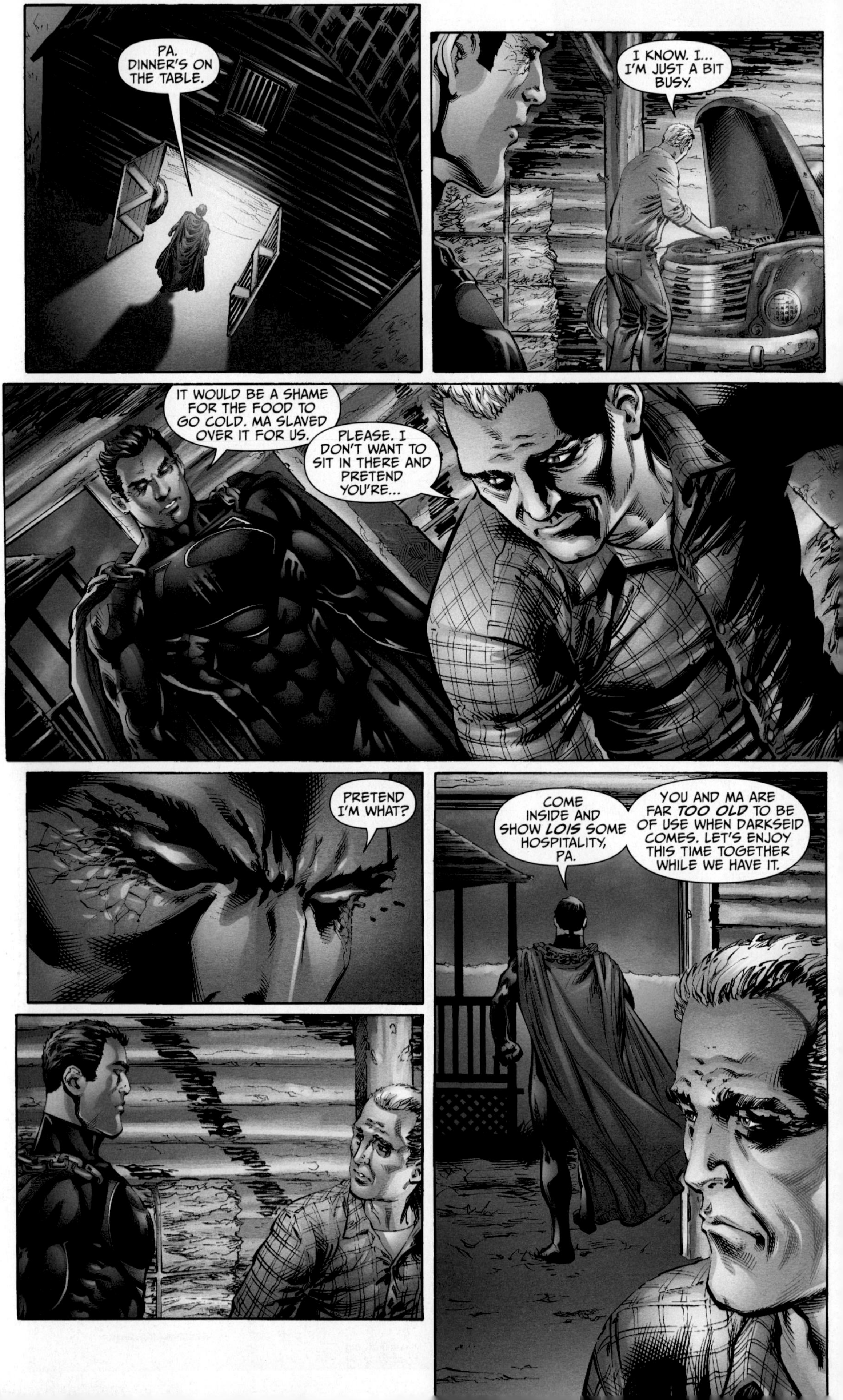
PA. DINNER'S ON THE TABLE.
I KNOW. I... I'M JUST A BIT BUSY.
IT WOULD BE A SHAME FOR THE FOOD TO GO COLD. MA SLAVED OVER IT FOR US.
PLEASE. I DON'T WANT TO SIT IN THERE AND PRETEND YOU'RE...
PRETEND I'M WHAT?
COME INSIDE AND SHOW LOIS SOME HOSPITALITY, PA.
YOU AND MA ARE FAR TOO OLD TO BE OF USE WHEN DARKSEID COMES. LET'S ENJOY THIS TIME TOGETHER WHILE WE HAVE IT.

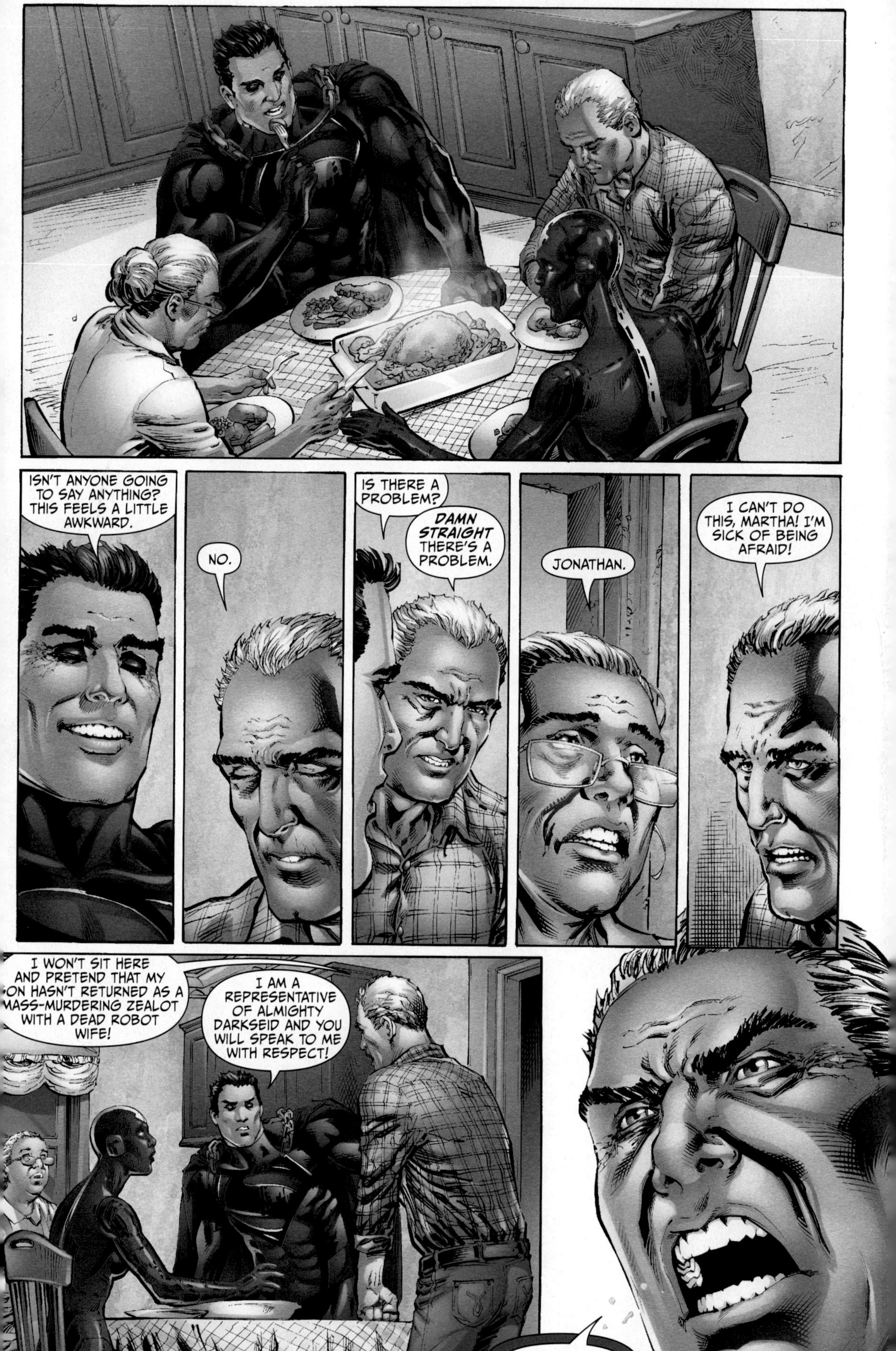
ISN'T ANYONE GOING TO SAY ANYTHING? THIS FEELS A LITTLE AWKWARD.
NO.
IS THERE A PROBLEM?
DAMN STRAIGHT THERE'S A PROBLEM.
JONATHAN.
I CAN'T DO THIS, MARTHA! I'M SICK OF BEING AFRAID!
I WON'T SIT HERE AND PRETEND THAT MY SON HASN'T RETURNED AS A MASS-MURDERING ZEALOT WITH A DEAD ROBOT WIFE!
I AM A REPRESENTATIVE OF ALMIGHTY DARKSEID AND YOU WILL SPEAK TO ME WITH RESPECT!
SCREW DARKSEID!!

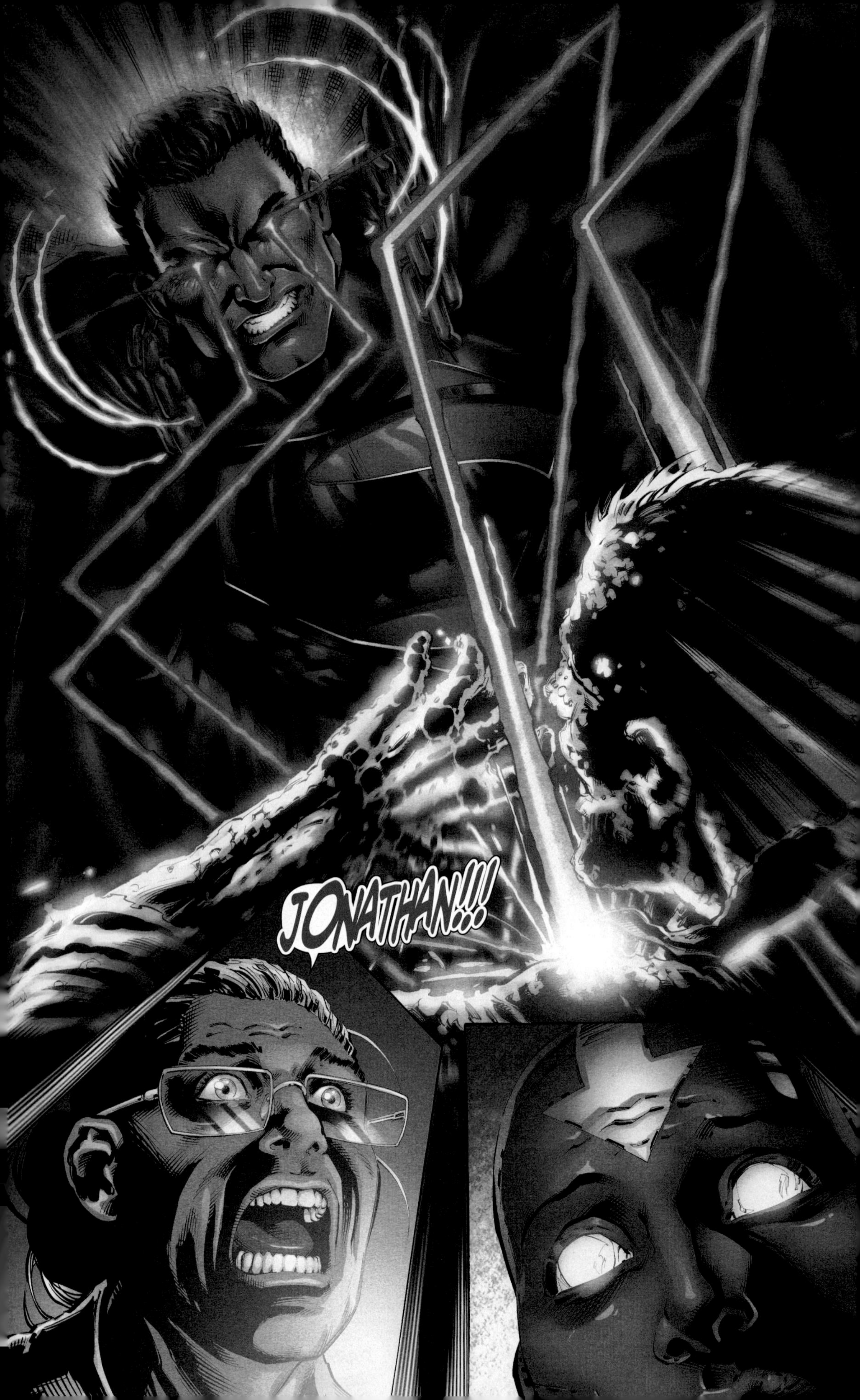
JONATHAN!!!

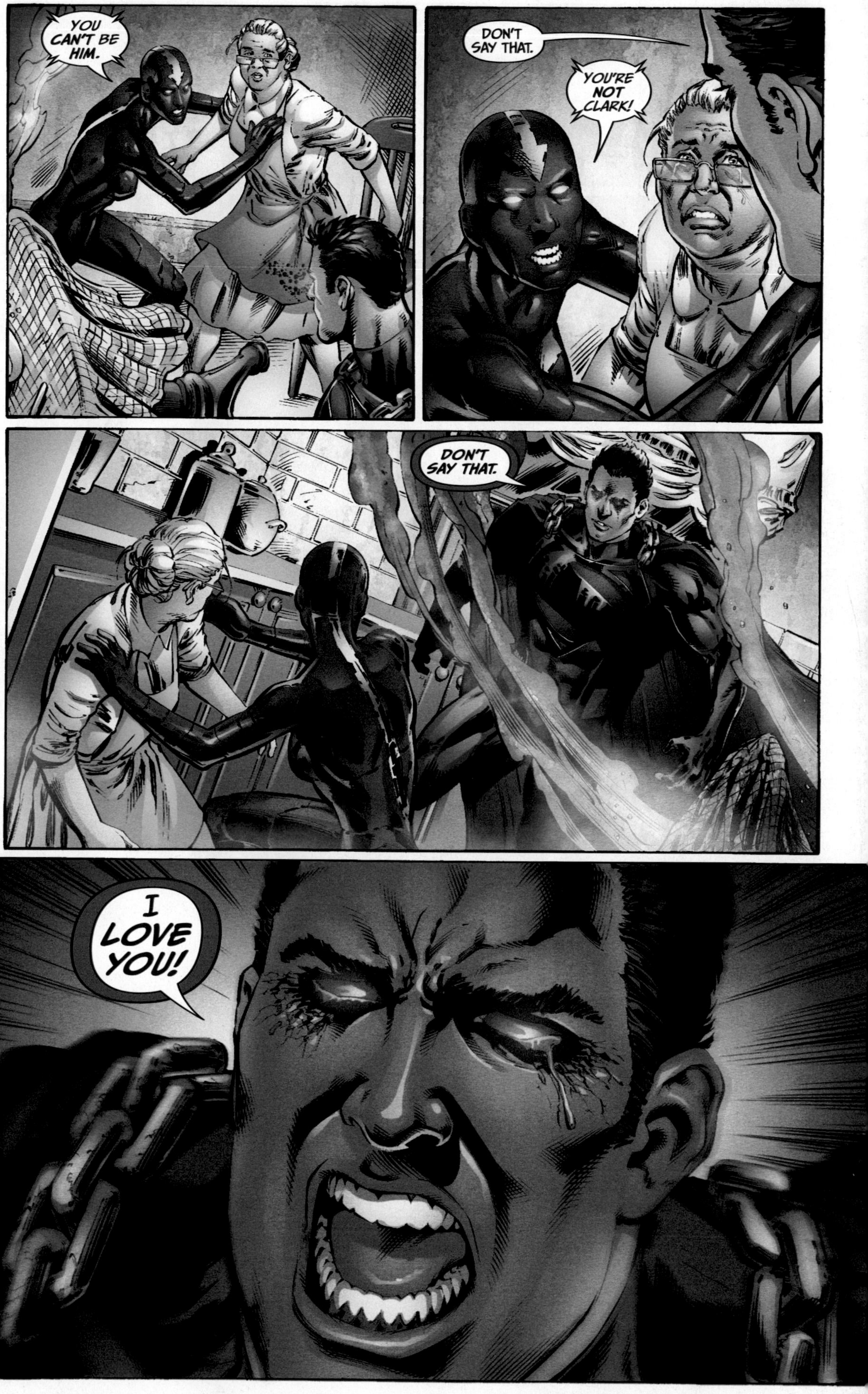
YOU CAN'T BE HIM.
DON'T SAY THAT.
YOU'RE NOT CLARK!
DON'T SAY THAT.
I LOVE YOU!

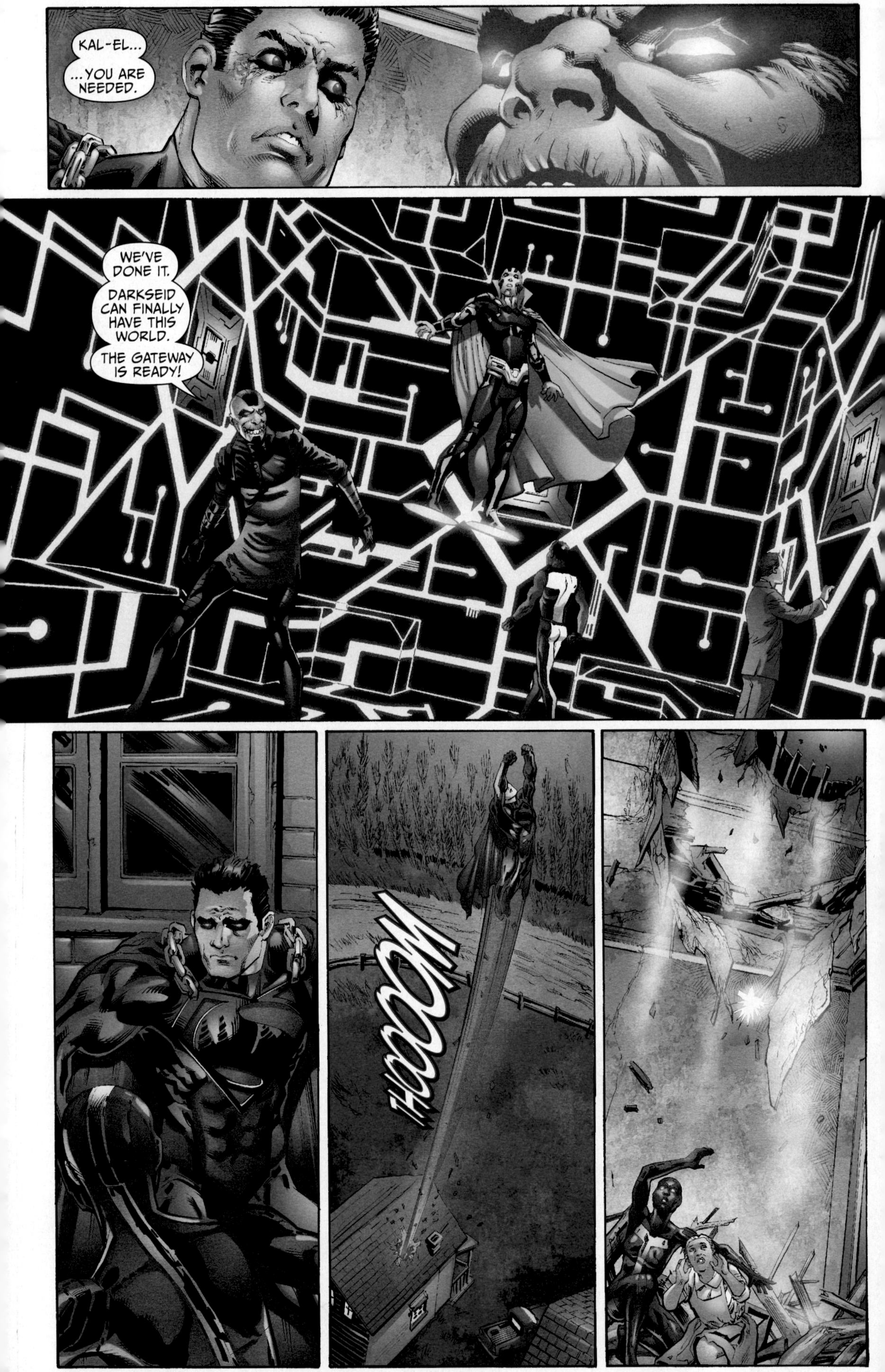
KAL-EL...
...YOU ARE NEEDED.
WE'VE DONE IT.
DARKSEID CAN FINALLY HAVE THIS WORLD.
THE GATEWAY IS READY!
WHOOOOM

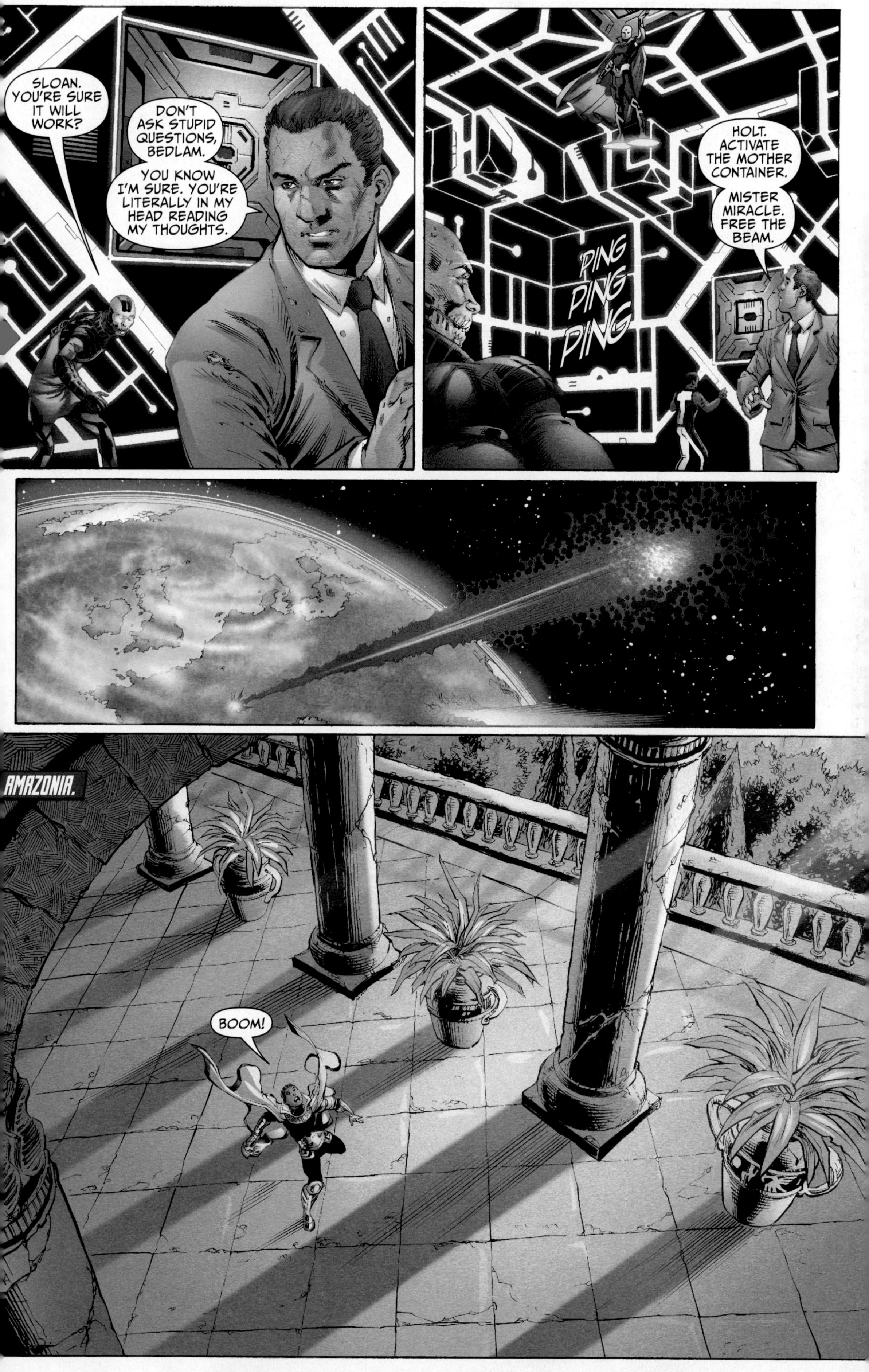
SLOAN. YOU'RE SURE IT WILL WORK?
DON'T ASK STUPID QUESTIONS, BEDLAM.
YOU KNOW I'M SURE. YOU'RE LITERALLY IN MY HEAD READING MY THOUGHTS.
HOLT. ACTIVATE THE MOTHER CONTAINER.
MISTER MIRACLE. FREE THE BEAM.
PING PING PING
AMAZONIA.
BOOM!

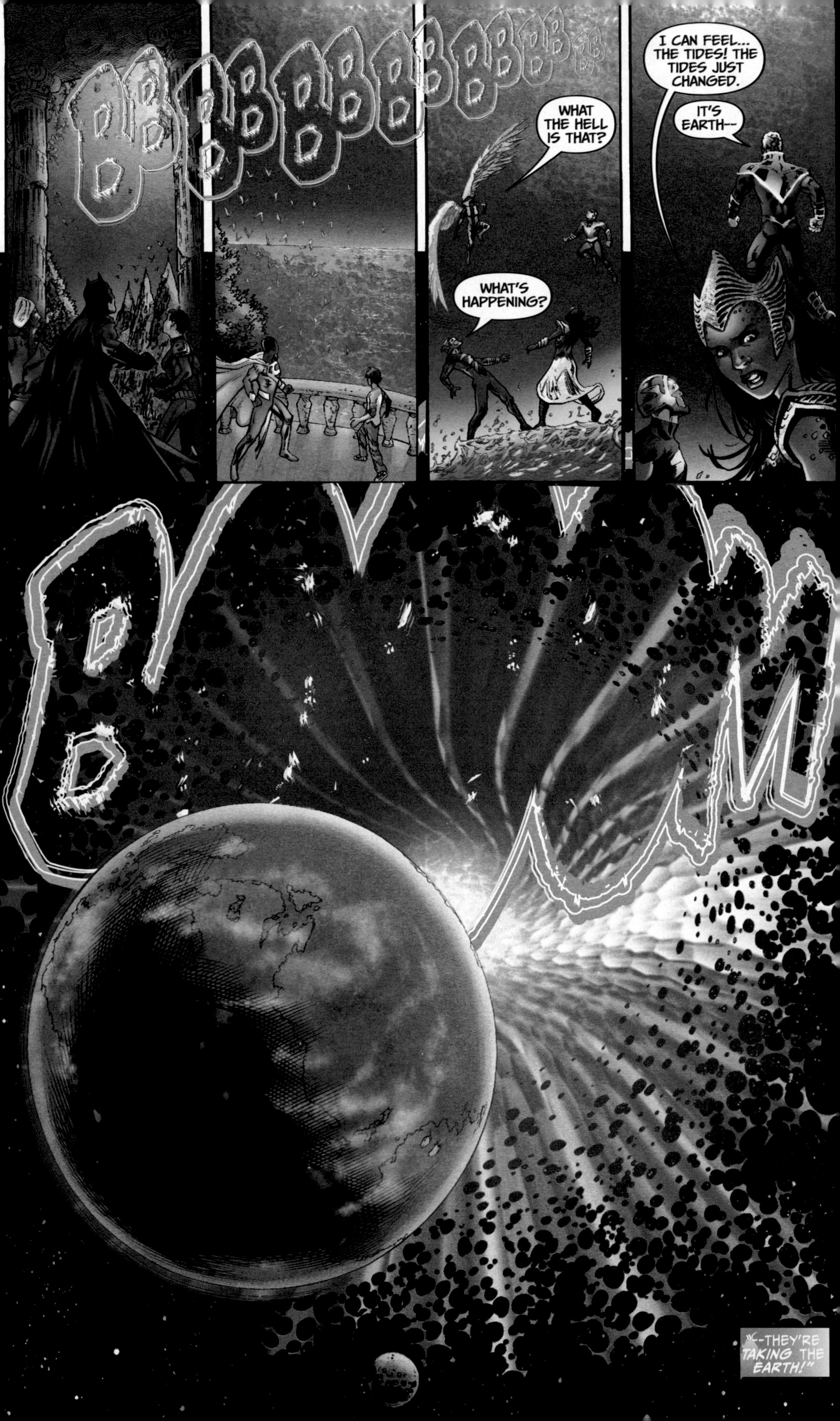
WHAT THE HELL IS THAT?
WHAT'S HAPPENING?
I CAN FEEL... THE TIDES! THE TIDES JUST CHANGED.
IT'S EARTH--
"--THEY'RE TAKING THE EARTH!"

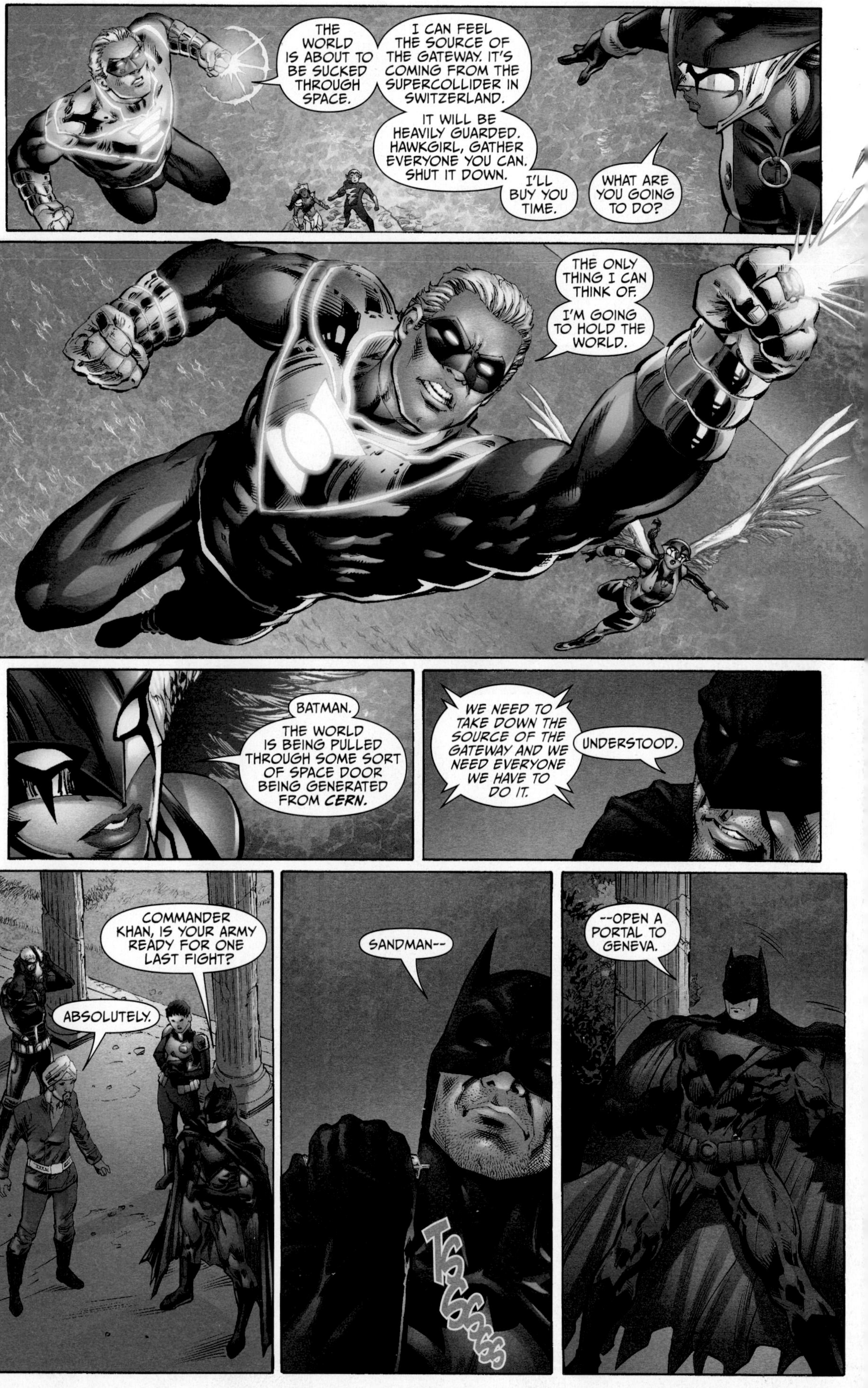
THE WORLD IS ABOUT TO BE SUCKED THROUGH SPACE.
I CAN FEEL THE SOURCE OF THE GATEWAY. IT'S COMING FROM THE SUPERCOLLIDER IN SWITZERLAND.
IT WILL BE HEAVILY GUARDED. HAWKGIRL, GATHER EVERYONE YOU CAN. SHUT IT DOWN.
I'LL BUY YOU TIME.
WHAT ARE YOU GOING TO DO?
THE ONLY THING I CAN THINK OF.
I'M GOING TO HOLD THE WORLD.
BATMAN.
THE WORLD IS BEING PULLED THROUGH SOME SORT OF SPACE DOOR BEING GENERATED FROM CERN.
WE NEED TO TAKE DOWN THE SOURCE OF THE GATEWAY AND WE NEED EVERYONE WE HAVE TO DO IT.
UNDERSTOOD.
COMMANDER KHAN, IS YOUR ARMY READY FOR ONE LAST FIGHT?
ABSOLUTELY.
SANDMAN--
TSSSSSS
--OPEN A PORTAL TO GENEVA.

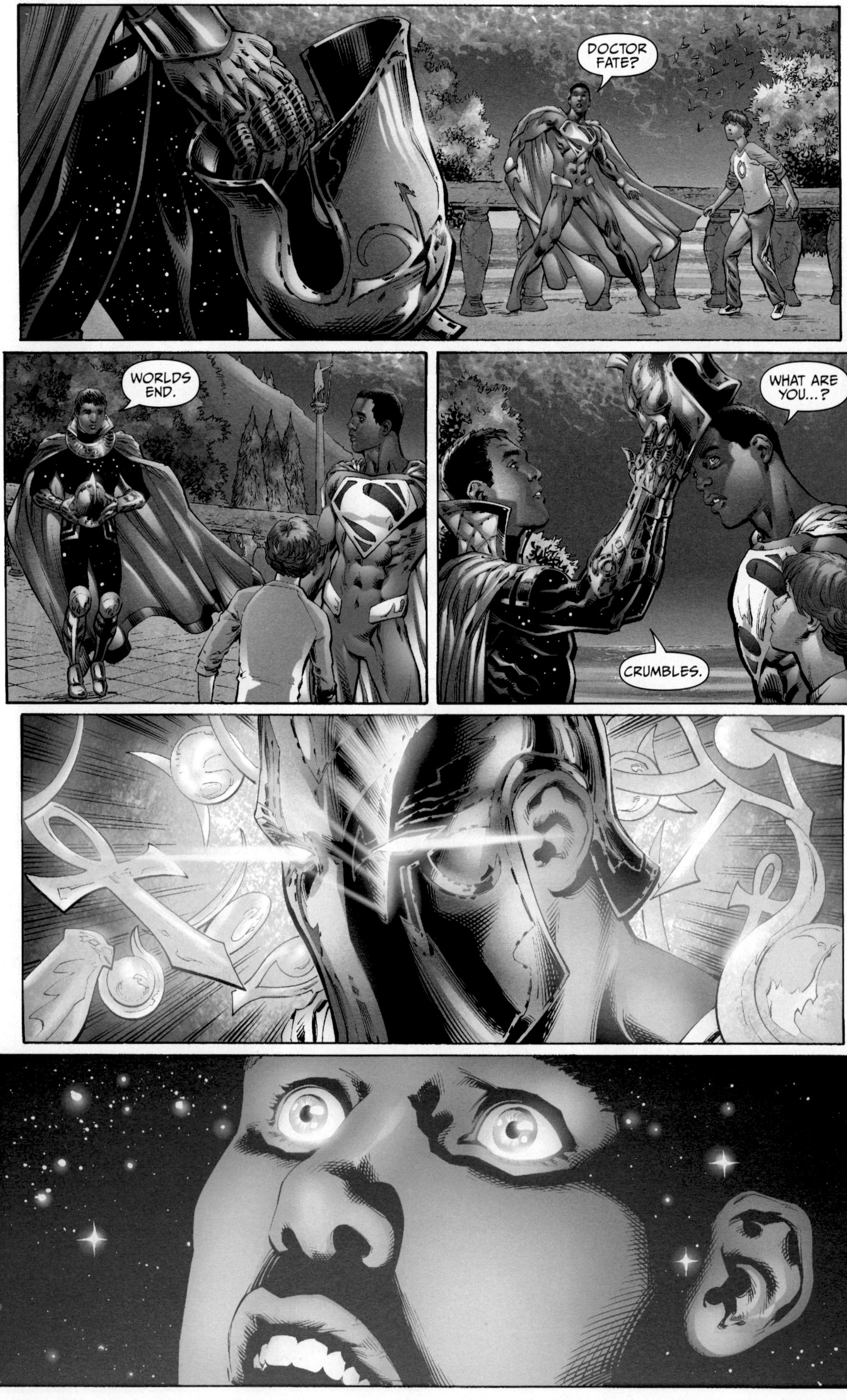
DOCTOR FATE?
WORLDS END.
WHAT ARE YOU...?
CRUMBLES.

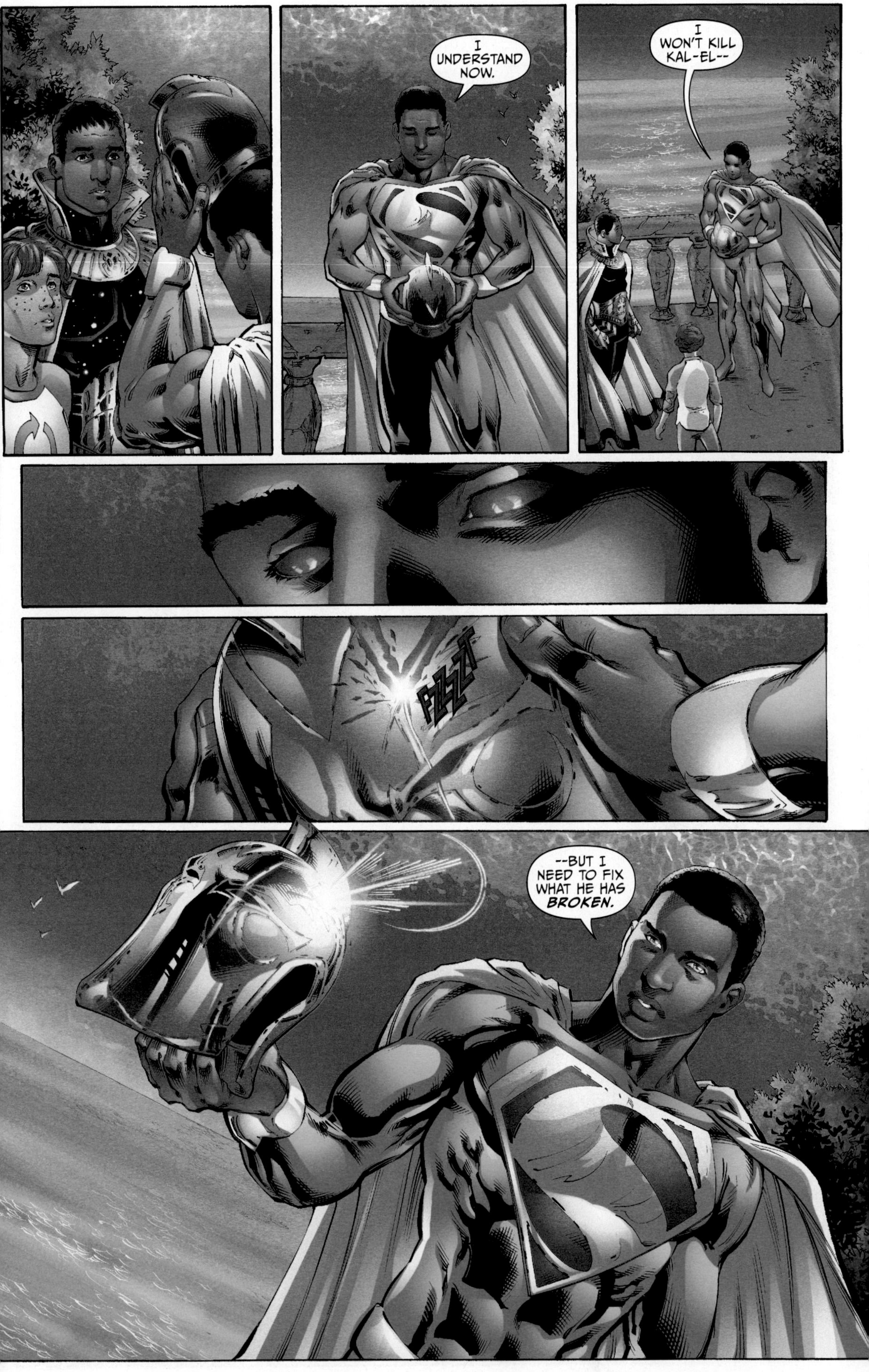
I UNDERSTAND NOW.
I WON'T KILL KAL-EL--
FZZZT
--BUT I NEED TO FIX WHAT HE HAS *BROKEN.*

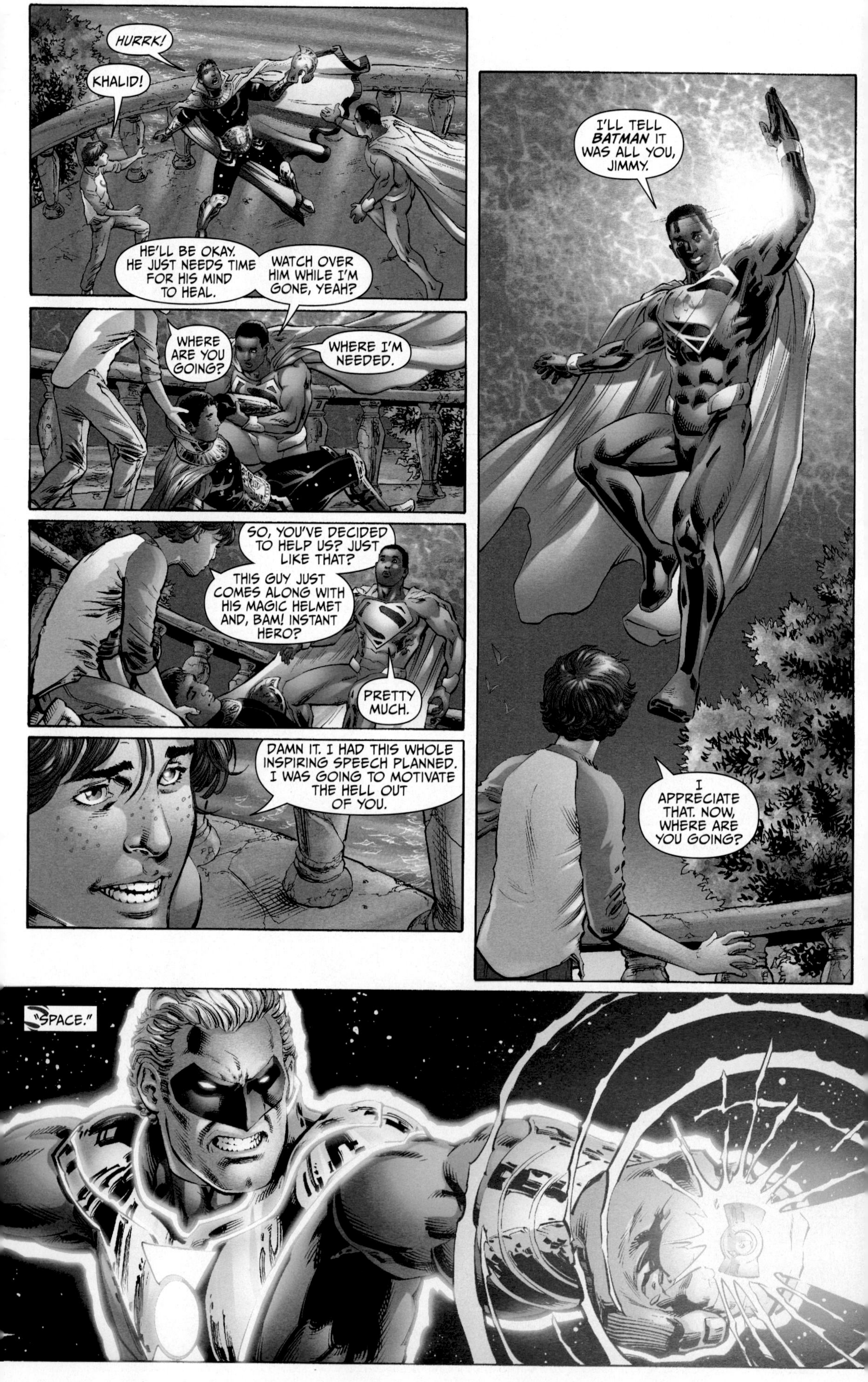
HURRK!
KHALID!
HE'LL BE OKAY. HE JUST NEEDS TIME FOR HIS MIND TO HEAL.
WATCH OVER HIM WHILE I'M GONE, YEAH?
WHERE ARE YOU GOING?
WHERE I'M NEEDED.
SO, YOU'VE DECIDED TO HELP US? JUST LIKE THAT?
THIS GUY JUST COMES ALONG WITH HIS MAGIC HELMET AND, BAM! INSTANT HERO?
PRETTY MUCH.
DAMN IT. I HAD THIS WHOLE INSPIRING SPEECH PLANNED. I WAS GOING TO MOTIVATE THE HELL OUT OF YOU.
I'LL TELL BATMAN IT WAS ALL YOU, JIMMY.
I APPRECIATE THAT. NOW, WHERE ARE YOU GOING?
"SPACE."

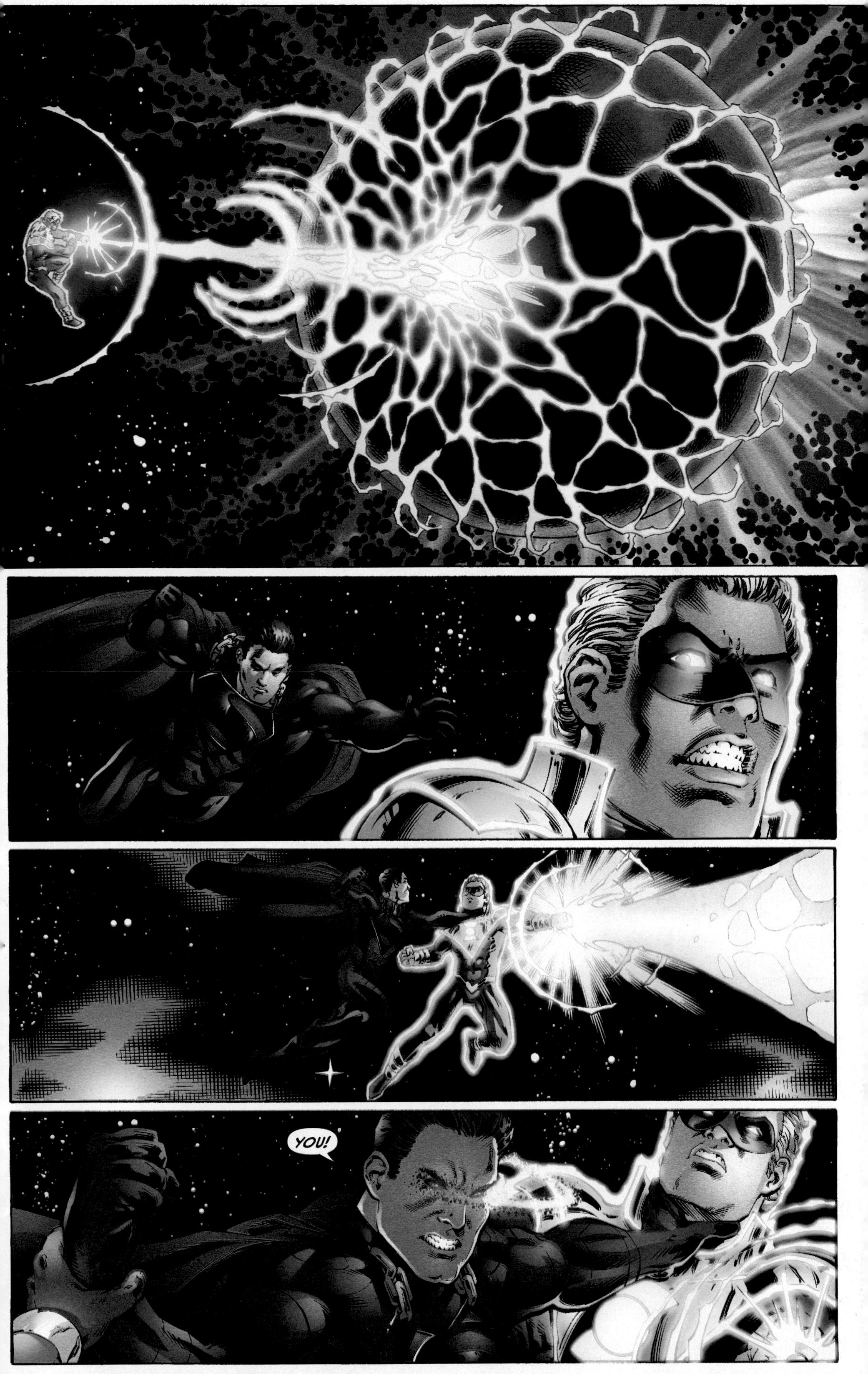
YOU!

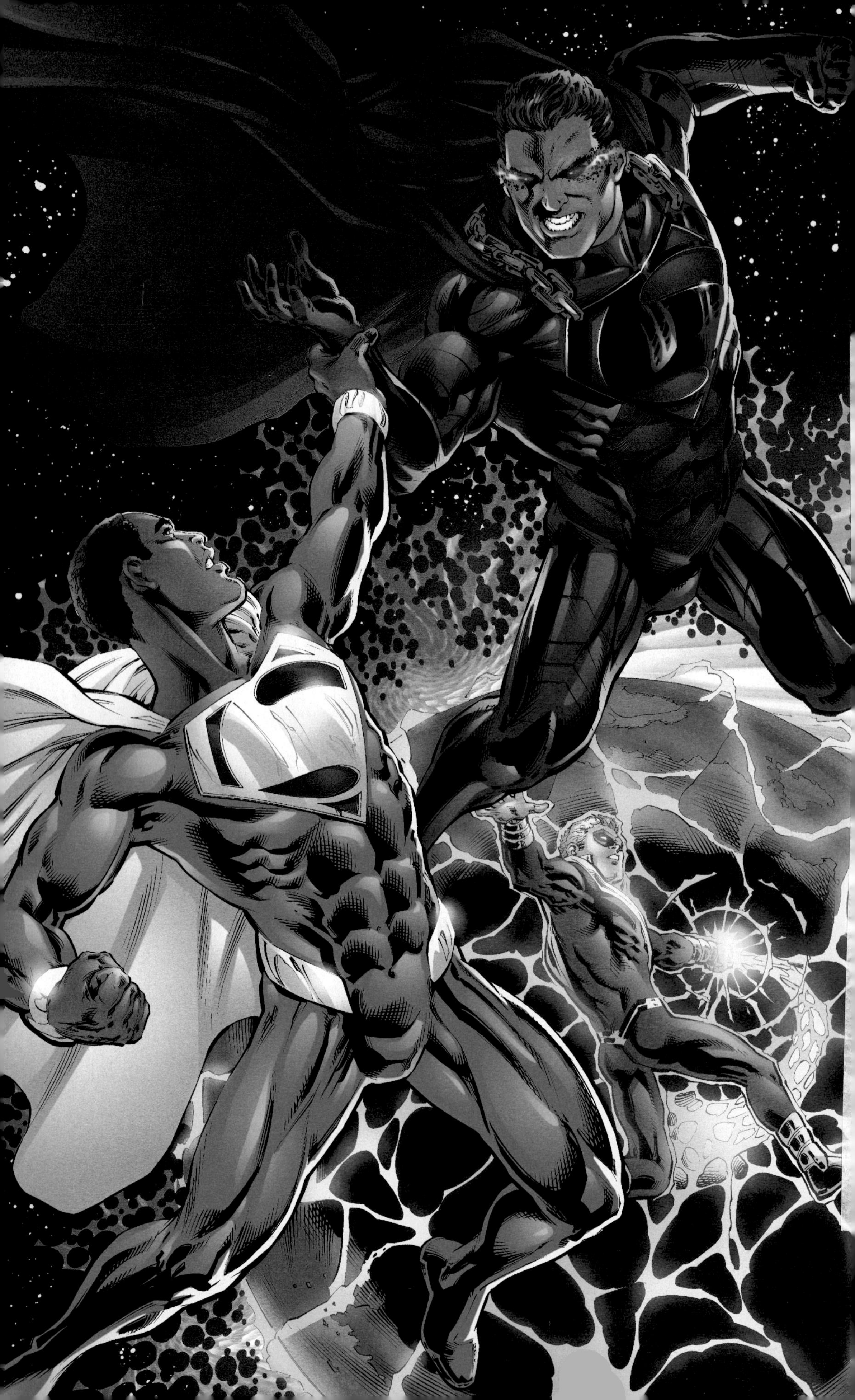

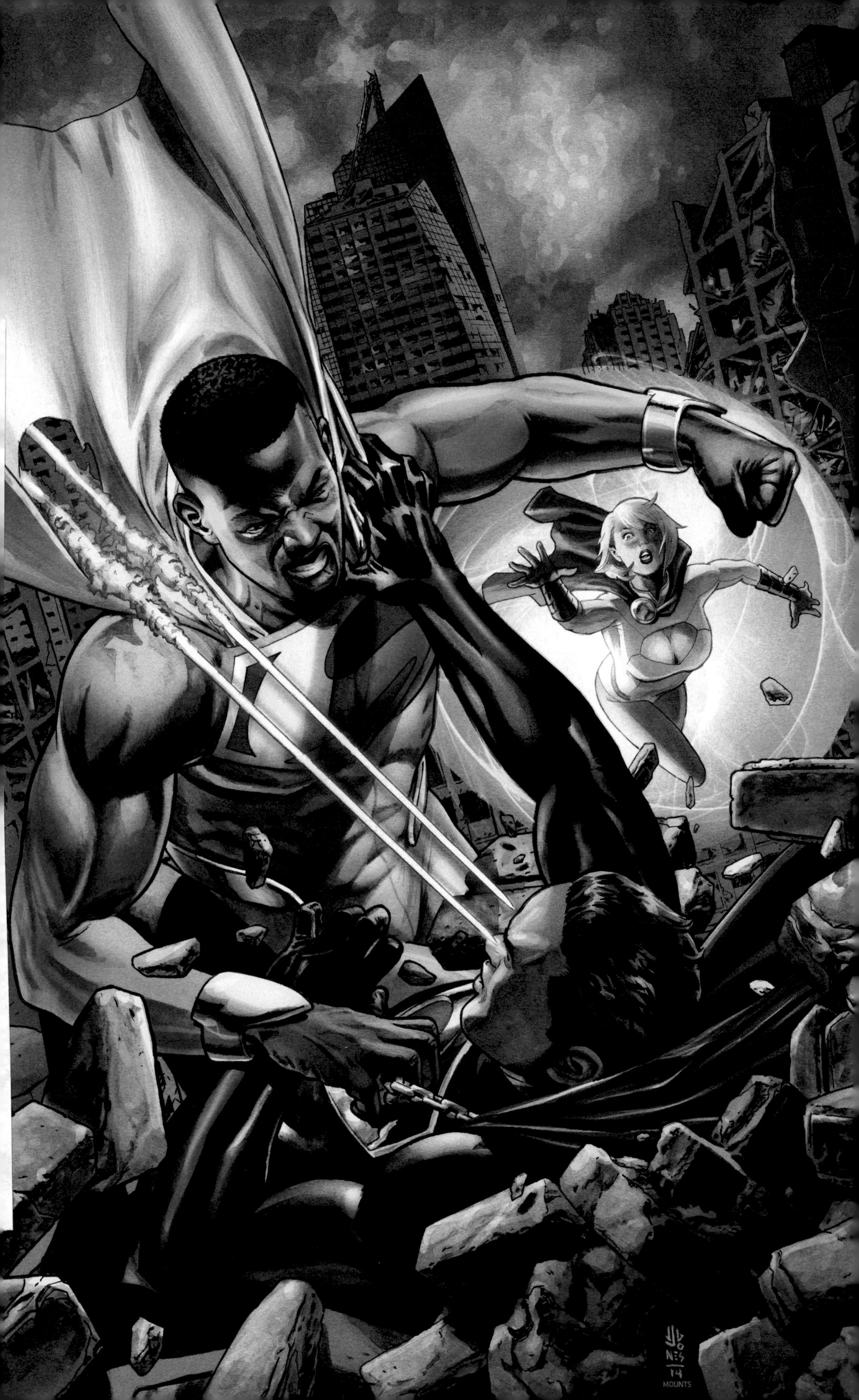
MOUNTS

THE KRYPTONIAN PART 6

TOM TAYLOR writer **NICOLA SCOTT** penciller **TREVOR SCOTT** inker **PETE PANTAZIS** colorist cover by **J.G. JONES** & **PAUL MOUNTS**

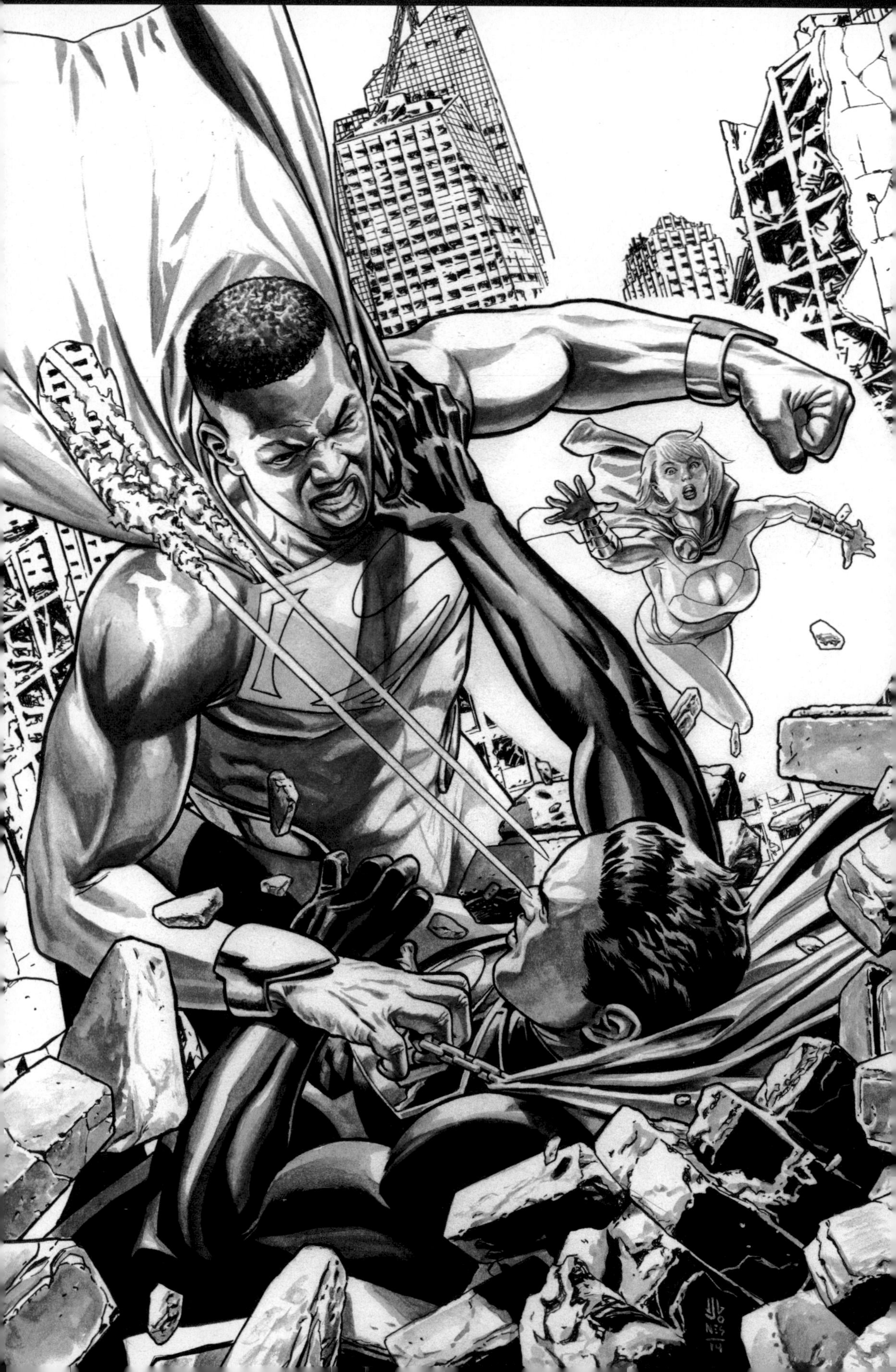

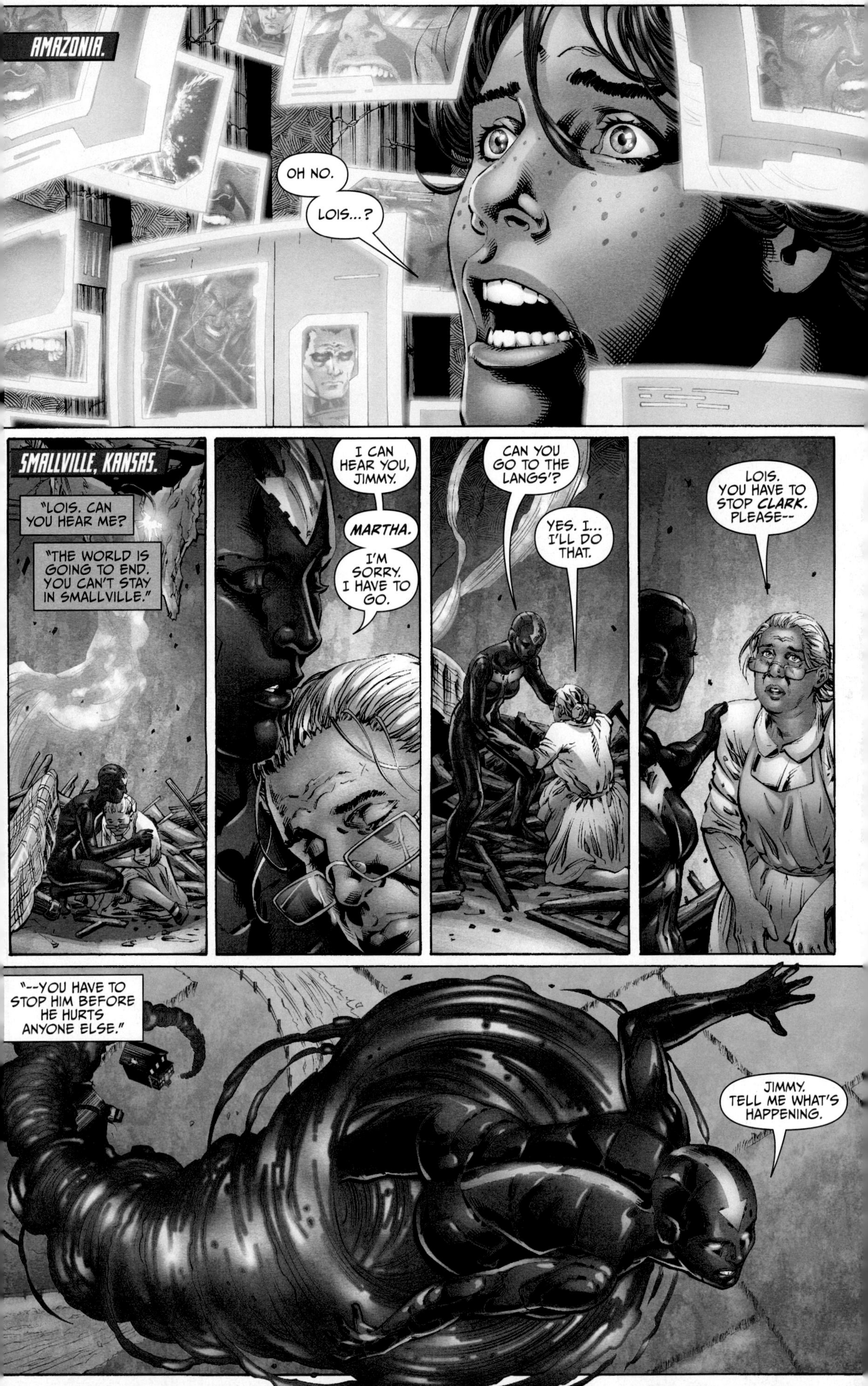
AMAZONIA.
OH NO.
LOIS...?
SMALLVILLE, KANSAS.
"LOIS. CAN YOU HEAR ME?
"THE WORLD IS GOING TO END. YOU CAN'T STAY IN SMALLVILLE."
I CAN HEAR YOU, JIMMY.
MARTHA.
I'M SORRY. I HAVE TO GO.
CAN YOU GO TO THE LANGS'?
YES. I... I'LL DO THAT.
LOIS. YOU HAVE TO STOP CLARK. PLEASE--
"--YOU HAVE TO STOP HIM BEFORE HE HURTS ANYONE ELSE."
JIMMY. TELL ME WHAT'S HAPPENING.

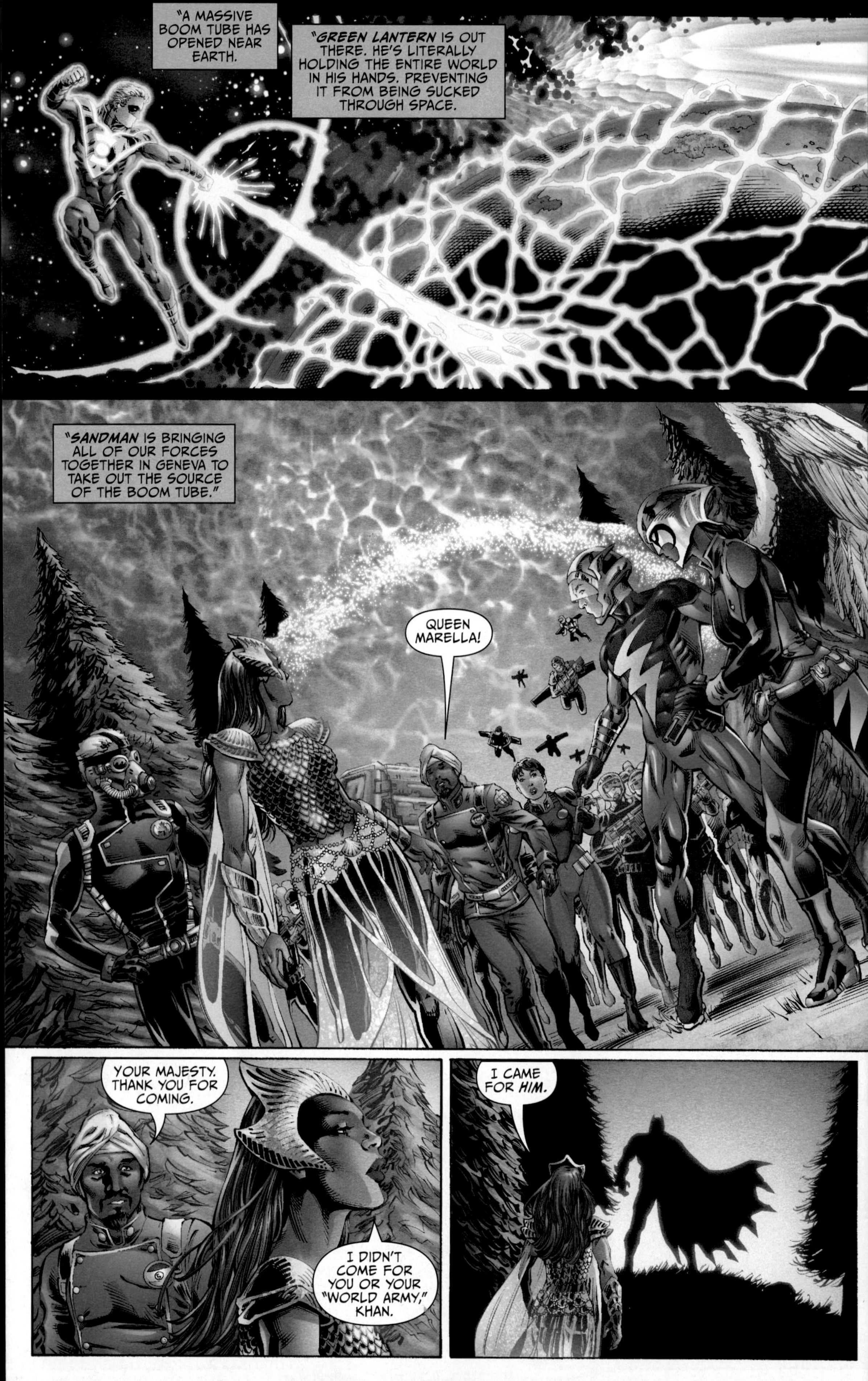
"A MASSIVE BOOM TUBE HAS OPENED NEAR EARTH.
"GREEN LANTERN IS OUT THERE. HE'S LITERALLY HOLDING THE ENTIRE WORLD IN HIS HANDS. PREVENTING IT FROM BEING SUCKED THROUGH SPACE.
"SANDMAN IS BRINGING ALL OF OUR FORCES TOGETHER IN GENEVA TO TAKE OUT THE SOURCE OF THE BOOM TUBE."
QUEEN MARELLA!
YOUR MAJESTY. THANK YOU FOR COMING.
I DIDN'T COME FOR YOU OR YOUR "WORLD ARMY," KHAN.
I CAME FOR HIM.

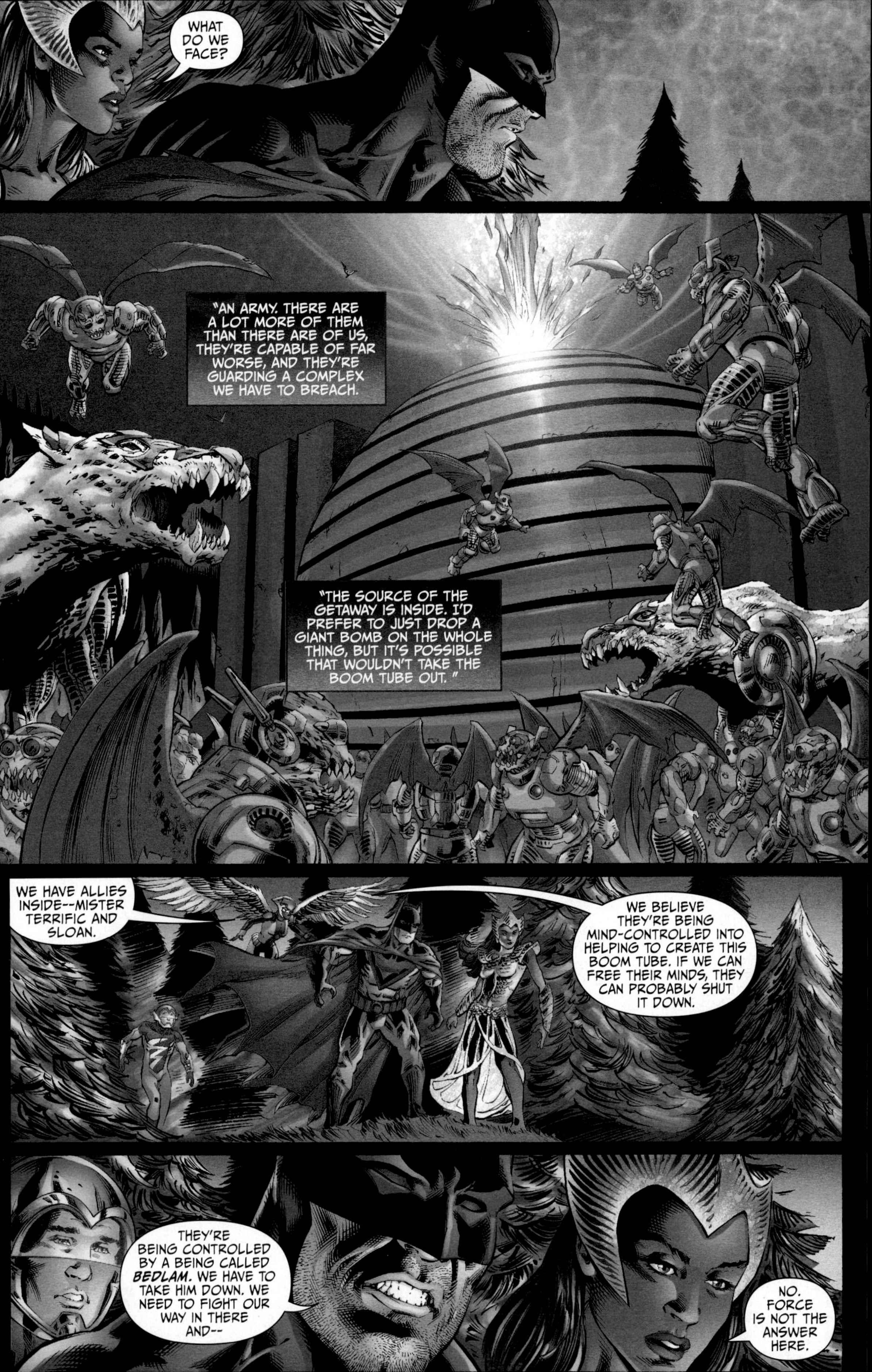
WHAT DO WE FACE?
"AN ARMY. THERE ARE A LOT MORE OF THEM THAN THERE ARE OF US, THEY'RE CAPABLE OF FAR WORSE, AND THEY'RE GUARDING A COMPLEX WE HAVE TO BREACH.
"THE SOURCE OF THE GETAWAY IS INSIDE. I'D PREFER TO JUST DROP A GIANT BOMB ON THE WHOLE THING, BUT IT'S POSSIBLE THAT WOULDN'T TAKE THE BOOM TUBE OUT."
WE HAVE ALLIES INSIDE--MISTER TERRIFIC AND SLOAN.
WE BELIEVE THEY'RE BEING MIND-CONTROLLED INTO HELPING TO CREATE THIS BOOM TUBE. IF WE CAN FREE THEIR MINDS, THEY CAN PROBABLY SHUT IT DOWN.
THEY'RE BEING CONTROLLED BY A BEING CALLED BEDLAM. WE HAVE TO TAKE HIM DOWN. WE NEED TO FIGHT OUR WAY IN THERE AND--
NO. FORCE IS NOT THE ANSWER HERE.

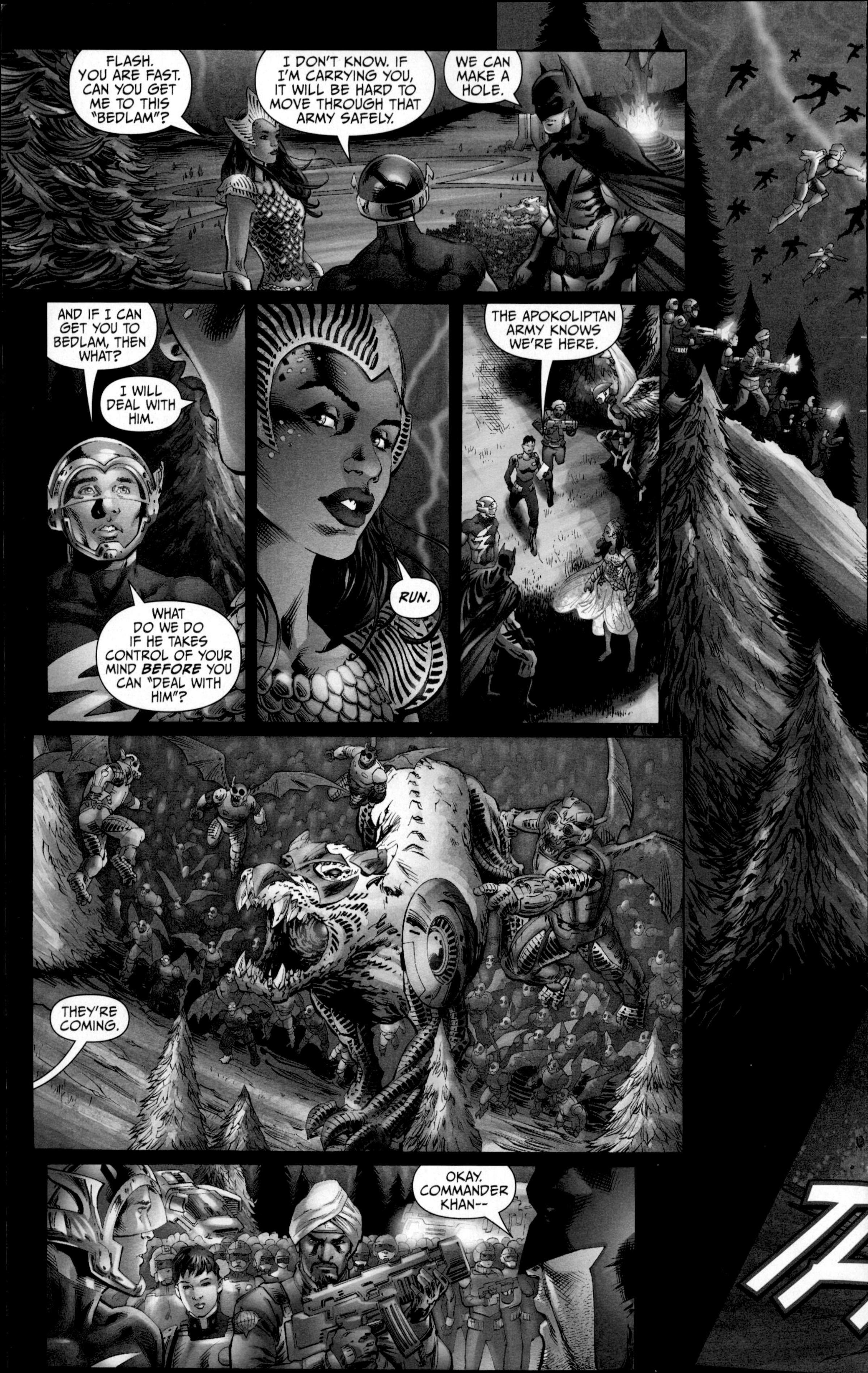
FLASH. YOU ARE FAST. CAN YOU GET ME TO THIS "BEDLAM"?
I DON'T KNOW. IF I'M CARRYING YOU, IT WILL BE HARD TO MOVE THROUGH THAT ARMY SAFELY.
WE CAN MAKE A HOLE.
AND IF I CAN GET YOU TO BEDLAM, THEN WHAT?
I WILL DEAL WITH HIM.
WHAT DO WE DO IF HE TAKES CONTROL OF YOUR MIND *BEFORE* YOU CAN "DEAL WITH HIM"?
RUN.
THE APOKOLIPTAN ARMY KNOWS WE'RE HERE.
THEY'RE COMING.
OKAY. COMMANDER KHAN--

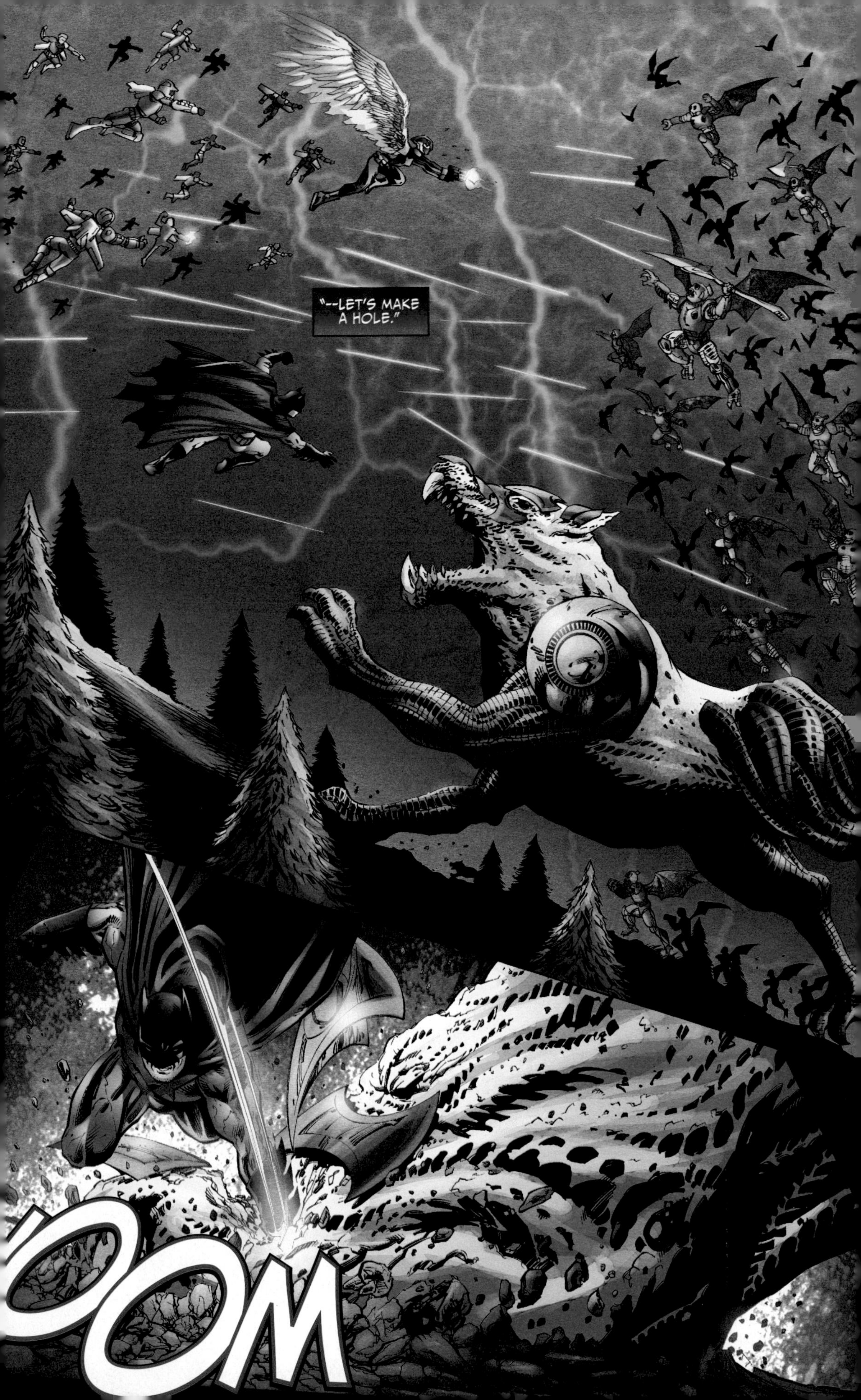
"--LET'S MAKE A HOLE."
OOM

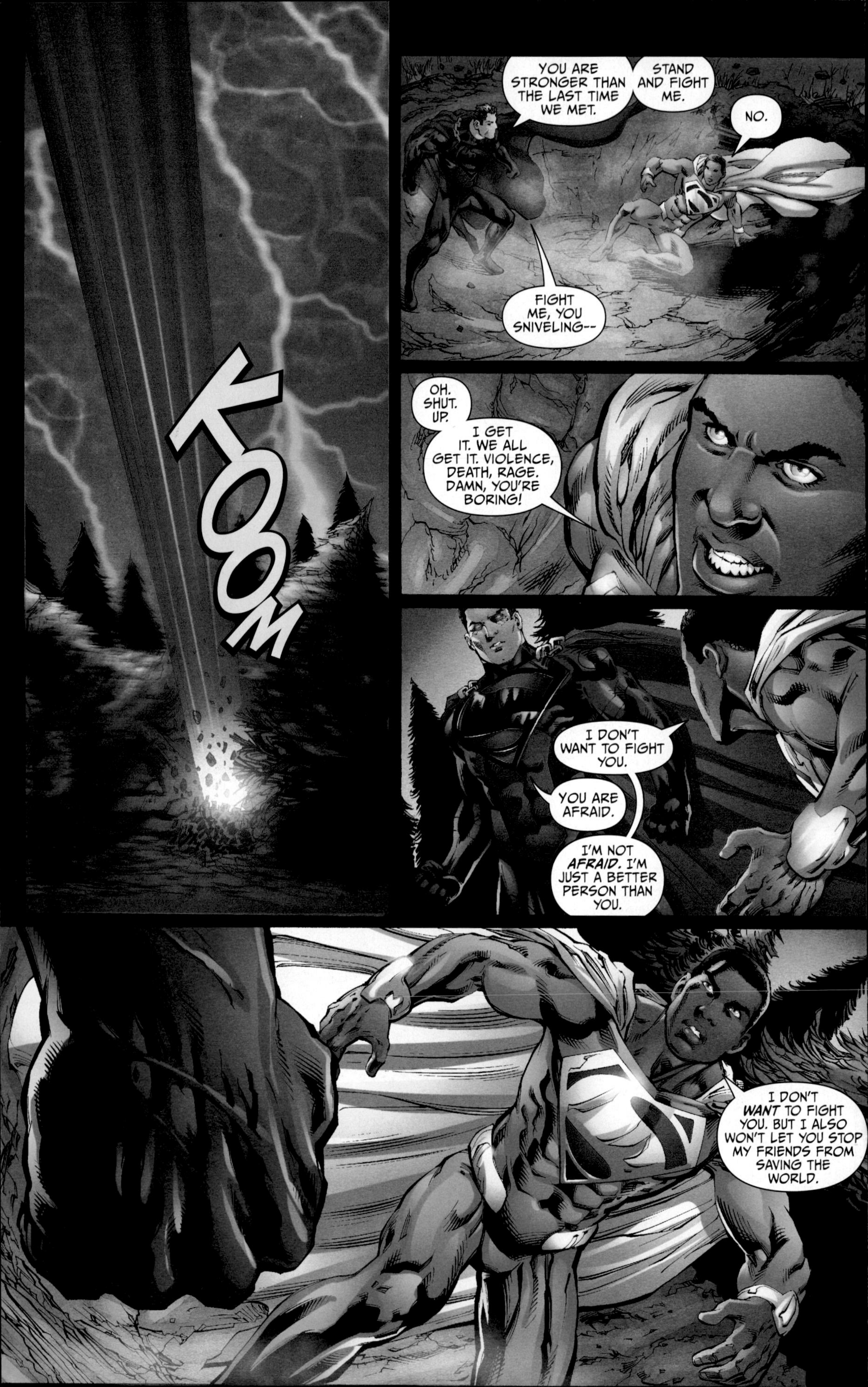
KOOM
YOU ARE STRONGER THAN THE LAST TIME WE MET.
STAND AND FIGHT ME.
NO.
FIGHT ME, YOU SNIVELING--
OH. SHUT. UP.
I GET IT. WE ALL GET IT. VIOLENCE, DEATH, RAGE. DAMN, YOU'RE BORING!
I DON'T WANT TO FIGHT YOU.
YOU ARE AFRAID.
I'M NOT **AFRAID.** I'M JUST A BETTER PERSON THAN YOU.
I DON'T **WANT** TO FIGHT YOU. BUT I ALSO WON'T LET YOU STOP MY FRIENDS FROM SAVING THE WORLD.

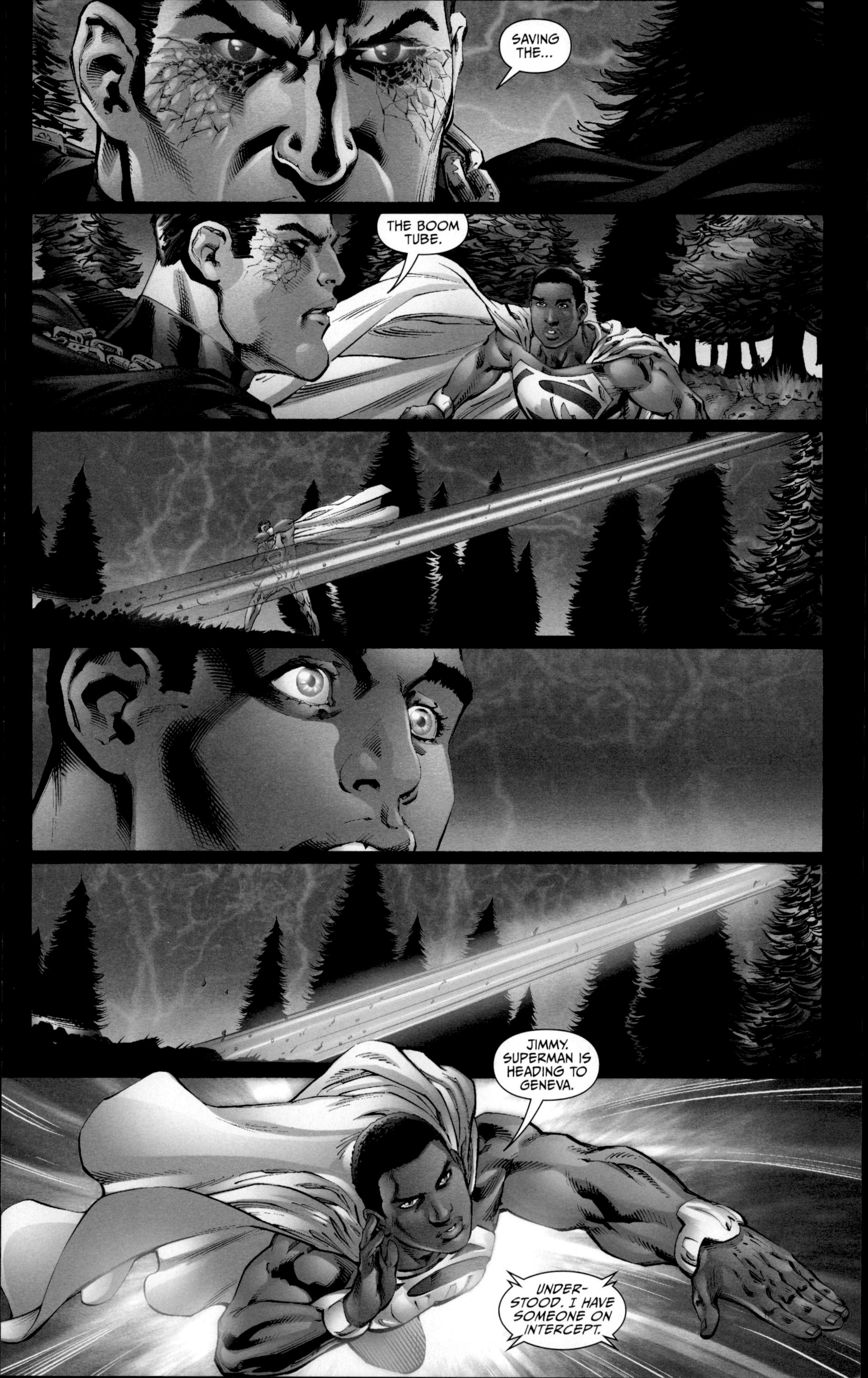
SAVING THE...
THE BOOM TUBE.
JIMMY. SUPERMAN IS HEADING TO GENEVA.
UNDER-STOOD. I HAVE SOMEONE ON INTERCEPT.

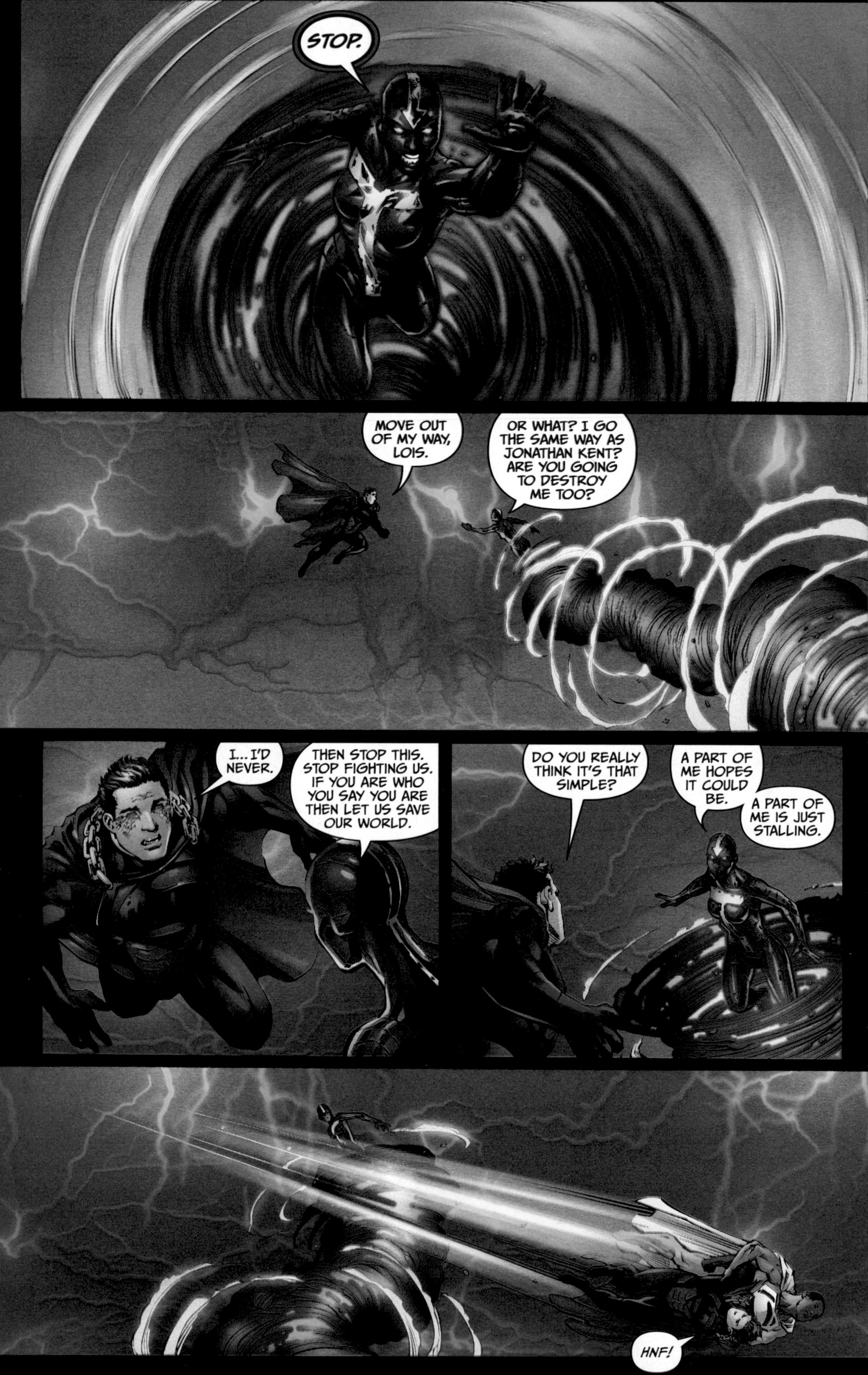
STOP.
MOVE OUT OF MY WAY, LOIS.
OR WHAT? I GO THE SAME WAY AS JONATHAN KENT? ARE YOU GOING TO DESTROY ME TOO?
I... I'D NEVER.
THEN STOP THIS. STOP FIGHTING US. IF YOU ARE WHO YOU SAY YOU ARE THEN LET US SAVE OUR WORLD.
DO YOU REALLY THINK IT'S THAT SIMPLE?
A PART OF ME HOPES IT COULD BE.
A PART OF ME IS JUST STALLING.
HNF!

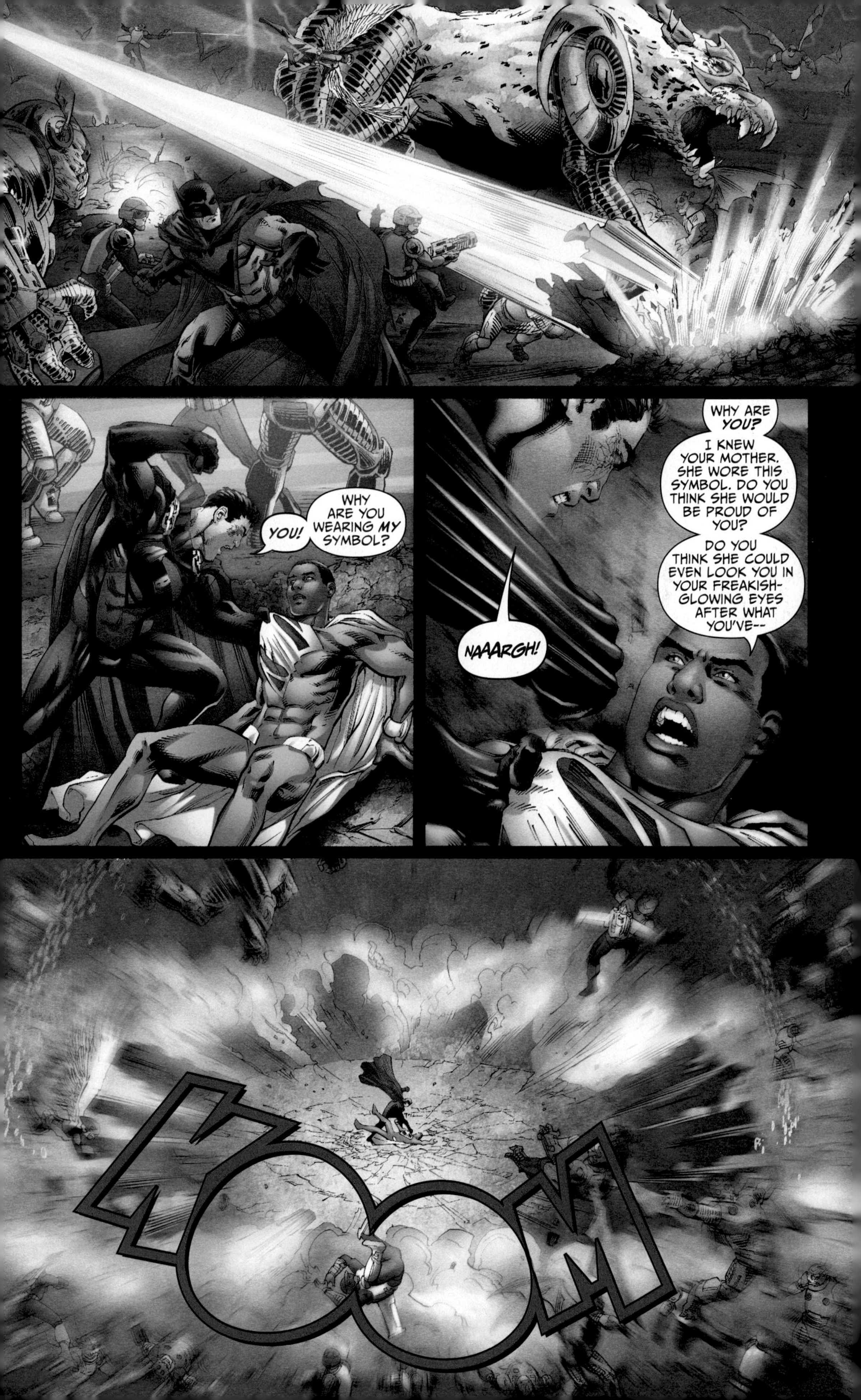
YOU!
WHY ARE YOU WEARING MY SYMBOL?
WHY ARE YOU?
I KNEW YOUR MOTHER. SHE WORE THIS SYMBOL. DO YOU THINK SHE WOULD BE PROUD OF YOU?
DO YOU THINK SHE COULD EVEN LOOK YOU IN YOUR FREAKISH-GLOWING EYES AFTER WHAT YOU'VE--
NAAARGH!
KOOM

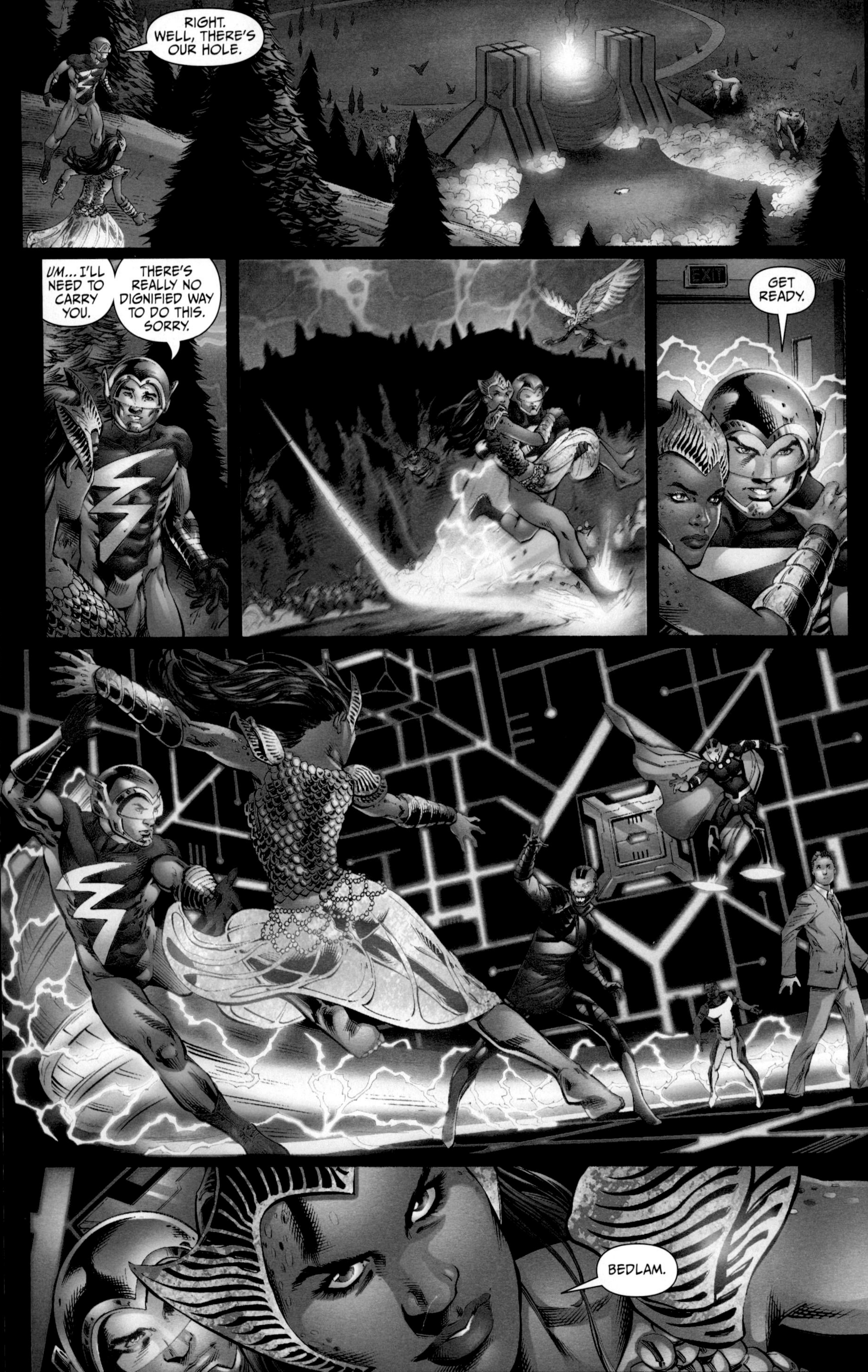
RIGHT. WELL, THERE'S OUR HOLE.
UM... I'LL NEED TO CARRY YOU.
THERE'S REALLY NO DIGNIFIED WAY TO DO THIS. SORRY.
EXIT
GET READY.
BEDLAM.

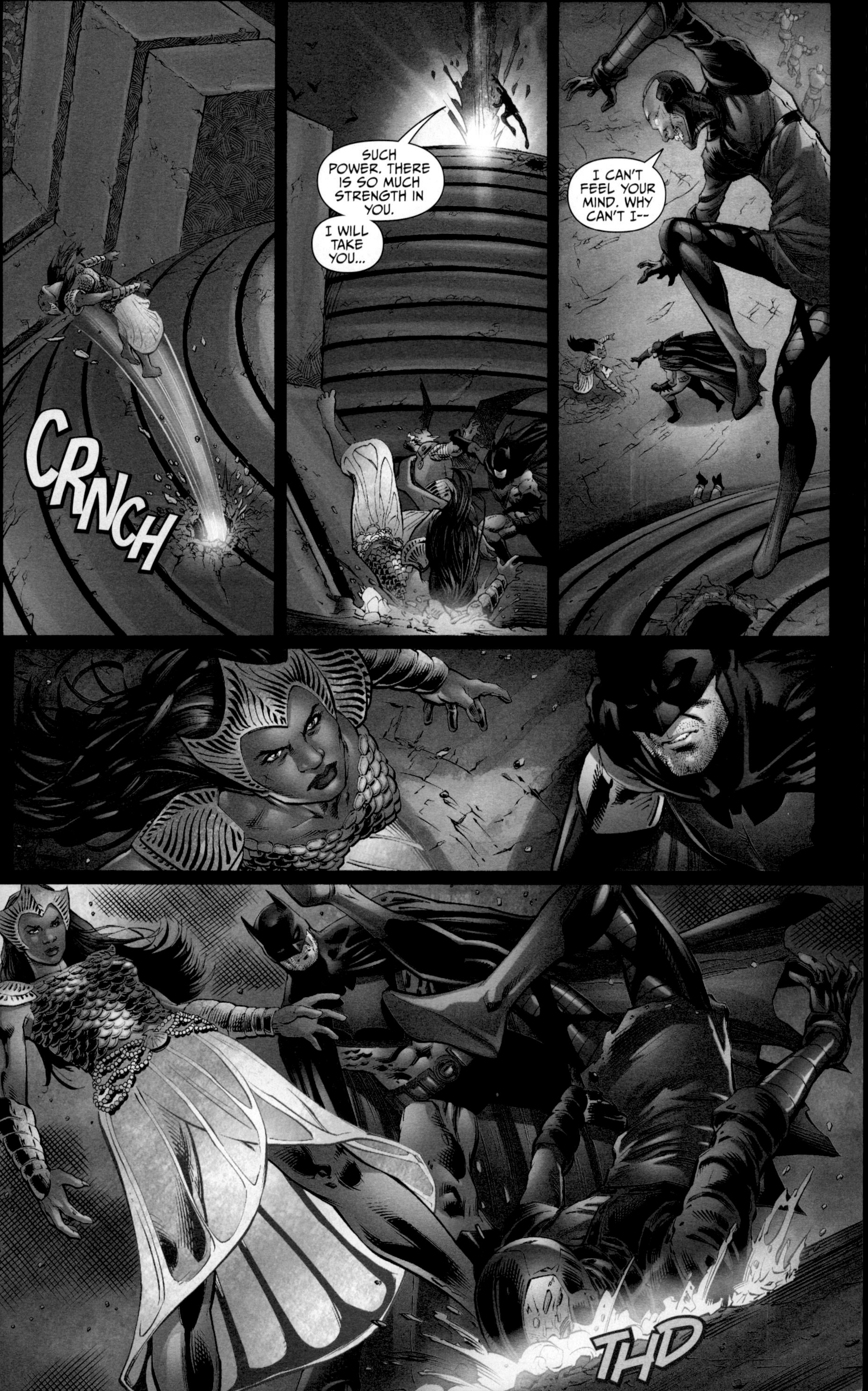
CRNCH
SUCH POWER. THERE IS SO MUCH STRENGTH IN YOU.
I WILL TAKE YOU...
I CAN'T FEEL YOUR MIND. WHY CAN'T I--
THD

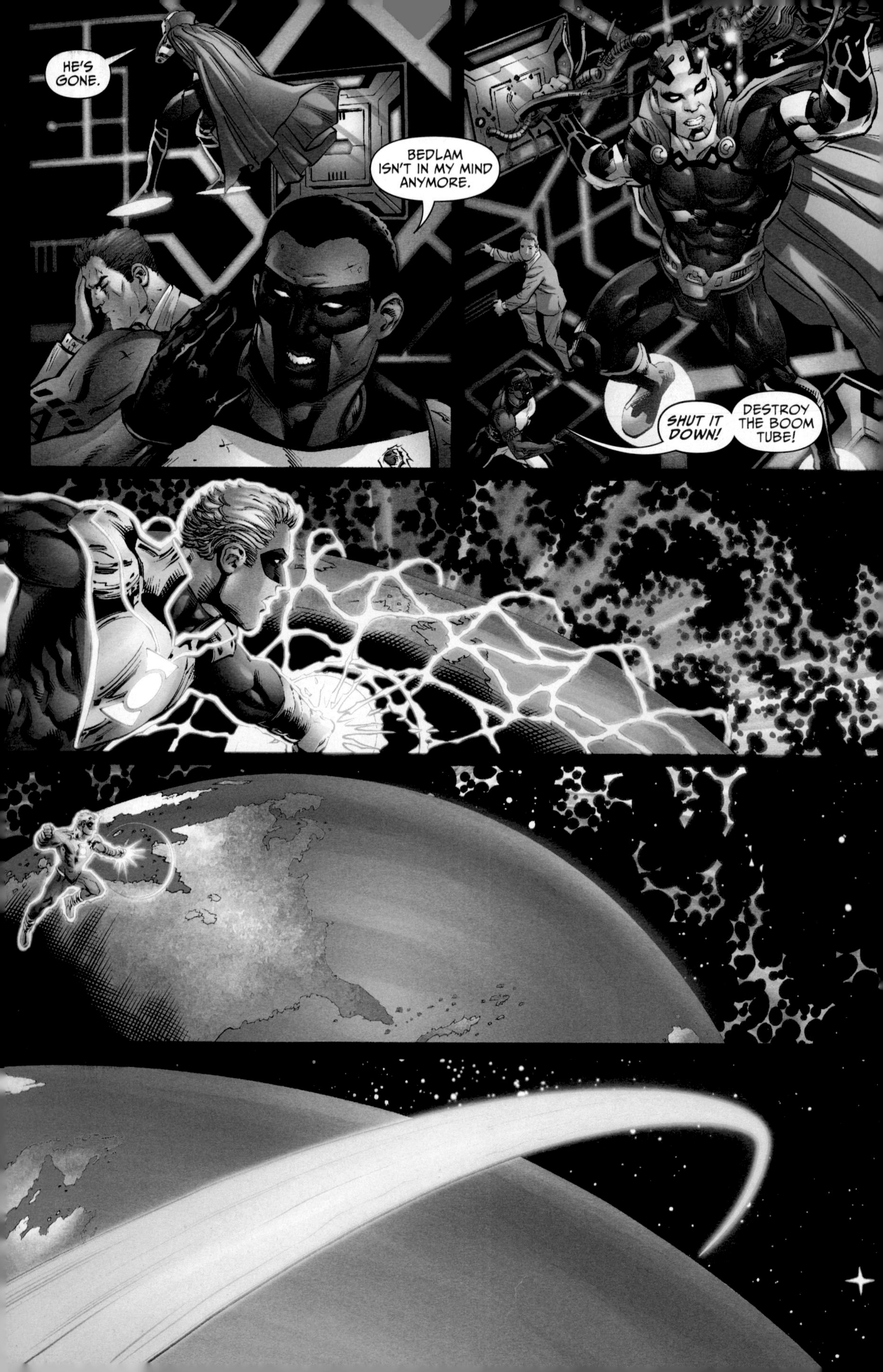
HE'S GONE.
BEDLAM ISN'T IN MY MIND ANYMORE.
SHUT IT DOWN!
DESTROY THE BOOM TUBE!

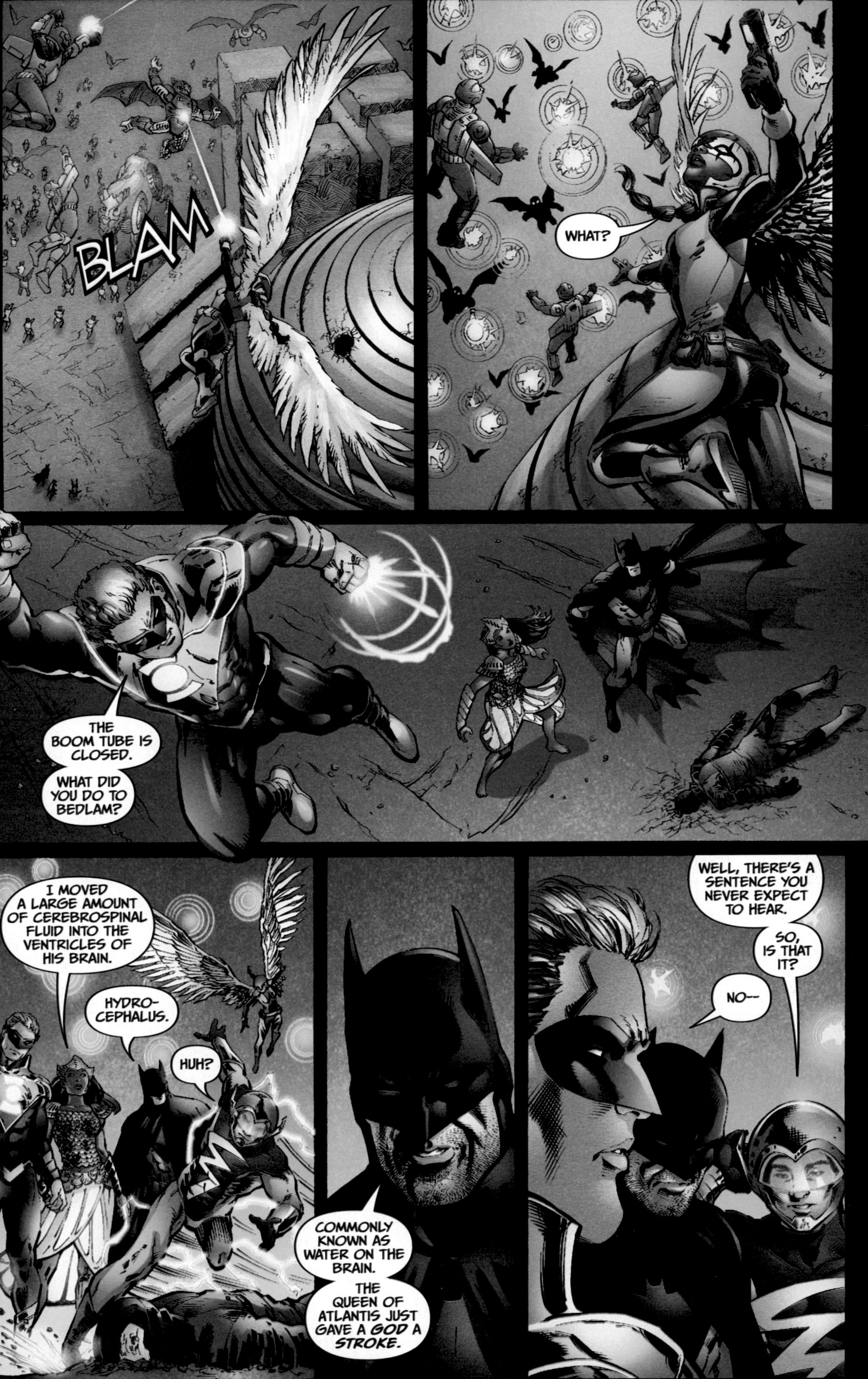
BLAM
WHAT?
THE BOOM TUBE IS CLOSED.
WHAT DID YOU DO TO BEDLAM?
I MOVED A LARGE AMOUNT OF CEREBROSPINAL FLUID INTO THE VENTRICLES OF HIS BRAIN.
HYDRO-CEPHALUS.
HUH?
COMMONLY KNOWN AS WATER ON THE BRAIN.
THE QUEEN OF ATLANTIS JUST GAVE A *GOD* A *STROKE*.
WELL, THERE'S A SENTENCE YOU NEVER EXPECT TO HEAR.
SO, IS THAT IT?
NO--

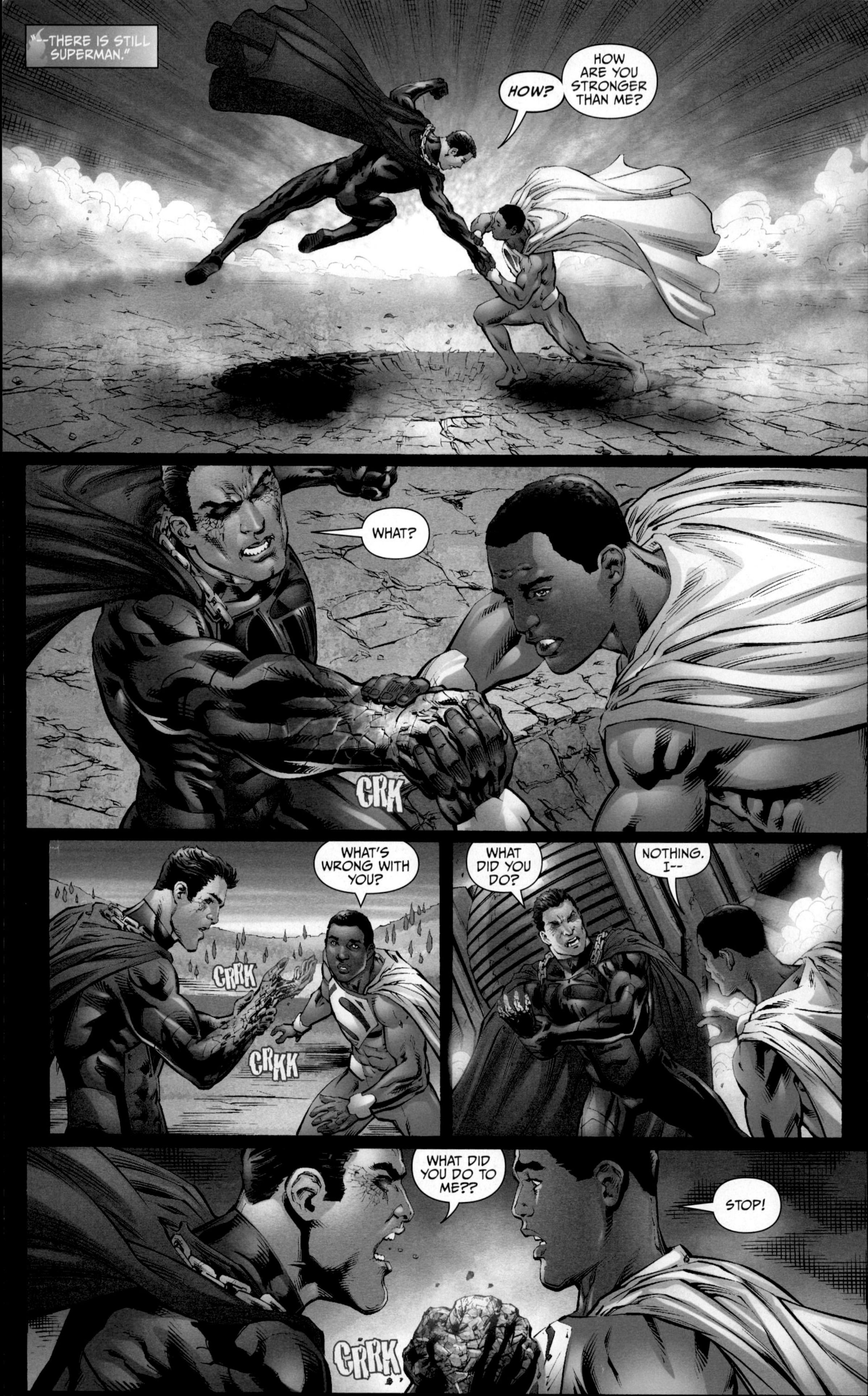
"--THERE IS STILL SUPERMAN."
HOW?
HOW ARE YOU STRONGER THAN ME?
WHAT?
CRK
WHAT'S WRONG WITH YOU?
CRRK
CRKK
WHAT DID YOU DO?
NOTHING. I--
WHAT DID YOU DO TO ME??
STOP!
CRRK

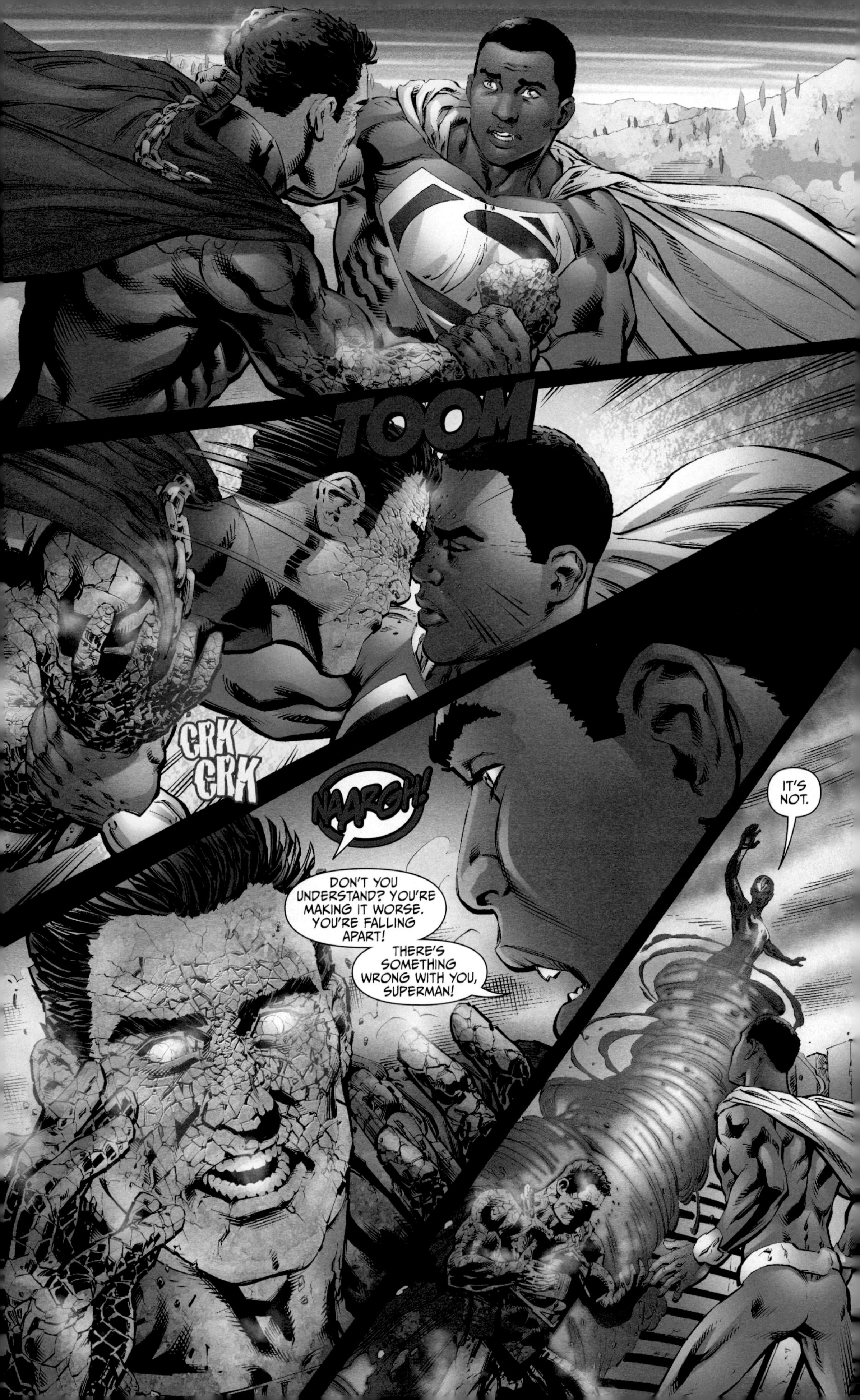
TOOM
CRK CRK
NAARGH!
DON'T YOU UNDERSTAND? YOU'RE MAKING IT WORSE. YOU'RE FALLING APART!
THERE'S SOMETHING WRONG WITH YOU, SUPERMAN!
IT'S NOT.

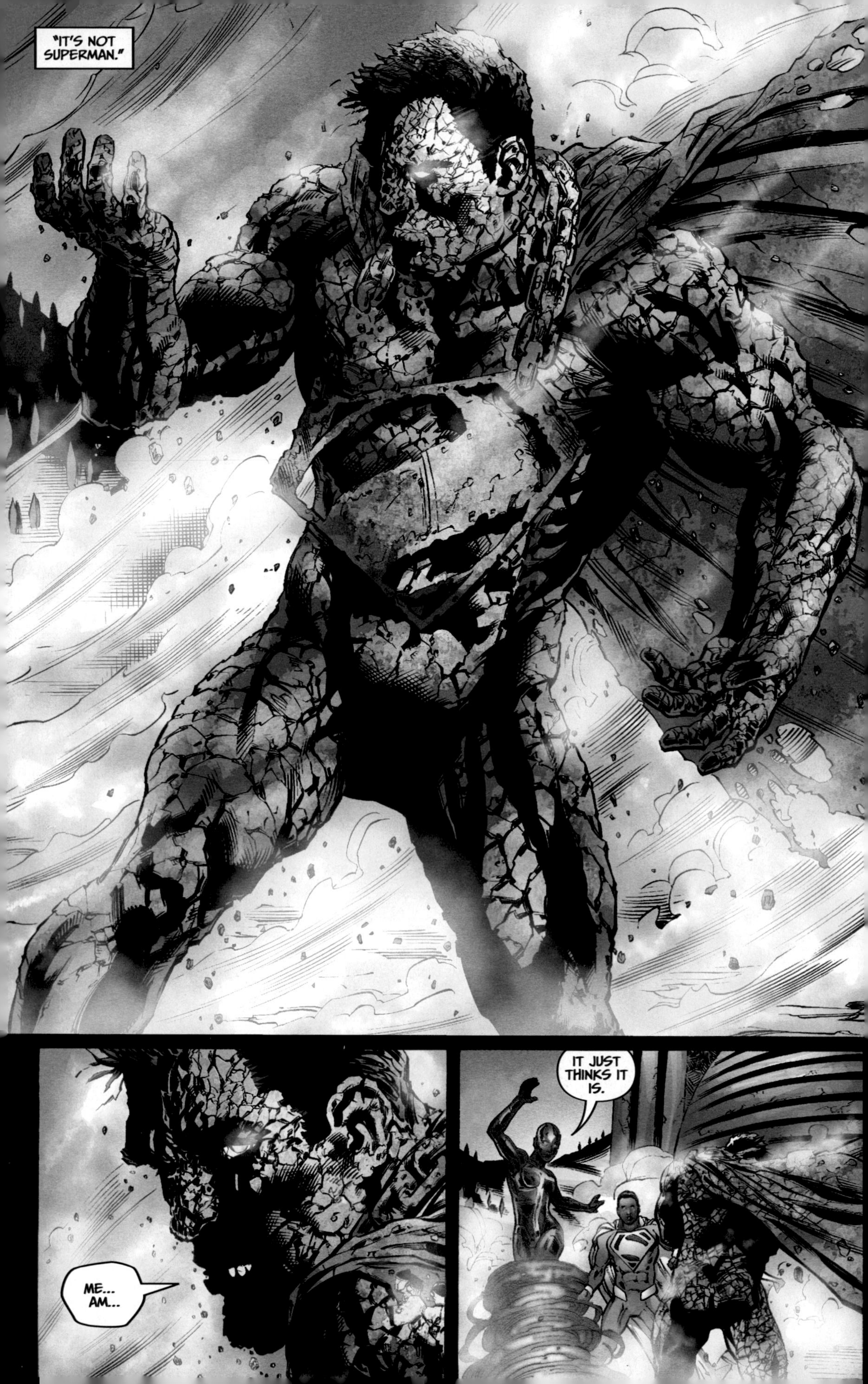
"IT'S NOT SUPERMAN."
ME... AM...
IT JUST THINKS IT IS.

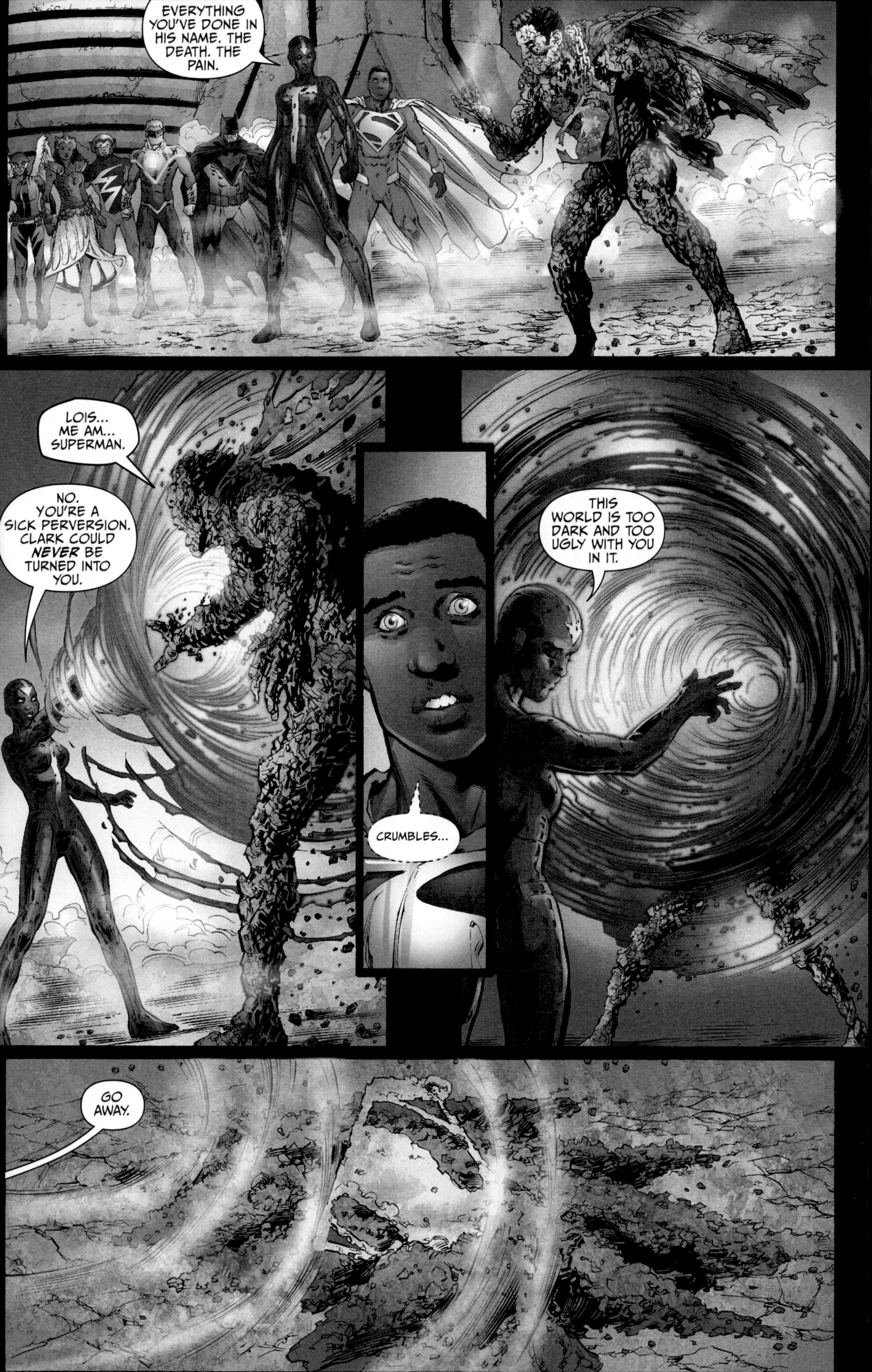
EVERYTHING YOU'VE DONE IN HIS NAME. THE DEATH. THE PAIN.
LOIS... ME AM... SUPERMAN.
NO. YOU'RE A SICK PERVERSION. CLARK COULD *NEVER* BE TURNED INTO YOU.
THIS WORLD IS TOO DARK AND TOO UGLY WITH YOU IN IT.
CRUMBLES...
GO AWAY.

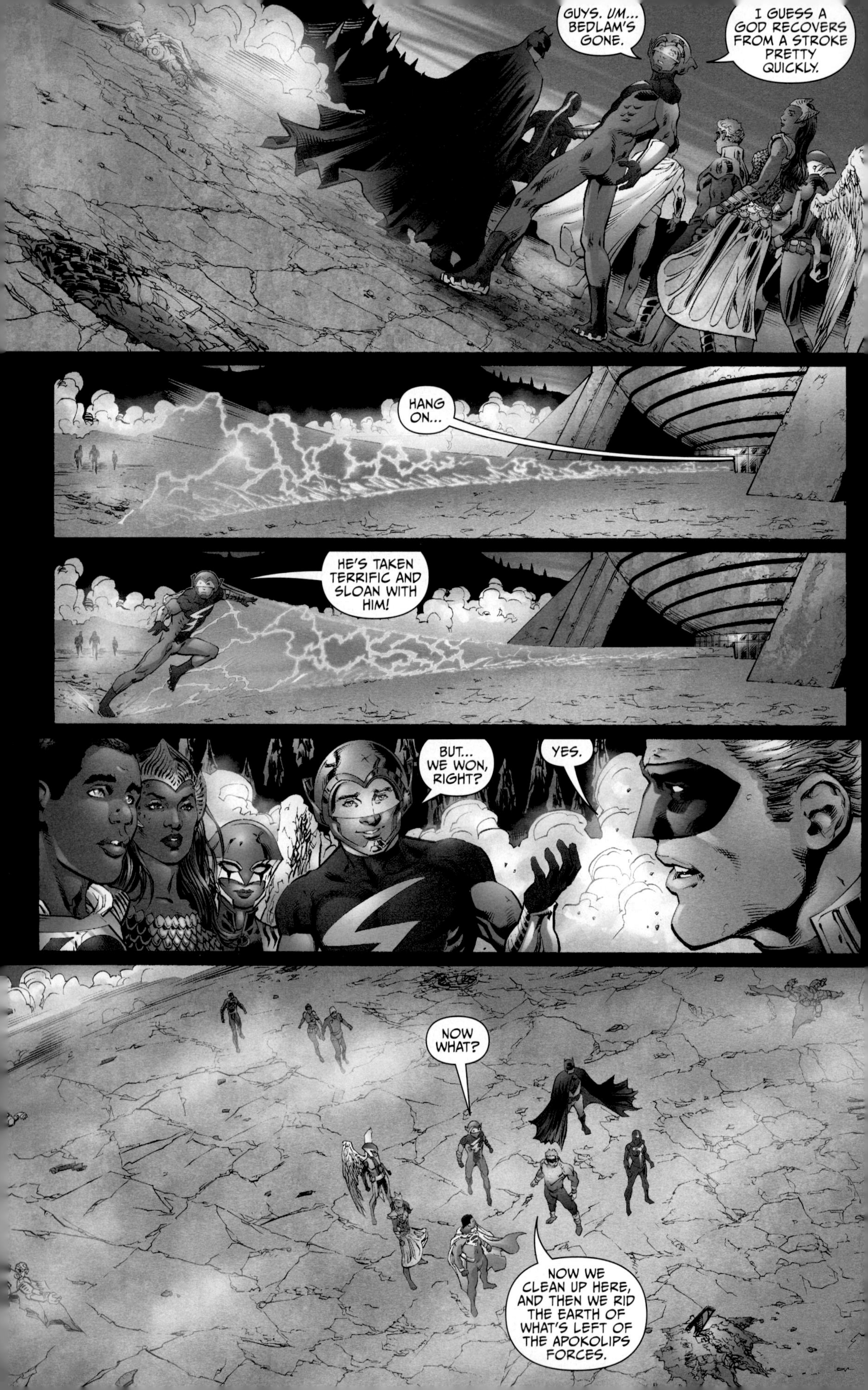
GUYS. UM... BEDLAM'S GONE.
I GUESS A GOD RECOVERS FROM A STROKE PRETTY QUICKLY.
HANG ON...
HE'S TAKEN TERRIFIC AND SLOAN WITH HIM!
BUT... WE WON, RIGHT?
YES.
NOW WHAT?
NOW WE CLEAN UP HERE, AND THEN WE RID THE EARTH OF WHAT'S LEFT OF THE APOKOLIPS FORCES.

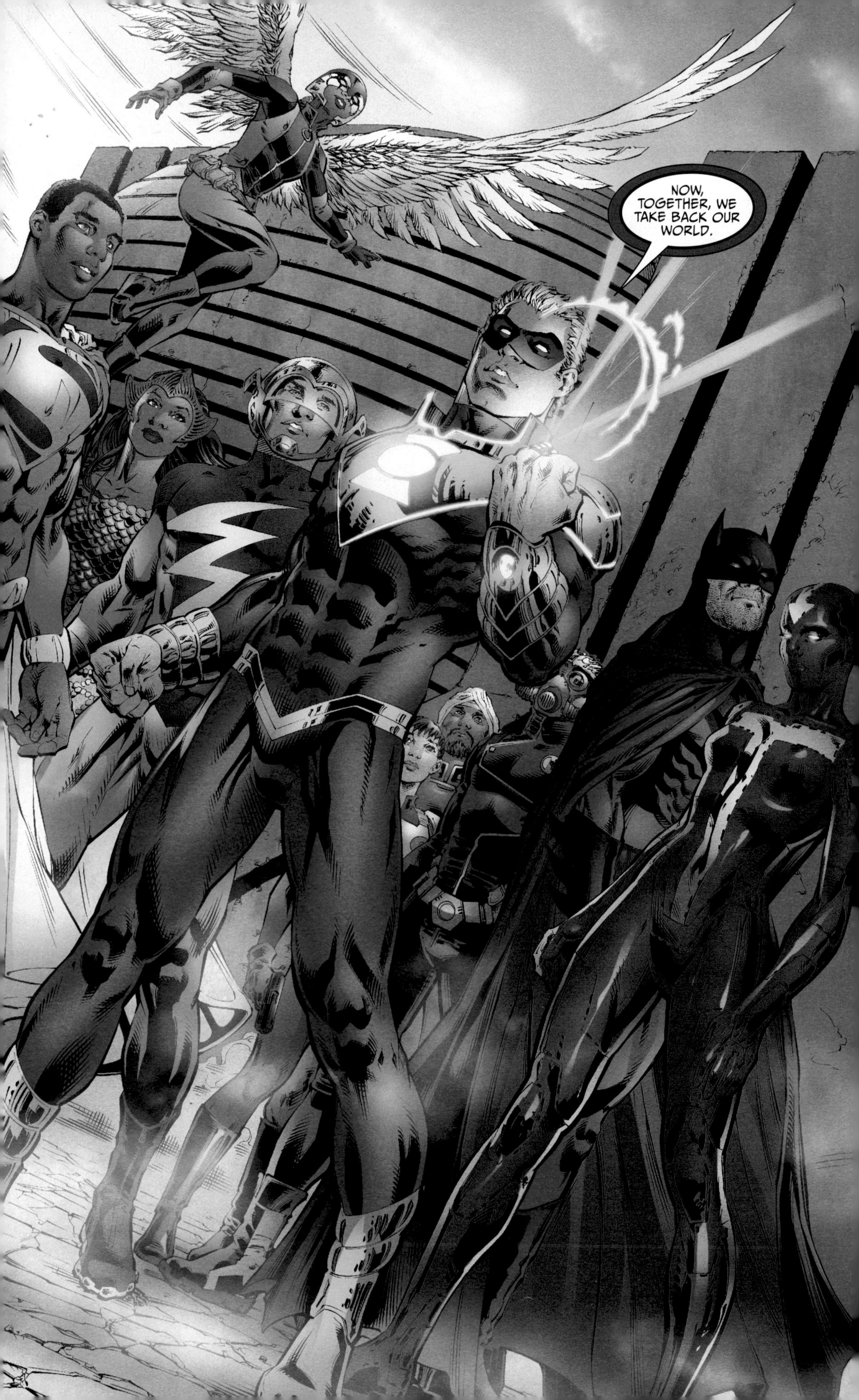
NOW, TOGETHER, WE TAKE BACK OUR WORLD.

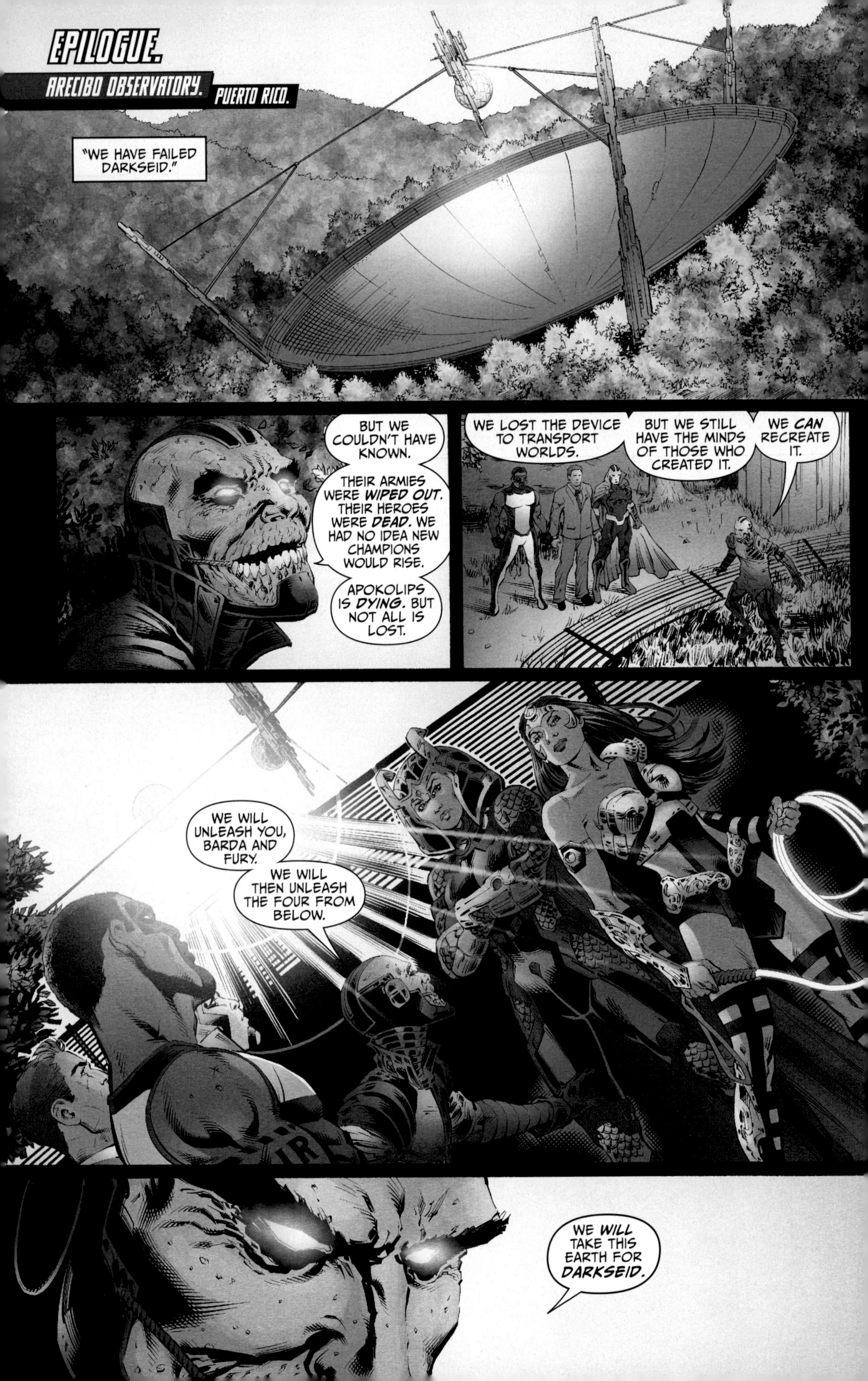
EPILOGUE.
ARECIBO OBSERVATORY.
PUERTO RICO.
"WE HAVE FAILED DARKSEID."
BUT WE COULDN'T HAVE KNOWN.
THEIR ARMIES WERE WIPED OUT. THEIR HEROES WERE DEAD. WE HAD NO IDEA NEW CHAMPIONS WOULD RISE.
APOKOLIPS IS DYING. BUT NOT ALL IS LOST.
WE LOST THE DEVICE TO TRANSPORT WORLDS.
BUT WE STILL HAVE THE MINDS OF THOSE WHO CREATED IT.
WE CAN RECREATE IT.
WE WILL UNLEASH YOU, BARDA AND FURY.
WE WILL THEN UNLEASH THE FOUR FROM BELOW.
WE WILL TAKE THIS EARTH FOR DARKSEID.

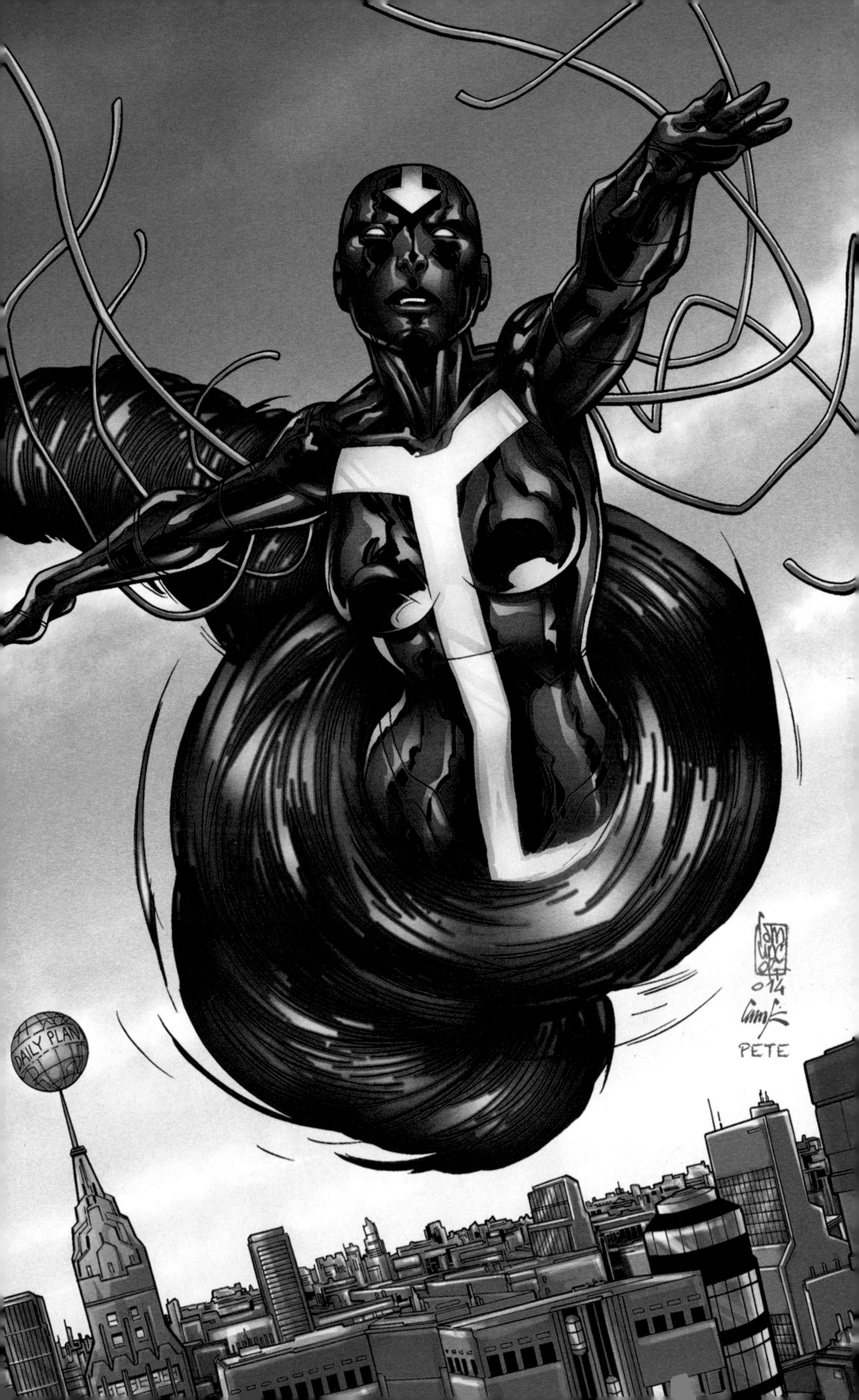
DAILY PLAN
PETE

POWER TO THE PEOPLE

DANIEL H. WILSON writer **EDDY BARROWS** penciller **EBER FERREIRA** inker **PETE PANTAZIS** colorist cover by **GIUSEPPE CAMUNCOLI** & **PETE PANTAZIS**

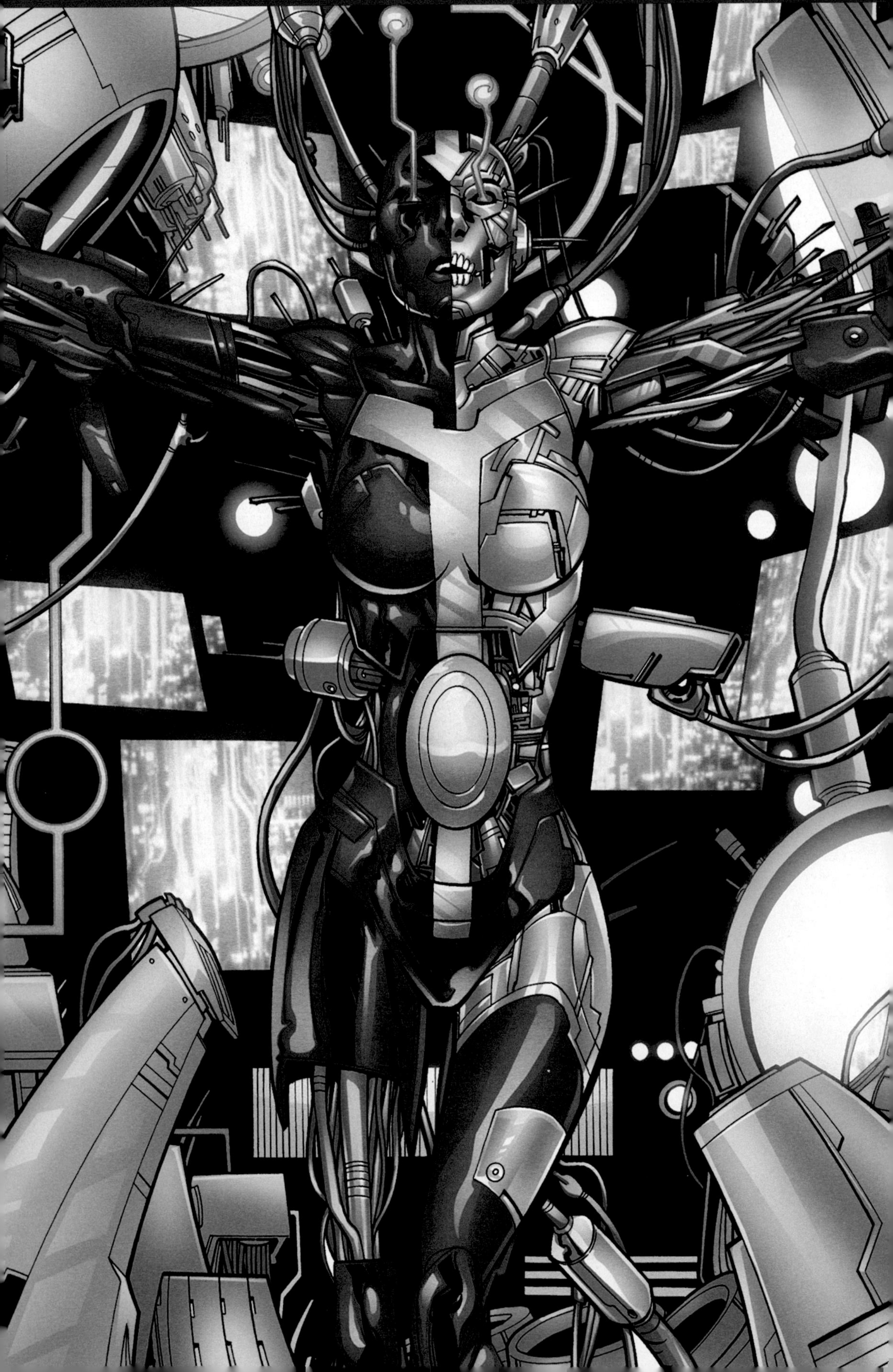

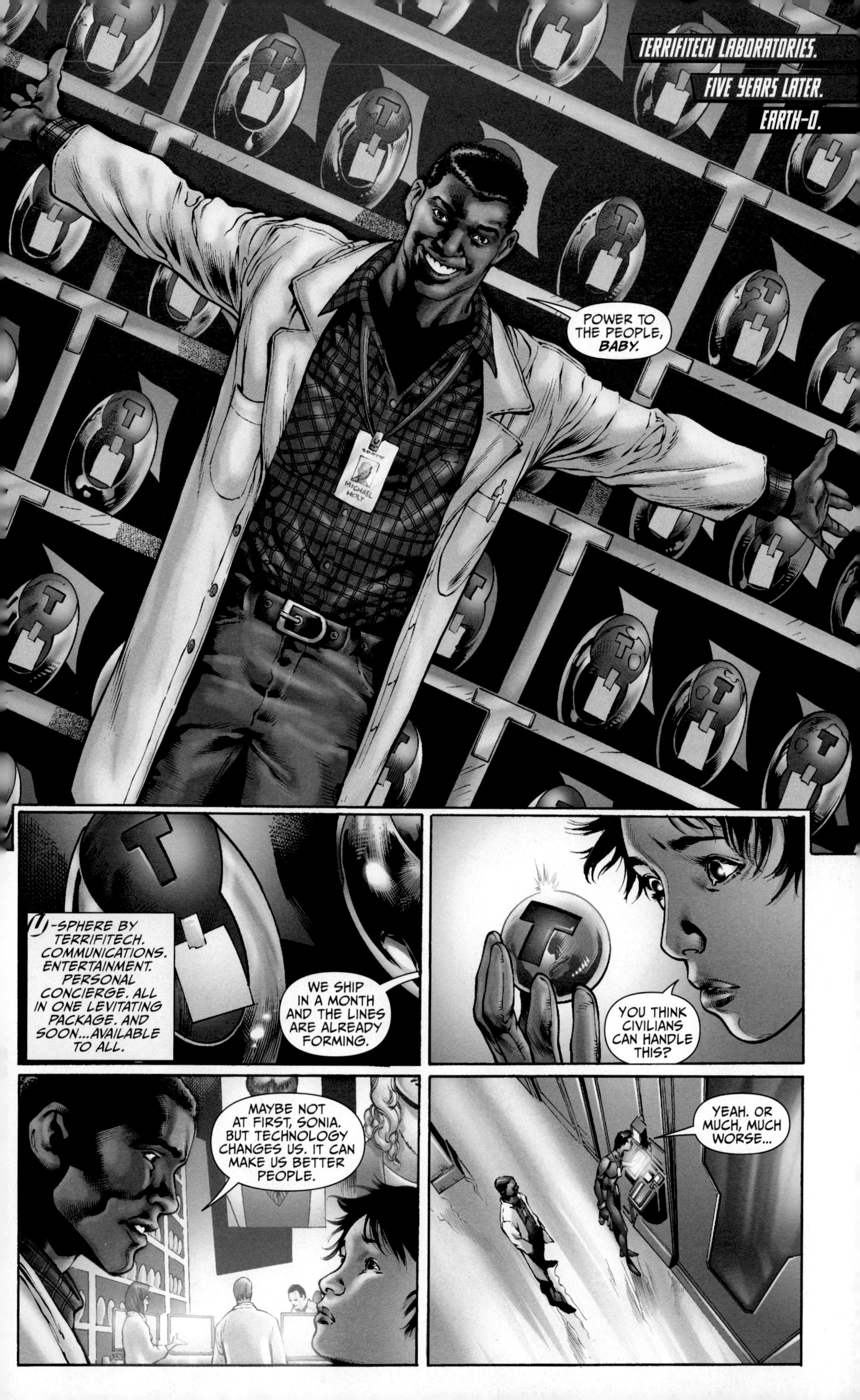
TERRIFITECH LABORATORIES.
FIVE YEARS LATER.
EARTH-0.
POWER TO THE PEOPLE, BABY.
MICHAEL HOLT
U-SPHERE BY TERRIFITECH. COMMUNICATIONS. ENTERTAINMENT. PERSONAL CONCIERGE. ALL IN ONE LEVITATING PACKAGE. AND SOON...AVAILABLE TO ALL.
WE SHIP IN A MONTH AND THE LINES ARE ALREADY FORMING.
YOU THINK CIVILIANS CAN HANDLE THIS?
MAYBE NOT AT FIRST, SONIA. BUT TECHNOLOGY CHANGES US. IT CAN MAKE US BETTER PEOPLE.
YEAH. OR MUCH, MUCH WORSE...

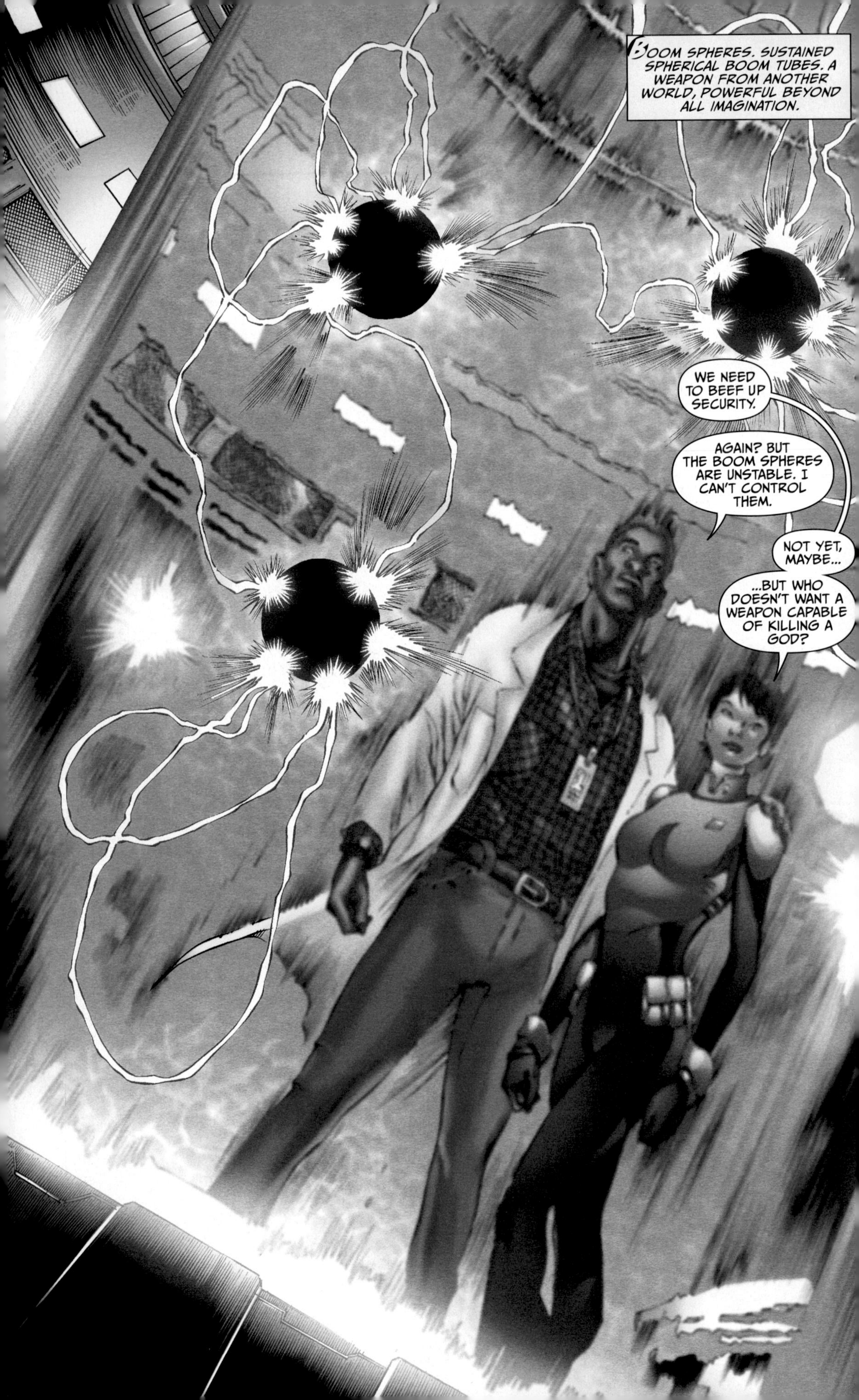
BOOM SPHERES. SUSTAINED SPHERICAL BOOM TUBES. A WEAPON FROM ANOTHER WORLD, POWERFUL BEYOND ALL IMAGINATION.
WE NEED TO BEEF UP SECURITY.
AGAIN? BUT THE BOOM SPHERES ARE UNSTABLE. I CAN'T CONTROL THEM.
NOT YET, MAYBE...
...BUT WHO DOESN'T WANT A WEAPON CAPABLE OF KILLING A GOD?

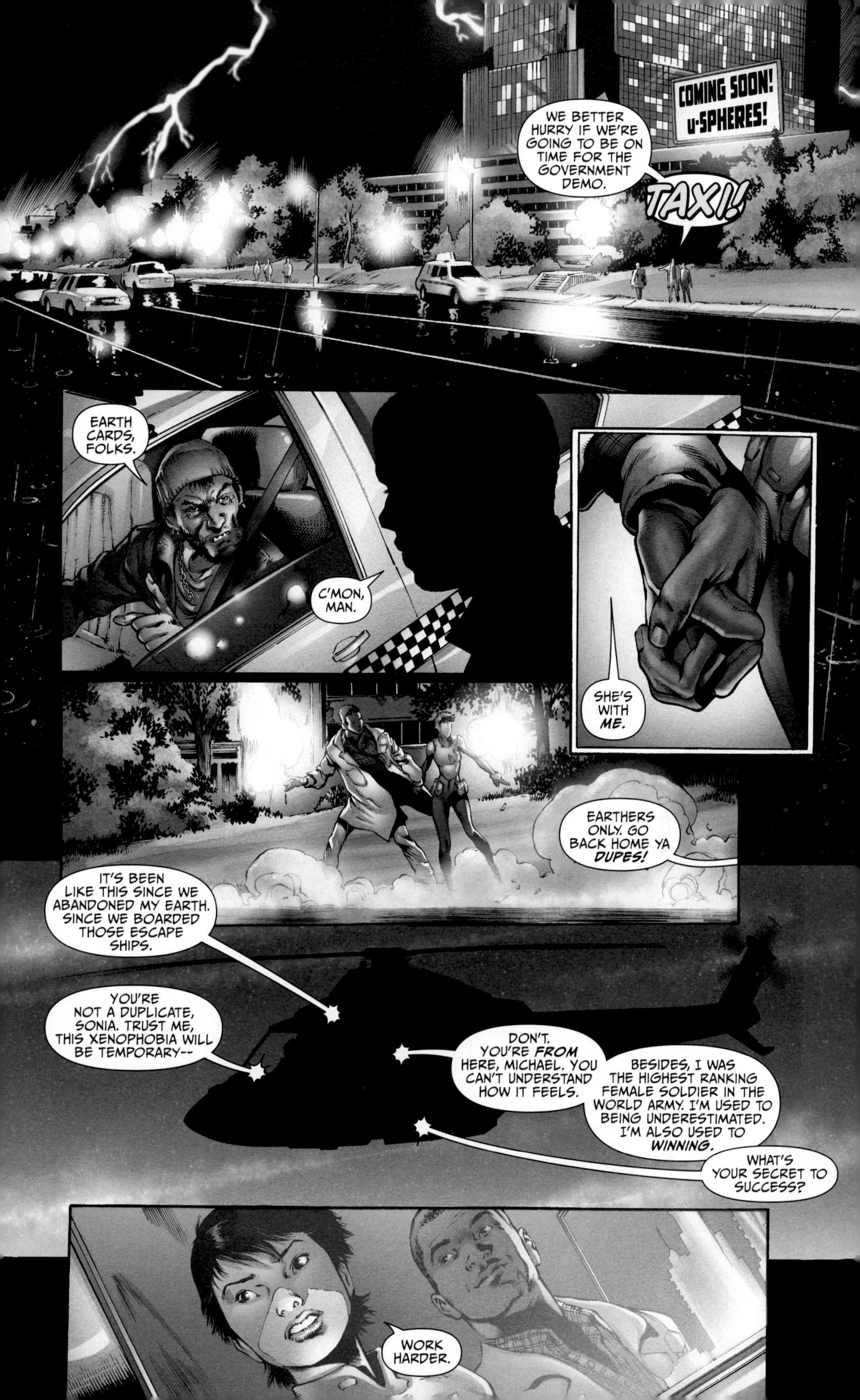
COMING SOON! u-SPHERES!
WE BETTER HURRY IF WE'RE GOING TO BE ON TIME FOR THE GOVERNMENT DEMO.
TAXI!
EARTH CARDS, FOLKS.
C'MON, MAN.
SHE'S WITH *ME.*
EARTHERS ONLY. GO BACK HOME YA *DUPES!*
IT'S BEEN LIKE THIS SINCE WE ABANDONED MY EARTH. SINCE WE BOARDED THOSE ESCAPE SHIPS.
YOU'RE NOT A DUPLICATE, SONIA. TRUST ME, THIS XENOPHOBIA WILL BE TEMPORARY--
DON'T. YOU'RE *FROM* HERE, MICHAEL. YOU CAN'T UNDERSTAND HOW IT FEELS.
BESIDES, I WAS THE HIGHEST RANKING FEMALE SOLDIER IN THE WORLD ARMY. I'M USED TO BEING UNDERESTIMATED. I'M ALSO USED TO *WINNING.*
WHAT'S YOUR SECRET TO SUCCESS?
WORK HARDER.

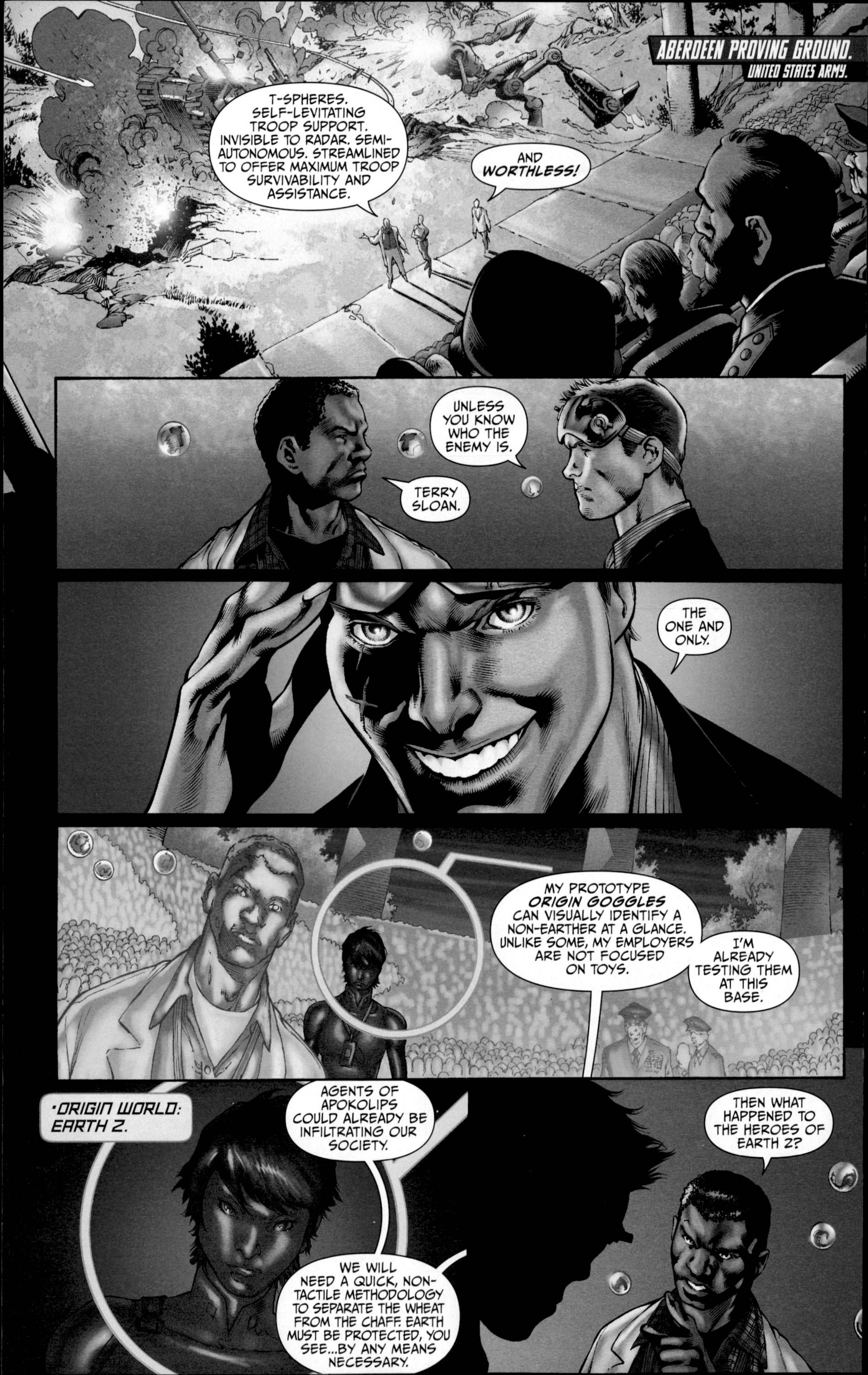
ABERDEEN PROVING GROUND.
UNITED STATES ARMY.
T-SPHERES. SELF-LEVITATING TROOP SUPPORT. INVISIBLE TO RADAR. SEMI-AUTONOMOUS. STREAMLINED TO OFFER MAXIMUM TROOP SURVIVABILITY AND ASSISTANCE.
AND WORTHLESS!
UNLESS YOU KNOW WHO THE ENEMY IS.
TERRY SLOAN.
THE ONE AND ONLY.
MY PROTOTYPE ORIGIN GOGGLES CAN VISUALLY IDENTIFY A NON-EARTHER AT A GLANCE. UNLIKE SOME, MY EMPLOYERS ARE NOT FOCUSED ON TOYS.
I'M ALREADY TESTING THEM AT THIS BASE.
•ORIGIN WORLD: EARTH 2.
AGENTS OF APOKOLIPS COULD ALREADY BE INFILTRATING OUR SOCIETY.
WE WILL NEED A QUICK, NON-TACTILE METHODOLOGY TO SEPARATE THE WHEAT FROM THE CHAFF. EARTH MUST BE PROTECTED, YOU SEE...BY ANY MEANS NECESSARY.
THEN WHAT HAPPENED TO THE HEROES OF EARTH 2?

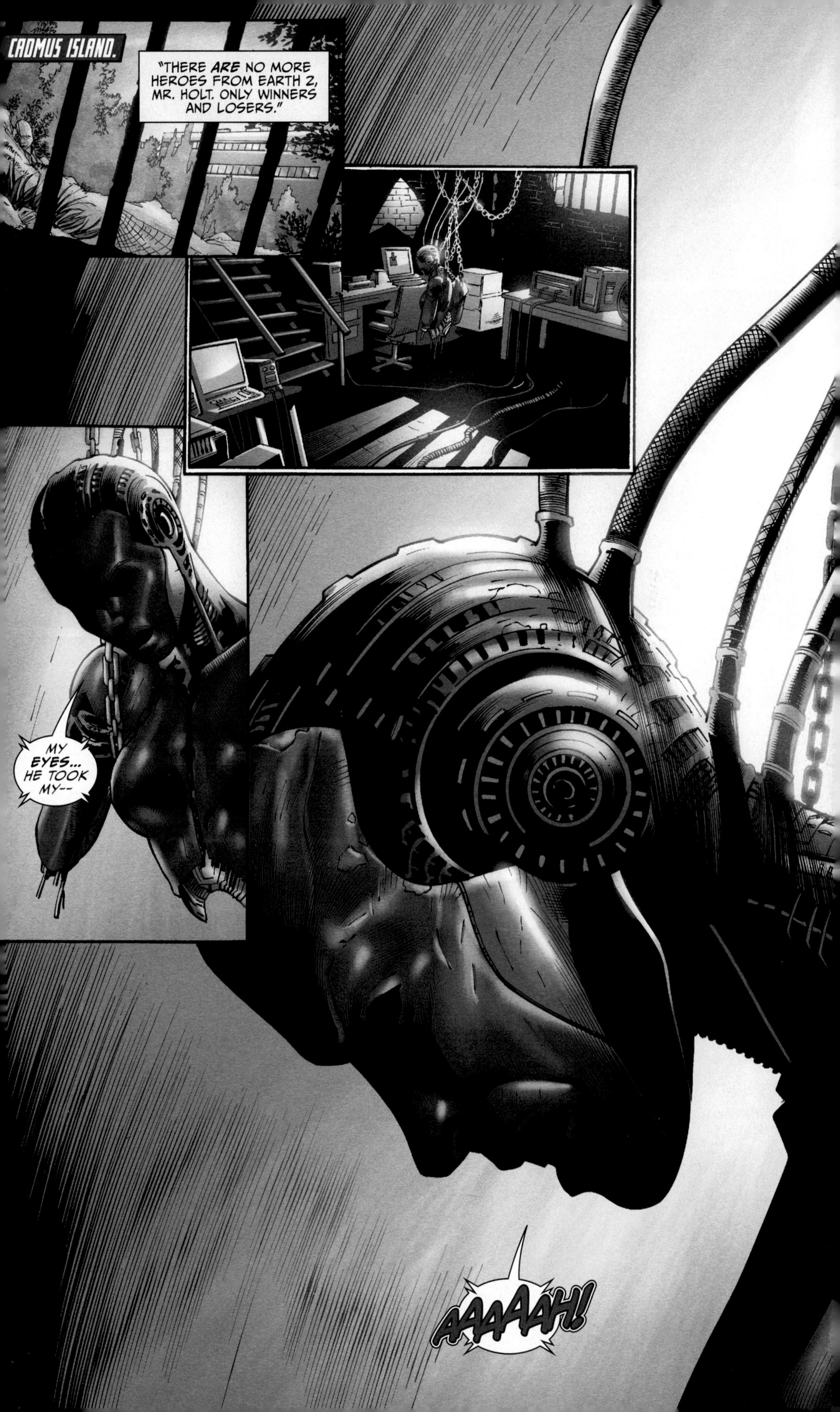
CADMUS ISLAND.
"THERE ARE NO MORE HEROES FROM EARTH 2, MR. HOLT. ONLY WINNERS AND LOSERS."
MY EYES... HE TOOK MY--
AAAAAH!

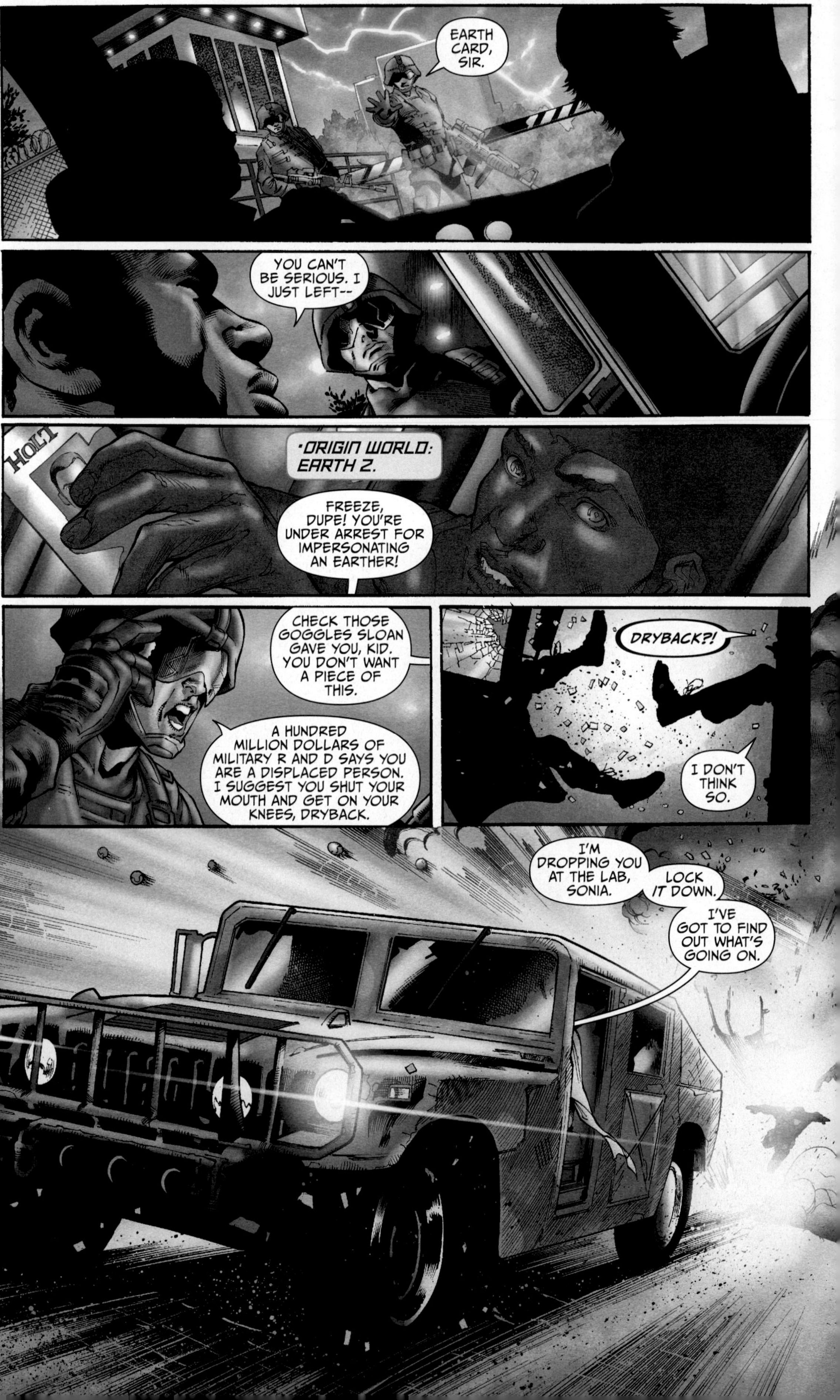
EARTH CARD, SIR.
YOU CAN'T BE SERIOUS. I JUST LEFT--
HOLT
·ORIGIN WORLD: EARTH 2.
FREEZE, DUPE! YOU'RE UNDER ARREST FOR IMPERSONATING AN EARTHER!
CHECK THOSE GOGGLES SLOAN GAVE YOU, KID. YOU DON'T WANT A PIECE OF THIS.
A HUNDRED MILLION DOLLARS OF MILITARY R AND D SAYS YOU ARE A DISPLACED PERSON. I SUGGEST YOU SHUT YOUR MOUTH AND GET ON YOUR KNEES, DRYBACK.
DRYBACK?!
I DON'T THINK SO.
I'M DROPPING YOU AT THE LAB, SONIA.
LOCK IT DOWN.
I'VE GOT TO FIND OUT WHAT'S GOING ON.

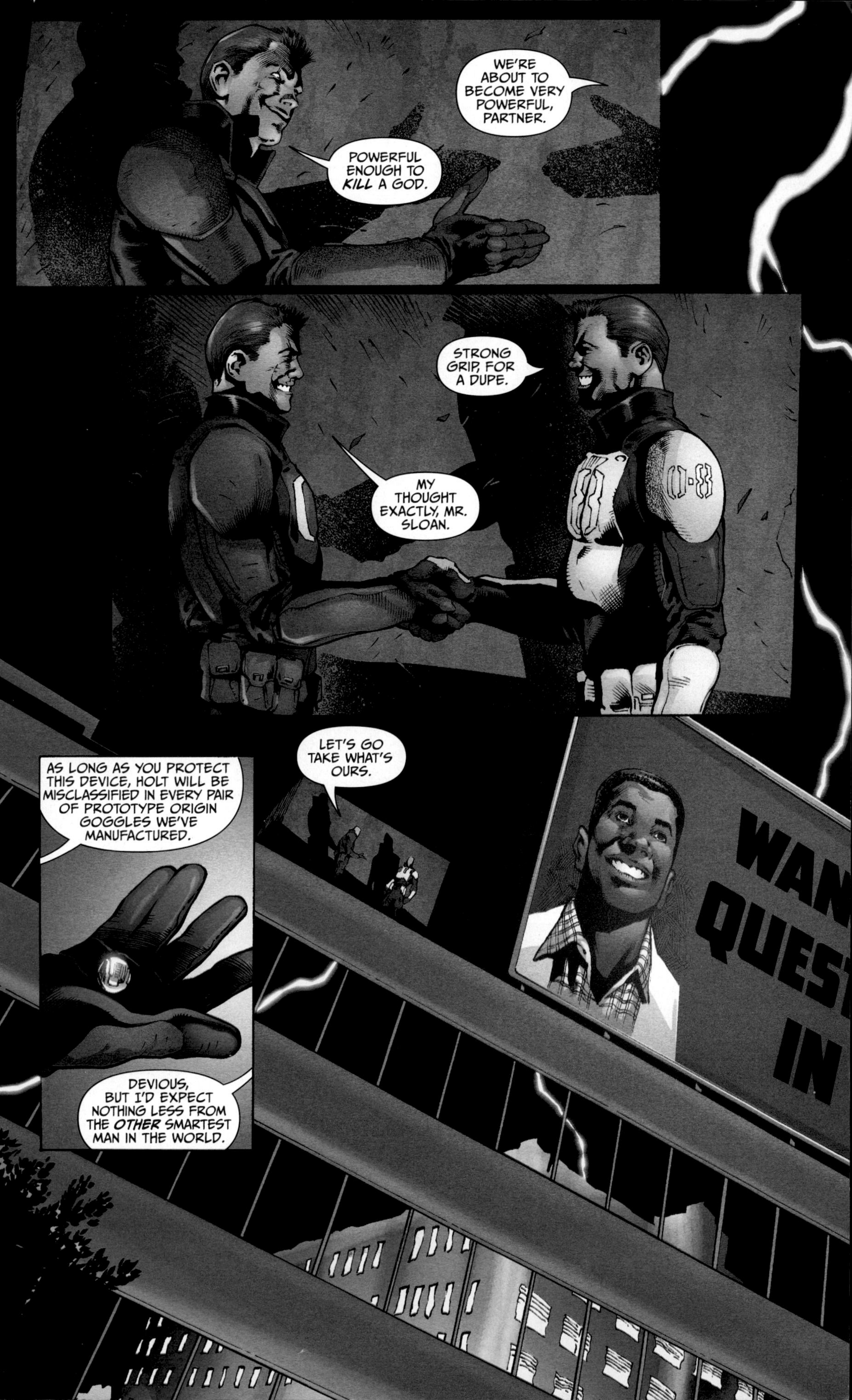
WE'RE ABOUT TO BECOME VERY POWERFUL, PARTNER.
POWERFUL ENOUGH TO KILL A GOD.
STRONG GRIP, FOR A DUPE.
MY THOUGHT EXACTLY, MR. SLOAN.
AS LONG AS YOU PROTECT THIS DEVICE, HOLT WILL BE MISCLASSIFIED IN EVERY PAIR OF PROTOTYPE ORIGIN GOGGLES WE'VE MANUFACTURED.
LET'S GO TAKE WHAT'S OURS.
DEVIOUS, BUT I'D EXPECT NOTHING LESS FROM THE OTHER SMARTEST MAN IN THE WORLD.

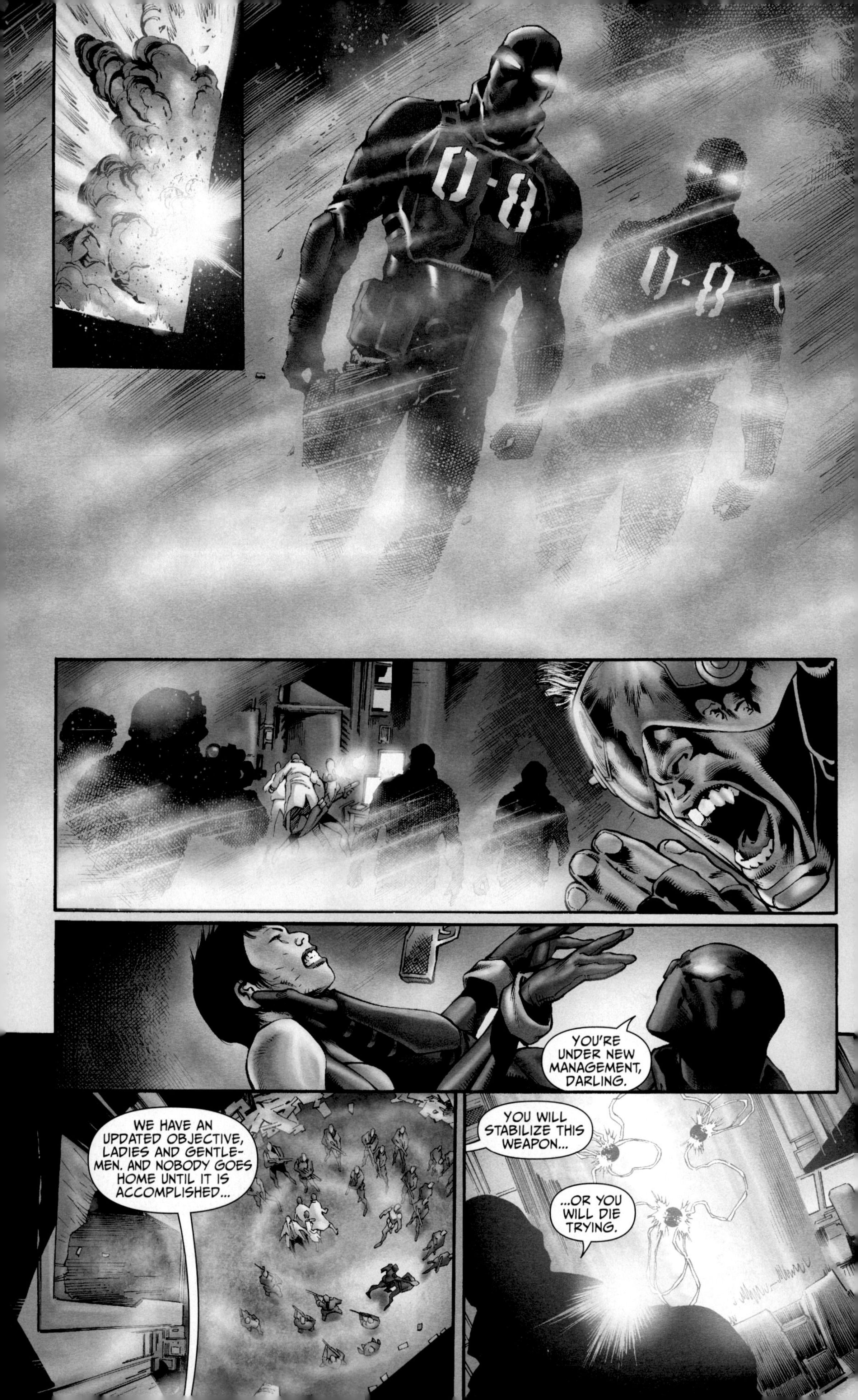
0-8
0-8
YOU'RE UNDER NEW MANAGEMENT, DARLING.
WE HAVE AN UPDATED OBJECTIVE, LADIES AND GENTLEMEN. AND NOBODY GOES HOME UNTIL IT IS ACCOMPLISHED...
YOU WILL STABILIZE THIS WEAPON...
...OR YOU WILL DIE TRYING.

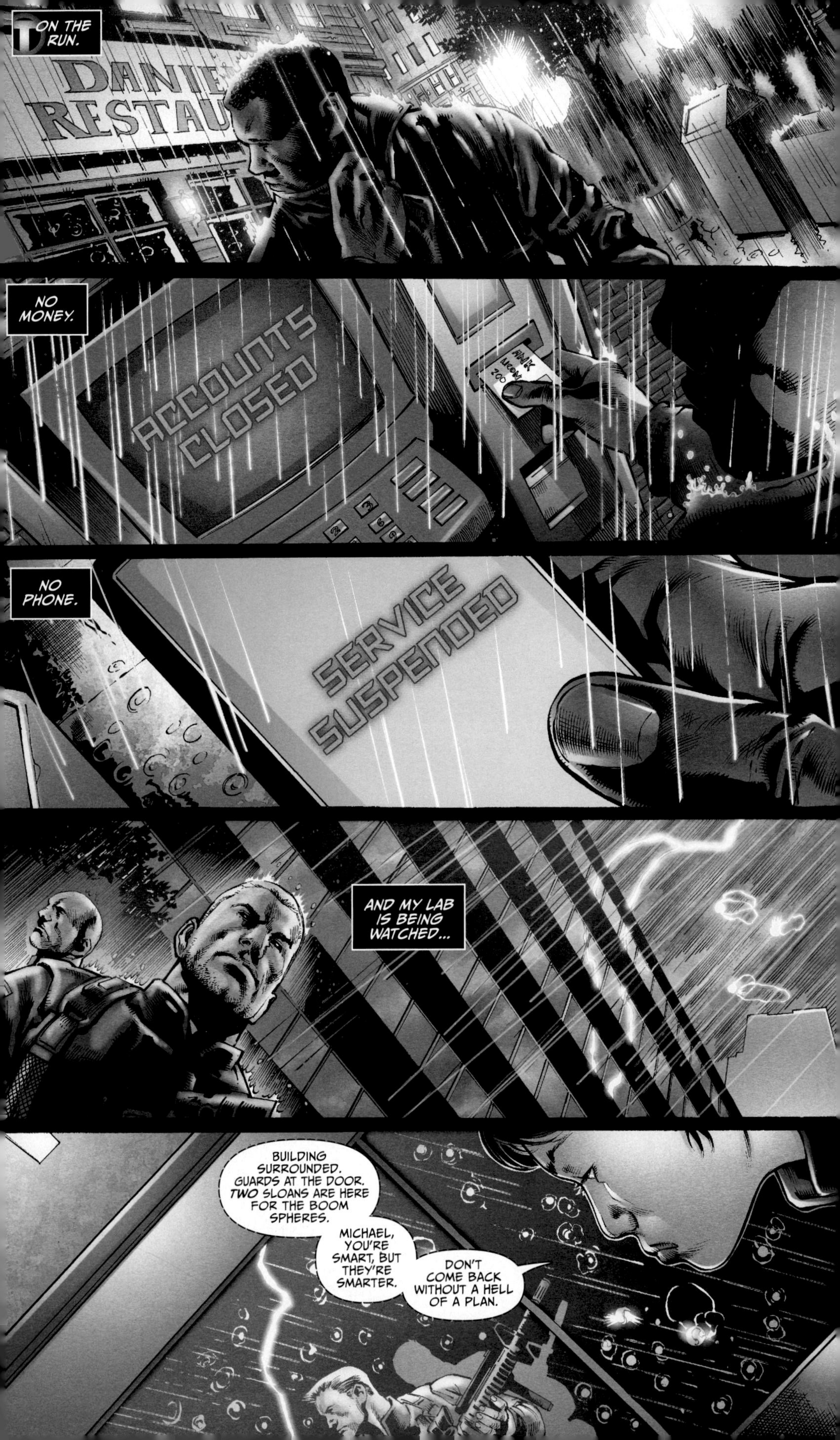

ON THE RUN.
DANIE
RESTAU
NO MONEY.
ACCOUNTS CLOSED
NO PHONE.
SERVICE SUSPENDED
AND MY LAB IS BEING WATCHED...
BUILDING SURROUNDED. GUARDS AT THE DOOR. TWO SLOANS ARE HERE FOR THE BOOM SPHERES.
MICHAEL, YOU'RE SMART, BUT THEY'RE SMARTER.
DON'T COME BACK WITHOUT A HELL OF A PLAN.

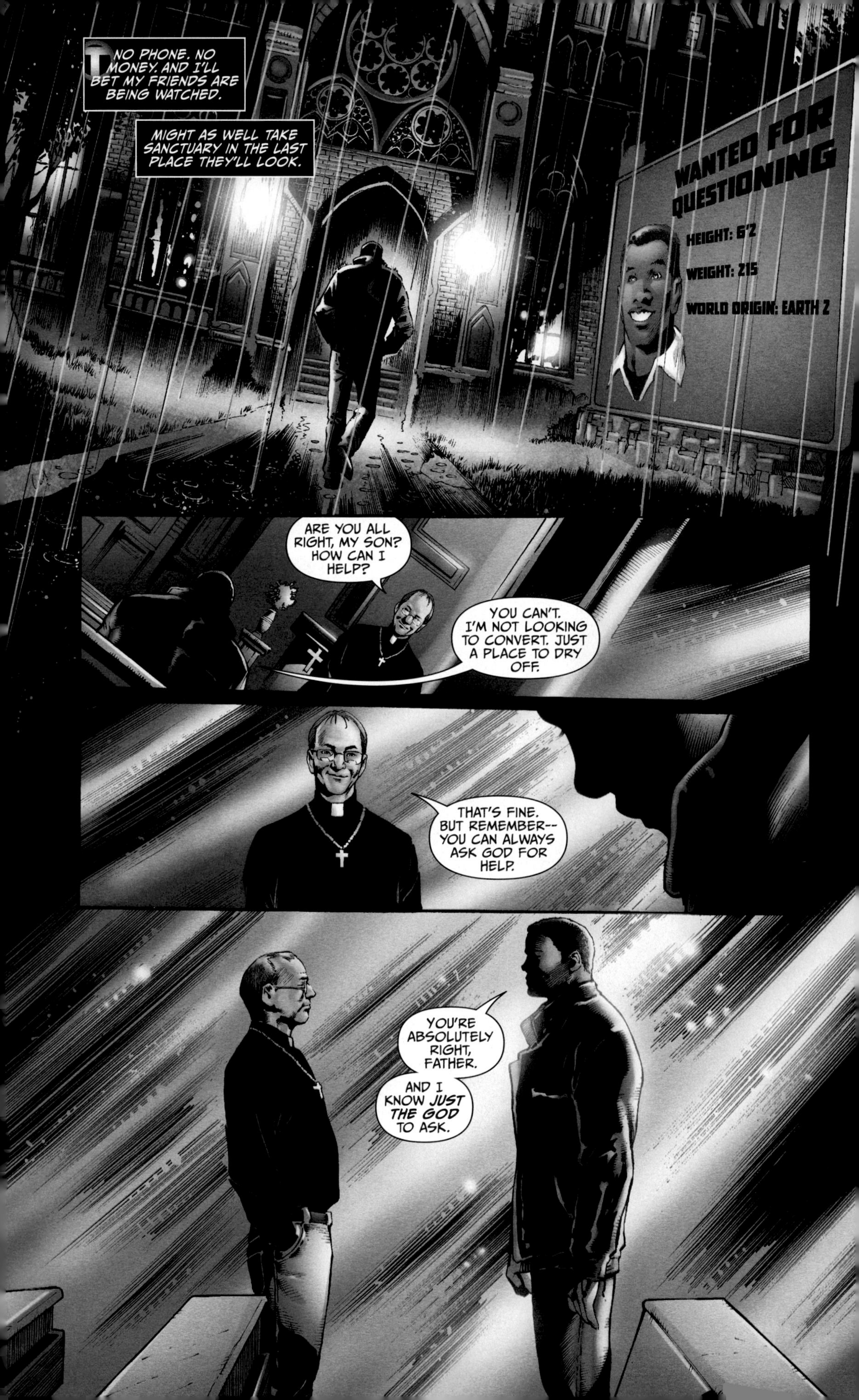
NO PHONE. NO MONEY. AND I'LL BET MY FRIENDS ARE BEING WATCHED.
MIGHT AS WELL TAKE SANCTUARY IN THE LAST PLACE THEY'LL LOOK.
WANTED FOR QUESTIONING
HEIGHT: 6'2
WEIGHT: 215
WORLD ORIGIN: EARTH 2
ARE YOU ALL RIGHT, MY SON? HOW CAN I HELP?
YOU CAN'T. I'M NOT LOOKING TO CONVERT. JUST A PLACE TO DRY OFF.
THAT'S FINE. BUT REMEMBER-- YOU CAN ALWAYS ASK GOD FOR HELP.
YOU'RE ABSOLUTELY RIGHT, FATHER.
AND I KNOW *JUST THE GOD* TO ASK.

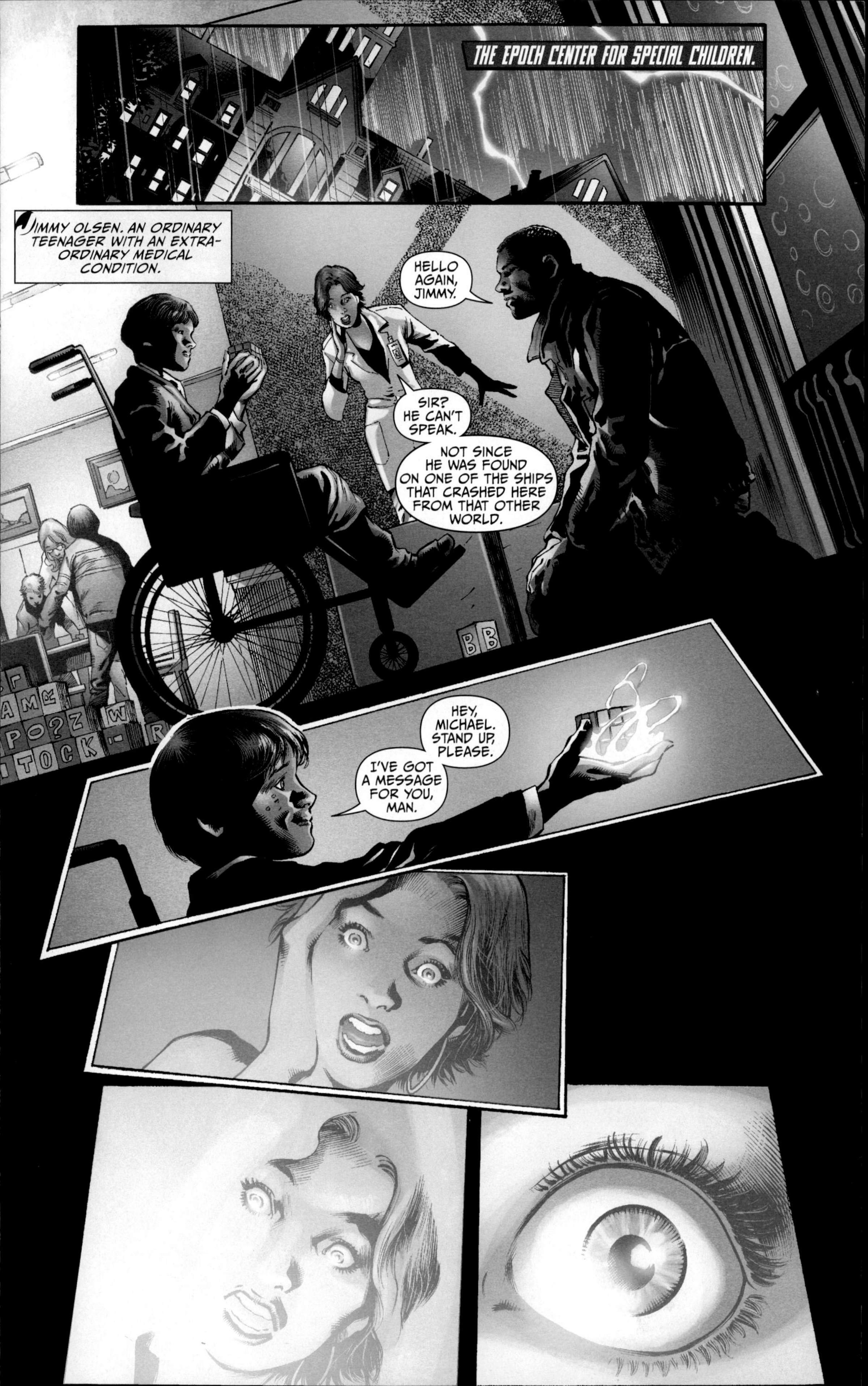
THE EPOCH CENTER FOR SPECIAL CHILDREN.
JIMMY OLSEN. AN ORDINARY TEENAGER WITH AN EXTRA-ORDINARY MEDICAL CONDITION.
HELLO AGAIN, JIMMY.
SIR? HE CAN'T SPEAK.
NOT SINCE HE WAS FOUND ON ONE OF THE SHIPS THAT CRASHED HERE FROM THAT OTHER WORLD.
HEY, MICHAEL. STAND UP, PLEASE.
I'VE GOT A MESSAGE FOR YOU, MAN.

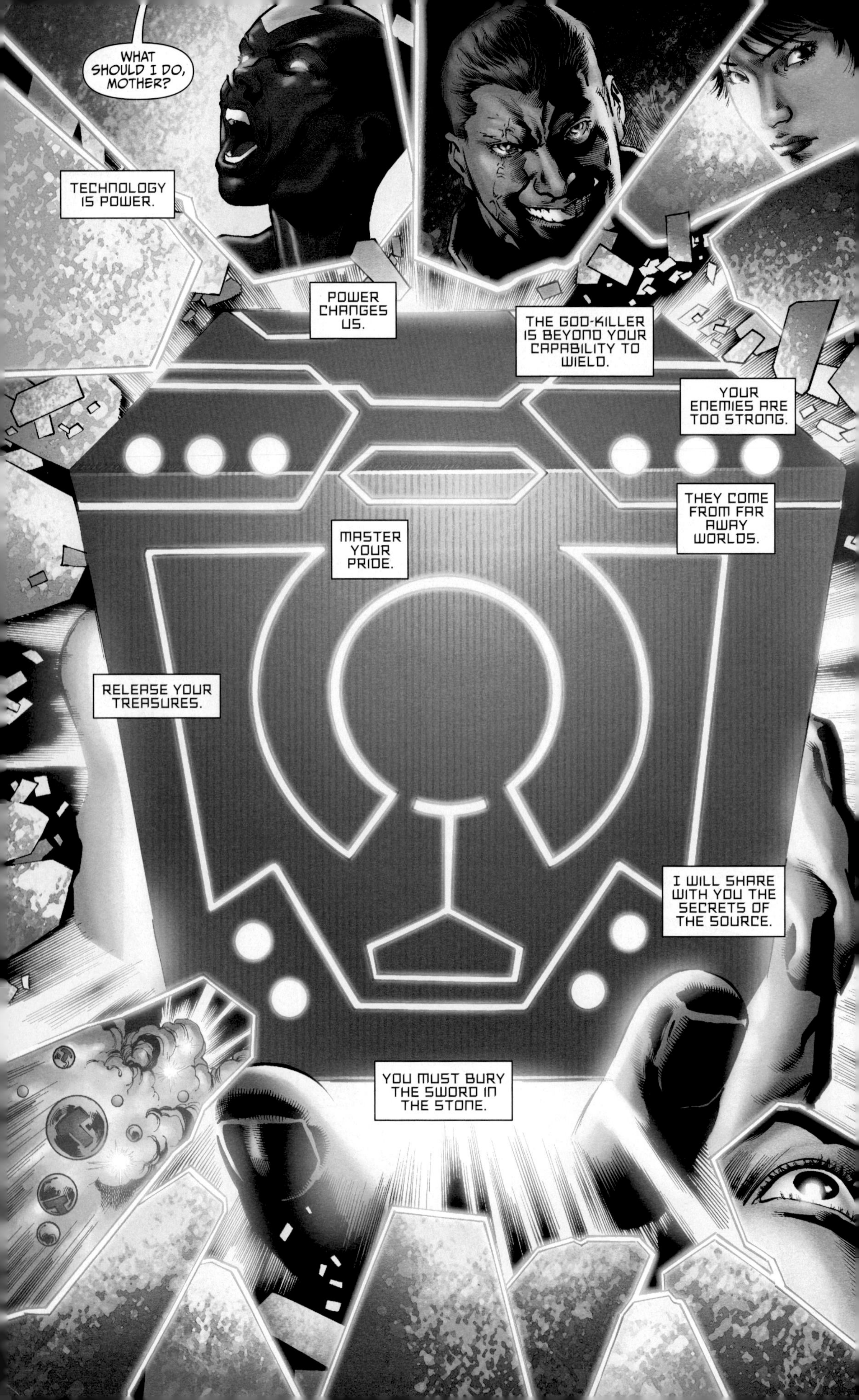
WHAT SHOULD I DO, MOTHER?
TECHNOLOGY IS POWER.
POWER CHANGES US.
THE GOD-KILLER IS BEYOND YOUR CAPABILITY TO WIELD.
YOUR ENEMIES ARE TOO STRONG.
THEY COME FROM FAR AWAY WORLDS.
MASTER YOUR PRIDE.
RELEASE YOUR TREASURES.
I WILL SHARE WITH YOU THE SECRETS OF THE SOURCE.
YOU MUST BURY THE SWORD IN THE STONE.

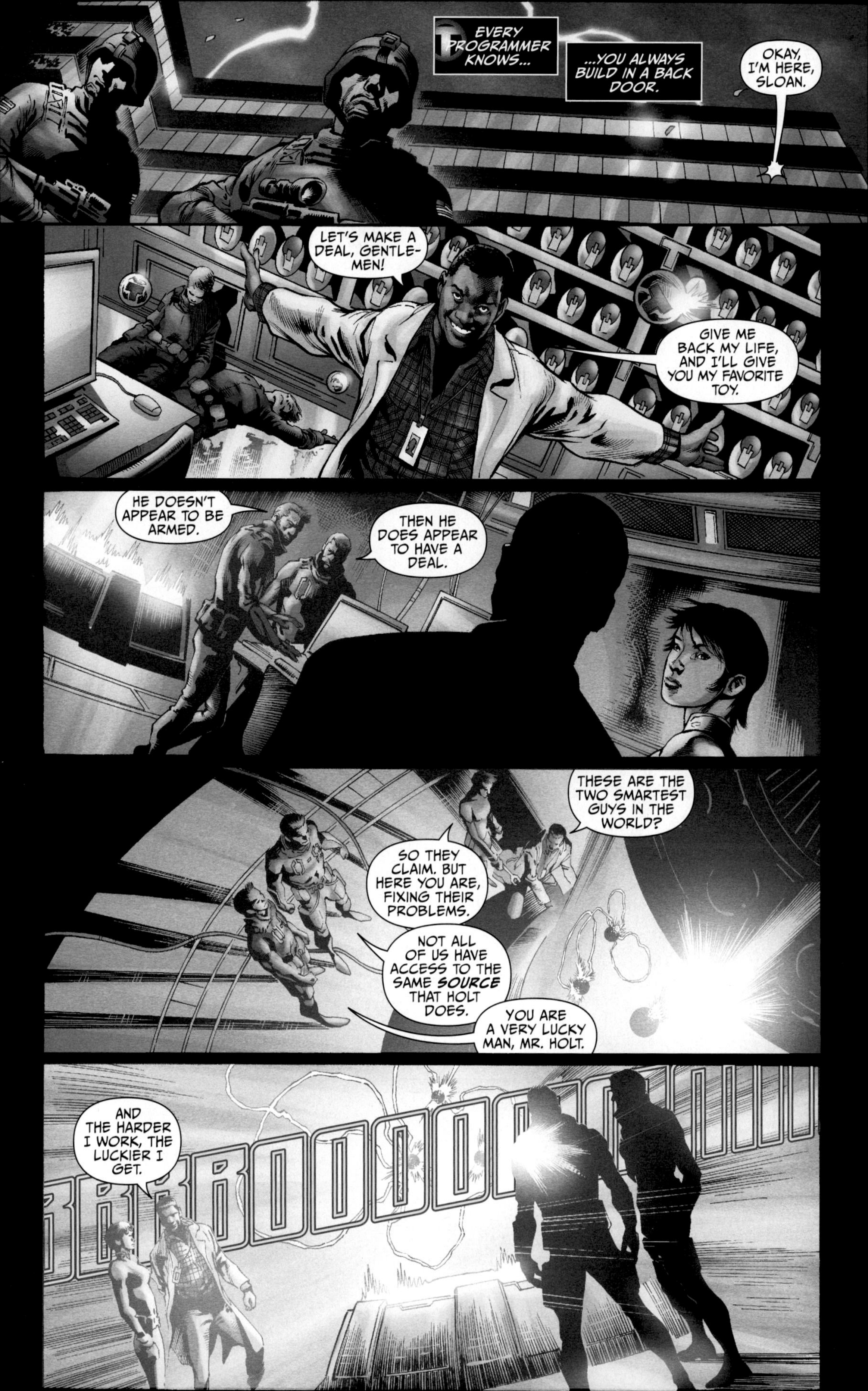
EVERY PROGRAMMER KNOWS...
...YOU ALWAYS BUILD IN A BACK DOOR.
OKAY, I'M HERE, SLOAN.
LET'S MAKE A DEAL, GENTLE-MEN!
GIVE ME BACK MY LIFE, AND I'LL GIVE YOU MY FAVORITE TOY.
HE DOESN'T APPEAR TO BE ARMED.
THEN HE DOES APPEAR TO HAVE A DEAL.
THESE ARE THE TWO SMARTEST GUYS IN THE WORLD?
SO THEY CLAIM. BUT HERE YOU ARE, FIXING THEIR PROBLEMS.
NOT ALL OF US HAVE ACCESS TO THE SAME SOURCE THAT HOLT DOES.
YOU ARE A VERY LUCKY MAN, MR. HOLT.
AND THE HARDER I WORK, THE LUCKIER I GET.

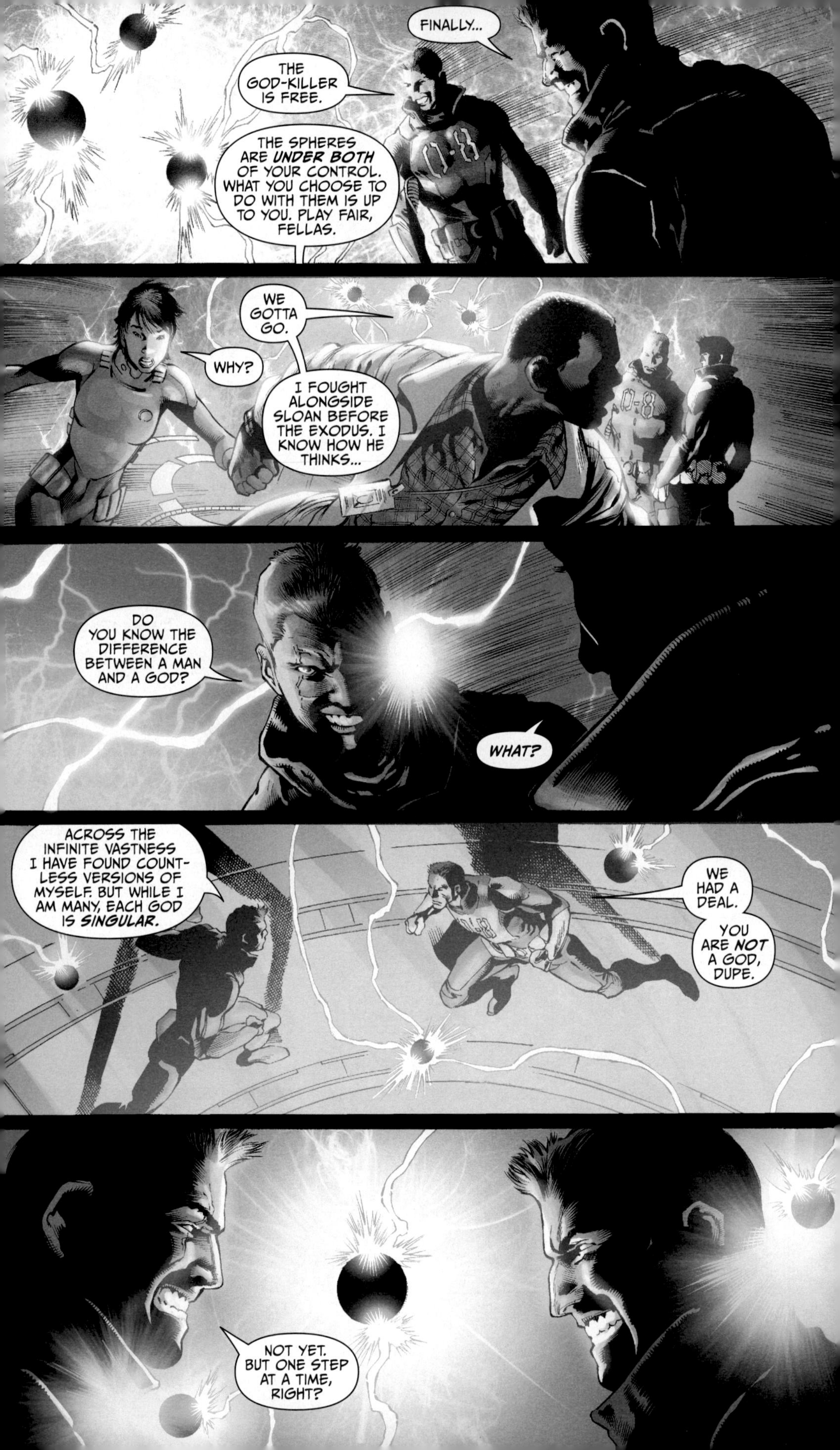
FINALLY...
THE GOD-KILLER IS FREE.
THE SPHERES ARE **UNDER BOTH** OF YOUR CONTROL. WHAT YOU CHOOSE TO DO WITH THEM IS UP TO YOU. PLAY FAIR, FELLAS.
WE GOTTA GO.
WHY?
I FOUGHT ALONGSIDE SLOAN BEFORE THE EXODUS. I KNOW HOW HE THINKS...
DO YOU KNOW THE DIFFERENCE BETWEEN A MAN AND A GOD?
WHAT?
ACROSS THE INFINITE VASTNESS I HAVE FOUND COUNTLESS VERSIONS OF MYSELF. BUT WHILE I AM MANY, EACH GOD IS ***SINGULAR.***
WE HAD A DEAL.
YOU ARE ***NOT*** A GOD, DUPE.
NOT YET. BUT ONE STEP AT A TIME, RIGHT?

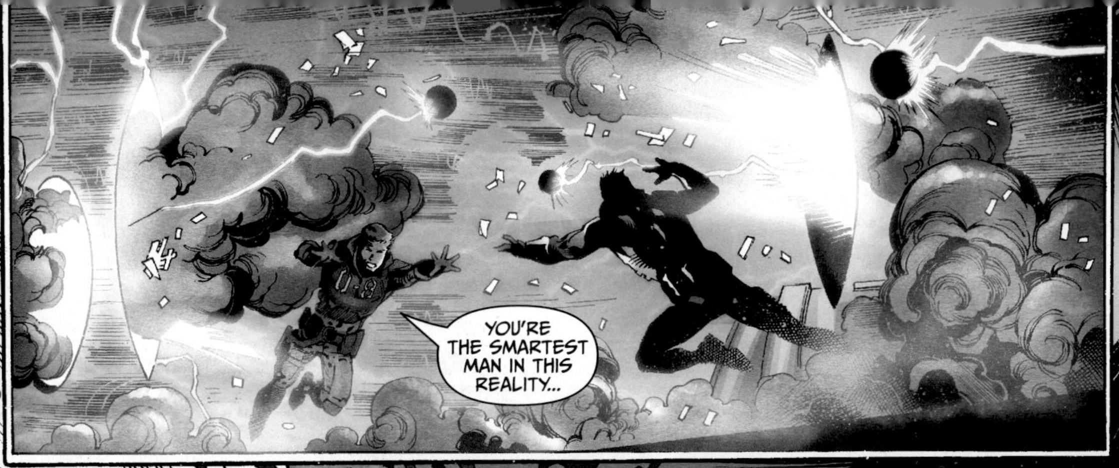
YOU'RE THE SMARTEST MAN IN THIS REALITY...

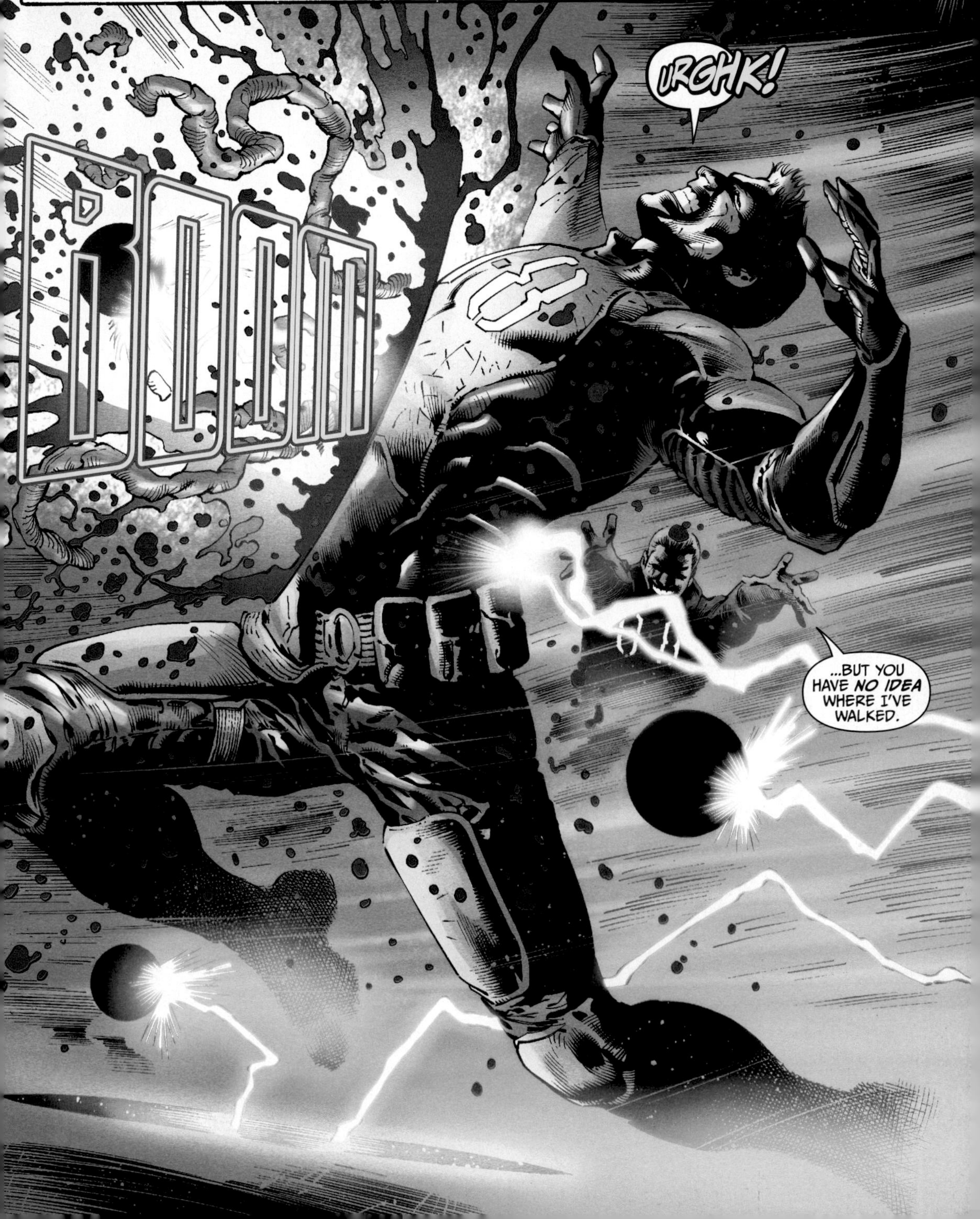
URGHK!
BOOM
...BUT YOU HAVE NO IDEA WHERE I'VE WALKED.

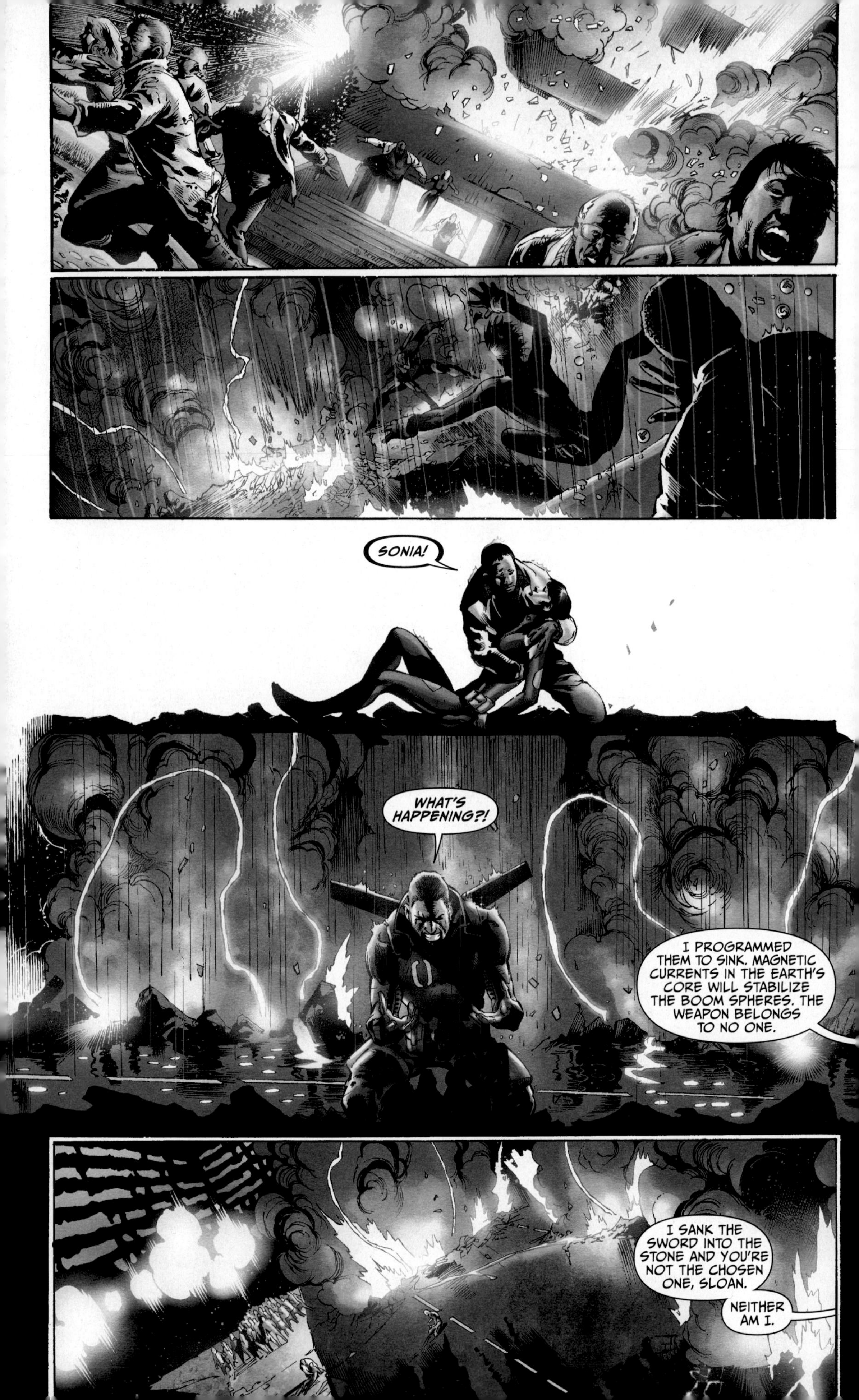
SONIA!
WHAT'S HAPPENING?!
I PROGRAMMED THEM TO SINK. MAGNETIC CURRENTS IN THE EARTH'S CORE WILL STABILIZE THE BOOM SPHERES. THE WEAPON BELONGS TO NO ONE.
I SANK THE SWORD INTO THE STONE AND YOU'RE NOT THE CHOSEN ONE, SLOAN.
NEITHER AM I.

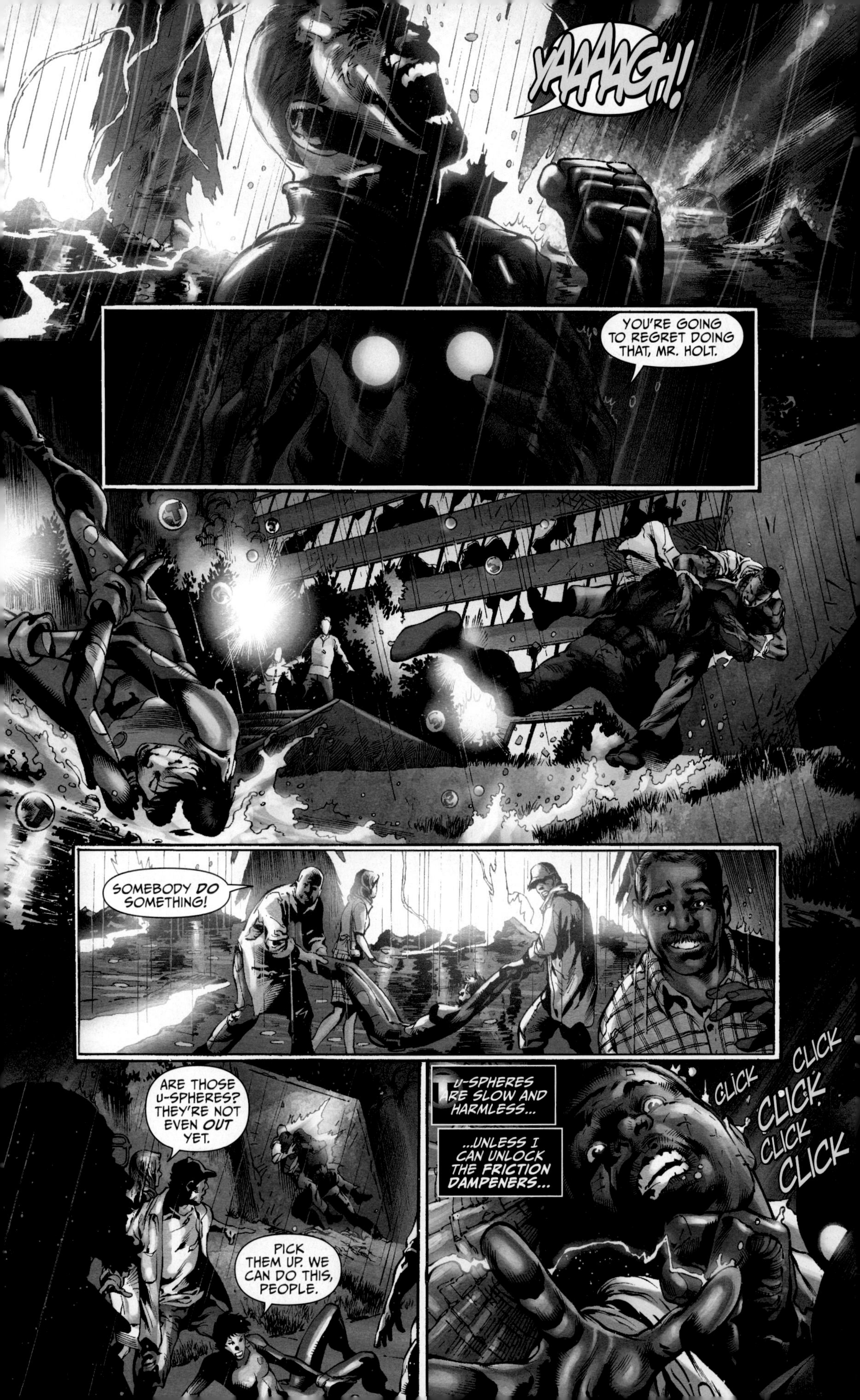
YAAAAGH!
YOU'RE GOING TO REGRET DOING THAT, MR. HOLT.
SOMEBODY DO SOMETHING!
ARE THOSE u-SPHERES? THEY'RE NOT EVEN OUT YET.
PICK THEM UP. WE CAN DO THIS, PEOPLE.
u-SPHERES ARE SLOW AND HARMLESS...
...UNLESS I CAN UNLOCK THE FRICTION DAMPENERS...
CLICK
CLICK
CLICK
CLICK
CLICK

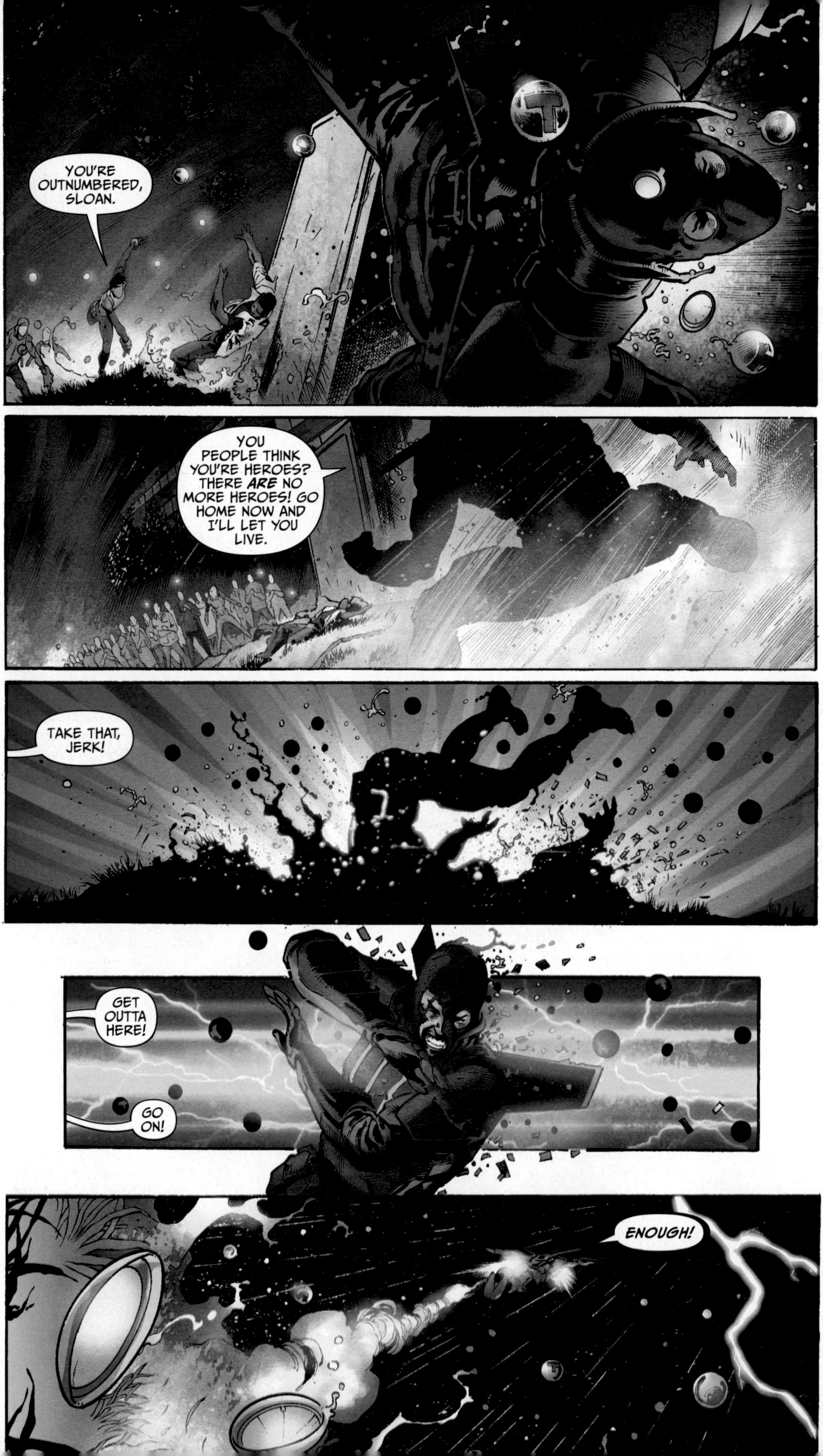
YOU'RE OUTNUMBERED, SLOAN.
YOU PEOPLE THINK YOU'RE HEROES? THERE *ARE* NO MORE HEROES! GO HOME NOW AND I'LL LET YOU LIVE.
TAKE THAT, JERK!
GET OUTTA HERE!
GO ON!
ENOUGH!

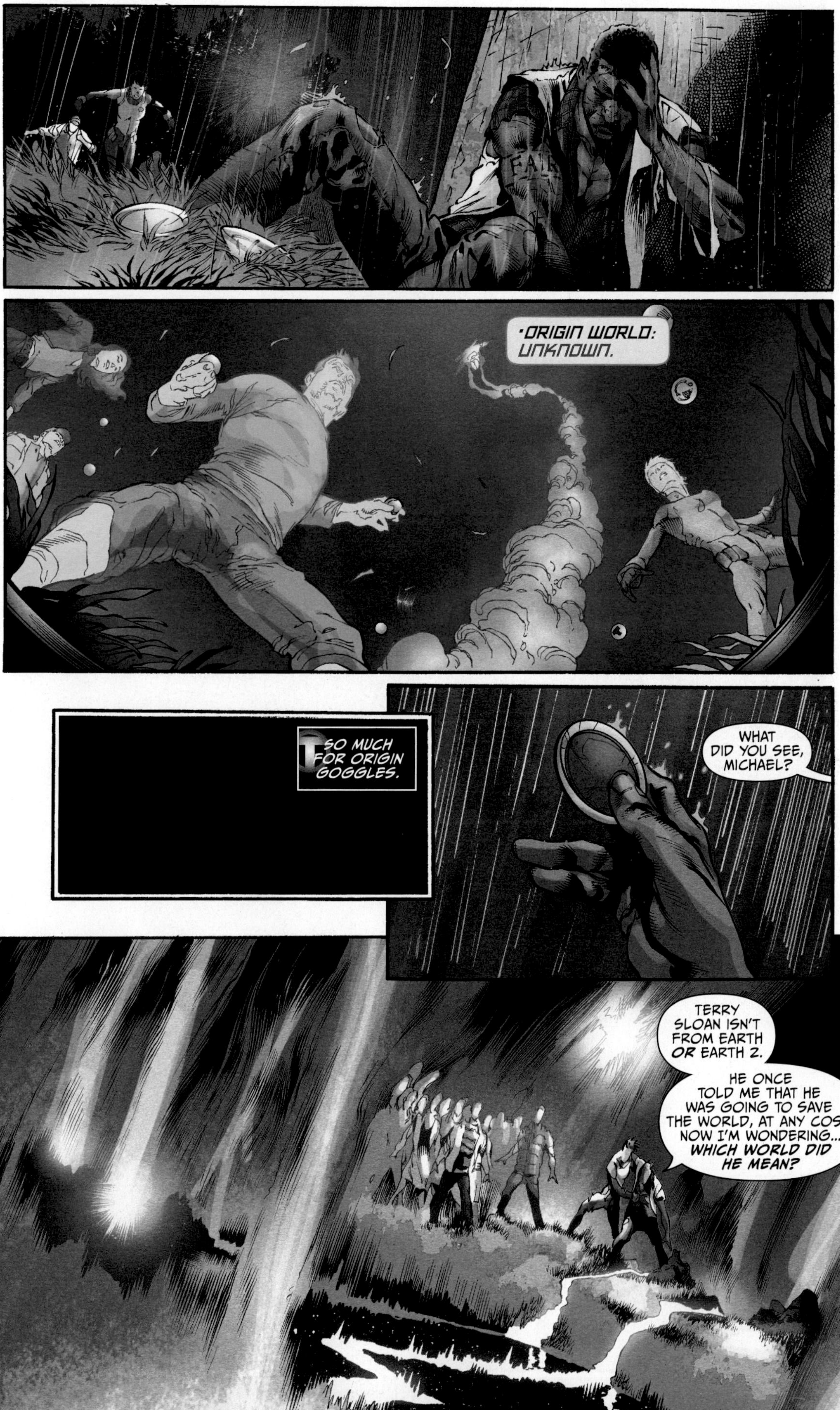
•ORIGIN WORLD: UNKNOWN.
SO MUCH FOR ORIGIN GOGGLES.
WHAT DID YOU SEE, MICHAEL?
TERRY SLOAN ISN'T FROM EARTH OR EARTH 2.
HE ONCE TOLD ME THAT HE WAS GOING TO SAVE THE WORLD, AT ANY COST. NOW I'M WONDERING... WHICH WORLD DID HE MEAN?

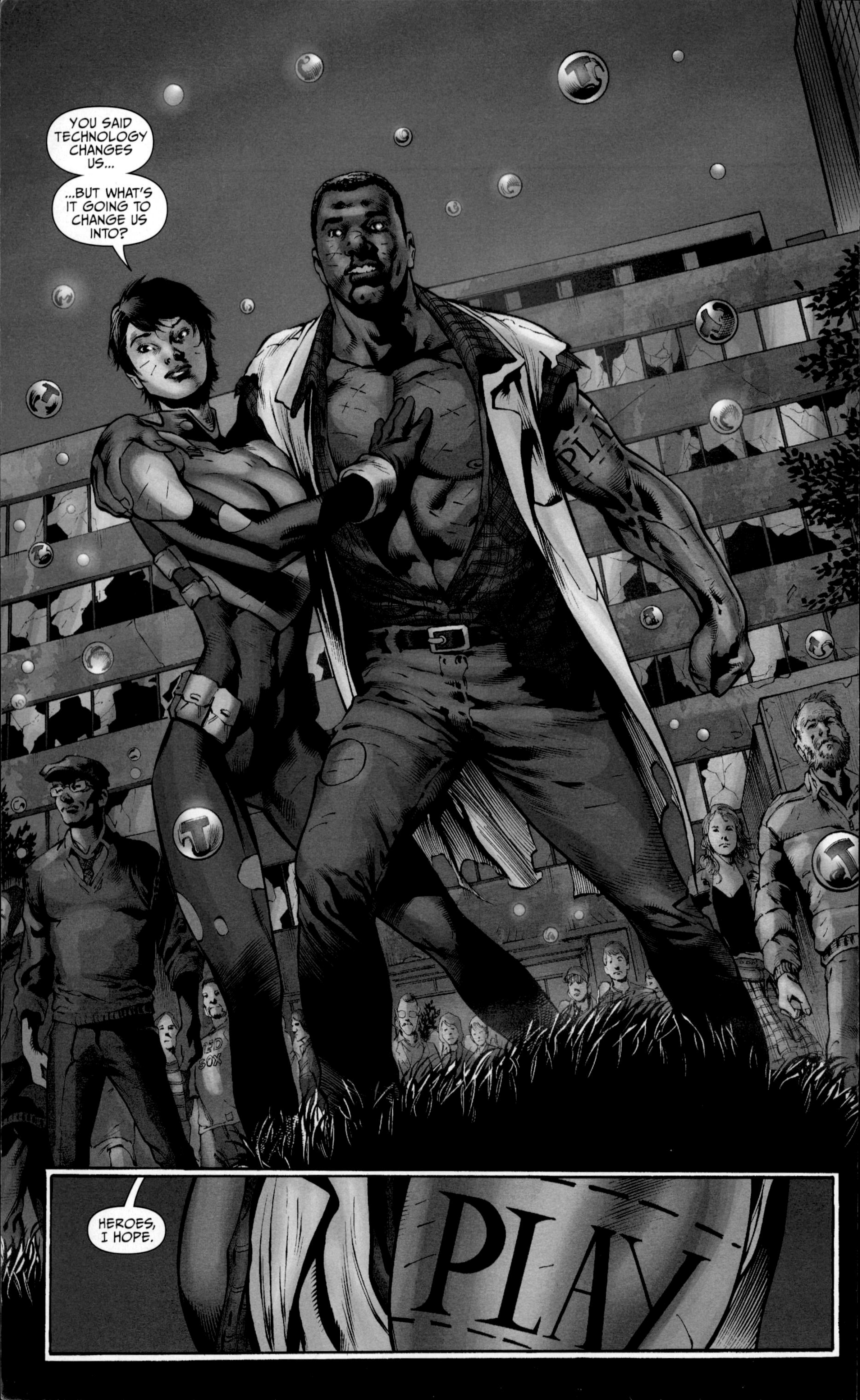

YOU SAID TECHNOLOGY CHANGES US...
...BUT WHAT'S IT GOING TO CHANGE US INTO?
PLA
HEROES, I HOPE.
PLAY

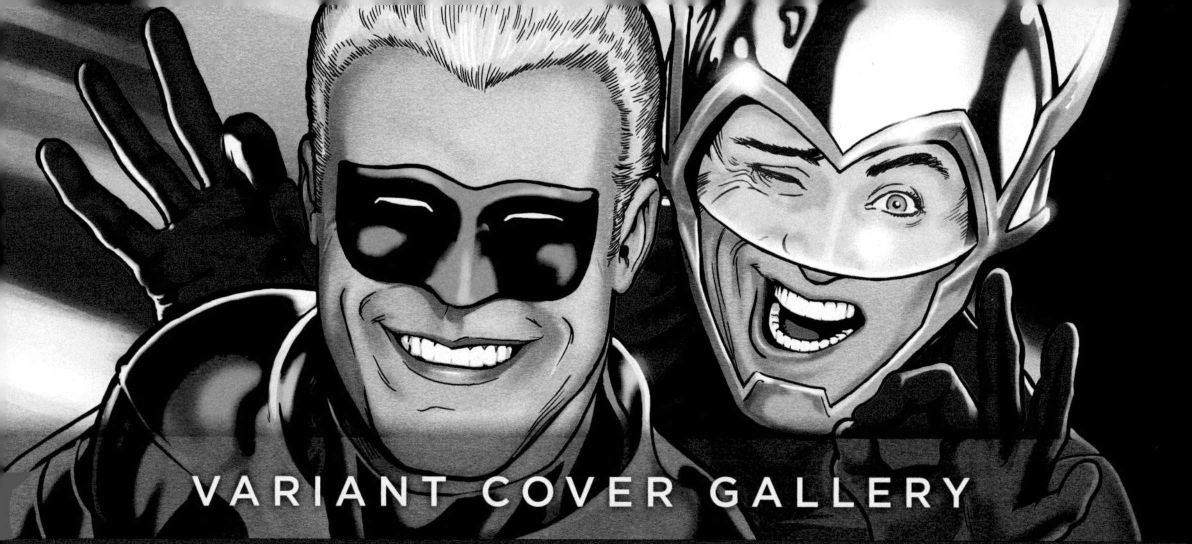

VARIANT COVER GALLERY

EARTH 2 #21
***Robot Chicken* variant by RC Stoodios**

EARTH 2 #22
MAD Magazine variant cover by John Kerschbaum

EARTH 2 #23
Batman '66 variant by Mike and Laura Allred

EARTH 2 #24
Bombshell variant by Ant Lucia

EARTH 2 #25
Batman 75th anniversary variant by Walt Simonson and Laura Martin

EARTH 2 #26
Selfie variant by Kevin Maguire

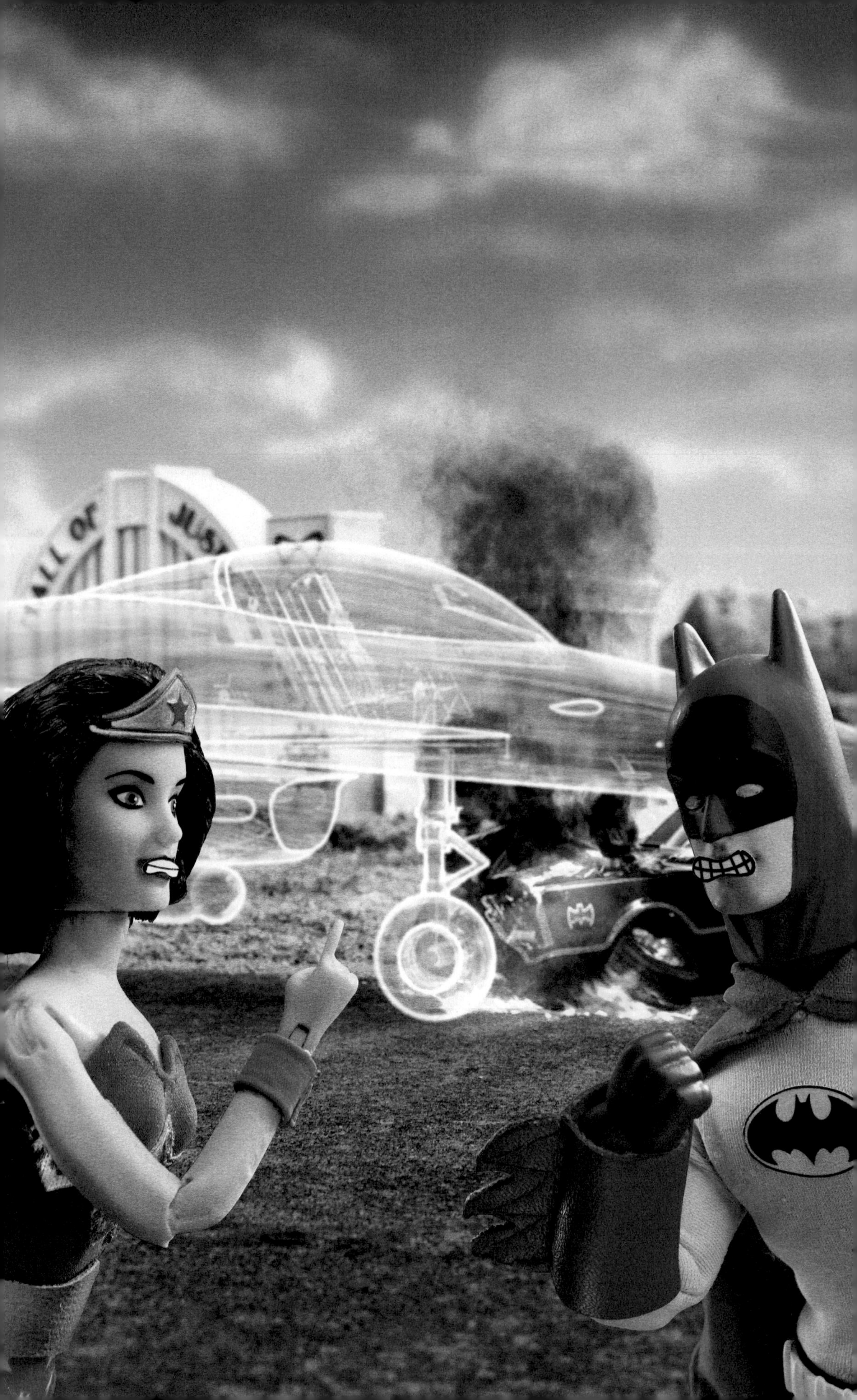
ALL OF JUS

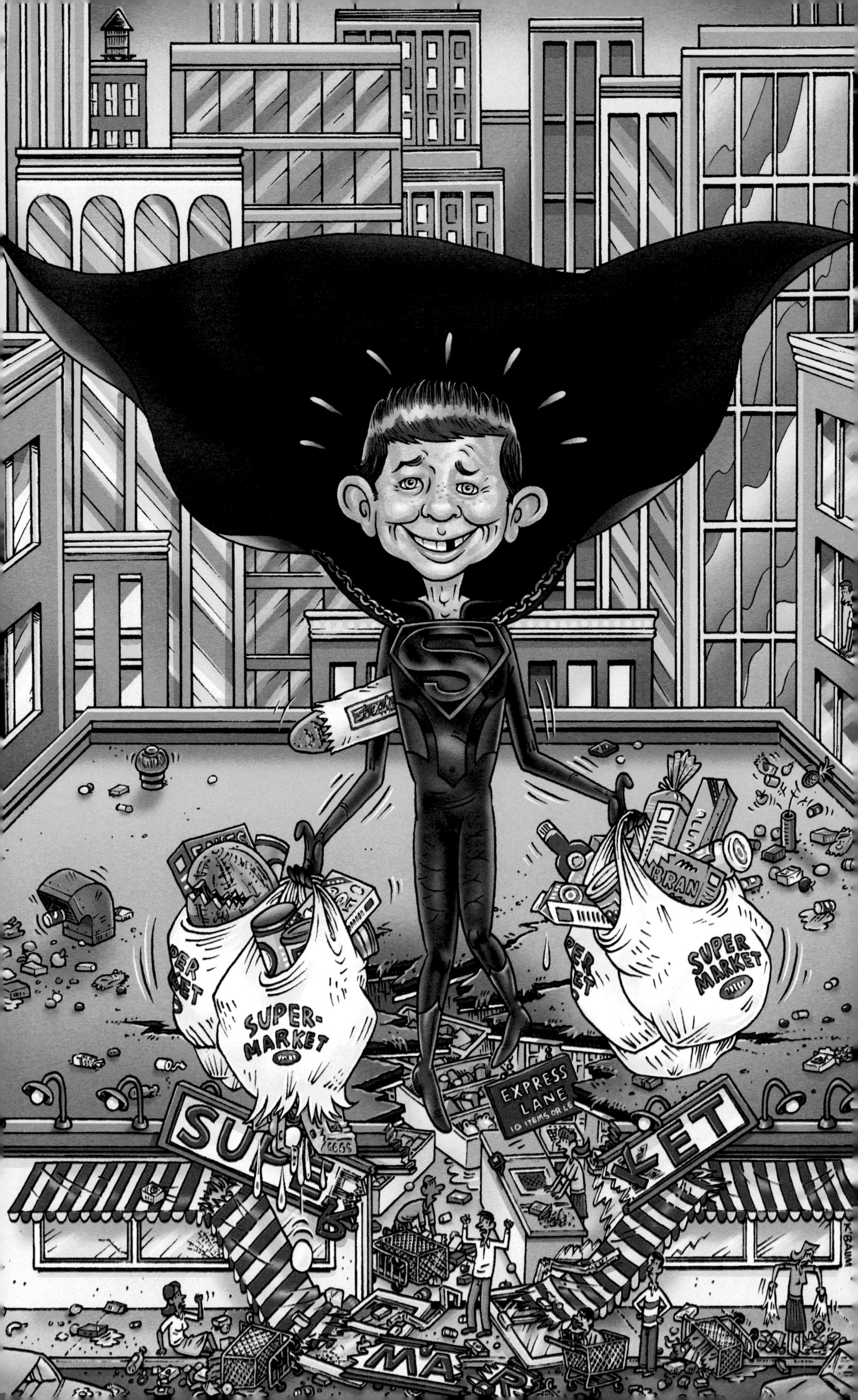
SUPER-
MARKET
SUPER
MARKET
BRAN
EXPRESS
LANE
10 ITEMS OR LE
KET
K BAUM

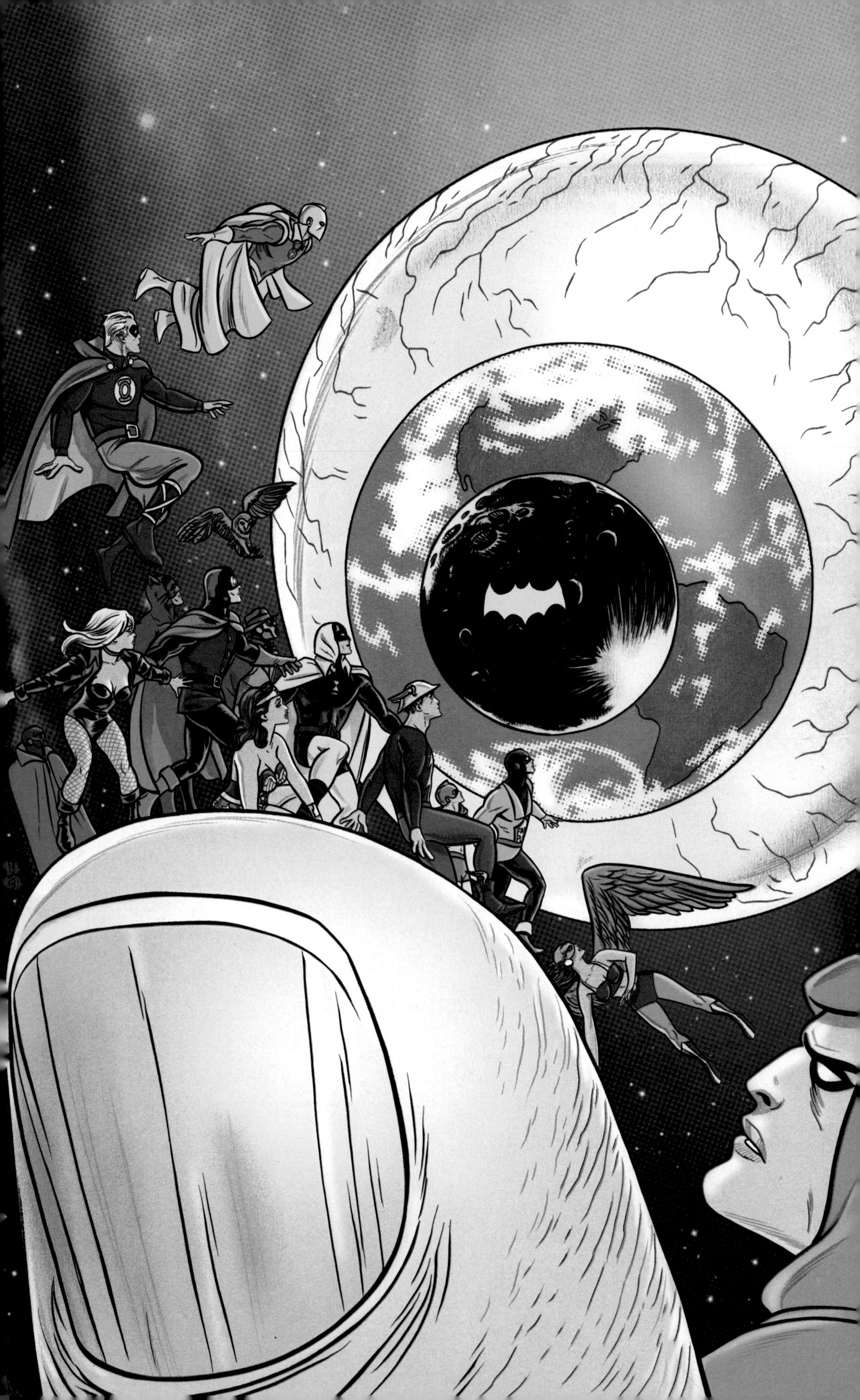

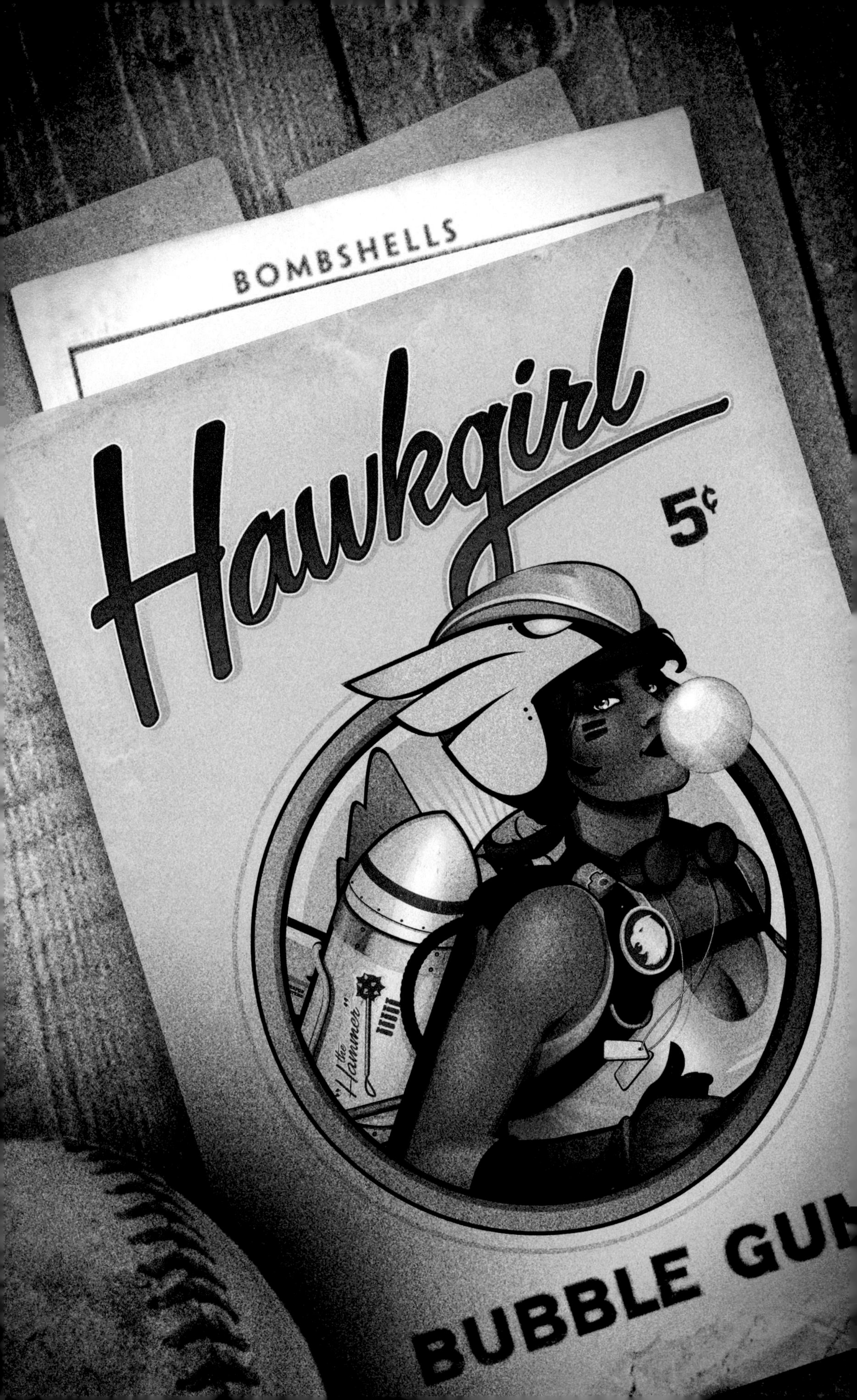
BOMBSHELLS
Hawkgirl
5¢
"the Hammer"
BUBBLE GU

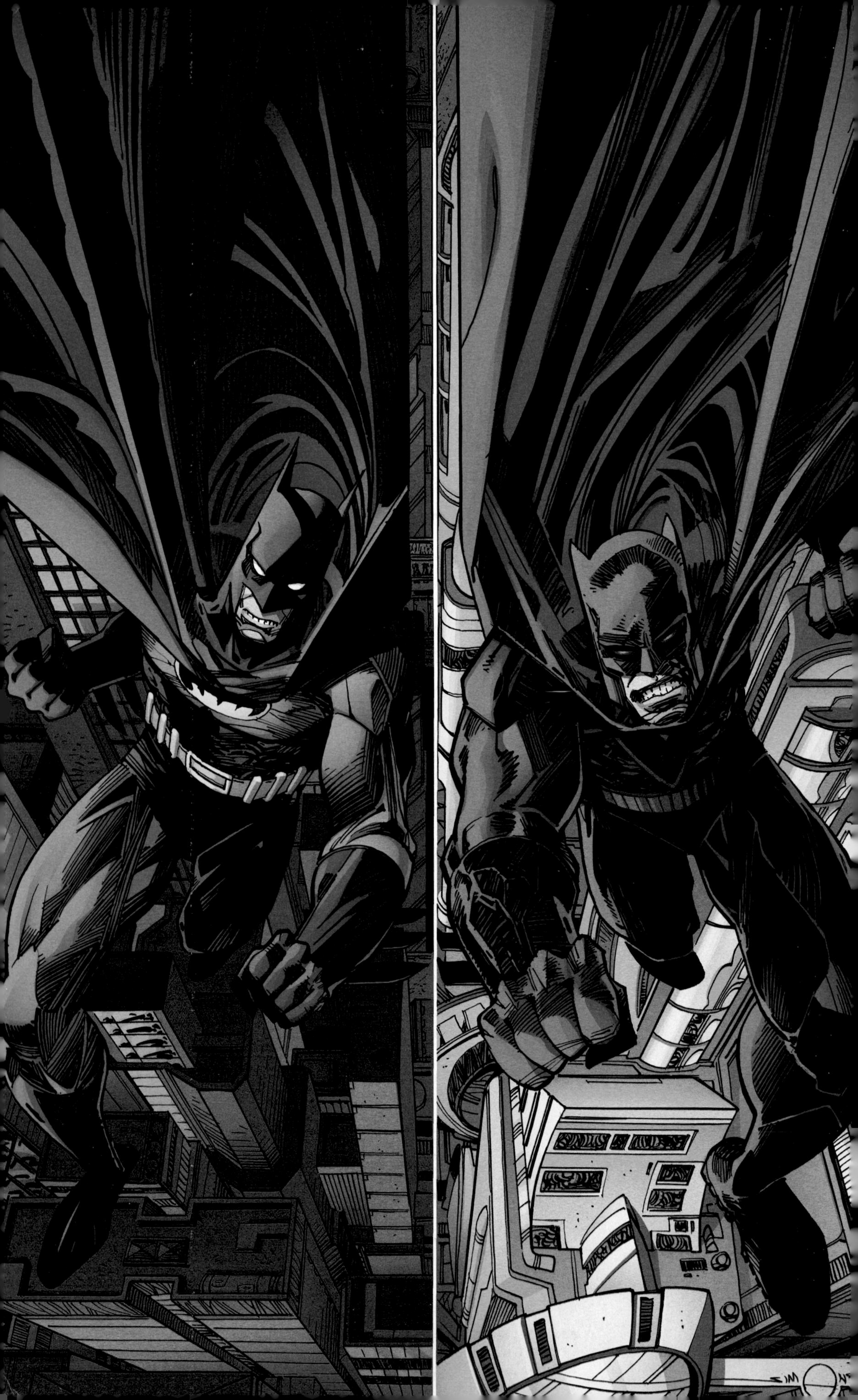

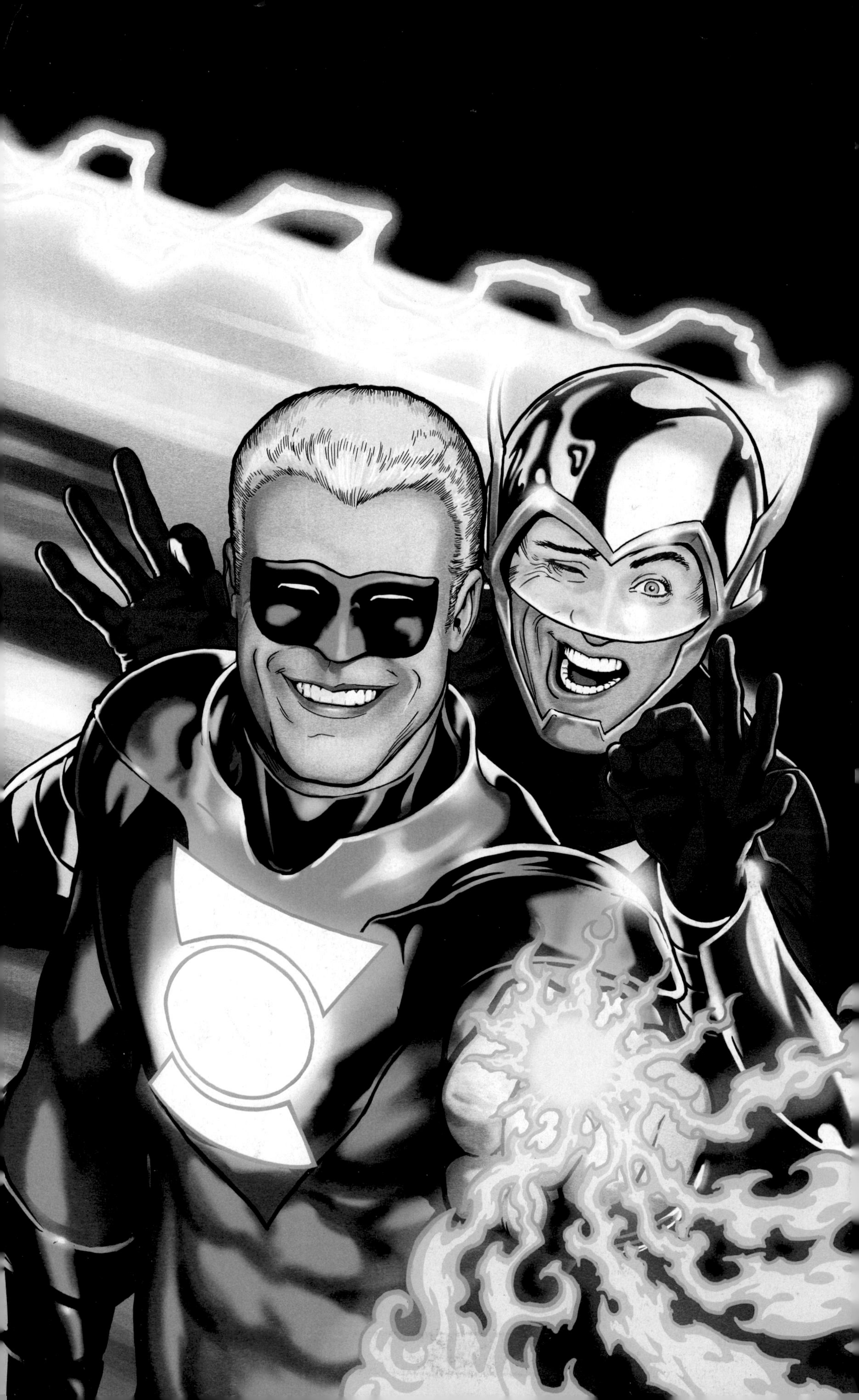

DC COMICS™

"Great characterization and exciting action sequences continue to be the hallmarks of this series, along with someinteresting meta commentary as well."—IGN

"EARTH 2 is an incredibly entertaining ride. The freedom to create a world from the ground up has allowed it to be one of the most exciting, diverse, and entertaining titles DC puts out." -CRAVEONLINE

START AT THE BEGINNING!
EARTH 2
VOLUME 1: THE GATHERING

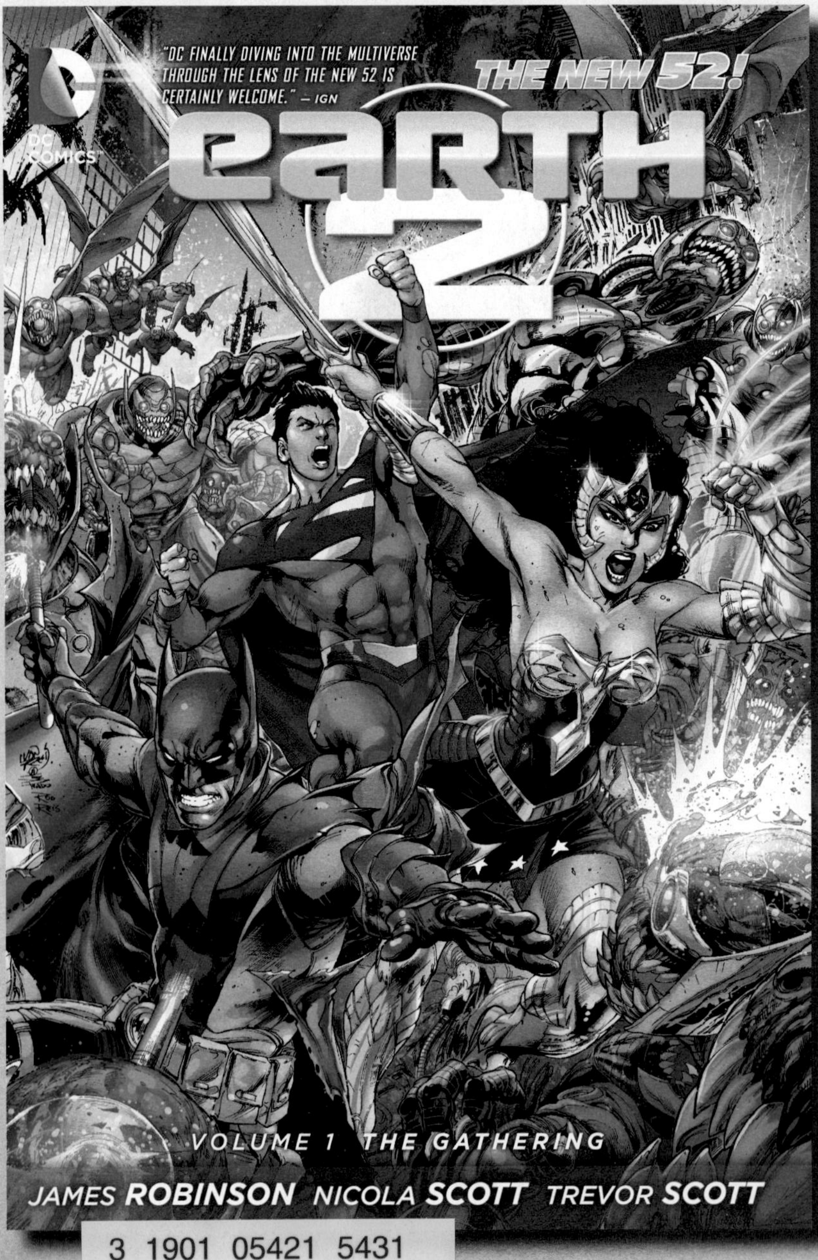
"DC FINALLY DIVING INTO THE MULTIVERSE THROUGH THE LENS OF THE NEW 52 IS CERTAINLY WELCOME." – IGN
DC COMICS
THE NEW 52!
EARTH 2
VOLUME 1 THE GATHERING
JAMES ROBINSON NICOLA SCOTT TREVOR SCOTT

EARTH 2 VOL. 2: THE TOWER OF FATE

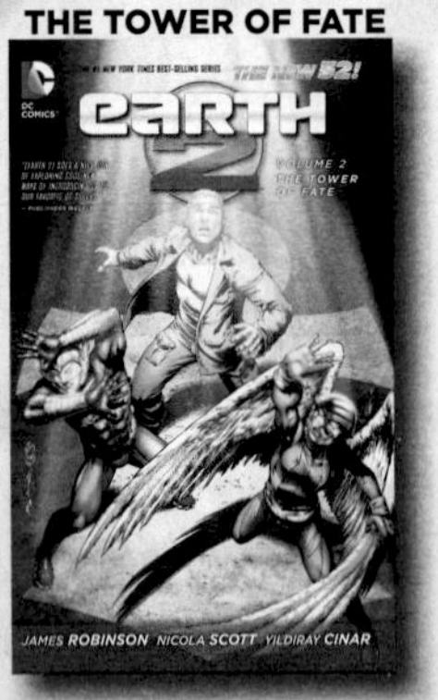
THE NEW 52!
EARTH 2
JAMES ROBINSON NICOLA SCOTT YILDIRAY CINAR

with JAMES ROBINSON, NICOLA SCOTT and YILDIRAY CINAR

EARTH 2 VOL. 3: BATTLE CRY

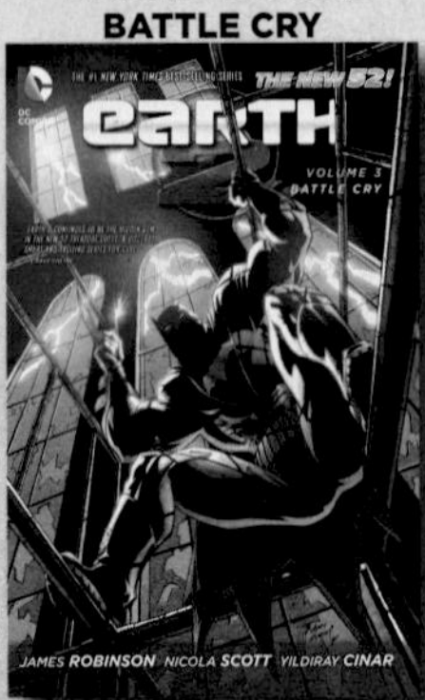
THE NEW 52!
EARTH
JAMES ROBINSON NICOLA SCOTT YILDIRAY CINAR

with JAMES ROBINSON, NICOLA SCOTT and YILDARAY CINAR

EARTH 2 VOL. 4: THE DARK AGE

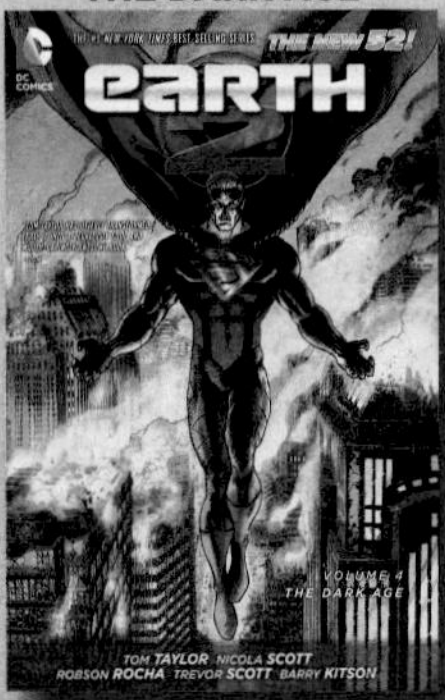
THE NEW 52!
EARTH
TOM TAYLOR NICOLA SCOTT
ROBSON ROCHA TREVOR SCOTT BARRY KITSON

with TOM TAYLOR and NICOLA SCOTT